EVERYBODY'S HEARD
ABOUT THE BIRD

EVERYBODY'S HEARD
ABOUT
THE BIRD

THE TRUE STORY OF
1960s ROCK ★ N ★ ROLL
IN MINNESOTA

★

RICK SHEFCHIK

University of Minnesota Press
MINNEAPOLIS · LONDON

The publication of this book was assisted by a bequest from Josiah H. Chase to honor his parents, Ellen Rankin Chase and Josiah Hook Chase, Minnesota territorial pioneers.

Published by the University of Minnesota Press
111 Third Avenue South, Suite 290
Minneapolis, MN 55401-2520
http://www.upress.umn.edu

Design and production by Mighty Media, Inc.
Interior and text design by Chris Long

Library of Congress Cataloging-in-Publication Data
Shefchik, Rick.
Everybody's heard about the bird : the true story of 1960s rock 'n' roll in Minnesota / Rick Shefchik.
Includes index.
ISBN 978-0-8166-9319-1 (hc)
1. Rock music—Minnesota—1961–1970—History and criticism. 2. Rock musicians—Minnesota.
3. Rock groups—Minnesota. I. Title.
ML3534.3.S53 2015
781.6609776'09046—dc23   2015024894

Printed in the United States of America on acid-free paper

The University of Minnesota is an equal-opportunity educator and employer.

21 20 19 18 17 16 15   10 9 8 7 6 5 4 3 2 1

For Mark Shefchik

CONTENTS

ST. PAUL, MINNESOTA
JANUARY 31, 1964

THE TRASHMEN—Tony Andreason, Bob Reed, Steve Wahrer, and Dal Winslow—looked around in amazement as they were escorted onstage by police at the 1964 WDGY Winter Carnival Spectacular.

The dance floor of the old St. Paul Auditorium was "a swirling mass of teenagers," as the *Pioneer Press* would describe it the next morning, but there really wasn't room to dance. Girls were screaming at the band, and those closest to the stage were clutching and tearing at the pants legs of The Trashmen's matching suits. Guys were yelling, pushing, and throwing punches. Police heard reports of a stabbing but could not confirm it. The band members heard a rumor that someone with a rifle had been removed from the

The spillover crowd of twenty thousand at the 1964 WDGY Winter Carnival Spectacular was front-page news in the *St. Paul Pioneer Press.* Courtesy of the Minnesota Historical Society, Minneapolis–St. Paul Newspaper Negatives Collection.

auditorium's balcony, but the noise from the crowd was so deafening that they would never have heard if a shot had been fired. The Trashmen could barely even hear themselves once they started to play.

Jan & Dean, the bushy-haired, striped-shirted surfer dudes from Los Angeles who had scored the Number 1 *Billboard* hit "Surf City" just the previous summer, had opened for The Trashmen (and hadn't been very happy about it). They had been preceded by Clyde McPhatter, the former lead singer of the Drifters who had racked up several Top 10 hits of his own; Linda Scott, whose "I've Told Every Little Star" had reached Number 3 in 1961; Joey Powers, who had made the Top 10 the previous month with "Midnight Mary"; and several local groups, including the popular Mike Waggoner and the Bops, and a promising outfit called the Underbeats.

But all that had been a precursor to what was amounting to the real coronation of the 1964 St. Paul Winter Carnival: The Trashmen accepting their crowns as the kings of rock 'n' roll—and not just in the Twin Cities, or the state of Minnesota, or even the five-state area including the Dakotas, Iowa, and Wisconsin. In a few days, the band would be heading to the West Coast as headliners on its first national tour. The Trashmen had already made one trip to the West Coast as unknowns, a pilgrimage a year earlier to learn about the surf sound that was sweeping the nation. They learned well: their massive hit single "Surfin' Bird" had been Number 1 on both the local WDGY and KDWB charts for weeks and was sitting in the Number 4 spot nationally. Disc jockey Bill Diehl, who was emceeing the Winter Carnival concert, had sources telling him that "Surfin' Bird" would jump to Number 1 when the new *Billboard* chart came out the next day.

The rococo-styled auditorium, which

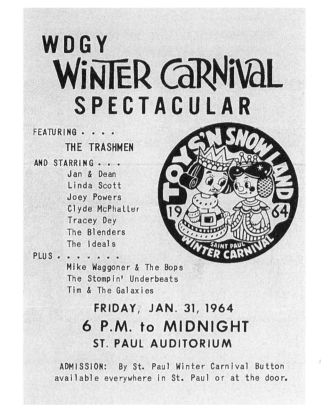

WDGY WINTER CARNIVAL SPECTACULAR

FEATURING . . . .
THE TRASHMEN

AND STARRING . . .
Jan & Dean
Linda Scott
Joey Powers
Clyde McPhatter
Tracey Dey
The Blenders
The Ideals

PLUS . . . .
Mike Waggoner & The Bops
The Stompin' Underbeats
Tim & The Galaxies

FRIDAY, JAN. 31, 1964
6 P.M. to MIDNIGHT
ST. PAUL AUDITORIUM

ADMISSION: By St. Paul Winter Carnival Button available everywhere in St. Paul or at the door.

For the price of a Winter Carnival button, nearly twenty thousand music fans crammed into the St. Paul Auditorium on January 31, 1964, to see a marathon concert featuring many local and national rock 'n' roll bands, headlined by the chart-topping Trashmen. Courtesy of Mike Jann.

was built in 1906 and had been expanded in 1931 to sixteen thousand seats to accommodate auto shows, hockey games, and circuses, was still not big enough to hold everyone who tried to jam into the building on that cold Friday night. Although the teens came and went during the six hours of music, the police estimated that seventeen thousand were inside when the doors were closed and The Trashmen hit the stage at 11 P.M., while another six thousand milled outside. Eight years earlier, Elvis Presley had drawn just three thousand for his first Twin Cities appearance in the building.

"It was insane—it really was," Andreason said fifty years later, the images of that night still burning vividly in his mind. "We were doing the show, and a girl grabs my leg. The boots we wore had zippers down the side, and they weren't very tight on me. She unzipped that and had that boot off me so fast—and I never got it back. So I took off the other one and threw it out into the crowd."

"It was crazy," recalled rhythm guitar player Winslow. "It was just a sea of people in that auditorium. I'm sure you couldn't hear. We couldn't hear anything we were singing."

"They were screaming so loud I don't know if they could really even hear us play," Andreason said.

They didn't play for long. Unlike the four-hour marathon jobs the band had played so many times at Minnesota's teen clubs, ballrooms, and roller rinks on their way up the rock 'n' roll ladder, this package show required them to play just a half-dozen numbers—which included "King of the Surf," the hastily composed B-side to "Surfin' Bird" that had turned into a hit on its own; a preview of their new single "Bird Dance Beat," allegedly written by their manager, George Garrett; and a couple of surf songs from their forthcoming album. It was all received with ear-damaging approval, but the loudest roar erupted when the diminutive, blond-haired Wahrer, the group's drummer and lead singer, put his mouth against his microphone, lowered his voice to a menacing growl, and barked, "A-well-a everybody's heard about the Bird . . ."

In an era of unself-conscious rock 'n' roll and good-time party songs, The Trashmen had hit paydirt with perhaps the goofiest blast of adrenaline-charged nonsense in rock history. "Surfin' Bird" had made the Twin Cities charts a couple of weeks before President John F. Kennedy's assassination and first cracked the *Billboard* Hot 100 on December 7, 1963. Despite—or perhaps because of—the nation's somber mood, the "papa-oo-mow-mow" refrain of "Surfin' Bird" had been embraced by the ascendant baby boom generation as a happy, mindless mantra.

The Beatles—unknown in America a month earlier—were looming on the horizon, scheduled to make their first U.S. visit in February. During that month, a former Hibbing, Minnesota, rock 'n' roll piano player, now playing folk guitar under the name Bob Dylan, would start writing a song called "Mr. Tambourine Man." Though the Beatles and Dylan would have an enormous impact on The Trashmen's future, their present could not have looked brighter. They would work nearly nonstop for the next three years, playing the surf clubs in Southern California, the frat parties at Columbia and Cornell, and seemingly every dance hall and rock 'n' roll joint in between. In the meantime, by 1965, estimates ranged from 350 to 500 Minnesota rock bands playing teen dances across the state. The members of the most successful of those bands made more money per week than their fathers did and drove Corvettes, Jaguars, and Thunderbirds.

By the time The Trashmen decided to call it quits in 1967, they had seen the music scene change in unimaginable ways, and they had seen their own audience stop dancing. Upper Midwest music fans began gravitating toward the bands that had been encouraged by The Trashmen's success but took their musical inspiration from the Beatles and Bob Dylan. The irony was that the Beatles and Dylan had idolized the same rock 'n' roll pioneers (Buddy Holly, Jerry Lee Lewis, the Everly Brothers, Little Richard, Chuck Berry) who had inspired The Trashmen. Yet The Trashmen were content to stay close to the roots of rock rather than attempt to reinvent it. That faithfulness cost them their audience in the midsixties, but it also set them up for a lucrative comeback decades later.

The success of The Trashmen in the 1960s cannot be overstated. They showed countless Minnesota musicians that four guys from flyover land could put a band together, cut a record, get airplay, and become stars, for however long it lasted. They also demonstrated the limitations of trying to launch a music career away from the coasts.

"There could have been fifty hits out of that town with the right producers," said Owen Husney, who played in the High Spirits, a midsixties band from St. Louis Park, and later became Prince's first manager.

This is the story of those 1960s-era Minnesota bands and how close some of them came to achieving the ultimate rock 'n' roll dream.

SUZIE BABY

IN THE BEGINNING was Augie Garcia.

When the eighteen-year-old Hispanic kid from the West Side Flats of St. Paul put together his first band in 1950, the term *rock 'n' roll* had not even been popularized; it would take hold in 1951, thanks to Cleveland disc jockey Alan Freed. Dubbed the Continentals, the group consisted of Garcia (who loved vocal harmony groups and traditional Mexican music), three Italian guys, and an Irishman. After a year playing Twin Cities clubs with his band, Garcia joined the Army and was shipped over to Korea. During his stint in the Army Garcia discovered the two elements that would combine to form his signature style: rhythm and blues music, and Bermuda shorts.

The troop transport taking Garcia and his fellow soldiers to the Korean War stopped in Hawaii, where he noticed many young men walking around in shorts. He liked the

Augie Garcia owned thirty-two pairs of Bermuda shorts, his signature stage outfit. Courtesy of the Minnesota Historical Society.

Augie Garcia's band played uninhibited rock 'n' roll at the River Road Club in Mendota. Photograph by Buzz Brown. Courtesy of the Minnesota Historical Society.

look and filed it away as a possible stage costume when he returned to the States and rejoined his band. Garcia had learned to play guitar from his uncle, Frank Garcia Pascquale, but it wasn't until he listened to Fats Domino records with his fellow G.I.'s in Korea that he got a sense of where pop music was going and how he could go with it. "You took that shuffle, that rhythm, and you put it with any tune, be it 'Pennies from Heaven' or 'Blueberry Hill,'" Garcia told interviewer Dave Hill in 1972. "You did blues to this shuffle, and then it was rhythm and blues."

Garcia almost didn't make it back from Korea to resume his musical career. During a ferocious battle, his bunker took a direct hit from a shell, and he was buried under logs, dirt, and rocks for nearly an hour and a half before fellow soldiers dug him out. "My back and neck hurt so badly that I felt like I'd been dragged around behind a car," he told Don Boxmeyer of the *St. Paul Pioneer Press* years later. Though Garcia was ultimately awarded a Purple Heart for his wounds, he didn't receive an early ticket home. He was on the

Elvis Presley drew a crowd of just three thousand to his initial visit to Minneapolis on May 13, 1956. Earlier that day, he had been upstaged by Augie Garcia's quintet before an even smaller crowd in St. Paul. Photograph by *Minneapolis Star Journal Tribune*. Courtesy of the Minnesota Historical Society.

front lines for two years before the cease-fire was declared. When he got back to St. Paul, he took a job digging ditches for Northern States Power, but he also resumed playing music—this time with what he called "that hard sock."

It was 1954, and "that hard sock" was beginning to be called rock 'n' roll. The Augie Garcia Quintet began gradually replacing original members with better players until Garcia had a wild, wailing combo that featured drummer Johnny Lopez, alto saxophonist Willie Brown, and two members who would become even more famous for their family connections: pianist James "Cornbread" Harris, father of songwriter-producer "Jimmy Jam" Harris, and bassist Maurice Turner, uncle of Prince. Garcia told Hill in 1972 that he intentionally recruited black musicians for his band: "They were the only ones that had the soul . . . it took a black cat to get up and do it all night and really dig it, you know?"

Garcia's role was to sing lead, play his Telecaster, and work the crowds. "I was the entertainer, the clown, the showman," Garcia told the *Star Tribune's* Chuck Haga in 1993. "I was jumpin' and cookin' on stage, up on top of the piano." The showmanship worked, spectacularly. Five nights a week, the band would pack crowds into a night spot in Mendota called the River Road Club, located beneath the Mendota Bridge and accessible only by a narrow, treacherous road. Wearing one of his thirty-two pairs of Bermuda shorts ("I had to cut the legs off everything—my black mohair suit, my tuxedo, everything," he told Haga) and knee-high socks, Garcia would stand with his back to Brown on Harris's piano and the two would blast their R&B licks to the far walls; alternately, Garcia would lie on his back on the stage and play his Fender Telecaster while he wriggled to the beat of Lopez's drums. The band played two shows a night; on Sundays (when only setups could be sold) the band played from 3 to 8 P.M., then ate dinner and cleaned up using the shower the club had installed for them. Then it was back onstage, where the band would play until 1 A.M.

Eventually word of this high-energy show attracted wider media attention. First, *Minneapolis Tribune* entertainment columnist Will Jones, who visited the River Road Club in 1955, encouraged his readers to see the "short, barrel-chested guitar player" who "works in Bermuda shorts, pink-and-charcoal argyle socks, a sleeveless toga, and a pair of moccasins." The next media figure to embrace Garcia was one of Minnesota's first rock 'n' roll disc jockeys, Joe "Mr. Rhythm" Zingale of wcow, a South St. Paul thousand-watt daytimer owned by brothers Al, Nick, and Vic Tedesco. Though wcow was a country station when Zingale arrived in 1955, he had been bitten by the same rhythm and blues bug that was infecting young people all over the country. Zingale, who greatly admired the music of the similarly smitten Garcia, flipped the wcow format from country to

R&B on Saturday afternoons and evenings—and became a ratings smash. "When he was on the air, there were hundreds and hundreds of people around the radio station just hanging out and listening to the music," according to Sam Sabean, then a young copywriter for the station who would later make a name for himself as deejay Sam Sherwood. Despite his success, Mr. Rhythm was not able to convince the Tedescos to go to an all-R&B format. They rightly assumed a station with a more powerful signal would simply usurp the format. That's precisely what happened when Crowell-Collier Broadcasting bought WCOW and renamed it KDWB three years later.

Zingale would soon move on to other markets, and ultimately he became owner of the Cleveland Nets of the short-lived World Team Tennis league in the 1970s. But while he was in St. Paul, he booked rhythm and blues shows for the St. Paul Auditorium, many featuring the Augie Garcia Quintet. Mr. Rhythm also used his connections to land Garcia a job that could have changed the course of his career: opening for Elvis Presley at the St. Paul Auditorium on Sunday, May 13, 1956. Promoter Thorstein Bjorn (T. B.) Skarning brought Presley to both St. Paul and Minneapolis on that Mother's Day, anticipating as many as twenty-five thousand teens to attend the two shows. Fewer than three thousand showed up for the matinee in St. Paul, which is perhaps why Presley's manager, the tight-fisted Colonel Tom Parker, was in no mood to watch Garcia's quintet win over the crowd with their smoking R&B and crazy antics.

The pairing of the outrageous Garcia Quintet and the newly crowned King of Rock 'n' Roll seemed a natural fit, but Garcia and his band proved too much competition for Presley, whose every career move was controlled by Parker. "They were expecting thousands and thousands of people," Garcia told Hill in 1972. "But what mostly filled it up was my friends. I could see them down in front from the stage." Fifteen minutes into the show, Garcia had the teens standing on their seats, but Parker abruptly pulled the band off the stage—literally. "[Parker] pulled me off the stage by my jacket," Garcia told Haga. "There wasn't supposed to be any competition."

Presley drew a similarly dismal three thousand or so at the evening show in Minneapolis, and Skarning lost his shirt. Garcia, however, was unscathed by the quick hook; he continued to pack the River Road Club through 1958, and he cut four singles for the North Star label of St. Paul. One of those, "Hi Yo Silver," received a good amount of airplay across the Midwest, and Garcia had a chance to take his act to Chicago. Several of his band members were married, however, and didn't want to leave town, so the band stayed put. Though he was disappointed, Garcia's own marriage a few years later helped him understand why his fellow musicians were reluctant to pull up stakes.

Garcia's career wound down in the early 1960s, but the musicians he inspired never forgot him. Though he was underage at the time, Mike Waggoner, who would go on to front the most popular Twin Cities rock 'n' roll band of the late '50s and early '60s, begged the owner of the Crystal Coliseum to let him come in and watch the Augie Garcia Quintet perform. He was permitted to sit in the ticket booth or the balcony and watch rock 'n' roll history being made. "I had never heard of a Minnesota rock band before his," Waggoner said. "He was a little bit of a character—the Bermuda shorts were unique. They played a variety of music. Today you would call it a dance-blues sound."

"I saw Augie Garcia," recalled Tony Andreason. "He and Mike Waggoner—we would watch them, and we were in absolute awe of them."

Meanwhile, Elvis Presley's dramatic rise and the spread of rock 'n' roll radio had captivated the kids of the postwar baby boom. Teens couldn't get enough of the hip, energetic, vaguely rebellious new music. It was the perfect sound track of the times, featured in movies starring James Dean, Marlon Brando, and Elvis, who played brooding loners living for cars, bikes, kicks, chicks, and whatever else life had to offer.

In Liverpool, John Lennon had discovered rock 'n' roll and, after finally meeting his idol in 1965, said, "Nothing really affected me until I heard Elvis." Paul McCartney, who successfully tried out for Lennon's band in 1958, said, "When we were kids growing up in Liverpool, all we ever wanted to be was Elvis Presley." The same was true for fifteen-year-old Bobby Zimmerman in Hibbing, Minnesota. "When I first heard Elvis's voice, I just knew that I wasn't going to work for anybody, and nobody was going to be my boss," he said some years later. "Hearing him for the first time was like busting out of jail."

And it wasn't just Elvis. The door had been kicked open for R&B singers like Chuck Berry, Little Richard, Ray Charles, Bo Diddley, Larry Williams, and Chuck Willis to get past the radio censors and reach white audiences, while rockabilly artists like Jerry Lee Lewis, Roy Orbison, Buddy Holly, and the Everly Brothers were showing music-obsessed kids how to sing, write songs, and play an instrument. A remarkable cross-pollination was taking place: in Hawthorne, California, Brian Wilson was adding Chuck Berry riffs to his Four Freshmen–inspired harmony lines; in London, teenagers Mick Jagger and Keith Richards were eschewing saccharine pop singers for American blues and R&B. In Minneapolis, high school kids Dal Winslow, Steve Wahrer, and Tony Andreason had started blending their country-western, rockabilly, pop, and blues influences in a series of bands that would lead, with the addition of bassist Bob Reed, to the formation of The Trashmen.

The passion for this new music (universally called rock 'n' roll by the mid-1950s) was

Buddy Holly's first visit to the Twin Cities (and first meeting with WDGY emcee Bill Diehl) was as a headliner on Alan Freed's Big Beat tour at the Minneapolis Auditorium on April 25, 1958. Courtesy of Joe Armstrong.

a global, generational phenomenon. Mike Waggoner, John Lennon, and Ringo Starr were born in 1940; Bob Dylan, Dal Winslow, and Steve Wahrer were born in 1941. Paul McCartney, Brian Wilson, and Bob Reed were born in 1942. George Harrison, Mick Jagger, Keith Richards, and Tony Andreason were born in 1943.

The music even reached Fargo, North Dakota, where Robert Thomas ("Bobby") Velline, also born in 1943, joined his older brother Bill's band in early 1959. Then just fifteen years old, Bobby had pestered his brother for months to be allowed to join the band, which was essentially a series of instrumental jam sessions at home with Bill Velline, bass player Dick Dunkirk (who was replaced after a few sessions by Jim Stillman), and drummer Bob Korum. Originally a saxophone player, Bobby bought a Harmony guitar for thirty dollars with money from his paper route, and Bill showed him how to play basic chords. Bill finally relented and let his little brother join the band as rhythm guitar player, primarily because Bobby—who would soon change his stage name to Bobby Vee—could really sing.

"I kind of backed into the band," Vee told his Website biographer. "I used to make all kinds of deals with my brother to come along and practice. When he finally let me join him (if I would promise to keep quiet), I was aware that they didn't know any of the songs lyrically and I just happened to know them all. I was fifteen years old and my ears were glued to the radio. It didn't take long before I started singing the songs and they started rockin' along."

Among the most popular hits of the day were the songs of Buddy Holly, a twenty-two-year-old guitar player from Lubbock, Texas, who burst on the rock 'n' roll scene in 1957 with his band, the Crickets. Their first single, "That'll Be the Day" (the title taken from a recurring John Wayne line in *The Searchers*), had gone to Number 1 in September 1957, followed by hits like "Peggy Sue," "Oh Boy," "Maybe Baby," and "Rave On" through 1958. Holly had first played Minnesota on April 25, 1958, at the Minneapolis Auditorium, as part of a package show put together by disc jockey Alan Freed that included Chuck Berry and Jerry Lee Lewis. In July, Holly appeared at the Duluth National Guard Armory.

"I had met Buddy Holly," said Bill Diehl, who at the time was becoming one of the most popular disc jockeys in the Twin Cities on WDGY. "He must have come through a couple of times before, but nobody paid much attention. He wasn't considered that big a star."

Yet Diehl, always on the lookout for rising talent, went to lunch with Holly at Freddie's Restaurant near the WDGY studios in downtown Minneapolis. "I liked Buddy Holly, and he liked me," said Diehl, who referred to Holly as the Glenn Miller of Rock for his unusu-

The ill-fated Winter Dance Party tour, starring Buddy Holly, Ritchie Valens, and the Big Bopper, made a stop at the Kato Ballroom in Mankato on January 25, 1959.

ally business-like approach to his musical career. "He wore the dark-rimmed glasses. He was very well spoken, very much like Elvis Presley, and I told him that. He said, 'Yes sir, no sir. Thank you for asking.' Always a polished gentleman. I talked to him about music. He liked the idea that his band was orderly. He was a very structured person. He wrote some music, too. He had a brain."

Holly returned to Minnesota in early 1959 with Dion and the Belmonts, Ritchie Valens, J. P. "Big Bopper" Richardson, and singer Frankie Sardo as part of the Winter Dance Party tour—so called because the performances were dances in ballrooms and armories rather than concerts. Kids would cluster in front of the stage, but the floor was open for dancing, and most of the teens danced. Bill Diehl emceed the January 25 show at the Kato Ballroom in Mankato. In attendance at that show was an enthralled Tom Klugherz, a thirteen-year-old aspiring guitarist who would soon be playing bass in a local band called the Jesters, later to become the Gestures. "I'm a big Buddy Holly fan—he was one of my idols," Klugherz said years later. "That was the big deal for John Lennon, too, when he was on the *Ed Sullivan Show*. He wanted to know, 'Is this the stage Buddy Holly stood on? Is this where he was?' It was a big deal to him."

On January 29, Holly and the Winter Dance Party drew an overcapacity crowd of two thousand to the Prom Ballroom in St. Paul, where Bill Diehl again emceed and found Holly's popularity soaring: "You think the Beatles had screamers. You should have seen Buddy Holly," Diehl said. Minnesota country-western singer Sherwin Linton told Larry Lehmer, author of the book *The Day the Music Died*, that he attended the show that night but could not get close enough to the stage to hear the music well because of the girls who would scream whenever Holly sang a verse. Holly was photographed backstage that night by twelve-year-old Tim Kehr, a friend of the ballroom's co-owner, Harry Given. Kehr would pop up again and again as Minnesota's rock music scene expanded in the 1960s.

From St. Paul, the Winter Dance Party bus took an oddly circuitous route: to Iowa for performances in Davenport and Fort Dodge, then 360 miles back north to Duluth, where Holly, Valens, Richardson, and the Belmonts played the Duluth Armory on the last night of January, when the temperatures plunged to 30 degrees below zero. Seventeen-year-old Bob Zimmerman attended that show, having made the seventy-five-mile trip south from his frozen birthplace of Hibbing to see Holly sing and play. A few months earlier, Zimmerman had kicked off his senior year in high school by performing Elvis/Little Richard–style rock 'n' roll on piano with his new band, the Satintones, consisting of his cousin and a couple of friends, all from Duluth. More recently, he had performed an R&B song at Hibbing High School's Jacket Jamboree, with a friend on lead guitar and three junior-college girls singing backup doo-wop vocals. A year earlier, Zimmerman had nearly been laughed and booed off the Hibbing High stage with his first rock 'n' roll band, the Golden Chords. This time, his performance had been received more hospitably; the ambitious curly-haired kid was starting to get the hang of performing. But Buddy Holly's performance at the Duluth Armory was on a completely different level.

"He was great. He was incredible," Dylan told *Rolling Stone* magazine a quarter-century later. "I mean, I'll never forget the image of seeing Buddy Holly up on the bandstand."

The performers left Duluth at midnight and embarked on another three-hundred-mile overnight drive to Appleton, Wisconsin, for a 1:30 P.M. matinee. When the bus broke down ten miles south of Hurley, Wisconsin, the musicians burned newspapers in the back of the bus to keep warm while waiting for help in temperatures of 25 below. Eventually the Appleton show had to be canceled, but they all made it to Green Bay for a show that night. A new bus took them

The Winter Dance Party made a stop at the Duluth Armory on January 31, 1959. Buddy Holly *(top)* was the headliner; he shared the bill with *(center)* J. P. Richardson (the Big Bopper) and Ritchie Valens *(bottom)*. All three were killed in a plane crash two nights later in Clear Lake, Iowa. Tommy Allsup of Buddy Holly's backing band is the second guitarist in each photograph. Courtesy of Sharon Johnson.

from Green Bay to Clear Lake, Iowa, but by this time Holly had seen enough of the Midwest winter through a frosted bus window. Following the show at the Surf Ballroom in Clear Lake on the night of February 2, Holly, Valens, and Richardson boarded a small chartered plane for the 360-mile trip to Moorhead, Minnesota. The plane was in the air for just a few minutes before crashing into a farm field, killing the three singers and pilot Roger Peterson.

Bob Reed was decorating a dance hall for a school party in Oakes, North Dakota, when he heard the news of the crash. Reed, who was a bass player for his high school band, the Corvairs, had planned to attend the Winter Dance Party at the Moorhead National Guard Armory with some friends. "All the sudden, we get it over the radio," said Reed. "There was this accident. It was just . . . it was a shock. Needless to say, we didn't go."

Tom Klugherz, who had seen Holly perform just ten days earlier in Mankato, said he was "really bummed" when he heard about the crash. His sorrow was shared by many. "I had a friend who was such a fanatic Buddy Holly fan that in school the next morning, somebody came up to him and said, 'Hey, Buddy Holly's plane crashed.' The guy did that because he knew he was a Buddy Holly fan. My friend knocked him out. He actually knocked the guy out—that's how serious a Buddy Holly fan he was. He didn't think that was funny at all. Then he found out it was true."

No one in Moorhead knew what to do. Word went out on local radio that the show had been canceled, but that generated a flood of phone calls to the stations pleading that the show go on as scheduled as a tribute to Holly, Valens, and Richardson. Promoter Rod Lucier, a deejay at Fargo's KVOX, stood to lose his $750 investment if the show was canceled. When the remaining members of the Winter Dance Party tour arrived by bus to hear the dreadful news, they decided they would rather perform than cancel. The show needed more acts, however. Singers Frankie Avalon and Jimmy Clanton were sent from Chicago to catch up with the show at its next stop, but they would not make it to Moorhead. Local deejays, including future WCCO radio personality Charlie Boone of KFGO in Fargo, put out a call for local rock 'n' rollers to fill in. Bassist Jim Stillman of Bill Velline's band called the station. When asked if the group had performing experience, Stillman lied and said yes. They were hired, along with the area's best-known local group, Terry Lee and the Poor Boys, and seven-year-old singer Ronnie Kerber. The Poor Boys had been playing in the Fargo–Moorhead area since 1955 and had been asked by promoter Lucier to join the show when news came of the plane crash. The Vellines had been jamming and learning songs since the previous summer but had never been on a stage before. They spent the afternoon rehearsing the half-dozen songs they knew best, then went downtown to buy matching stage outfits: black peg pants with tight cuffs, sweater vests (Bobby's red, the others black), and black-and-white-striped angora ties.

That night's show played to an overflow crowd of two thousand, many of them attracted no doubt by the national publicity the crash created. "I don't know if people came to the Armory expecting to see coffins laid out in front," Boone told Larry Lehmer in *The Day the Music Died.* "But there was a curiosity factor."

"It was a rock 'n' roll wake," Bobby Vee said years later. "Charlie did a masterful job of presenting what would seem like an impossible evening."

"The atmosphere of the show was almost surreal, I felt, with the Big Three's deaths so fresh in everyone's minds," Bob Becker (aka Terry Lee) told Midwest rock historian Jim Oldsberg in 1995. "There was excitement, but there was also a sadness in the air. Probably more bewilderment than sadness, actually."

Fifteen-year-old Bobby Vee began touring small towns around Fargo after his first public performance subbing for Buddy Holly at the Winter Dance Party tour in Fargo on February 3, 1959. Courtesy of Tom Tourville.

Ronnie Kerber opened the show by singing the recent Laurie London hit "He's Got the Whole World in His Hands" and received a tremendous ovation; he would eventually form a Fargo rock band called the Mods and have a big local hit in 1966 with a song called "Should I." When it was time for the Vellines' band to be introduced, emcee Boone turned and asked them what they called themselves. Bobby Velline came up with the name the Shadows on the spot. Their brief set, consisting of briskly played Top 40 hits by Elvis Presley, Little Richard, and the Everly Brothers, lifted the mood of the crowd, primarily because young Bobby Velline had Buddy Holly's singing style down cold, including Holly's trademark hiccup phrasing.

Burnell "Bing" Bengtsson, who owned the Starlight Drive-In Theater in Fargo and also booked and managed local rock 'n' roll bands (including Bob Reed's Corvairs), called Bobby

Velline's performance "haunting," according to Lehmer. "When he sang, he sounded like Buddy Holly," Bengtsson recalled. "Everybody gasped. It was really a strange feeling." Terry Lee and the Poor Boys played next, followed by Frankie Sardo, who performed a maudlin version of Valens's hit ballad "Donna" that cheered no one. Then came a makeshift version of the Crickets, led by Waylon Jennings—the bass player in Holly's band who lost a coin flip for a seat on the doomed plane. Dion and the Belmonts closed what would go down as one of the most significant—and melancholy—concerts in rock 'n' roll history.

The Shadows received no pay for helping to save the Moorhead leg of the Winter Dance Party, but they did take advantage of the unexpected exposure. Following the show, Bengtsson offered an audition to both Terry Lee and the Poor Boys and the Shadows; the Poor Boys missed the morning tryout because they had played a job the night before and didn't get up in time. The Shadows showed up, and Bengtsson agreed to start booking them.

No one voice or band was going to fill the hole that Holly's death left in the rock 'n' roll world—which had already suffered serious blows in just a few short years. Elvis Presley had been drafted and was still in the U.S. Army, serving a two-year hitch in Germany that would not conclude for another year. Jerry Lee Lewis's career had almost foundered after he married his thirteen-year-old cousin in 1957. Richard Wayne Penniman (Little Richard), a huge source of inspiration to Bob Dylan and the Beatles, temporarily gave up secular music and began studying theology in 1958. Chuck Berry was arrested in 1959 for violating the Mann Act with a fourteen-year-old girl and ultimately served time in prison in the early 1960s. Holly had been rock 'n' roll's best hope for sustaining its popularity, and now he was gone.

Bill Diehl never forgot how Holly's death impacted Minnesota's rock-loving teens. "I'll tell you what it was like," he said. "I was on the air, and the next day the word came that Buddy Holly, J. P. Richardson, and Ritchie Valens were dead. And I had all the current records lying right there. I went on the air at 4 o'clock. Fans could come into the Builder's Exchange and watch the broadcast. I look at this mob of girls—and I don't remember if there were any boys—crying their eyes out. Awww, it hit me so hard I was starting to cry on the air" (Diehl paused and wiped his eyes as he recalled his emotions that afternoon more than fifty years earlier) "and I'm doing it again! I was not blood brothers with Buddy Holly, but it was the sight of these girls. Just crying and crying. That's how it hit me. We played their records over and over. Maybe two weeks later I had to go through the same thing again."

He was referring to the "Three Stars," released in April by Tommy Dee with Carol Kay and the Teen-aires, featuring Dee's spoken tributes to the three singers over a slow guitar line, followed by Kay's mournful refrain "Gee, we're gonna miss you. Everybody sends their love." The song peaked at Number 11 on the *Billboard* chart in May 1959. "They go on, 'Buddy's in heaven,' and I look up and there's a crowd—when I say 'a crowd,' I mean they went back to the elevators—crying again."

Meanwhile, the Shadows were gaining performing experience in Fargo and beyond. On Valentine's Day 1959, the band earned sixty dollars playing a job in a high school gym in Breckenridge, Minnesota. Benches were pushed together to form a stage, but during the band's performance the benches separated and their amplifiers fell to the floor. That experience was typical for Upper Midwestern rock bands of the era, as was the hardship of driving miles across snowy, icy roads to an armory or a ballroom in rattletrap vehicles (in the case of the Shadows, a 1951 Oldsmobile) to play several hours of cover songs for rock 'n' roll–loving teenagers.

The Twin Cities area was beginning to spawn a number of rock 'n' roll bands, including Mike Waggoner and the Bops, the Delricos, the Dorados, Damon Lee and the Diablos, and a stable of bands that recorded on a small Minneapolis label called Gaity Records: the String Kings, the Sonics, the Flames, the Glenrays, the Big M's, and a pair of black vocal groups, the Valquins and the Wisdoms. Gaity owner David Hersk recorded the groups on a sixty-five-dollar tape recorder in the basement of his parents' house at 1501 Newton Avenue in North Minneapolis. "In high school when I had my bar mitzvah, the guy who taught me Hebrew had a Wilcox [recording] machine and put the lessons on discs," Hersk said. "I became interested and got the bug, I guess."

Hersk offered bands a standard deal: five hundred dollars bought you one thousand copies of your record and paid for the studio time. Airplay was exceedingly rare for the few rock 'n' roll records made by Twin Cities bands in the late 1950s, but they were a valuable promotional tool. Bands could sell or give away the 45 rpm records at their dance jobs. "The Glenrays got airplay, but none of my pop stuff was really what I'd call high airplay, or very successful," Hersk said. "Back then, playlists were very selective. If you had ten or twenty records, you played them over and over. I knew all those guys at KDWB and WDGY, but it was difficult. When I think about it, there was nothing special about our records."

Yet Gaity's records were wild, raw, free, and they rocked. The groups were mostly just having fun. They didn't expect to get on the air—and the black groups couldn't. "It was very tough for them," Hersk said of the Big M's, the Wisdoms, and the Valquins. "They got no airplay—none. I wish Motown had been around. I would have licensed them. I'm sure Berry Gordy would have picked them up. I never saw them live, because they only played for high school dances. They never played at the Crystal Coliseum, never played at the Prom. I didn't give it that much thought as to why. They didn't stay together too long." Their lack of success in 1959 translated into big bucks on the modern collectors' market, however. A copy of the Valquins' "Falling Star" 45 on Gaity can fetch $650, while a copy of the Wisdoms' "Lost in Dreams" / "Two Hearts Make One Love" on Gaity goes for $600.

Kay Bank began as a recording studio for jazz and polka bands in the midfifties before evolving into the primary studio in Minneapolis to record rock 'n' roll. Courtesy of Steven Wiese.

Though he launched Minnesota's rock 'n' roll recording boom, Hersk was out of the record business by 1964. "There was no reason to keep Gaity going," he said. "The business had changed so much. The bands and music had changed completely. My last part at Gaity had been the folk music binge. Maybe my interest in music had changed."

The prime location to record a record in Minneapolis was Kay Bank Studio, near the corner of Nicollet Avenue and East Twenty-sixth Street in Minneapolis, two blocks from the Minneapolis College of Art and Design. Kay Bank Studio began its life as the Garrick vaudeville and movie theater in the 1920s. The young daughter of the theater owner is said to have died there, and generations of musicians have reported sudden drops in temperature, unexplained footsteps on the stairway, and piano keys played by unseen hands. The building was abandoned for many years before being purchased in 1954 by twenty-one-year-old Bruce Swedien, who was studying electrical engineering with a minor in music at the University of Minnesota. He was also recording jazz and polka bands as a part-time job at Schmitt Music's studio. Swedien bought Schmitt's equipment and moved it into the former Garrick Theater, converting it into the best recording studio in the Upper Midwest. He recorded anyone who had the desire—and the money—to put their music to disc, including longtime WCCO radio pianist Jeanne Arland Peterson, who, with her husband Willie conducting the band, recorded "Summer Love" and "Right Side

Up, Upside Down" under the moniker of Jeannie Arlen and the Vocalarks in late 1954.
Other early artists in the studio included Art Fitch and his Polka Dot Boys, Leo and his
Pioneers, and Norm Wilke's Little Fishermen. Swedien also recorded tracks by jazz greats
Art Blakey and Herbie Mann.

In 1957, Swedien was hired by RCA in Chicago and went on to a spectacular career
as a recording engineer. He earned his first Grammy nomination for the Four Seasons
and their hit "Big Girls Don't Cry" in 1962. He later engineered the hits "Oh Girl" and
"Have You Seen Her" by the Chi-Lites, and he engineered every album that Quincy Jones
produced for Michael Jackson, including *Thriller*, generally credited as the best-selling
album of all time. Swedien was ultimately nominated for thirteen Grammy awards and
won five.

When he left for Chicago in 1957, Swedien sold the studio to Vernon Bank, who
renamed it after his wife, Kay. The Banks had begun making recordings at weddings in
the late 1940s, eventually shifting to recording choir and polka music. "Vern Bank was my
competitor, but we became good friends," said David Hersk. "We shared equipment. Our
rates were identical. He gave me a price on record pressing. We were a tight-knit family,
Vern and us. We had a very good relationship."

Vern Bank's partners in the purchase of the studio were brothers Amos and Daniel
Heilicher, who had been in business together since the 1930s, when they printed and sold
scorecards at University of Minnesota football games for a dime apiece. They progressed
to pinball machines and then jukeboxes, selling the used records from the machines
when customers stopped playing them. After World War II, the Heilichers opened a
record store at Third and Hennepin in downtown Minneapolis. Their big break came
in 1947 when they acquired the Mercury Records distributorship for Minnesota and
the Dakotas. By the 1950s, the Heilichers had become regional distributors for Mercury,
Columbia, RCA, and other labels, putting records in jukeboxes and racks at department
and variety stores.

Though neither of the Heilichers was particularly musical, the next logical step for
them was to start a record label and buy into a recording studio. They also built a record-
pressing plant on Washington Avenue North in Minneapolis. They named their label
Soma, perhaps because *Dan* spelled backward would have been a less appealing name
than *Amos* spelled backward. The year was 1957, and the tastes of established Upper Midwest musicians ran toward country-western and polka music, with a little jazz thrown in.
Early Soma artists included local TV and radio country singer Ernest "Slim Jim" Iverson
and old-time music acts Fezz Fristche, Jerry Dostal, Elmer Scheid, the Jolly Lumberjacks,

Happy Hugo and His Polkateers, and the Chesney Brothers. Vern Bank and the Heilichers didn't care who came in to record; they offered essentially the same deal to each artist, regardless of quality or sales potential: three hours of studio time and one thousand copies of a two-sided 45 rpm record for $495. Soma sent one hundred copies to Midwest radio stations, one hundred copies to regional record dealers, and kept one hundred for promotional ventures; the artist kept the remaining seven hundred. Heilicher would include review cards with the promo copies he sent to radio stations and record stores, asking for feedback. If the reports were favorable, Soma would sign a new deal with the artist to press more records and do heavier distribution.

Bobby and Bill Velline arrived at Kay Bank Studio on June 1, 1959, to record as many songs as they could from 9 A.M. to noon. They managed to lay down four tracks during the session. The A-side of the group's single was a catchy vocal tune that Bobby had written in study hall at Fargo Central, called "Suzie Baby"; the B-side was an instrumental Bill wrote called "Flyin' High." There were certainly echoes of Buddy Holly in Bobby's smooth vocal delivery, and Bill's slinky guitar line wafted over and around the melody in a tasteful, memorable way. The record, released on the Soma label under the name Bobby Vee and the Shadows, caught on quickly in the Twin Cities, thanks in part to the Heilichers' local influence. It became the first chart hit for a song recorded at Kay Bank and bearing the Soma logo, the lowercase letters s, o, m, and a in tilted boxes on a black background with the words SOMA RECORD CO. MINNEAPOLIS, MINNESOTA around the top of the label.

Within a few weeks, Bobby Vee and the Shadows were receiving offers to sign with major record companies, and Amos Heilicher was listening, because he knew Soma was not capable of distributing enough copies of "Suzie Baby" to keep up with demand. While the offers were coming together, the Shadows spent the summer promoting "Suzie Baby" in their Minnesota–Iowa–Dakotas backyard. Meanwhile, Terry Lee and the Poor Boys, the Fargo band that shared the stage with the Vellines back in February at the Winter Dance Party, also made their way to Kay Bank to cut a rock 'n' roll record for Soma. The A-side was "My Little Sue," written by Bob ("Terry") Becker; the B-side was an instrumental written by lead guitarist Dave Pederson called "Driftin'." The Poor Boys' record had a tougher rock sound, more akin to Gene Vincent than to Buddy Holly, and became a hit on KFGO in Fargo but did not spread to other markets the way "Suzie Baby" did.

The Poor Boys and the Shadows had one other unusual connection in common. Ron Joelson, a friend of Becker and the other Poor Boys, knew the band was looking for a piano player and introduced them to a guy he had met at Camp Herzl, a summer camp in

Webster, Wisconsin, established in 1946 for Jewish youth. The seventeen-year-old piano player's name was Bob Zimmerman, but he introduced himself to the band as Elston Gunnn—with three *n*'s. Zimmerman had come to Fargo to stay with Joelson, but Joelson's mother couldn't stand listening to him sing and play, so he took an apartment in town and was working as a busboy at the Red Apple Cafe. The audition with the Poor Boys was not promising.

"He could only play in the key of C, I recall," Becker said in Jim Oldsberg's 1995 fanzine *Lost and Found #4*. "He tried to sing one song once, and we unanimously said, 'Oh my God!' and that was it." Even if the Poor Boys had liked his playing and singing (which they likened to Ernest Tubb, as Zimmerman would descend on a note, hit it for an instant, and then slide under it), few locations could provide a piano, and Zimmerman didn't own one. The Poor Boys did bring him to a couple of jobs, including one at the Crystal Ballroom in Fargo. Owner Ralph "Doc" Chinn gave Zimmerman a listen and said, "That guy's gotta go."

Before becoming Bob Dylan, the folk singer Bobby Zimmerman *(right)* performed with his band the Golden Chords at local venues, including Hibbing High School. Courtesy of Monte Edwardson and Leroy Hoikkala.

And so he did—to another audition, this time with Bobby Vee and the Shadows, who were also interested in adding a piano player. "Elston Gunnn" was given a tryout, after meeting Bill Velline at Sam Paper's Recordland store and telling him he had recently toured with Conway Twitty. They brought him to KFGO in Fargo for an audition because there was a piano in the studio. The verdict: not bad, at least in the key of C. They bought him a black shirt to match the rest of the band and brought him to a church basement job in Gwinner, North Dakota. The only piano available there was an old upright that was badly out of tune, but the Shadows appreciated finally having a piano player for their Jerry Lee Lewis songs. Zimmerman accompanied the band to their next job near Fargo, but the equipment issue surfaced again. They couldn't arrange their bookings around halls where a piano was available; Zimmerman had to buy a piano if he was going to stay with the group. Elston Gunn didn't have that kind of money. Vee and Zimmerman parted amicably; the piano player accepted fifteen dollars for each of the two nights he played with the Shadows and caught a bus back to Hibbing. "It was even suggested at one point that he had been fired," Bobby Vee recalled years later. "Not true. The truth is simple . . . it just didn't work out."

Once back on the Iron Range, Zimmerman told a few friends that he cut a record called "Suzie Baby," and his professional name was now Bobby Vee. He continued that ruse for a time when he moved to Minneapolis in September to begin his freshman year at the University of Minnesota, but few there believed him. Just as well: by that time, Zimmerman had decided there was no future in rock 'n' roll. "I was playing rock 'n' roll when I was thirteen and fourteen and fifteen, but I had to quit when I was sixteen or seventeen because I couldn't make it that way," he told the *Chicago Tribune* in 1965. "The image of the day was Frankie Avalon or Fabian, or this whole athletic supercleanness bit, you know, which if you didn't have that, you couldn't make any friends. . . . I played semiprofessionally piano with rock 'n' roll groups. About 1958 or 1959, I discovered Odetta, Harry Belafonte, that stuff, and I became a folk singer."

After hearing Odetta's first album, he traded in his electric guitar for a flat-top Gibson acoustic. He would soon drop the name Zimmerman and forever after go by the name Bob Dylan. After a year immersing himself in traditional folk music and writing his first derivative yet promising songs, Dylan moved to New York City, where he would seek out his new idol, Woody Guthrie, become a fixture in the city's folk clubs, and sign a recording contract with Columbia. He would rarely return to Minnesota, but he would return to rock 'n' roll and have a profound effect on the rock 'n' rollers he left behind.

Bobby Vee had that "supercleanness" look that Zimmerman felt was necessary to succeed in rock 'n' roll. He also had a hit. Joe Sadd, a Midwest promotion man for Liberty Records (the same label for which Minnesota native Eddie Cochran recorded), sent "Suzie Baby" to Thomas "Snuff" Garrett, one of the label's in-house producers. Garrett, just nineteen years old, had moved to Los Angeles from Dallas and had once worked as a deejay in Lubbock, Texas, where he met Buddy Holly. Liberty signed Vee to a one-record deal with an option for a second single and bought the "Suzie Baby" master from Soma. The record was reissued nationally in early August 1959, reached Number 77, and remained on the *Billboard* singles chart for four weeks. It was a somewhat disappointing performance after the record's success in Minneapolis, but Garrett still believed that Vee could fill some of the void left by Holly.

While "Suzie Baby" was in re-release, Vee returned to Kay Bank with the Shadows and recorded several more tracks, including "Remember the Day," "Love Must Have Passed Me By," and "Laurie," since there was no word yet on whether Liberty was going to pick up Vee's option. Then it was back to touring the Midwest with the Shadows. Vee and Jim Stillman got into a bitter argument at St. Paul's Prom Ballroom over something Stillman had said to emcee Bill Diehl—a man no bandleader could afford to aggravate. Vee fired Stillman and brought original jam session member Dick Dunkirk back to play bass.

Snuff Garrett finally called Vee in December 1959 and asked him to come to Los Angeles to record a second single for Liberty, a cover of Adam Faith's "What Do You Want" backed with "My Love Loves Me," written by Sonny Curtis, Buddy Holly's former lead guitarist. After that session, Vee again returned to the Midwest to tour with the Shadows. He and brother Bill started the Vee record label, and in February they released the single "What'll I Do" / "Leave Me Alone" under the name Bill Velline and the Shadows, though Bobby played on the record and wrote the B-side. Both songs are in the Ricky Nelson midtempo pop ballad style, and it is clear from these recordings that only one of the Velline brothers was a gifted pop singer; Bill sounded like an amateur at a barn dance talent show.

In March 1960, Garrett sent Vee and the Shadows to Clovis, New Mexico, to record with Buddy Holly's producer and collaborator, Norman Petty. Vee told author Jim Oldsberg that the Clovis sessions felt much more comfortable than the L.A. sessions—more like recording at Kay Bank. When Vee went back to Los Angeles to record the other side of the album, however, Garrett began pushing more pop-oriented material with strings, accurately pointing out that Holly had been going in that direction before he died. Rockabilly was fading away, replaced by professional songwriters—most of them working out of the Brill Building in New York City—who were cranking out pop tunes with a more gentle rock 'n' roll beat. The Clovis tracks were scrapped. At that point, the Shadows decided the time was right to drop manager Bing Bengtsson, who had taken a staff job at Kay Bank Studios. Neither Liberty nor Bengtsson seemed particularly interested in the Shadows.

Vee's first Liberty album, *Bobby Vee Sings Your Favorites*, took off in the fall of 1960, propelled by his first Top 5 single, a smooth pop cover of the Clovers' "Devil or Angel." Garrett then turned to Brill Building songwriters for Vee's next records, including the upbeat "Rubber Ball" by Aaron Schroeder that reached Number 6 in January 1961 and his back-to-back breakthrough hits in late 1961: the Number 1 smash "Take Good Care of My Baby," written by Carole King and Gerry Goffin, followed by the Number 2 hit "Run to Him," written by Goffin and Jack Keller. By that time, Vee was becoming a mature crooner whose vocal style retained only traces of the Buddy Holly influence.

Yet Vee was not willing to give up on his hometown rock 'n' roll band. As recounted in Oldsberg's *Lost and Found #4*, the Shadows hired a new lead singer, Ken Harvey, and continued to play the Midwest ballroom circuit while Vee was in California. Bobby Vee booked the band into Cuca Recording Studio in Sauk City, Wisconsin, a primarily polka and ethnic music studio started in 1959 by James Kirchstein. The Shadows recorded ten tracks at Cuca; four were eventually released by Liberty in 1962 on two all-instrumental singles, "Toy Soldier" / "Loco" and "Mind Reader" / "Card Shark." Neither sold, and the Shadows broke up a year later.

Selling Bobby Vee and the Shadows to a bigger label was not a blow for Amos and Danny Heilicher. Instead, it demonstrated to them that there was money to be made recording contemporary rock and pop music at their Kay Bank Studio and distributing it on their Soma record

Dave Dudley *(right)* was a fixture on the stage of Minneapolis's Flame Cafe before recording his 1963 hit "Six Days on the Road" at Kay Bank Studio. Courtesy of Cheri Lindberg.

label. Two more national hits followed. The first was "Mule Skinner Blues" by a band from Madison, Wisconsin, called the Fendermen. With no drummer or bass player, guitarists Phil Humphrey and Jim Sundquist cut a heavily echoed novelty version of the Jimmie Rodgers country blues song in Kirchstein's basement studio in Sauk City and released it on the Cuca label. Despite Humphrey's yodeling hillbilly vocal and Sundquist's speedy lead guitar work, the record languished until deejay Lindy Shannon began playing it on WKBH in La Crosse, Wisconsin. It sold thousands of copies and came to the attention of the Heilichers, who signed the Fendermen to Soma records and had them re-record the song at Kay Bank. The new version—just as corny, echoey, and irresistible as the first—reached the Top 5 on the *Billboard* singles chart in July 1960. The Fendermen eventually cut an album on Soma, but no more hits followed, and within two years Humphrey and Sundquist split up.

Soma's next hit was the classic truck-driving anthem "Six Days on the Road," sung by Spencer, Wisconsin, native Dave Dudley (born David Pedruska), who traveled around the Midwest as a country singer and disc jockey before landing in Minneapolis. Dudley held down a shift as a deejay on the country-western station KEVE and played with his band the Country Gentlemen at the Gay 90's bar on Hennepin Avenue and the Flame Cafe on Nicollet Avenue. Dudley had recorded on the King label as far back as 1955, with little success. His career was further impeded in 1960 when he was struck and injured by a hit-and-run driver while loading his guitar into his car outside the Flame Cafe. He spent a year recuperating but returned to recording in 1961 with a single on the Velline's Vee label called "Maybe I Do," a standard country weeper that peaked at Number 28 on the *Billboard* country chart. The B-side was "I Wouldn't Wait Around," a peppy rockabilly-styled tune. Both songs were cowritten by George Garrett, who owned the Nic-O-Lake Record Shop at the corner of Nicollet Avenue and Lake Street in Minneapolis.

Dudley followed "Maybe I Do" with a single called "Under Cover of the Night," an obvious imitation of Leroy Van Dyke's 1961 hit "Walk on By." It reached Number 18 on the country charts and brought him to the attention of Jim Madison, who owned a small Twin Cities record label called Golden Wing, which was distributed by Soma. Dudley signed with Madison as a producer, talent scout, A&R man, and recording artist in 1962. His first single on Golden Wing was an attempt to cash in on the folk music surge, doing country versions of traditional folk songs "Barbara Allen" and "John Henry." The record went nowhere. Dudley needed to find a song in the pure country-western style or his career as a recording artist was in jeopardy.

"Six Days on the Road" was cowritten by Earl Green and Carl Montgomery, brother of country singer Melba Montgomery and songwriter Earl "Peanut" Montgomery. Green and Montgomery had actually worked as interstate truckers, making a regular six-day run between Alabama and Pittsburgh hauling floor tile. They eventually wrote a song about the experience and called it "Six Days on the Road." The song was first recorded in 1961 by obscure country artist Paul Davis, but the arrangement was bouncy and lacking in personality. Green and Montgomery offered the song to Cajun singer Jimmy C. Newman during a visit to the Grand Ole Opry. Newman turned it down but suggested that it might be right for his friend Dave Dudley. Dudley was going into Kay Bank Studios on April 1, 1963, to cut his next single, "I Feel a Cry Coming On," funded by the fourteen thousand dollars he had received in his hit-and-run insurance settlement. He put "Six Days on the Road" in his guitar case as a backup tune in case there was time to record it at the end of the session.

Dudley's deep, almost leering baritone was a perfect fit for the lyrics about dodging scales and cops, taking little white pills to stay awake, and passing up "a lot of women" on his drive back home. His recording is also notable for the twangy string popping of nineteen-year-old lead guitarist Jimmy Colvard. Colvard was living in St. Paul and playing at the Flame Cafe with his own trio, then sitting in with the house band that backed the visiting country stars. Dudley liked the innovative string-snapping style Colvard used, and when he found extra time at the end of the session, he had Colvard pluck the distinctive opening riff to "Six Days on the Road." "Jimmy Colvard was a real great guitar player," said the Trashmen's Tony Andreason. "He played 'Six Days on the Road' with his fingernails, using a Gretsch Country Gentleman. He became a really well-compensated studio musician in Nashville. He was so good, everybody knew who he was."

Dudley's version of "Six Days on the Road" was released on the Soma-affiliated Golden Wing label in May and became a country-western smash, reaching Number 2 on the country chart and Number 32 on the pop chart in July 1963. He also released an album for Soma (on the Golden Wing label), which reached Number 16 on the *Billboard* country album chart. Again, a larger label came in quickly and snapped up Soma's new star; this time it was Mercury Records, for whom Dudley recorded twenty albums and dozens of singles over the next decade.

The Heilicher brothers were beginning to suspect that there was more money to be made in this pop music business than they had first estimated. They wouldn't part with their next stars so easily.

FROM THE LAND OF 10,000 HITS

EVERYBODY'S HEARD
ABOUT THE BIRD

MONOPHONIC
33⅓ RPM

FOR PROMOTIONAL USE ONLY

HIGH FIDELITY
SIDE ONE

CHAPTER
2

THE RAJAH OF THE RECORDS

THE BIGGEST AND MOST POPULAR RADIO STATION in Minnesota for most of the twentieth century was WCCO-AM, the fifty-thousand-watt clear-channel behemoth primarily known for its news, sports, and genial personalities. From Minnesota Gophers football games in the '30s and '40s to Minnesota Twins baseball and Minnesota Vikings football in the '60s, all dials seemed to be tuned to 830. WCCO played inoffensive pop music, too, but news, jokes, and conversation were the primary filler between the big games. It was often said that airline pilots flying over the Twin Cities in the 1950s could watch the lights go out all over Minneapolis and St. Paul after Cedric Adams wrapped up his 10 P.M. newscast on WCCO radio, and water levels would drop due to simultaneous toilet flushings.

Bill Diehl started his media career at the *St. Paul Pioneer Press,* where he progressed from copyediting to movie columnist in 1950. Courtesy of *St. Paul Pioneer Press.*

Nothing seemed capable of challenging the self-proclaimed Good Neighbor for supremacy of the Twin Cities airwaves—not until rock 'n' roll came along.

In the mid-1950s, radio stations WLOL, WMIN, and WCOW experimented with rock 'n' roll, but most broadcasters considered the music a passing fad, something advertisers wouldn't support and young listeners would grow out of. The more inquisitive and adventurous young music lovers in Minnesota were tuning in to late-night rhythm and blues broadcasts from exotic southern stations in Arkansas, Tennessee, and Louisiana. But rock 'n' roll continued to lap at the shores of the Land of Ten Thousand Lakes until two Twin Cities AM radio stations, WDGY and KDWB, jumped in with both feet and began competing furiously for the huge teen audience. A big part of the appeal of these rock 'n' roll stations was their wisecracking, hip-talking deejays, who knew how to keep the young listeners entertained and coming back for more. The stations promoted their personalities, and no Twin Cities radio personality was savvier about promotion than WDGY's Bill Diehl.

Diehl always thought of himself as a newspaperman first, since his career with the *St. Paul Dispatch* and *Pioneer Press* lasted from 1943 until 1996, a year after he retired from his last radio job. His journey to Top 40 radio was a long and somewhat circuitous one. Diehl was born in St. Paul in 1926 and graduated from St. Paul Central High School in 1943. By then he had earned the reputation as one of the hardest-working and shrewdest newspaper carriers on the streets of St. Paul. "I started carrying newspapers when I was eleven," Diehl said. "I carried the old *St. Paul Shopper* and the *Shopping News and Guide.* I had about 250 papers—you wonder why my back is bent? In 1939, one of my buddies, Bud Moffatt, who lived over on Hillcrest, a classmate of mine at Central, said his brother Bill Moffatt was giving up his newspaper route. In those days getting a newspaper route—we were fresh out of a terrible depression, not even out of it yet, in fact it was getting worse—to get a little outside income was terrific."

Diehl told his pal that he wanted the newspaper route, which involved delivering eleven daily and twenty-three Sunday copies of the *Minneapolis Evening Tribune*. He was still just thirteen years old, but he had a bicycle with a basket that could carry the papers. Bill Moffatt agreed to give Diehl the route and drove him around in his car to show him the territory. "He had a car, he was only fifteen, and he smoked Phillip Morris cigarettes in the brownish box, which I thought was just terrific—wow," Diehl said. "But that route never seemed to end. It stretched from Grand Avenue to Montreal, and from Lexington up to Cleveland. You look on a map, it's a fourth of the city of St. Paul."

No problem. Diehl was so dedicated to completing his route each day that he had to be pulled off the streets during the Armistice Day blizzard that killed forty-nine Minnesotans on November 11, 1940. Later that year the *Evening Tribune* was bought by the *Minneapolis Star-Journal*, owned by the Cowles family of Des Moines, Iowa, and Diehl found himself delivering papers for the company that had previously been the competition. Though he considered that paper the enemy, he hit on a rich vein of new subscribers: a new apartment complex called the Highland Village opened in St. Paul, and Diehl quickly began snapping up new accounts. His success did not go unnoticed at his hometown paper. One day a man from the *Dispatch–Pioneer Press* came to the Diehl house on Hillcrest and offered him a morning and evening route. "I was thrilled to think I was going to get a *Dispatch* route, because they delivered to everybody, where the *Star-Journal* was here and here and here," Diehl said. "I wanted to have a route where I delivered to everybody, and I was seeing dollar signs."

The Highland Village was considered a battleground between the St. Paul and Minneapolis papers, because many of the new residents had moved to town to work at the St. Paul Ford plant and had no loyalty to either city. Diehl came up with an aggressive approach to increasing his subscribers. In exchange for giving the manager of the complex a free morning, evening, and Sunday paper, Diehl was notified whenever a new resident moved in. If the potential new customer turned down the paper, Diehl offered to give the resident a free paper for a week. If they still weren't interested at the end of the week, they were under no obligation and Diehl absorbed the loss. But Diehl estimates he sold the subscription "eight times out of ten—because the wife would get used to the recipes and features and say, 'I want that paper.'"

Diehl's route became so large—beginning with eighty customers, it soon reached 250—that he had to hire an assistant to help him deliver all the papers. As the route grew, Diehl developed what would be a lifelong bond to both the St. Paul newspapers and the business itself. "I got up in the morning at about 4 o'clock. I got down to the corner about 4:30, and in the distance, winter or summer, rain or shine, here were these two headlights coming in the vicinity of Grand Avenue and Cleveland, way down there," Diehl recalled more than sixty years later. "The truck would come, and I'd see them stop, and they'd throw out their bundles, and I knew they were coming. I'm standing out there and I'm freezing, just freezing—there were 20-below mornings—and off in the distance I'd see these two dim truck headlights coming closer, and I'd say, 'The *Pioneer Press* is coming, coming, coming.' It wasn't like this with the evening paper, because I could go into Roith's Pharmacy and warm up. But the paper would finally come, and they'd throw the papers off, and I'll tell you, I would go, 'Thank you,' and grab that bundle of papers and slide my hands in. They were literally hot off the press. And they were warm. They'd come out of a warm building. I'd leave my hands in there until I could move my fingers again. If you are that close to a paper and you needed it to warm your hands, there's a bond. There's a bond that's built, and it still exists."

When Diehl's route topped 250 papers, he was summoned to the downtown offices of the *Dispatch–Pioneer Press* by associate publisher Hal Shugard. Diehl was worried that he was going to be fired, but Shugard simply wanted to know how on earth Diehl had built up such a successful paper route. When Diehl said he was offering a week of free papers out of his own pocket, Shugard was so impressed with his initiative that he said, "When you graduate from high school, you come down and see me. You've got a job here at the *Pioneer Press and Dispatch*."

Shugard was as good as his word, but when Diehl gave up his route after graduating from Central in 1943, he was not given a job in the newsroom as he'd hoped but, rather, was assigned to collect delinquent accounts for the circulation department. A seventeen-year-old with a crew cut and a leather jacket, Diehl was sent to some of the worst neighborhoods in town to try to collect money from hard-core deadbeats who threatened him, insulted him, and—in at least one instance—invited him upstairs to take money off the dresser in a bedroom where two couples were having sexual intercourse.

Desperate to get out of debt collection, Diehl continued to angle for a job as a copy boy in the fourth-floor newsroom. Finally he was told there was a spot for him. He reported to managing editor Fred Heaberlin. "He was just the sweetest guy," Diehl said. "He'd hold his lips like that—he had little dimples, he always chewed gum—and he'd say, 'Bill, ah, I want you to get over there, ah . . .'" Diehl started out taking movie listings and then moved up to occasional headline writing for copy desk chief Edwin Olwin: "Nicest guy in the world—steely salt-and-pepper hair, dark olive complexion, and he liked me. I was always very respectable to him. Not all the guys on the copy desk liked me. The rumor was around that I was a Ridder." Diehl had a flair for puns, which at the time were seldom seen in newspaper headlines. Many of the stories he was given came from municipal court.

Diehl interviewed hundreds of Hollywood stars for the *Pioneer Press,* including Minnesota native Judy Garland. Courtesy of *St. Paul Pioneer Press.*

"There was this guy who slammed into several cars, and he was a saxophone player," Diehl said. "They arrested him for drunkenness. I put the headline on it: 'Sax player goes on toot.'" Another story about a shirt that had been stolen several times before being recognized by its original owner ended up with the headline "Shirt tale has happy ending." Olwin told Diehl he wanted him on the desk as much as possible.

"That woke up some of the old-timers," Diehl said. "They were used to 'Man dies, 86.'"

By 1948, one of his assignments was to edit the movie column of Jules Steele, whom Diehl described as "a real old guy. He was getting everything wrong, and I'd get his column and correct it." Diehl had acquired a love of movies from his mother and had grown up watching classic films starring Charlie Chaplin and Gloria Swanson. Features editor Quint Jones eventually suggested to Heaberlin that Diehl begin writing a full-page movie column on Sundays. "I sampled around and we're losing the young readers," Jones said. "I want Bill to write a column about movie stars. He can make it a little sassy if he wants, with some pinup pictures, and jokes and movie gossip—anything he can pick up." The column was an immediate success, and in 1950 Diehl was named movie editor and reviewer for the *Pioneer Press*, a job he held for the next thirty-five years.

By then, he had already dipped his toe into radio as well. In March 1948, Diehl received a call from Sev Widman, one of the most irreverent radio announcers in the Twin Cities, about subbing for him on WMIN while Widman took two weeks of vacation. Widman, who had created a big band and jazz show on WMIN in 1941 called "Studio Party Wham" with his friend Leigh Kamman, was actually talking with WDGY about making a station switch. Diehl loved Widman's show (Widman made a point of munching on popcorn while he was talking, even though the WMIN brass disapproved) and was flattered to receive the call.

"I'm going on vacation for a couple of weeks and I'm wondering if you'd like to take over," Widman told Diehl. "I read your column in the Sunday paper, and it's full of jokes. You sound like a lot of fun. I've heard you've got a pretty good voice. You know how to do a radio show, don't you?" Diehl lied and said, "Oh, yes."

"Okay, come on up," Widman said. "The records are here in the studio. Get up there a little early and you can pick out the records you want to play right from the studio library. You'll be it for two weeks." Diehl went to the public library and found a book on how to be a radio broadcaster, and the two weeks went well. Then Widman called and asked Diehl to do another week. By that point, Diehl had heard that Widman was talking to WDGY. But he'd also heard that WMIN's general manager, Frank Devaney, liked the job he was doing. When the announcement came that Widman had taken a job at WDGY, WMIN program director Norm Page asked Diehl if he'd like to do a regular shift at WMIN—the all-night show, 1 A.M. to 5 A.M. The show would be sponsored by Harold Chevrolet, and Diehl would use the on-air name Hub Cap.

He turned it down flat, saying he wasn't going to change his name and he wasn't going to work the overnight shift. Devaney told him that was the only shift available, but Diehl kept subbing on the morning show until Devaney offered him the 6 to 9 A.M. weekday shift on a permanent basis. That fit his schedule perfectly; he could go from the WMIN studios in the Hamm Building to the *Pioneer Press* at 9 A.M., work on the copy desk, go out and review movies, then return and write his column.

Everything went well for Diehl at WMIN until the winter of 1950, when he refused to do a commercial spot that he was convinced was deceptive, based on calls he had received from listeners. Frank Devaney insisted he read the spot, but each day it came up on the log, Diehl ignored it, until Devaney fired him while he was on the air, effective at the end of the week. "I started my program and I said, 'Well, folks, I just was fired,'" Diehl said. "'The management here told me I'm fired. There's a dispute about a certain commercial I refuse to do and I've been fired. I'm not joking, this is not a broadcast stunt. There are a lot of stunts these days, but I have been fired, and I'm through as of Saturday.' I said, 'I'm so sorry, I'm going to miss so many of you, your calls and your letters.' And the switchboard lit up, and I said, 'Yes, I'm really fired.' Devaney called again and said, 'Tell him he's fired, and stop talking about it.'

"I didn't stop talking about it. I said, 'Well, I've got to tell you, it's a chapter in my life and I've just been fired.' [Engineer] Bill Jessie got on the phone and said, 'Devaney just called again and he's beside himself.' This is all going out on the radio. 'He told me to censor you, to cut you, every time you say you've been fired.' I said, 'Okay, cut my mic. And here's the forecast for tomorrow, it's going to be a beautiful day—and by the way, folks, I was fired today, and I'm done as of Friday—sunshine and then rain maybe moving in tomorrow. And the outlook for next week—well, the outlook for next week is, I'm fired.' And Jessie said Devaney called again, saying, 'I told you to cut him when he says that,' and Jessie said, 'I'm an engineer, not a censor. How am I supposed to know when he's going to say it?' So they finally told me I was out that day."

Diehl wasn't out of the broadcasting business for long. Three weeks later he got a call from Stanley E. Hubbard of KSTP, who had started the market's first television station in 1948. Hubbard asked Diehl to host a summer television show on the entertainment business. "You know how to do a TV show, don't you?" Hubbard asked. Once again Diehl lied, took the job, and went back to the public library to find a book on how to be a television broadcaster. He was also writer, producer, and director of the show, which was sponsored by Majestic Cleaners, with thirty locations in the Twin Cities. His prop was a map of the Twin Cities with little black squares at each location. "I would say, 'This is *Screen Story*, brought to you by Majestic Cleaners, always a location near you,'" Diehl said. "And then they would cut to the map. 'Here, at Fiftieth and Fourth Street, here at Randolph and Lexington, here, here, here . . .' I had to point out each location, and I had to do each one twice."

When the show had run its course at the end of the summer, Hubbard asked Diehl to stay on as a full-time KSTP personality, but Diehl was not about to give up his solid newspaper job to join a broadcast medium in its infancy. He offered to work nights or weekends, but Hubbard didn't want anyone with divided loyalties. Diehl thought Hubbard might change his mind, but he did not. "That was his final word," Diehl said. "I picked the *Pioneer Press*."

Shortly thereafter, Frank Devaney called from WMIN, saying all was forgiven, and offered Diehl his old job back—same hours, same pay. Diehl took it and remained with WMIN until 1955. Then he jumped to WTCN radio and television, where Sev Widman had landed as program director. The studios were at the Calhoun Beach Club in Minneapolis, where Diehl did both radio and television news. He had recently married, so when Widman came to him and said he was temporarily moving him to the Night Owl radio slot from midnight to five in the morning, Diehl didn't think he could afford to turn it down. There he learned how to entertain the audience with sound bites culled by producer Sheldon Post from ABC's daytime programming. A few months later he was back to daytime work, hosting a 6 to 7 P.M. TV talk show sponsored by White Owl cigars. The panel format worked well, but sponsor and cohost Bernie Slater, who ran a downtown Minneapolis cigar store, thought Diehl looked unconvincing holding the product.

"Have you ever smoked a cigar?" Slater asked after the first show.

"No," Diehl admitted.

"I could tell by the way you were handling it, the way you looked at it," Slater said. "It's the worst. But we'll do it."

In the fall of 1956 Diehl hosted the ABC affiliate's election coverage. Once an hour he had to switch from the white tuxedo with black bow tie he was issued as studio host to a black tuxedo and a white tie for a one-minute Buick commercial, then back to the white tuxedo again. The TV work was wearing on him, so when he received a call from Jack Thayer of WDGY radio, he was ready to listen. Thayer had been a star deejay at WLOL, the primary rock 'n' roll station in the Twin Cities. When radio pioneer Todd Storz bought WDGY and brought his revolutionary Top 40 format to the Minneapolis–St. Paul market in 1956, he hired Thayer as his program director. Thayer wanted Diehl to be part of his team.

WDGY had begun its existence as KMFT in 1924, broadcasting over a World War I surplus transmitter from the sun porch of the home of its owner, North Minneapolis jeweler and optometrist George W. Young. Befitting his large ego, Young changed the call letters to his own initials (Dr. George Young) in 1926. Dr. Young was a showy character, wearing colorful shirts and gaudy diamonds and talking to bystanders from a loudspeaker mounted on his maroon Rolls-Royce. He flew his own airplane, though he was not much of a pilot and injured himself in crashes. "He was a screwball, but everything he touched turned to money," his first engineer, Gordon Volkenant, told interviewer Jerry Haines for a college thesis written in 1970. WDGY gradually increased its power and expanded its programing from musical performances by local artists to political speeches, religious shows, football games, and boxing matches. Young moved the broadcast studios into a succession of Minneapolis hotels before finally building a studio on the second floor of his optometry building on West Broadway in 1933. Local country-western singer Slim Jim Iverson was the station's primary draw in those years.

In 1938, WCCO radio had outgrown its studios on the twelfth floor of the Nicollet Hotel and moved to a new building, so Young moved WDGY into WCCO's old studio. In 1941, WDGY settled at its well-known 1130 frequency and a year later was granted permission to broadcast all night. The station was unaffiliated with a national network, except for a brief time in 1938 when it carried Mutual Network programming like *The Lone Ranger*. To reach their target audience of working-class city folk and farmers—"the leather jacket crowd," as the station referred to them—WDGY played mostly country-western, old-time, and jazz music.

When Young died of cancer at his Lake Minnetonka home in 1945, the station was acquired by the Twin City Broadcasting Corporation, owned by the Stuart family of Nebraska. A new directional antenna in Bloomington increased WDGY's reach, and its power was upped to fifty thousand watts during the daytime and twenty-five thousand watts at night—though the new northward-aimed antenna and the evening wattage cutback cost the station many of its loyal listeners in southern Minnesota. In an attempt to reach a "quality" audience, the new owners cut out the station's weekday morning religious programming in favor of classical music and began airing a wider variety of music, ranging from waltzes and polkas to pop standards and hillbilly tunes. A twice-weekly half-hour show called *Sepia Serenade* in 1948 even featured black recording artists, but like other Twin Cities radio stations, WDGY mostly adhered to an unspoken agreement not to play "race music." That policy remained in place well into the 1950s.

The Stuarts, who had driven off the station's old audience and failed to attract enough new listeners, sold the station in 1952 to a group headed by Clarence "Swanny" Hagman, who had worked at WTCN radio for ten years before moving to WLOL in 1947. Owner Ralph Atlass had adopted a prototypical version of the Top 40 record format at WLOL, and Hagman brought that to WDGY. Due to the emerging popularity of television, there was decreased interest in dramatic or comedy programing on radio; playing recorded music was becoming the best alternative.

In 1954, WDGY lost its lease at the Nicollet Hotel and moved its studios to the Bloomington transmitter site. The Top 40 format never took off for the Hagman group because the station didn't fully commit to it, interspersing music with sports, religious programming, farm news, and traditional radio variety and drama programming. It remained for the next owner—R. Todd Storz, the thirty-two-year-old son of the owner of Storz Brewing in Omaha, Nebraska—to execute the Top 40 format to perfection.

The story goes that Storz "invented" Top 40 radio after listening to the same handful of songs being played on a jukebox in an Omaha bar. But as reported in Ben Fong-Torres's book *The Hits Just Keep On Coming: The History of Top 40 Radio*, Storz first got the idea while serving in the Army Signal Corps during World War II. He then acquired University of Omaha research done in 1950 that said music was a major reason people turned on their radios. Storz and his father bought KOWH in Omaha in 1949, dumped all network programming, and adopted an all-music format, putting the top ten songs in heavy rotation. "I became convinced that people demand their favorites over and over while in the Army during the Second World War," Storz told *Television* magazine in 1957. "I remember vividly what used to happen in restaurants here in the States. The customers would throw their nickels into the juke box and come up repeatedly with the same tune." Storz expanded his Top 10 idea after buying station WTIX in New Orleans in 1953. A competing station aired a Top 20 show, so Storz added twenty more songs, started his show an hour earlier, and stayed on the air an hour later. Top 40 was born. In 1954, Storz bought AM giant WHB in Kansas City, which sent its signal throughout the Midwest. The advent of Bill Haley and His Comets, Elvis Presley, and rock 'n' roll was ideally timed for the spread of the Top 40 format. Switching to Top 40, WHB moved from fourth to first place in the Kansas City market within six months.

Storz's next purchase was WDGY, bought in 1956 for $212,000. He immediately canned the classical music show and the Mutual network programming (including *Bob and Ray*, which outraged fans of the deadpan comedy duo) and dumped sports, moving former Minnesota Gophers football coach Wes Fesler to promotions—all in favor of wall-to-wall pop music. In addition to bringing a full-fledged Top 40 rock 'n' roll format to the Twin Cities, Storz blitzed the market with contests for cash. Listeners who heard their home address read on the air had one minute to call the station for their cash prize. WDGY's ratings shot up, and other local stations began similar contests. WCCO was particularly competitive, hiring an announcer named Big Bill Cash to handle its contests. WDGY countered by reading WCCO's clues on the air; then WCCO changed its clues to include its call letters: "I always listen to WCCO." WDGY stopped broadcasting its competitor's clues, but the tide had already turned; WDGY jumped to second in the ratings within three months of the format change. The contest wars ceased within a year when the FCC considered blocking Storz's acquisition of WQAM in Miami because it considered the giveaways "a deterioration in the quality of the service previously rendered to the public."

Even after WDGY rose to number two in the market behind WCCO, the station's sales-men met with stiff resistance from advertisers to buy time on a station because rock 'n' roll was a tacit violation of the "no race music" agreement. Jim Ramsburg, an early WDGY disc jockey, told Jerry Haines in 1970 that "we were given strict orders never to utter the phrase 'rock 'n' roll,' because it was black slang for sex. For that matter, we were discour-aged from using the term 'teenager,' too. By that time Elvis had hit it big with 'Heartbreak Hotel' and 'Hound Dog'—a cover of a black record—followed. Covering black music was standard operating procedure in those days. Pat Boone made a fortune covering Fats Domino records. Finally, in the late '50s, Sam Cooke broke the color barrier in the Mid-west with 'You Send Me' and black artists began to appear regularly on Top 40 charts. In summary, it was a conservative, white bread market with only a handful of stations in those days."

Storz brought in top-shelf talent from the Twin Cities and other markets to staff WDGY. He didn't think he could lure the best announcers to the wilds of Bloomington, so he moved WDGY's studios to the second floor of the Builders' Exchange building in downtown Minneapolis. Thayer's courtship of Bill Diehl was part of the Storz effort to upgrade the station's talent. "WDGY was already heating up," said Diehl. "People were talking about it, and it was aimed at the young, young listener, with rock 'n' roll. Rock 'n' roll was barely in its infancy. Elvis was a name, but we didn't know—he'd had maybe one good song at that point."

Diehl went to lunch with Thayer at Charlie's Cafe Exceptionale, one of the swankiest restaurants in Minneapolis. Thayer bought Diehl a steak and they talked about radio, but Diehl was so nervous he didn't even ask about the job opportunity. Thayer called him later and said, "You never once mentioned trying to do the program. What are you going to hit me with for a salary? Are you holding back? Are you going to come or not? I'm eager to get you. Is this a waiting game you're playing?" Not at all, Diehl said. He went to the WDGY studios to accept the offer. Thayer told him he was going to be on the air from 9 P.M. to midnight. "I want you to play the Top 40, the records that are there," Thayer said. "Keep up a little line of chatter."

Diehl was excited to be on a fifty-thousand-watt station and immediately accepted the job. After just four weeks on the air, Thayer met with Diehl again. "I'm wasting you," Thayer said. "You've got energy, you've got drive, you've got the voice, you've got the idea." WDGY's top show—the 4 to 7 P.M. shift—was hosted by Don Loughnane, who'd been brought in by Storz from New Orleans to be the station's program director and was more management-oriented. "Quite frankly, we were holding it open, waiting for somebody

YOUR FAVORITE WDGY PERSONALITIES

STAN MACK
6-9

DAN DANIEL
9-11 2-4

DON KELLY
11-2

BILL DIEHL
4-7 TOP 40 SHOW

TOM WYNN
7-10

Wonderful Music everyday on
WDGY

Bill Diehl was recruited away from WTCN by WDGY in 1956 and soon took over the key 4 to 7 p.m. Top 40 show. Courtesy of Tim Warden.

to come along," Thayer said. "I want you in there doing our Top 40 show." The 4–7 shift fit Diehl's newspaper schedule perfectly. He took the promotion.

"He threw a figure at me for a salary," Diehl said. "People think the salaries were great in those days—it was a salary, let's let it go at that. I was impressed. I was very eager to get a few bucks together. I was still newly married, in a way. I knew my first wife, Marilyn, was not totally happy." They were living in a $75-a-month furnished apartment in Highland Village. "That's all I could afford," Diehl said. "I didn't have any money." The carpeting was threadbare, the furnishings were falling apart, and so was the marriage. When WTCN put Diehl on the late-night shift, he came home from the newspaper at 4 P.M. to eat dinner with Marilyn, who usually served frozen dinners on TV trays while they watched *West Point Story* together. "Then I'd say, 'Thank you, nice meal,' and I'd nod off until 9:30 . . . and then go to WTCN in the Calhoun Beach Hotel," Diehl said. "She gave up after a while. She wanted a divorce."

Things might have looked bleak at the time, but taking over WDGY's Top 40 show was the beginning of the most exciting and creative years of Bill Diehl's life. He figured that from 4 to 7 P.M. he was required to play forty records, but after timing it out, he realized he could play even more if he talked over the intro and outro on the records. "Some of them

In addition to his deejay duties, Diehl emceed a variety of events, including WDGY promotions at the Minnesota State Fair. Promotional graphic courtesy of Richard Tvedten.

started cold, which made me grind my teeth," he said. "And others would have 'La-da-da, La-da-dah, Wise men say . . .' There'd be 10, 12, 15 seconds of intro, and while that was on, I'd get rid of all the—'This is the Top 40 Show, Bill Diehl.'"

The WDGY call letters were being pronounced as "Wee-Gee" by the disc jockeys, but Diehl came up with another idea. "Hi, this is Bill Diehl on WDGY," he'd say. "You know what WDGY stands for? Where Diehl Greets You! WDGY."

It didn't make the other disc jockeys too happy, including morning man Stanley Mack, who said, "It doesn't mean that at all!" But it caught on, and Diehl still meets people who grew up identifying his name with the call letters WDGY. His most memorable bit of radio patter came to him at the same time. "I wanted to get an identity," he said. "They had talked about me being Hub Cap, and that had always kind of intrigued me. Milton Berle was 'The Clown Prince of Television.' So I figured out something, and I came up with this in a week: 'It's the Top 40 Show. I'm Bill Diehl, the Rajah of the Records, the Deacon of the Discs, the Purveyor of the Platters, and the Wizard of Wax, with all the musical facts.'"

The handle stuck. Almost sixty years later, people who grew up listening to WDGY remember Diehl as the Rajah of the Records, the Deacon of the Discs, and so on. It might seem corny now, but Diehl's slick jive between records set the tone for the entire market: "From 4 to 7, we go from 40 to 1," he'd say on a typical day. "Last week's Number 39, this week—oh, down a notch, it's Don and Phil Everly. When I hear an alarm clock, 'Wake Up, Little Susie!'"

"This is it," Thayer said the first time Diehl used that intro. "This is what I want. Oh, this is just what I've been praying for. That's great! I want that every afternoon. And give me a different one for each record."

"What? There are forty records," Diehl said.

"Just introduce them with those puns," Thayer said. "You're good at the puns."

"But some of those records are on there for three or four weeks," Diehl said. "I'm going to run out."

"Oh, once in a while, repeat one."

Once he'd created his on-air persona, Diehl found himself in demand for personal appearances. It started with a phone call in June 1958 from the Chamber of Commerce in St. James, Minnesota. They had a local band signed up to play a teen dance at the St. James Armory, and they wanted Diehl to emcee the event, because all the kids in St. James listened to his show. Diehl said he'd do it. "What do you charge?" they asked him. Diehl hadn't even thought about asking for a fee. On the spot, he decided to ask for fifty dollars. "For the next ten years, fifty dollars was it," Diehl said. "I never changed. I always got fifty dollars whether it was down in Iowa, on the border, up at the Fiesta Ballroom in Montevideo—fifty bucks, flat fee." St. James agreed to the price, so Diehl began promoting the upcoming show on the air. Jack Thayer liked the idea, seeing it as a good way to attract more listeners. Then the St. James chamber called again to ask which highway Diehl would be driving when he came into town, and what time he'd be arriving.

"Why is that important?" Diehl asked. "Does the dance start at 8?"

"No, no, no, we just want to do something, ha, ha, ha," the chamber rep said.

"So I got in my car that night," Diehl said. "It was a beautiful evening, sunshine, and I drove down there. And as I approached St. James, Minnesota, here were kids on both sides of the roadway, adults, too: 'Bill Diehl! Bill Diehl!' It was that much of a novelty."

The dance was a success. A week later, Diehl got a call from George Neuwirth, who owned George's Ballroom in New Ulm. Neuwirth wanted Diehl to emcee a dance on Friday night, but he didn't have a band lined up. He asked Diehl to find a band and agreed to his $50 fee, but wanted the appearance mentioned on WDGY.

Diehl always gave away promo copies of record albums and singles whenever he hosted a dance job. Courtesy of *St. Paul Pioneer Press.*

"This guy wants me to get a band and go down there and mention them on the air," Diehl told Thayer.

"Well, if they're starting to ask you to mention them on the air, we gotta ask for a commercial fee on that," Thayer said. "I don't want to get in trouble with the FCC. Let's set a fee of $10 a spot for five thirty-second spots."

It was a dirt-cheap rate ("On WCCO, that wouldn't even turn on the lights," Diehl said), and Neuwirth accepted it. Diehl cut a promo spot for the dance in his usual style of jive patter ("Let's rock, let's roll, let's bop, let's stroll . . .") and once again, the dance drew a big crowd. It wasn't long before word spread to ballroom owners across the state, who were used to hosting polka bands and swing orchestras, that they could make a lot of money booking rock 'n' roll bands—particularly if they hired Bill Diehl to emcee and promote the show on WDGY. He began lining up bands and making appearances for Hoot Gibson, who owned the Pla-Mor Ballroom in Rochester, Herb Martinka at the Kato Ballroom in Mankato, and Nate and Billie Ehrlich at the Monterey Ballroom in Owatonna.

"Little Nate Ehrlich stood about this tall, always smoking a wet cigar, and he could never remember names, so everybody was Spook," Diehl said. "'Okay, Spook.' He was married to a tall, thin woman named Billie. So there they were, like something out of a comedy. Every Sunday night we had dances at the Monterey Ballroom. I'd collect $50 for Bill Diehl, $50 for the radio station, and then, if the band wanted me to, I'd collect $100 for them and give it to them later. It was always $200, and if Nate Ehrlich got 260 kids in at a dollar, it was an easy sixty bucks for him. He sometimes got close to three hundred."

One night Diehl counted his pay after a dance at the Monterey and found $55 in his envelope. It was snowing heavily that night, but Diehl turned his car around in the parking lot, almost getting stuck, and went back to the ballroom.

"Nate, you overpaid me," he said.

"Bill, get out of here," Ehrlich said.

"You paid me $55 instead of $50."

"You're an honest man. Get out of here!"

Later Diehl asked him why he'd told him to leave.

"You had no business being near me if you were an honest man," Ehrlich said.

Diehl ran into many eccentric characters during his years as a rock 'n' roll emcee. One was a crusty Dutchman named Elmer Wagner, a dairy farmer who ran the Paradise Ballroom at Lake Waconia. He hired Diehl to bring in a band and emcee a dance. They drew a decent crowd of about two hundred kids the first night, charging a dollar and a quarter—top price at that time. At the end of the evening, Wagner sat at a table with the money in a stack and started dividing it up.

"Let's see now—here's the patrolman," Wagner said. "He gets ten. And the cashier. She gets fifteen."

"Don't forget WDGY, now," Diehl said.

"Fifty dollars for WDGY," Wagner said. "And $125 for the band. And $50 for Bill Diehl. Dat's it? Dat's the money. Well, dat's somepthin'. The cop gets, and the cashier gets, and the radio station gets, and the band gets, and Bill Diehl gets. And Elmer Wagner, he owns the ballroom, and he gets nottin'."

Soon Diehl was lining up bands and emceeing shows as often as seven nights a week, crisscrossing the state to host shows at ballrooms, teen clubs, and armories. He kept little books with the names and phone numbers of all the bands worth booking, and where they were scheduled to play.

"The bands were from all around the Twin Cities," Diehl said. "One band would tell another band. The first one I really worked with was Mike Waggoner and the Bops. He knew how honest I was. I never charged a penny. I would call them up and say, 'You're working at the Pla-Mor Ballroom in Rochester. Are you available Friday night? Yep? Okay, I'll call the ballroom.' I would call the ballroom and tell them that's the band that was coming, whether it was the Accents, the Underbeats, T. C. Atlantic, the Avanties, Mike Glieden, Danny's Reasons, or Showtime. The bands would call me, or if I got a call from a ballroom operator saying, 'I need a band Friday night,' I would call the bands. 'Are you available?' 'No.' I would keep dialing until I got a band. I'd call the ballroom back and tell them, 'You got a band, here they are. They'll be there at 8 o'clock and they need a hundred and a quarter. Or they want a hundred and a half.' Or when I was there I'd tell them, 'You've got the Accents coming next week.' 'But my kids are talking about the Underbeats.' 'You got them the following week.' It was hard keeping everybody happy.

"The worst night of the week was Friday night or Saturday night if it was snowing," said Diehl. "You'd wait for the phone to ring—'This is the God-knows-

Kato Ballroom

Mankato, Minnesota

TEEN AGE DANCING
Every Sunday Night - 8 to 11 P.M.

Sunday, January 24
THE UNDERBEATS
(Sweet Words of Love)

Sunday, January 31
THE TRASHMEN
(Surfin' Bird)

CARNIVAL DANCE
Sunday, February 7   Hats, Balloons, Leis
THE AVANTIES
(The Slide)

Sunday, February 14
THE ACCENTS
(Why)

The above attractions only $1.00 admission

COME AS YOU ARE!

Listen to Bill Diehl, WDGY

By 1964, Bill Diehl had regular emcee gigs at many ballrooms and dance halls within 135 miles of the Twin Cities. Courtesy of Tom Tourville.

Bill Diehl and his fellow WDGY disc jockeys were integral to the success of The Trashmen's "Surfin' Bird," giving the band extensive airplay and interview opportunities that helped push the record to Number 1 in the Twin Cities. The "Wee Gee Tigers" gathered on January 12, 1964, to greet the band: *(from left)* Jack Chapman, Bill Diehl, Hal Raymond, J. Walter Beethoven, Johnny Dollar, and Perry St. John. Courtesy of Dal Winslow.

what ballroom. It's 8 o'clock and the band isn't here.' 'Oh, Jesus.' And then ten minutes later—'Hi, this is Skip Dahlin of the Accents. We're in the ditch, here in so-and-so, but we're getting dug out and we'll be there.' Now I've got to call the ballroom. 'Well, what do I do now with the kids?' It was just awful, back and forth."

It wasn't just the bands that were on the road, dealing with the harsh Minnesota-Wisconsin-Iowa elements. On Friday nights Diehl emceed three separate shows in two different states. How did he do it? "Driving fast," Diehl said. "I would go out to the Bloomington K.C. Hall, get there at a quarter to 8 while the band would be setting up. I'd have them do a fast rock 'n' roll number, talk, and I'd start giving away albums right away, and make a lot of noise: 'Next week we're here with Mike Glieden and the Rhythm Kings, and I said, 'We'll be back,' and I made my appearance. I'd talk to the guy who ran the place and tell them what his band was the next week. Then I'd drive like hell out to Danceland in Excelsior. Big Reggie out there—Ray Colihan—he didn't care, he was half in the bag all the time anyway. I'd get there five minutes, ten minutes of 9, stay there for maybe a half hour, and they'd be happy. He made good money at Danceland. Then I'd drive like hell to Frederick, Wisconsin, which really wasn't that far away [about ninety miles from Excelsior]. Two guys ran the roller rink. They were great guys; they didn't care what time I got there. I'd get there about 9:45, but I'd stay till midnight, which is what they wanted. They ran their dance 9 to midnight. I did that every Friday night. I'd go out on Tuesday nights, sometimes to Danceland, sometimes to Schlief's Little City out on Highway 55. It was a regular adult ballroom. They'd put a rock 'n' roll band in there. I'd get there about 8, rock till about 9, then drive like hell to Danceland. I had Danceland every Tuesday, Thursday, and Saturday night."

Butch Maness, bass player for Mike Waggoner and the Bops, viewed Diehl as a celebrity with cash in his pocket and a very polished act. "He was kind of a ladies' man," Maness said. "It seemed like every time we played someplace, there was some lady who wanted to go somewhere and have fun with him. He always drove a Cadillac. He was a good guy and fun to work with. He had the voice for it, too. During our breaks, he'd do some talking, talk about other things coming up. He'd maybe pick out a certain couple that [were] really good dancers, we'd play, they'd dance again, and he'd give them records or some other item he might have brought along."

"Bill Diehl was very nice, very honest, very helpful," said Dal Winslow of The Trashmen. "If he didn't like what you were doing, he'd tell you. He was a wheeler-dealer, but why not? He had a golden goose right there. He'd take some of these promo records out to several gigs on the weekends, and they'd pay him, and he'd give away all these free records. We were satisfied. We were doing well. Without him, it would have been harder to get jobs. That's why we rode on his wave for a while, because KDWB wasn't quite doing the same thing."

WDGY's phenomenal turnaround brought other radio owners to the realization that rock 'n' roll was not just a passing fad, but a lucrative way for advertisers to ply loose cash from the pockets of free-spending baby boomers. Joe "Mr. Rhythm" Zingale had given WCOW a taste of rock 'n' roll on his weekend show in 1956, but it took a few more years before the station was ready to go toe to toe with WDGY for the teen audience.

The Tedesco brothers had started WCOW as a country and western music station in 1951, based near the stockyards in South St. Paul. All the announcers took corny western nicknames, including Arizona Al Tedesco, Valley City Vic Tedesco, Nevada Nick Tedesco, and Denver Don Doty, the station's program director. There was also a young newsman on the staff named Sam Sabean, who was born in Melrose, Minnesota, in 1930, moved to St. Paul with his family when he was in grade school, and graduated from Washington High School. Then he joined the Navy with twelve of his buddies and ended up serving on the USS *Juneau*, which fired the first shot of the Korean War. "I was there for two years in the combat zone," Sabean recalled. "The USS *Juneau* sank seventeen ships, and we took down twenty-some Russian MiG fighters that fought for the Commies. Then we took out a whole squadron of torpedo boats that were bound and determined to sink the *Juneau*, because *Time* magazine labeled us the Galloping Ghost of the Korean Coast. They were determined to put their torpedoes in our side, but we took out their gunboats one by one, then we went and picked up the survivors."

Sabean was discharged in 1952, and he and his buddies enrolled at Hamline to play football. Accused by the dean of being lazy, Sabean dropped out of Hamline and enrolled in the American Institute broadcasting school. His first job was at WCOW as a commercial copywriter, and then he was promoted to newsman. "Don Doty gave me my first shot on a Saturday afternoon newscast," Sabean said. "I was scared stiff—I butchered it up."

He improved, of course, earning a cowboy nickname and show of his own: Hobo Sam and His Bum Program. He left WCOW for a year to go into the film business, but the station lured him back in 1956 as deejay and station manager—this time with the on-air name Sam Sherwood. By then the station had changed its call letters to WISK (same as the new liquid laundry soap, in a misguided attempt to attract a female audience), switched its format from all country to easy listening and light pop, and affiliated with the Mutual network, which WDGY had just dropped. The studios were now on White

Bear Avenue in St. Paul, and the frequency soon shifted from 1590 AM to 630 AM. It was still a five-thousand-watt daytime-only station, but WISK would shortly become a giant under another set of call letters.

In June 1959, the Tedescos gave up on WISK and sold the station to Crowell-Collier Broadcasting, which owned pioneer rock 'n' roll station KFWB in Los Angeles. The company's national program director was Chuck Blore, who had learned the Top 40 format from Gordon McLendon, a legendary Texas broadcaster who'd tweaked and refined Todd Storz's original idea. Blore came up with the catchphrase "Color Radio" for KFWB's Top 40 format and dubbed his crew of deejays "Seven Swingin' Gentlemen." Both of those concepts were imported to the Twin Cities by September 1959 when Crowell-Collier took over the former WISK and changed the station's format to Top 40 and its call letters to KDWB.

"I was a disc jockey when Crowell-Collier bought the station and turned it into the rock 'n' roll station that competed with WDGY," Sabean said. "Chuck Blore was a genius. All of us guys had to go to his rock 'n' roll disc jockey school. We had to pass his level to be able to earn a position on the air. We would sit in the one studio while the rest of the disc jockeys were there critiquing the guy performing. I was scared stiff. Finally, when you knew you hit his pace, Chuck would jump up and down and get so excited. He said, 'You're in, you're one of us!'"

Sabean said Blore was looking for entertainers. He taught his deejays how to produce and write their comedy material a day in advance and then deliver it like it was off the top of their heads. The disc jockeys at Crowell-Collier stations were considered "auto-entertainers" rather than disc jockeys. "We had an amazing advantage," Sabean said. "Our home office was on Hollywood Boulevard. All the stars would come down there. We'd go to a meeting at KFWB, and every rock 'n' roll star on the charts was there."

For several weeks before the KDWB changeover, WDGY announcers were reading commercials for some mysterious product called Formula 63. It was finally revealed that Formula 63 was actually the station's new competitor, broadcasting at 630 on the AM dial—at which point those spots were quickly dumped. On September 15, 1959, KDWB switched over to rock 'n' roll by playing the French version of "Charlie Brown" by the Coasters for two days straight. Then KDWB's original Seven Swingin' Gentlemen assumed their shifts: Sabean, Hal Murray, Phil Page, Bob Chasteen, Bob Friend, Randy Cook, and Dick Halvorson.

"The original cast are all dead now," Sabean said. "Lou Waters and I are the only remaining living souls."

Lou Waters, who for twenty years anchored news programs on CNN, began his professional broadcasting career in his home state of Minnesota, using his original name, Lou

Riegert. Born in Edina, Riegert became a radio fan listening to rock 'n' roll on WDGY. After graduating from high school in 1956, he studied architectural engineering but was lured to the fun of broadcasting by campus radio station WMMR, a closed circuit station that broadcast to the dormitories. Abandoning his architectural studies, Riegert was hired as a five-dollar-an-hour newsman at WMIN. When his union, AFTRA, went on strike two months later, local deejay Dick Driscoll suggested Riegert apply at KDWB, which was looking for a newsman and weekend deejay.

"Don French, the program director, hired me as a weekend mobile news guy, three days a week in a news cruiser mobile unit, and disc jockey on the week-

KDWB brought the Seven Swingin' Gentlemen deejay format to the Twin Cities on the cover of the promotional LP *KDWB Disc/Coveries*. One of the station's deejays, Lou Riegert, played a big part in the future of the Gestures before switching to TV news as Lou Waters.

ends," Waters said. "That gave me a new thing to learn about. That was in 1959. It was a time when disc jockeys were more personalities, very entertaining and very innovative."

He wasn't one of the original Seven Swingin' Gentlemen, but when 9-to-noon jock Phil Page got fired, Lou Riegert moved into the weekday lineup at 6 to 9 P.M., opposite Bill Diehl's Top 40 show on WDGY. "I started out learning from guys who'd been in the business for years all around me," Waters said. "I felt rather diminished by them. They apparently liked my youth and energy. I used wild tracks, doors slamming, adding voices. The programing had to do with each of the personalities, scripting what they did. We had homework, had to plan out our shows—no sitting there thinking, 'Maybe I'll come up with something.'"

"WDGY was the leader," Sabean said. "We were so much different. They were yelling and screaming. We went on with our entertainment and gained momentum very fast."

All the elements of a vibrant music scene were now in place: a successful record label, a competent recording studio, a growing number of local rock 'n' roll bands, plenty of venues for live music, and two radio stations that desperately wanted to capture the young rock 'n' roll listeners.

"The Heilichers had the distribution," said Owen Husney, guitarist for the High Spirits, a St. Louis Park band that recorded on the Soma label in the mid-'60s. "They owned the Kay Bank Studio. They owned the Record Lane stores, which became Musicland. Now you had people with distribution building the Musicland empire. They had access to the acts, and they had the studio. Many of these acts recorded at other studios as the town got going, but a lot recorded at Kay Bank and went to Soma. You had the fertile ground."

Throughout the 1960s, KDWB and WDGY would battle each other furiously—and not always good-naturedly—for the hearts, minds, and pocketbooks of the baby boom generation. One of the best ways to reach the young listeners was to play records by their friends, classmates, and peers—the local rock 'n' roll bands. "We played local records because the promotion people brought them to us," said Sabean, who became KDWB's program director in the early 1960s. "The local bands—the corporate office had nothing to say about the music we played. Lou and Bobby [Dale] ruled the music. We played more of the local stuff at night. We weren't as involved in the local bands as WDGY. Bill Diehl had those all corralled with him." Diehl had similar freedom to play local records at WDGY. "If they had a record that was worthwhile, I'd play it," he said. "I was the music director at WDGY, and I'd give them every break I could if the record was halfway good. They'd be billed 'As heard on WDGY.'"

The More-Tishans from Stillwater got a few spins on WDGY with their record "Nowhere to Run." It was clear to rhythm guitarist Chris Nelson that Diehl's approval had a lot to do with whether a record became a local hit or never made the charts. "Bill Diehl was a big, big personality in the Twin Cities," Nelson said. "We played a couple dances with Dino Day, who hosted a TV show in Twin Cities called *Date with Dino*. But it was just never the same as with Bill Diehl. Nobody ever got as big as Bill Diehl."

It wouldn't be long before dozens of bands were heading for the recording studios and bringing the resulting 45-rpm disks to the jocks at WDGY and KDWB. Most of those records became promotional tools, to be sold or given away at dances; some made the local charts and enabled the bands to raise their appearance fees.

A rare few became national smashes and changed lives forever.

BATTLE OF THE BANDS

AUGIE GARCIA'S TRAILBLAZING CAREER inspired the next generation of Minnesota rockers to follow his lead. Of those, Mike Waggoner was the king.

A good-looking young man with a strong, pliable singing voice and a lot of energy, Waggoner grew up in a family of country-western musicians living near Hinckley, Minnesota. He learned to play guitar by the age of ten and performed with his dad's band, the Three Jacks, singing Hank Williams songs and country-folk tunes like "Old Shep," the same song that Elvis Presley sang at a singing contest when he was ten years old. He made appearances on several Twin Cities TV talent shows, including one hosted by David Stone of KSTP-TV's *Sunset Valley Barn Dance.* Then Waggoner's family moved to Richfield in the mid-1950s. "I went from a school with twenty-two kids to one with seven hundred," he said. "I was a hick from the country. The only thing I had that would allow me to make

Mike Waggoner put together his band, the Bops, with his brother Colly and several of their Richfield High School pals in 1956. Courtesy of Tom Tourville.

some friends was I could sing and play guitar. I started doing that at pep fests and talent shows at Richfield every year."

Waggoner describes Richfield of the 1950s as a first-ring suburb where working-class men were returning from World War II and Korea to build two-bedroom houses. Southdale was under construction, kids were learning to drive, television was taking hold, and more radio stations were popping up on the dial. "The mid-to-late-teen kids were eager to establish themselves as something different from their parents," Waggoner said. "I came along at a wonderful time as a representative of something that was happening."

Waggoner's tastes began gravitating toward rock 'n' roll. He listened to WLOL's midnight-to-6 A.M. *Nightwatch* show hosted by Carl Peterson, who lived next door to Waggoner's aunt and uncle. But local stations didn't play enough rock to satisfy Waggoner. "To better improve my library of tunes, I listened to WLS [in Chicago]," he said. "I found a place out by the airport toward Old Shakopee Road with high enough elevation that I could listen to the radio at night. I'd listen to the songs that weren't being played in the Twin Cities. I'd write down titles and artists and brought it to my friend at Hub Record Store, and he'd order those for me. It was late '50s stuff—Chuck Berry, Carl Perkins, Presley, Ronnie Hawkins—the real deal. They were simple tunes, three-chord, four-chord songs with a danceable beat."

He eventually put together a band of like-minded Richfield High buddies, including his younger brother Colin "Colly" Waggoner, who was just fourteen but already a whiz on lead guitar. "Colly was a very gifted fellow, self-taught—we both learned from our dad—and delightfully talented," Waggoner said. "He was such an asset to our early years. He could listen to a song three times and have it nailed." The other Bops were Lyle Gudmanson on drums, Rusty Bates on stand-up bass, Dick Benedict on rhythm guitar, and Doug Barton on saxophone.

Carl Peterson began booking the band for record hops. One of their first jobs was at St. Richard's School on Penn Avenue South. Waggoner hadn't come up with a name for the band yet, and, much like Charlie Boone with Bobby Vee and the Shadows at Fargo, Peterson turned to the band just before introducing them and asked, "What's your name?" Waggoner quickly thought of songs the band was playing, remembered Gene Vincent's "Dance to the Bop," and told Peterson they were the Bops.

They started out playing local dance spots like the Bloomington Roller Rink, the Richfield VFW, and the Ford Union Hall in St. Paul. After Waggoner graduated from high school in 1958, he had to replace his bass player and drummer. Sheldon Hasse took over on stand-up bass and John Lentz became the band's new drummer. "As we got to be more active as a band, we had the good fortune to be invited to play venues that were much larger, like the Marigold Ballroom in Minneapolis and the Kato Ballroom in Mankato," Waggoner said. "We traveled regionally."

They were booked to play the opening weekend at Mr. Lucky's, a teen club on Lake Street and Nicollet Avenue in Minneapolis that would soon become the hub of the Twin Cities live rock 'n' roll scene. They also landed a regular Friday night gig at the Crystal Coliseum, a Quonset hut roller rink off Highway 100 with a portable stage, and they played every other Saturday at the Prom Ballroom in St. Paul. The Prom, like the Pla-Mor Ballroom in Rochester and the Turf Ballroom in Austin, was starting to cater to teenage dancers, but management wasn't ready to give up on the older couples who liked the

The Diablos were one of the Twin Cities' early rock bands, fronted by singer/guitarist Damon Lee and including future members of the Accents. Courtesy of Steve Brown.

smooth big band sounds. For a while, the two styles were mixed. "They had a split stage for an orchestra like Jules Herman or Frankie Sherman, and a rock 'n' roll band," Waggoner said. "They recognized the fact that music was changing. Each band would play half the night on a huge, lovely hardwood floor stage with tiered seats around it. It was elegant dancers, and teens in white bucks and poodle skirts. I'm not terribly sure when I was eighteen I'd want to go somewhere with my parents, but some of the younger-thinking older people just absolutely loved the rock 'n' roll we were playing."

Competition for rock 'n' roll gigs was heating up among the local bands. Waggoner admired and studied the other bands that got their start in the 1950s. The Delricos from South St. Paul recorded a couple of sides on Gaity Records ("They were playing a little more poppy stuff, a white version of black music," Waggoner said), and featured lead guitarist and singer Darwin Eckholm, who later changed his name to Donald K. Martin and had a long career as a radio deejay on both KDWB and WDGY. The Glenrays from St. Paul functioned as the house band at Gaity recording studios. "They had a real good band," Waggoner said. "They had a sax or two." The Glenrays and their manager, Clarence Hajney, landed a nice promotional splash on the cover of the *St. Paul Pioneer Press*'s Sunday magazine on May 3, 1959.

Damon Lee and the Diablos were a tough-sounding rockabilly band from Minneapolis that included future Accents members Ken Sand on guitar and Tom Nystrom on drums. "Damon's a great guy, nice as can be," Waggoner said a few months before Lee's death in San Antonio on November 22, 2014. "I sold him my first band trailer. He turned out to be one of the great, great blues players. Back in the day, he was playing similar music to ourselves." Another early combo, the Dorados, were "a wonderful band," Waggoner said. "We used to tease lead guitar player Donny Dax because he could clone Chuck Berry and Lonnie Mack licks on guitar, even the mistakes."

A very early iteration of The Trashmen used the name String Kings, but there was a different group with the same name, a wild rockabilly group that was the house band at Bashland, a barn in South St. Paul, "almost on the way to Hastings," Waggoner said. "It was discovered by a disc jockey from WLOL with the air name Throckmorton. He talked people into having bands out there. He was a real gypsy; nobody had seen or heard anybody like him in the Twin Cities. He had a cot and lived at the radio station in the engineering area." The Big M's, who were primarily black but featured white guitar phenom Eddie Lovejoy, also played frequently at Bashland.

"They had battles of the bands, but you didn't open for anybody," Waggoner said. "You just played. We played on the same bill with the Everly Brothers, Del Shannon, Sandy Nelson, Conway Twitty, Clyde McPhatter, plus the locals. It was always fun to see them. I was always into, 'How does this band look? How do they present themselves? What kind of equipment do they have?' You knew they were going to be good or they wouldn't be there. 'What can I learn from them to make us a little more showy?' I was always reasonably anal—always, always worried about how do we look and how do we sound. 'Do we have the right equipment? What does it look like from the crowd, from the stage? Do we stand around and talk to each other?'"

In the battle for Twin Cities rock 'n' roll band supremacy, the Bops quickly worked their way to the top. They were the first band Bill Diehl worked with regularly at his live appearances. Diehl and Waggoner became close friends and remained so through the years. "Bill was the go-to guy to get stage time, and he was a good businessman," Waggoner said. "I learned a lot from him about promotion. He was very helpful to many, many of the Twin Cities bands. Just a delightful guy, wonderful guy. Bill meant the world to me. When our son was less than a year old, Bill came over to the house and had a gift for him. He was the tried-and-true professional and could read the room as well as anybody I ever worked with. He was well dressed and always on time."

So were the Bops. They wore suits to most of their gigs, bought at Teeners on Hennepin Avenue in downtown Minneapolis. "That was a real wonderful dress-up era," Waggoner said. "I was always proud to be onstage. The people paid good money to come see us, and I thought we owed them respect." Their professionalism was recognized by the Ballroom Operators Association, which gave the Bops their Band of the Year award four years in a row, from 1961–1964.

"We were self-contained, had our own sound and our own lights," Waggoner said. "We were very dependable. We always put on a good show; we were always there on time. To a businessperson, a sole proprietorship running ballrooms, that's incredibly important. Many of them don't even know you. They've never seen you. They call up, you make a deal, sign a contract, and we never missed a show."

Heavily echoed vocals were a big part of the rock 'n' roll sound of the late '50s and early '60s. The Bops achieved a unique stage version of that studio sound using a pair of Echoplex machines, a moveable recording tape head that could change the delay time of the sound. They put one on Colly's guitar, the other on Mike's vocals.

To learn a new song, Waggoner would buy the record and listen to it for the three elements that he thought were most important: the hook, the style and tempo of the song, and the presentation. "We'd try to capture the three pillars that would hold the song up," Waggoner said. "I or a band member or girlfriends or wives would write the chords down and type them out—copiers weren't available—and many times she'd hand-write out a lyric sheet for everybody. We'd listen to the words and make notes where the changes were. One of the things all the band members possessed, God bless us, we were given the gift that we could play by ear. In the early days there was no songbooks.

"We all discovered early in the day we didn't have to play these songs note for note," Waggoner said. "You could have three different bands play 'Little Latin Lupe Lu.' We all took the songs and made them our own. My brother could capture the familiar licks, but we would change the tempo to a degree and rekey it. Many times, if they did the instrumental once, we did it two or three times. They were two-minute songs. Otherwise, you'd do seventy tunes a night."

In 1961 the Bops went into Kay Bank Studio to record their first single, "Baby Baby," which did not receive much local airplay. Courtesy of Denny Johnson of Minniepaulmusic.com.

They were introduced to Bobby Vee's first manager, Bing Bengtsson, who took them into Kay Bank Studios in March 1961 to make a record. The A-side was to be "Basher #5," a hot guitar instrumental written by Colly Waggoner. They put a Dale Hawkins rockabilly tune called "Baby Baby" on the B-side of the single and released it on the Vee label. When the band gave the record to Bill Diehl at WDGY and Sam Sherwood at KDWB, however, the disc jockeys played the vocal number, "Baby, Baby," instead of the instrumental A-side. Airplay was minimal, and the song did not chart locally—not surprising for the times. The few local groups that had recorded 45s did so primarily hoping to get a couple of spins on WDGY, KDWB, or WCCO, thus raising their profile enough to charge more for dance jobs.

Waggoner and the other '50s-spawned rock 'n' roll bands couldn't have foreseen it, but change was afoot in the '60s. The speed, danger, and sexual overtones of rock 'n' roll—even the term was a euphemism for sex—were being toned down in favor of teen romance and novelty numbers. Vocalists with their own backing bands were fading away in favor of the teen idol—Dion, Fabian, Bobby Rydell, Frankie Avalon, Paul Anka, Bobby Darin, Neil Sedaka, and Gene Pitney—who toured with anonymous musicians behind him. In addition, folk music was beginning its transition from campus cult status to a significant force in the music industry. "Michael (Row the Boat Ashore)" by the Highwaymen hit Number 1 on the *Billboard* singles chart in September 1961, taking a more traditional and authentic approach to the music than the form's previous standard-bearers—the striped-shirted, pop-oriented Kingston Trio. The following year Peter, Paul, and Mary scored their first two hit singles, "Lemon Tree" and "If I Had a Hammer," and Hibbing's Bob Dylan released his debut album on Columbia. Dylan had completely turned his back on his rock 'n' roll roots, even writing a song for his second album called "Talkin' World War III Blues" that included a satirical swipe at the Top 40 groups of the day: "Turned on my record player, it was Rock-a-day Johnny singin', 'Tell your ma, tell your pa our love's a-gonna grow, ooh-wah, ooh-wah.'"

There were a few self-contained rock 'n' roll bands with no obvious frontman, but the instrumental breaks were usually taken by the band's saxophone player, going back as far as Bill Haley and His Comets in 1954. As the '60s dawned, rock 'n' roll bands like the Champs, Johnny and the Hurricanes, and the Wailers continued to feature the sax solo. But in the summer of 1960, an instrumental band from Tacoma, Washington, called the Ventures, featuring two electric guitars, electric bass, and drums, scored a huge hit with a song called "Walk, Don't Run." The song had been written and recorded by jazz guitar great Johnny Smith in 1955 and covered in 1957 by country guitar legend Chet Atkins. Neither of those versions made much of a dent on the national consciousness, but when the Ventures climbed the national charts with their rock 'n' roll take on the song, it inspired a generation of guitar players. Almost overnight, instrumental guitar bands were being formed around the country. Coupled with Californian Dick Dale's invention the same year of surf-style lead guitar—reverb-soaked, lightning-fast staccato picking—the direction of American rock 'n' roll was leading away from rockabilly and rhythm and blues.

"All of a sudden, along came 'Walk, Don't Run' by the Ventures, and that really got me going," said Tom "Zippy" Caplan, who at the time was a fourteen-year-old aspiring guitarist in St. Paul. "I started picking it up by ear. The Ventures were something brand new."

"It started for me with the instrumental guitar stuff," said Bob Folschow, who would become lead guitarist with the Castaways. "The Ventures, Duane Eddy, Link Wray, covering all that stuff."

Even Mosrite guitars—the brand played by the Ventures and featured prominently on their album covers—became the guitar of choice for many young players. "The second guitar I bought was one of the very first Mosrite guitars," said Dale Menten, who would soon join his first band, the Jesters, in Mankato. "I learned to play 'Walk, Don't Run' on that guitar. I found it very difficult to play—I'd use the whammy bar, and the whole guitar would be out of tune. I guess I won't whammy anymore."

"What really started me was when I got into the Ventures," said Larry Wiegand of the Rave-Ons and, later, Crow. "When I heard 'Walk, Don't Run,' that's when I started wanting to play music. I didn't know how to play, but I wanted to. At first all we did was instrumentals. We just played Ventures songs."

Certain communities were hotbeds of rock 'n' roll start-ups, with young guitar players, bass players, keyboard players, and drummers jumping from one band to another until they found a good fit. In addition to being home to the Bops, Richfield spawned the Knights, the Castaways, and Robbie and the Rave-Ons. Lonnie Knight, born in 1948 in Camden, New Jersey, was a member of all three groups at different times. "I know there were a lot of us in Richfield, and a lot I didn't know about until much later on," he said. "There was a music store in Richfield called Del's Music, owned by two brothers, Del and Len Upsahl. Either Len or Del himself was going door-to-door soliciting guitar students. I was eleven or twelve at the time. I begged my folks to let me take lessons from him. I still have my very first guitar, an old late '50s Harmony folk guitar."

Knight's father played a coronet once a year on Christmas morning and loved classical music, and while Knight was taken with *Scheherazade*, he didn't really get hooked until he heard Link Wray's "Rawhide." Then it was the Everly Brothers and Buddy Holly. "I have a Christmas morning photograph: my little brother got a big helicopter, my sister got a transistor radio, and I got a Fender Jazzmaster," he said. "My dad and I went to Thorgaard-Anderson that fall and looked at guitars. Dad said we couldn't afford it, but on Christmas morning, there it was."

When Knight was in junior high, he was playing pickup baseball in a field across the street from the current site of the Southdale Mall, where the Key Cadillac dealership is now. "I ran into a guy named Dick Roby," Knight said. "We talked, and I said, 'I'd rather be playing guitar.' He said, 'I play, too.' He lived across the street on Xerxes, so we went to his house. He had a couple guitars, we started playing, and decided within a couple of hours to start a band. We liked the same music. We got Denny Craswell on drums, Dick switched to bass, and we got Roy Hensley. Our first job, whether we got paid or not, was at Miller's Pizza on 68th and Penn Avenue in Richfield. We were doing some sort of folky things, 'Michael (Row the Boat Ashore),' we did a couple of Ventures tunes, and we tried to do 'Rawhide' by Link Wray."

That was the start of the Castaways. Knight would remain with the band just a short time, before switching to a band called, coincidentally, the Knights, with brothers Larry and Dick Wiegand, also of Richfield. Then all three got an offer from singer Robbie Hardell to join Robbie and the Rave-Ons.

Another Minneapolis suburb bursting with musicians and bands was St. Louis Park. David Rivkin, born in 1948, was originally interested in folk music and went to the Ten O'Clock Scholar folk club in Dinkytown to see Bob Dylan several times before Dylan left for New York. He formed a folk duo with fellow St. Louis Park High School student Don

The Chancellors formed in St. Louis Park in 1963. From left: David Rivkin, Dan Holm, Mike Judge, and John Hughes. Courtesy of Tom Tourville.

Garon. "There was another guy in the group for a while, Greg Geffner," Rivkin said. "We thought we were the Kingston Trio. We'd play at parties, weddings, bar mitzvahs, weird little places like the Women's Club, on weekends."

Rivkin was interested in Elvis Presley and Buddy Holly, but he was playing acoustic guitar, and jealous of his cousin's electric guitar. "I brought my acoustic over there, and he whips out this electric," Rivkin said. "I was, 'Wow, what's that?' I followed him and got an electric guitar. My musical tastes were changing—everyone's musical tastes were changing. Not just me, it was the whole society."

After moving from South Minneapolis to St. Louis Park, Rivkin heard a drummer who lived a block away practicing in his basement. He walked by the house a couple of times and finally got the courage to go in and introduce himself. The drummer was John Hughes. He was playing in a group with a couple of neighborhood kids—Dan Holm on bass and, later, Mike Judge on rhythm guitar—that would name itself the Chancellors. "Eventually I joined the band," Rivkin said. "We started doing old R&B songs. There were probably only ten bands in the Twin Cities back then. It wasn't a cool thing to be into a band like now. Only if you were into music. There was no fame involved. It was just fun. We wanted to be the Beach Boys, of course."

The Chancellors were the first band to be booked by partners Dick Shapiro and Ira Heilicher—Amos's son—of Path Musical Productions, who got them gigs paying $500–$600 every weekend all over Minnesota. They recorded a cover version of the Righteous Brothers' "Little Latin Lupe Lu" at Kay Bank on October 13, 1964.

Another St. Louis Park resident, Owen Husney, was a self-described nerdy guy who got picked on a lot and played the clarinet in the school band. He was living in a 900-square-foot home after his parents had gone broke. "I was completely lost," he said. "When I was fifteen years old, my parents managed to send me to Camp Tikvah in Aitkin,

The High Spirits (Owen Husney, Cliff Siegel, Rick Beresford, Doug Ahrens, Jay Luttio, and Rick Levinson) formed in St. Louis Park before the Beatles came to America. Courtesy of Tom Tourville.

Minnesota. It didn't cost if you were a counselor-in-training." On the bus to camp he met another counselor-in-training named Cliff Siegel, who was so disgusted with Husney that he called his mother and begged to come home. His mother wouldn't come to get him, however, so they tolerated each other.

"There were these guitar players who would come through camp, kind of vagabond guys," Husney said. "For ten bucks, they were hired to wander from camp to camp playing these folk songs like 'Michael (Row the Boat Ashore),' 'Hang Down Your Head, Tom Dooley,' and all that shit. I remember specifically sitting there at the campfire just mesmerized by these guys playing, because they were super into what they were doing. As I turned to see if the rest of the kids dug it like I did, I noticed the little girls were staring in that special way. It just freakin' clicked with me." The performance had the same effect on Cliff Siegel. The two discussed their newfound love for music, then Husney left camp early, sold his clarinet, and bought a cherry red Silvertone guitar. He took it into his basement and, with the help of a friend who was an accomplished acoustic guitarist, spent the entire winter learning how to play. "When I emerged the next spring, I had learned all the surf songs and Beach Boys songs," Husney said. "When I came out, I had the ability to play guitar."

Husney met David Rivkin, who by then was playing in the Chancellors, and after hearing him play his red Fender Jaguar guitar, became more determined than ever to form a band. "I made attempts at getting into a few bands and got thrown out of one because I wasn't quite good enough," Husney said. He called Siegel and told him he was learning to play guitar.

"Come on over," Siegel said. "When I came home from camp, I started singing."

"Cliff and I were like magic," Husney said. "We knew we were passionate. You have to have passion and a very high work ethic. You have to fucking love what you do. We decided to form a band." The original High Spirits included Husney on lead guitar, Doug Ahrens on drums, Jay Luttio on keyboards, Rick Beresford (stage name Beckett) on bass, Rick Levinson (stage name Anthony) on rhythm guitar, and "Little" Cliff Siegel (stage name Stone) on vocals.

Bloomington was another suburb bursting with talented young musicians. The Accents were formed from several earlier Bloomington bands, including the Rivals and the Blue Kings, each of which featured Skip Dahlin on bass. In 1961, Dahlin recruited drummer and vocalist Tom Nystrom, who played in the Bloomington High School band. Guitarist Ken Sand was playing in a Bloomington group called the Trippletones, then joined Damon Lee and the Diablos, who were also from Bloomington. When Sand left the Diablos in 1962, Lee invited Nystrom and Dahlin to join his band. That lasted until Lee moved to Kansas City to join a blues band, so Sand, Dahlin, and Nystrom got together, added keyboard player Bill Miller, and started the Accents.

Charles Schoen started the Del Counts in Minneapolis in 1961. He'd injured his leg badly in a car accident when he was nine and missed a year and a half of school, so he had plenty of time to learn how to play the guitar his dad played in bars with Uncle Otto, who played violin. One night at dinner Schoen's mother said to his father, "Chuck, your son can play guitar and sing like you do." In junior high school Schoen started playing upright bass in addition to his Kay electric guitar through a Supro amp. His tastes ranged across the board, from Elvis to Marvin Rainwater ("I just liked music"). When he started the Del Counts, he named the band after his first drummer, Del Leon LaFave. "We were called the Del Counts from the start," Schoen said. "Del counted the songs—funny how that came about. Del was also the first personnel change. He was throwing in too many fills. He was too busy. We talked to him about it, and he got madder than hell. I said, 'It doesn't do any good to get mad, because in this situation, you're not right about it. People don't dance to rolls, they dance to a beat.'"

As the unquestioned leader of the Del Counts, Schoen replaced LaFave. He asked Bill Soley, whose dad owned Soley Iron Works, to play bass. Soley said, "Okay, I'll tell my dad." Soley's father bought him a bass and an amp, and Schoen taught him how to play it. He then added a guy from two blocks up the street named Tom Aspenwall, who had a guitar and amp. They played their first job at the Margaret Berry House, run by the Minneapolis League of Catholic Women. "I think we got, like, thirty bucks," Schoen said. "We drew good-size crowds."

LaFave was replaced by Tony Preese, whose father owned Tony's Shoe Repair in downtown Minneapolis. The band rehearsed there after hours and was discovered by promoter/booker Marsh Edelstein of Marsh Productions as he was walking by the shop. "Mind if I listen to you for a while?" he asked. Edelstein was running battles of the bands at the Marigold Ballroom in downtown Minneapolis, featuring as many as ten bands at a time, including groups like the Castaways, Underbeats, Avanties, Chancellors, and More-Tishans.

"You moved up depending on how the crowd was responding," Schoen said. "We started out being the first band. Within probably seven or eight months, we were up to number eight. Toward the end, we'd finish out the night."

Greg Maland and Dave Maetzold attended Minneapolis Washburn High School together and formed the Avanties in 1960. Because they were grouped together alphabetically in chorus, they started hanging around with each other after school. "Greg would buy all these 45s in a ten-cent bin because he couldn't afford to buy a record that was current," Maetzold said. "He didn't have much money, and neither did I. After school we'd listen to all these records. That influenced us in what style of music we liked."

They got their hands on an electric guitar, plugged it into a stereo, and thought the amplified notes sounded almost as cool as the radio and the records they were listening to. They started to copy songs and work out the chording. They had a friend who received a guitar and amp as a birthday gift but had no interest in it, so Maetzold and Maland rented the gear for next to nothing. They now had two guitars but needed a drummer. They tried out several and ended up choosing Doug "Froggy" Nelson, who got his nickname from the TV show *Andy's Gang* ("Plunk your magic twanger, Froggy!"). Four years younger than his bandmates, Nelson had learned to play his instrument in a drum and bugle corps. "That's where he learned a certain style beat that the Avanties used," Maetzold said. "When he was younger, he was messing around with a home-made bomb, put something into a pipe, and it blew off part of his thumb and index finger, so he started playing drums as therapy. That's how he got interested in drumming."

The original group—two guitars and drums—called themselves the Tempest Trio. Maetzold thought a car name would be cool, as there was already a popular Twin Cities band called the Corvets, and came up with the Avanti. "It was a fairly new sports car," Maetzold said. "I looked up *avanti* in the dictionary, and it said 'to move forward or advance.' Plus, it was the first letter in the alphabet."

They played parties, developed a following, and began to put some cash in their pockets when people passed the hat. "All of a sudden we realized we're having fun and getting money, too," Maetzold said. "We could go to a party for free and they would pay us. We started to play at some school dances, homecoming, and stuff—the same kids we played for at parties."

When they graduated from high school in 1961, Maetzold started at the University of Minnesota and offered the band's services to the campus fraternities, guaranteeing cheap live music and a good time. "When we'd take a break, we'd go to the next house on fraternity row, and we'd see the group playing there," Maetzold said. "Every frat would have a party on weekends, and back then there was beer allowed in the fraternities. They were great parties, and we got to hear a lot of bands. Those guys probably started their groups like we did."

Instead of going to college, Maland took a series of menial jobs, including working as a fry cook at Bridgeman's. He and Maetzold would go out to see national artists when they did Twin Cities shows. One night they went to Mr. Lucky's and saw Jerry Lee Lewis. "Greg could play piano really great, but this was when he was playing guitar," Maetzold said. "When he saw Jerry Lee play there, he was really impressed." By this time the group had added Bob Ohde on guitar, and Maetzold had switched to bass. Maland and Maetzold began following the Dorados to watch their outstanding electric piano player, Gary Nielsen (who occasionally played with Jim Thaxter and the Travelers, and later sat in and recorded a few times with The Trashmen). Maland decided to start renting an electric piano from a music store. "Whenever he'd go pick it up or drop it off, he'd run into other keyboard players doing the same thing," Maetzold said. "Back then you didn't have the money to buy an instrument at full price." Soon Maland would switch to the organ, the distinctive sound that would set the Avanties apart from the other bands in the Twin Cities.

Another of the most successful Minneapolis bands was taking shape at the same time. The Underbeats were started by Jim Johnson and Russell Hagen. Johnson grew up in Waterloo, Iowa, where he and his sister used to sit on the doorstep and harmonize on songs by Hank Williams, Ernest Tubb, and Roy Acuff. "I had a natural knack for harmony," Johnson said. When he moved to Minneapolis at age twelve in 1954, there wasn't much going on in music. "Doris Day and Perry Como," he said. "Then 1955 is when Elvis, Bo Diddly, and Little Richard came along. They caught me right away. But I still liked country. When I have second thoughts, I think maybe I should have gone that way."

Johnson got his first guitar at fifteen from his brother-in-law. He stripped it down, sanded it and varnished it, and taught himself to play along with the radio. "There was one guitar in the whole damn neighborhood," he said. "You just had to be lucky enough to run into somebody who knew how to play. An influence on me was Donny Dax of the Dorados. I ran into him one night. He's the one who turned me on to the unwound G string. I learned to bend it like Chuck Berry."

Johnson played trumpet in junior high school but was demoted from first chair when the music changed from B-flat to E-flat in senior high school. He attended vocational school for a year and a half but couldn't stand it and quit when he turned sixteen, halfway through eleventh grade. "I just started playing," he said. "I knew I wanted to make music. I kind of had a knack. I started playing guitar at home. That's what I wanted to do. It was just me and my dad—my mom left. He said I'd be nothing but a goddamn bum with that guitar."

He met Russell Hagen, who lived in Brooklyn Center, at a friend's house in Columbia Heights. Because they both played guitar, "right away we locked." The next day, Russell picked up Johnson in his mom's '55 Cadillac. "I thought, 'This kid's got to be rich,'" Johnson said. Hagen had hung around the black neighborhoods and had been exposed to R&B music. "To get B. B. King records, you had to go to the ghetto, to the basement record shops," Johnson said. "As soon as we started playing, I ended up staying there more than I stayed at home."

Johnson's first guitar was a Danelectro. Then he went to Torp's Music in St. Paul and bought a Fender Stratocaster. Hagen was more into country music, influenced by his father who played steel guitar. Johnson was being pulled in two musical directions. "We had a choice: country or rhythm and blues?" Johnson said. "We chose R&B. Ike and Tina's 'I Think It's Gonna Work Out Fine,' Little Richard, and Chuck Berry sent us in that direction. A country song would catch my ear every now and then, and I had to learn it. We always had a couple of country songs in there."

As the duo quickly improved, Johnson met Doni Larson, who was dating Hagen's sister, Barbara. (She was eventually married to Johnson for a short time.) Johnson asked

The Underbeats were formed in 1962 by Jim Johnson and Russ Hagen of North Minneapolis. Hagen and original drummer Bob "Duke" Duane soon left for the military, and the band solidified around *(from left)* Ray Berg, Rod Eaton, Doni Larson, and Johnson. Courtesy of Doni Larson.

Larson if he could play bass. "I don't know," Larson said but decided to give it a try, buying a Magnatone bass and Amplex amp. They added Bob "Duke" Duane on drums. "We would practice in Russell's basement," Johnson said. "We played 'Walk, Don't Run,' the Fireballs, instrumental things. I was still bashful about singing, so Russell sang, but he had a bit of a pitch problem. But he was funky. I did better but I was shy about it."

For some reason that he can't recall, Johnson and Hagen decided, "Let's go into the Army on the buddy plan. We can play guitars all over the world." Johnson talked to his dad, who said, "What, are you crazy?" Hagen went ahead and joined, but Johnson stayed behind. "All three of us were going into the service, but Jim and I changed our minds," Larson said. "Then he came out of his shell. He became the musical leader, and I took over the business." They also lost Duane to the military. He and Larson plugged the holes with Ray Berg on guitar and Rod Eaton on drums. "That was the first Underbeats," Johnson said. "We rehearsed and rehearsed, more than anybody. We came out running. Our first gig was Bill's Roller Rink in Anoka. I didn't want to do it. I didn't think we were ready."

He and Hagen chose the name Underbeats. "Me and Russell were underdogs," Johnson said. "We wanted it to be kind of cool, something with Beats. 'What's an Underbeat? I don't know, but it sounds cool, so let's go with it. Okay, we're Underbeats.' I still think to this day, 'Geez, couldn't we have thought of something better?' I don't know. It still seems to hang in there. I could do better now, but I'm seventy."

In St. Paul, Tom "Zippy" Caplan made the transition from folk group to Ventures-style instrumental rock 'n' roll in 1961. He'd first started playing acoustic guitar after hearing a duo sing and play Jan and Arnie's "Jenny Lee" at the junior high school auditorium. "It was so impressive to me, because I was a small guy, not good at sports, and here these guys are singing and playing a song I knew," Caplan said. "I thought, God, that's really neat. I've got to learn how to play the acoustic guitar."

Like so many other guitar players of his era, his first guitar was a Harmony acoustic. "It cost twenty bucks," Caplan said. "I took lessons from a guy in St. Paul who had played classical style. I would take the bus down with my guitar, this young kid, probably about twelve. I took eight lessons and quit. The guy was teaching me 'Mary Had a Little Lamb,' and I said, 'The hell with it.'"

He formed a trio called the Uniques with Ron Butwin on drums and Caplan and John Sklar on acoustic guitars. "We played at a club in downtown St. Paul," Butwin said. "Folk music was very popular at that time, so we were playing rock-oriented folk music." Butwin's father, Ray, had designed and developed the leather-sleeved outerwear that became the ubiquitous letter jacket—an essential item of clothing (sans the letter) for the preppie gang known as the Baldies. Ray Butwin would not allow Ron to work for the St. Paul–based Butwin Company, however, preferring that Ron learn life's lessons on his own.

The Uniques played folk for about a year, and then the Ventures came along. "I have this total recollection from 1960," Butwin said. "We're on a road trip in the South with the family, my sister and I are in the back seat, and all of a sudden I hear 'duh-duh-duh, duh-duh-duh, duh duh duh duh [the "Walk, Don't Run" riff]. The drummer started it out. That's kind of neat. The drums were simple but cool. I got back from the trip, and Tom was already working on the song."

By this time, a group of young musicians had developed around Highland Village in St. Paul. "It was a small community of guys like me that was bubbling under and getting ready to break out," Caplan said. "We were just learning how to play instruments. Butwin knew John Sklar. He was big into the Ventures, too. We decided to play local parties and whatever else. It all started like that. It fell into place partially by accident. Back in the first half of the '60s, everybody knew everybody. It was all intermixed."

They met Rick Youngberg, who started a band called the Deacons, and jammed with him at Youngberg's house. Later they met Bill Strandlof, singer and lead guitar player with Keith Zeller and the Starlighters, who also knew Youngberg. "We were all friends, jamming together," Caplan said. When the Uniques switched over from acoustic to electric guitars, Caplan bought a Fender Jazzmaster and a blond Fender Bandmaster amp. The band added bass player Larry "Red" Cable to become a four-piece rock 'n' roll band. "We thought we were fantastic," Butwin said. "We went in and did an acetate album of songs we were doing, Ventures and non-Ventures. And we thought, 'Oh, God, we must be so damn good.' And then years later Tom and I listened to that record. Oh my God, we were beginners, and we thought that was good. It may have been that I was off rhythm, or Zippy was off rhythm, or the guitars had the wrong chords totally. But we were popular in St. Paul."

As a four-piece rock 'n' roll band, the Uniques began getting dance bookings instead of parties. They even booked themselves into the Ford Union Hall in Highland Village. "By then it's 1961, '62, and all these bands are coming up, partially because of the Ventures, and groups like the Surfaris," Caplan said. "Bill Diehl had these Battle of the Bands at armories and arenas. We played a lot at White Bear Lake. It was the Uniques, Keith Zeller, the Black Hawks, Tim and the Galaxies, Mike Waggoner and the Bops, and the early beginnings of the Underbeats, the Accents, and the Avanties. We did several car shows with Keith Zeller. Everybody hung around together and jammed together. Everybody was friends with everybody. If we weren't playing on a Saturday afternoon, I talked to Rick Youngberg. If there were new records out, we'd call each other and jam. It was almost like a family situation. We were all working together to move the thing forward. The St. Paul people eventually met the Minneapolis people, and it kept growing. What was going in Minneapolis was basically the same story. Eventually the St. Paul groups played Minneapolis, and the Minneapolis groups played St. Paul. By the mid-'60s it was a Twin Cities scene."

It was not just the Twin Cities. In Mankato, Dale Menten was learning to play guitar and write songs, and forming friendships with Tom Klugherz, Gus Dewey, and young Bruce Waterston, who would become the Gestures. In Ely, the Bulinksi brothers, Bill and Earl, had moved from Chicago in 1960 and formed a rock band called the Electras. In Duluth, Steve Tamasy, George McLellan, George Johnson, and Dennis Brady formed a group called the Rebel Rousers, in honor of Duane Eddy, and would soon change the band's name to the Titans, add guitarist Rick Colborn, and write original material inspired by the West Coast surf guitar style.

Minnesota was not that different from other regional hubs: Pittsburgh had Tommy James and the Shondells, Boston had the Remains and the Barbarians, and Cleveland had the Outsiders and the McCoys. Chicago was the nearest geographic match, and there were similarities between those two markets as well. As Minnesota groups were multiplying, Chicago spawned breakout teen rock bands like the Buckinghams, the Cryan' Shames, the Shadows of Knight, the Ides of March, the American Breed, and the New Colony Six, each of which had national hits without having to leave the Midwest. Like WDGY and KDWB, Chicago also had two giant rock 'n' roll radio stations—WLS and WCFL—that gave the best local bands the airplay that allowed them to flourish.

That's where the comparisons between Minnesota and Chicago end, however. With its much larger population, Chicago had far more record labels and recording studios, and the city was firmly established as one of America's premier soul and blues cities. Chicago was home to major soul recording artists like Curtis Mayfield and the Impressions, Jerry Butler, Major Lance, Betty Everett, and Gene Chandler. Chicago was even better known for blues, represented primarily by the world-famous Chess record label (revered particularly by British rock bands of the era). Artists like Muddy Waters, Bo Diddley, Howlin' Wolf, Willie Dixon, Otis Rush, Sonny Boy Williamson, and Buddy Guy were household names in the blues world (and did in fact influence many Minnesota rock bands). And, of course, rock 'n' roll's patron saint, Chuck Berry, recorded for Chess in Chicago. Berry's influence on Minnesota's rock 'n' roll bands was deep and profound, but it had begun to lessen as the '60s progressed.

Soul and R&B success would come to Minnesota a decade later. Though they made little commercial impact in the 1960s, the talented soul and blues groups working in Twin Cities clubs and dance halls had a significant influence on what would come to be called

Mixer ≈≈≈≈≈≈ *Dance*

Back by Popular Demand

The "UNIQUES"

on

FRIDAY FEBRUARY 28th

at

FORD UNION HALL

2191 Ford Parkway

Across from Ford Plant in Highland Village, St. Paul

8:00 P.M. to 12 Midnite

Clip and Save Coupon   See other side for map

- -

Valuable Coupon worth **25¢**   Toward one ticket

DANCE — FRIDAY - FEB. 28th

"THE UNIQUES"   № 4699

8:00 P.M. to 12 Midnite

FORD UNION HALL — 2191 Ford Parkway

One Coupon Per Person   Highland Village, St. Paul

The Uniques, formed by guitarist Zippy Caplan and drummer Ron Butwin, was one of the bands that formed the St. Paul rock 'n' roll scene in the early 1960s. Courtesy of Denny Johnson of Minniepaul-music.com.

the Minneapolis Sound in the late 1970s and beyond. Artists like Prince, Jimmy Jam Harris, Terry Lewis, Morris Day, and André Cymone created a hybrid rock-soul-R&B style that was a clear stepchild of the rock 'n' roll and horn-rock bands heard throughout Minnesota in the 1960s, and the soul music that was pouring out of AM radios throughout the '60s and '70s. Indeed, David Rivkin of the Chancellors and Owen Husney of the High Spirits would be integral to the development of Prince's career as producer and manager.

Even as styles were gradually changing in Minnesota rock music, Mike Waggoner and the Bops remained on top of the heap, working hard and making good money. The younger bands idolized them. "One of the big early thrills of my life was when Mike Waggoner gave me a call," Lonnie Knight said. "Colly was sick, and Mike asked me if I would fill in at a ballroom out in Bloomington. I was scared to death to play with Mike Waggoner and the Bops—they were legendary."

Their fame eventually brought them and the other successful bands of the era to the grudging attention of the Minneapolis Musicians' Local 73, run by Biddy Bastien, a bassist who once worked with big band drummer Gene Krupa. "We had to join the union," Waggoner said. "You had to try out for the union. It was on the second floor in [a building in] Minneapolis someplace. They weren't going to let us join the union, because we couldn't read music, and the unions were set up basically for sidemen. They had a little roster. If somebody came to town and needed to a hire a musician, they'd call the musicians' union and say, 'I need a tuba player,' and they'd look through the list, give them a couple of names, and you'd go out and read their music and go home. [Bastien] said, 'I don't know how we're going to use you guys, because you don't read music.' But we joined the union."

The union had personnel minimums for each venue under its jurisdiction. The Leamington Hotel, for instance, required a minimum of seven musicians, so when the Bops were hired to play the wcco State Tournament dances there—drawing a thousand kids—they had to bring extra players. "I don't know how they came up with this ratio," Waggoner said. "Maybe it was square feet. I used to hire two or three guys out of the Dorados, I used the Accents a couple of times, [drummer] Tommy Nystrom and [keyboardist] Bill Miller. That's what you had to do."

Even Bill Diehl ran up against the musicians' union. After several years of lining up bands for ballrooms and other venues, Diehl got a call from Bastien, asking him if he was a booker. Diehl said, no, but he helped bands find jobs. "I said, 'They're a bunch of young kids, and I'm trying to help them,'" Diehl said. Bastien didn't see it that way. He told Diehl he was going to put him out of business unless he got a booking license. He was told to come to the union's office in downtown Minneapolis and explain the situation. Before a panel consisting of Bastien and three other union officials, Diehl explained how he matched up the bands with the ballroom operators.

"Well, where's the contract?" Bastien asked.

"Word of mouth," Diehl replied. "Handshake. There's no formal contract or anything."

Bastien asked him how much he took from the ballroom operators for providing bands, and Diehl replied, "Nothing."

"But you're functioning for them. How much do you get from the band? Are you getting the required 10 percent?"

"No. I never took a penny."

Diehl said they didn't believe him, so he suggested they call in Mike Waggoner, who had just been in to see Bastien.

"Ask Mike," Diehl said. "He sometimes plays two dates a week through me."

They asked Waggoner to come back in and put him and Diehl in chairs facing away from each other.

"You turn and face this way, and don't try to make any signals to Mike," Diehl was told.

"How much does Bill Diehl charge you commission?" they asked Waggoner.

"Oh, Bill doesn't charge us anything."

"Well, who lines up the dates?"

"Well, Bill helps us get the dates. And when we're there, we ask when we can come back. Sometimes they want us in a month, and then we tell Bill. And then Bill sometimes says, Surprise, surprise, surprise, you're wanted at the Turf Ballroom in Austin, Minnesota, and would you go down there for $135 or $140? He never charges us."

"What do you do it for?" they asked Diehl.

"These kids deserve a break," he said. "They're trying to get started. I'm getting my money. I appear with them, I get my $50 for my time, and I pay the station."

The union insisted, however, that Diehl had to pay a booker's fee and get a license. "I whispered in the ear of each of the kids, 'Keep it to yourselves, but I'm supposed to collect ten bucks minimum on the booking.' And I never collected a penny. I suppose if there's retroactivity, they'll come and get me."

Butch Maness joined the Bops on bass when Sheldon Hasse entered the Air Force. Maness had started his career in 1959, playing bass in Anoka's first rock band, the Corals, along with two of his buddies from Anoka High School, Steve DeMarais on lead guitar and Jack Richardson on lead and rhythm guitar. Another band inspired by the Ventures, the Corals changed their name in 1960 to the Trespassers after a Ventures song called "No Trespassing." They played private parties,

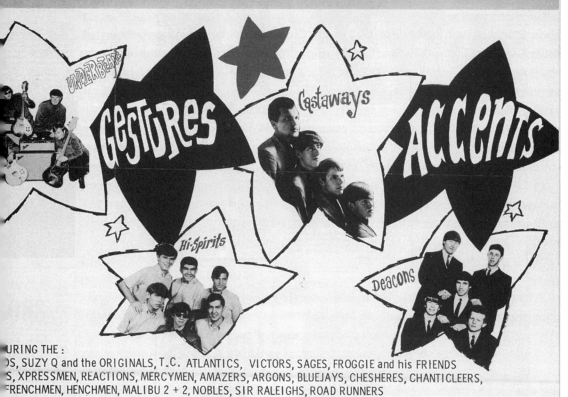

UNDERBEATS

GESTURES

Castaways

ACCENTS

Hi-Spirits

Deacons

URING THE :

)S, SUZY Q and the ORIGINALS, T.C. ATLANTICS, VICTORS, SAGES, FROGGIE and his FRIENDS

S, XPRESSMEN, REACTIONS, MERCYMEN, AMAZERS, ARGONS, BLUEJAYS, CHESHERES, CHANTICLEERS,

FRENCHMEN, HENCHMEN, MALIBU 2 + 2, NOBLES, SIR RALEIGHS, ROAD RUNNERS

) AND MANY MORE

E OF THE MIDWEST'S STARS"

698·8653
927·6187

)NE NUMBERS FOR ALL YOUR ENTERTAINMENT NEEDS

Bill Diehl's involvement in the local music scene eventually led him to form the Central Booking Agency, which promoted several of the region's top acts, including the Accents, the Underbeats, and Gregory Dee and the Avanties. Courtesy of Steve Kaplan.

then got their break at Bill's Roller Rink in Anoka, when Maness suggested to owner Bill Barrett that he'd draw more kids to the Friday night sock hops with a live band. Once they joined the union, the Trespassers began playing the teen clubs and ballrooms around the Twin Cities. Their drummer, Jim Cudd, joined the service and the Trespassers briefly hired future Trashmen drummer Steve Wahrer while Wahrer waited for Tony Andreason and Jim Thaxter to return from military duty. Wahrer was then replaced by a series of drummers who didn't pan out.

Maness played bass with The Trashmen a couple of times while they searched for a permanent bass player, but he had no intention of leaving the Trespassers. Then Mike Waggoner called. "That was my idol," Maness said. "I thought that was the best band in the world. I saw them at the Crystal Coliseum. Wow. We played different places where I got to know Mike and Colly. I patterned my playing after Sheldon, so when I went down to practice, I sounded like Sheldon, but it was me. I was in. We all kind of knew each other. Steve, the lead guitarist with the Trespassers, would play with Mike when he needed a guitar player. If we weren't playing, we'd go out to the dances to see what they were playing, how they were dressed, and see what girls were hanging out. The only reason a guy learned to play guitar was to pick up chicks.

"Everything back then was so natural, everything was so innocent," said Maness. "Nobody drank, nobody smoked. Every place we played was nonalcoholic or a teen center. We played proms and high school benefit dances, homecomings, you name it."

"Mike Waggoner and the Bops, Jim Thaxter and the Travelers, the Dorados—they were big, but there weren't that many bands," Larry Wiegand said. "When I started playing, there were only about twenty bands that I was aware of. By the time I got out of high school, there were five hundred. We were part of the front edge of the [baby] boomers. I think there was something about the boomers, but I can't say why. We were young, living at home, and carefree. There was just kids everywhere. It was just sort of a happy thing."

"The king around here at the time was Mike Waggoner and the Bops," said Tony Andreason. "He was absolutely our idol. And Colly Waggoner was very good, if not maybe the best picker around. Over time, when Colly couldn't play a job, then Mike would call me and I'd play." Andreason was still with Jim Thaxter and the Travelers at that time, but along with fellow Travelers Wahrer and Winslow, he was about to quit and form the most popular band Minnesota had ever known.

EVERYBODY'S HEARD ABOUT THE BIRD

FROM THE LAND OF 10,000 HITS

MONOPHONIC
33⅓ RPM
CHAPTER 4
FOR PROMOTIONAL USE ONLY
HIGH FIDELITY
SIDE ONE

TRASHMAN'S BLUES

OF THE FOUR FOUNDING MEMBERS of Minnesota's first great rock 'n' roll band, only Tony Andreason was born in Minnesota.

Andreason's father, Arthur, was from Rhinelander, Wisconsin, and had been a successful vaudeville accordion player. He and his partner, John Bolster, appeared on stages as the Jazz Twins with stars like Red Skelton and Jack Benny. "He was an incredible player, the smoothest I've ever seen," Andreason said. "Just brilliant." Yet Arthur Andreason eventually settled down in Minneapolis, married a local girl named Gertrude, and opened the Victory service station in North Minneapolis. Tony Andreason was born in 1943 at the Swedish Hospital in Minneapolis, one of three Andreason kids, including a younger sister and brother. "I had a great childhood and great parents," Andreason said. "I don't have any hard luck stories to talk about. I really don't."

He worked at his dad's service station throughout his school years, paying into Social Security starting when he was fourteen. "Back then, kids, teenagers, you had to get a job, and I don't see that happening anymore," Andreason said. "I shoveled lots, mowed lawns, trimmed with a hand trimmer. I worked at my dad's station and made twenty bucks a week, at a buck an hour. That went up to a buck-ten an hour, before taxes. And then if I played on the weekend and made fifteen bucks during the course of the week, I'd make thirty-five bucks that week. Sometimes I'd make forty bucks. I cashed checks back then for people who were working for seventy-five/eighty bucks a week. If you were making a hundred bucks a week, that was a lot of money."

Andreason was a fast runner who played football at Minneapolis Patrick Henry High School, and even got a tryout with the Gophers when he enrolled in college, but he was brittle and easily injured. "When I was a kid, I was bullied a lot," Andreason said. "My name was Anthony and I had zits. I was skinny, and people would beat me up on a regular basis, so my dad sent me to boxing school." He took boxing lessons from University of Minnesota instructor Earl Kaehn, a lightweight who had trained and managed the Fighting Flanagan Brothers from St. Paul. "He was a wonderful guy, a very devout Catholic, said the rosary three or four times a day," Andreason said. "Even when he was in his seventies and eighties, he could still hit. So he taught us how to box and get in shape, so then we knew how to defend ourselves. We wouldn't start anything, but we could finish it. If bullies know you're willing, and they're going to get hit, and it's not going to be easy, they're not going to fool around with you."

Of course, that didn't prevent a kid from getting into the occasional fight with a friend. One day Andreason was in the bathtub when his father came and told him his pal Charlie Harper was outside in the driveway, waiting to settle a fight that had started earlier in the day. Andreason didn't want to trade any more punches, but his father told him he had to "go out there and take care of it." So Andreason dried off, put clothes on, and went outside. He and Harper knocked each other around until they were both beat up and decided they'd had enough. In the process, however, his father's fence was knocked down. The next day the fathers of both boys summoned them back to the Andreasons' driveway. "This is what you're going to do to fix this fence," Andreason's father said. "This is what it's going to cost, and this is where you're going to go to get the lumber, and this is where you're going to go to get the paint. You're going to fix it like it was before this all started, and you're going to pay for it." And so they did—and in doing so, cemented a friendship that lasted years.

Discipline was always firm but fair at the Andreasons' house. When Tony was a sophomore in high school, his car was stolen. The police came to Patrick Henry High and hauled him down to his dad's service station, saying that someone had identified him as the driver in a hit-and-run accident. Andreason's car was found, but the driver had run away. Andreason insisted he'd been in a Modern Problems class at the time, and his teacher eventually confirmed it, but Andreason's dad didn't need to hear an alibi. "It wasn't my kid," Andreason's father told the police. "It wasn't him. He wouldn't run away. I know my kid."

"I never forgot that," Andreason said. "I knew that he was watching my back."

Tony's first musical instrument was his aunt's ukulele; once he'd mastered that, he got his first guitar, a Harmony acoustic, when he was in sixth grade—"when guitars were not a popular instrument." He took lessons at the North Side School of Music from Len Gates, who played with Slim Jim and Cactus Slim on KSTP-TV's *Sunset Valley Barn Dance*. A teacher introduced him to a novice guitar player named Mike Jann, who lived in nearby Robbinsdale and attended DeLaSalle High School in downtown Minneapolis.

"I heard Tony was really something," said Jann, who was four years older than Andreason. "They said you should check him out. Early on when I first met him, I knew this guy knows what it's all about. There's talent there. My eyes just popped out. 'Wow! Show me how you did this and do that.' We'd get together and jam, because it's more fun with two or three than on your own. We were doing mostly country material, probably pre-rock in 1955, 1956." Jann was a big fan of *Sunset Valley Barn Dance*, and it turned out that Andreason watched it, too. After jamming on country standards for a while, the duo began playing at parties and church suppers. "We'd play any chance we got, but most of it was in the basement of his folks' house," Jann said. "It was tough carrying that amp up and down the steps."

Andreason's first electric guitar was a Kay, with a Premier amp, bought for him by his father. Jann's first guitar was a Sears Roebuck acoustic. For an amp, Jann used the tuner chopped out of a homemade console radio. He then talked his father into buying him a Gibson Les Paul and a proper amp at Schmitt Music. "Along about this time, whenever Fenders came on the scene, I noticed the lead player on the Barn Dance was playing a Stratocaster, and so was the lead guitar player on Lawrence Welk," Jann said. "I said, 'Tony, there's something going on'—we weren't even sure it was a guitar—'You gotta get one of those Fenders.'" Jann remembers calling the music store to find out how late they stayed open. The owner agreed to remain past his 7 P.M. closing time when Jann and Andreason assured him they were on their way with $300 cash to buy a Fender Strat. Jann—hoping he'd get a chance to just hold the new guitar and strum a couple of chords—drove Andreason to the store, where he bought a sunburst-finish Strat.

"He was a little on the shy side in public," Jann said. "When we'd jam, he'd sing, but in public, no. He made me sing. He would rather play—lead or backup. He knew a few instrumentals that always went over well. I'd play rhythm. The crowd went wild. They really didn't, but they didn't throw anything at us, either."

"Mike wasn't a lead player, but that's what I wanted to do, play lead," Andreason said. "Mike was really into country music. He would sing like Johnny Cash. I started playing like Luther Perkins [Johnny Cash's lead guitar player]."

They had more church supper jobs lined up when Andreason broke his arm throwing a snowball. Jann had to wait months for Andreason's arm to heal so they could start playing again. "What could I do but wait it out, like the sports guys?" Jann said. "You wait till he heals."

Andreason got back to playing again in the spring of 1959. Jann worked part-time at a Super Valu grocery store across the street from Arthur Andreason's service station, where Tony worked part-time. One of the women at the grocery store was married to a member of the local Knights of Columbus, who sponsored an annual talent show in a room over "one of the seedy bars in the neighborhood," according to Jann. Their competition was several accordion players. "That was the big thing," Jann said. "All the kids took accordion lessons. Then here comes these two guys with guitars."

Andreason and Jann performed Homer and Jethro's parody version of "On Top of Old Smokey." They defeated all the accordion players for the first prize, a recording session at the same Kay Bank Studio where Bobby Vee recorded "Suzie Baby" that June. Jann drove them to the studio, because Andreason still wasn't old enough to have a license. "We put a couple songs on the acetate that we were pretty excited about," Jann said. They recorded three songs: "I Couldn't Care Less Than I Do Now," "The Third Man Theme," and "Guitar Boogie Shuffle."

That was the high point of the Andreason-Jann collaboration. Although they traveled together to Nashville that summer and managed to meet with country picker/producer/executive Chet Atkins, Jann returned to his journalism studies at the University of Minnesota that fall, and Andreason started playing more rock 'n' roll. He entertained at Patrick Henry pep fests with brothers Gene Ruffenock on piano and Jim Ruffenock on drums, and Harold Leslin on sax. "The teachers would get upset with us because we were playing too loud—I mean, really angry," Andreason said. "By today's standards, it wasn't loud at all."

The word was getting around North Minneapolis and neighboring Robbinsdale that Andreason could really play his guitar. He started getting calls from friends of friends to sit in and jam. That's how he met Robbinsdale High classmates Dal Winslow and Steve Wahrer.

Tony Andreason *(left)* and Mike Jann *(right)* were a country-style guitar duo in 1959 when they visited their hero, Chet Atkins, in Nashville. Courtesy of Mike Jann.

Dallas Maynard "Dal" Winslow was born in 1941 in Burwell, Nebraska, a town of five hundred in the middle of the Nebraska Sandhills. His father was the movie projectionist at the Rodeo Theater in Burwell, a town once known for attracting thousands to its summer rodeos. His mother taught kindergarten through eighth grade in the country schoolhouse. After scraping for every cent they could during the war years, the family moved into the basement of Winslow's uncle's house in Kearney, Nebraska. Winslow's dad worked as the projectionist at Kearney's drive-in theater, his mother—when she wasn't teaching—worked in the concession stand, and Dal cleaned up ramps and polished car windows with a bottle of Windex for nickels and dimes.

Being a kid in Kearney was a great experience, Winslow said. "You take your bike a mile out of town and you're on the Platte River, and you're shooting or spearfishing," he said. "It was a very good atmosphere to grow up. Nobody locked their doors or anything like that. Of course, with my dad as a movie projectionist, we got to go to movies free every week. I saw every movie up in the balcony. For a quarter you could get popcorn, pop, and candy."

Eventually, Winslow's dad lost his job when a union projectionist with more seniority came to town and claimed the position. He found a projectionist job in Minneapolis and moved into the Seville Hotel in downtown Minneapolis. Winslow's mother sold the house, packed up everything, and pulled a trailer to the Twin Cities. They found a home in Richfield, where his mother was hired as a teacher, and a year later moved to Robbinsdale. Winslow was in the eighth grade at the time. "Coming from a small town to a suburb of the big city, I just thought that was like *Blackboard Jungle,* Winslow said. "Here are all these guys with leather coats and so on—I, a country kid, scared to death."

At Robbinsdale, he met another country kid named Steve Wahrer, who'd moved to the Twin Cities from Keokuk, Iowa, when his father took a job with a Twin Cities box company. Wahrer was blond, thin, wiry, and very smart; he would earn a journalism scholarship to Hamline by the time he graduated from high school. "Wahrer and Winslow were in the same homeroom—you went by alphabet, so all the W's were in the same," Winslow said. "My friends' names were Larry Westveer, Jerry With, all W's. I didn't know any Andersons or Bennetts."

Wahrer was a drummer from the beginning with the school band and then in the Robbinsdale city band, playing drum-and-bugle-corps snare. In early pictures, Wahrer is always seen holding the sticks in marching style. "He always drummed that way," Winslow said. "Eventually, he turned the sticks around and started using the butt-end of the sticks. He was a very loud drummer and really had his own style. But initially, he used to comment on a lot of the drummers who came along: 'Well, they're holding the sticks wrong. That's not the way a real drummer holds the sticks.'"

Winslow's father had been a saxophone player; in Nebraska, Winslow had played the trumpet, and his mother forced him to go to piano lessons every week. "Sometimes I'd skip them and get a good whipping," he said. "In fact, I told her in later years that the one thing I wanted to do was go back and get my music theory and play piano. I took piano lessons at MacPhail. They had a program where you could come over during the noon hour and take piano lessons when I was working downtown. She thought that was hilarious. She said, 'I used to have to force you to go to piano lessons every week.'"

During his last year in Nebraska, Winslow played cello in the city band. After moving to the Twin Cities, he didn't play an instrument for a couple of years. But when Elvis Presley became a phenomenon in 1956, Winslow got hooked on rock 'n' roll. "I saw these guys playing guitar, and said, 'I gotta do that.'"

When he met Steve Wahrer, Winslow was playing an old Kay acoustic guitar that he bought at a pawnshop. "Go out and get an electric," Wahrer told Winslow. "We can't play rock 'n' roll on acoustic guitars." Winslow spent money he didn't have ("I probably charged it") on a Stratocaster like the one Buddy Holly played. "That's gotta be the guitar," Winslow told himself. "There was no technical regard whatsoever. That was a guitar that had three pickups on it and could play loud."

He learned chords in the basement by playing along with the records he and Wahrer bought. Wahrer had an older friend who played, and sometimes they'd get together and play a few rock 'n' roll songs, like "At the Hop" by Danny and the Juniors. "It was definitely rock 'n' roll that got us going," Winslow said.

In the spring of 1958, Wahrer briefly drummed with Robbinsdale's first rock 'n' roll band, the Blue Kats (Bob Ruth, Jud Sheridan, Doug Fredin, and Bob Elster). When Wahrer left, George Seibert took over on drums; Seibert then entered the service and was replaced by Forrest "Punky" Cole. At that point the band changed its name to the Sonics and became the first rock band to record with David Hersk's Gaity records.

Wahrer was asked to play with a couple of jazz combos, and eventually Winslow sat in, too. They formed a short-lived group called Jerry Wing and the Citations. Then through the local network of musicians they met Tony Andreason. "Dal was just a guy I met over at Edina who was playing with some guys who got together," Andreason said. "And somebody knew me. I think what happened a lot of times is, somebody would get an opportunity to play somewhere but didn't have a band. Somebody would call me a week or two beforehand and say, 'I've got a job. Can you play it on Saturday night?' I'd say, 'Yeah.' So we'd get together and maybe practice once. 'What songs do you know, and what songs do I know?' Everybody knew 'Johnny B. Goode,' and all that stuff. And so we'd put together four hours of music. You'd write 'em down as you'd rehearse 'em, and we'd get forty or fifty songs that we would do. We would meet all these different people, and you'd get together with the people you like to play with. Others weren't very serious about it, and we wanted to practice all the time."

"We sat down and started messing around, and then we just kinda evolved," Winslow said. "That movie that Tom Hanks had out, *That Thing You Do*, it's really kind of a true story. It's really how these bands form. People kind of move in, move out, eventually the ball stops, here's the big opportunity, and whoever's there at the time, that's who moves forward. That's what happened to us."

"You know what it did? It kept us out of trouble when we were teenagers," Andreason said. "All we were interested in were cars, girls—of course—and playing the guitar, playing music. So we rehearsed all the time. Finally, we thought we'd really hit it. We played lots of parties and everything for free. I think our first paying job was at the Crystal Coliseum. I think I made seven bucks."

The duo of Mike Jann and Tony Andreason had run its course. Jann was swamped with homework at the University of Minnesota and had little time to play, but Andreason, still in high school, was ready to play whenever and wherever he could. They rehearsed in Winslow's basement or Andreason's garage while trying out several names, including the String Kings and the Ravons. "It was supposed to be pronounced The Rave-Ons, but when you looked at it, it said Ravens," Winslow said.

They eventually coalesced around Jim Thaxter, a young singer and guitar player who was managed by his father. Along with piano player Tom Diehl, the band billed itself as Jim Thaxter and the Travelers. They didn't have a bass player; instead, Thaxter tuned his

JIM THAXTER AND THE TRAVELERS

Before they were The Trashmen, Dal Winslow, Steve Wahrer, and Tony Andreason joined with keyboardist Tom Diehl and guitarist Jim Thaxter to form Jim Thaxter and the Travelers. Courtesy of Mike Jann/ Sundazed Records.

Fender Duo-Sonic down and played the bass riffs. Andreason played lead guitar, Winslow played rhythm, and Wahrer drummed and often sang the lead vocal.

"Tom Diehl would do the Jerry Lee Lewis piano," Andreason said. "Steve could sing Jerry Lee Lewis better than Lewis. Really. We were doing a lot of offbeat Jerry Lee Lewis songs—not just 'Great Balls of Fire,' but 'Twistin',' 'Breathless,' and 'High School Confidential.' We did those just about every night. Steve could do that stuff—he was just an amazing singer. He was a little guy, about 125 pounds, but he had this big voice, and he had energy. He could play and play at that intensity all night. It was like he never got tired."

"With Steve singing Jerry Lee Lewis better than Jerry Lee Lewis, and playing drums at the same time, it was really a good draw," Winslow said. "He would sing every Lewis song that he heard, until the one time he saw Lewis, and Lewis said he would never do 'Breathless' again. So Steve said, 'I'm not doing it, either.'"

Mike Jann went to see the Travelers one night at the Crystal Coliseum. "I remember going out on a Friday night after the grocery store gig to see them in a battle of the bands," Jann said. "I could see our duo disbanding, splitting. Not that we wouldn't jam, but playing for money, buying uniforms, dressing alike—it started then."

Winslow and Wahrer graduated from Robbinsdale High School in 1960 and eventually moved into a duplex on South Lake Street with five other guys. Wahrer enrolled at Hamline; Andreason was still a junior at Patrick Henry. "I started working for Northwest Bank at that time in the bookkeeping area, but I had no idea what I wanted to do," Winslow said. "I knew I didn't want to go to college. To tell you the truth, I was pretty much fed up with school when I graduated from high school, even though I graduated on the Honor Society." One particular incident had soured him on formal education. He had good grades but was not allowed to go on an Honor Society trip to Washington, D.C., because he wasn't involved in enough extracurricular activities. "I don't really want to belong to a lot of committees," Winslow told the counselor. "I'm that type of person."

"You have to learn how to socialize and go out with people and work on committees and join the German club," the counselor said.

"Then you can take your Honor Society and shove it," Winslow said.

He already had enough classes to graduate, so he cut his senior year schedule down to three classes. "I lived a block from school, so I'd just go home," Winslow said. "My senior year of school I was just a slacker."

Jim Thaxter and the Travelers were on their way to becoming one of the most popular bands in the Twin Cities when they met David Anthony Wachter, an ambitious twenty-two-year-old booking agent from Columbia Heights who was just starting to gather a roster of acts and went by the professional name of David Anthony. He had always been interested in music. "Because it makes everybody happy," Anthony said. "It gives a really good feeling to people, you know. Going to polka dances and people would just run to get on the dance floor. It was fantastic."

On Saturday mornings he'd hit the streets ahead of the garbage trucks and salvage discarded old radios. On Sunday nights he'd have as many as five radios going at one time, tuned into the clear-channel music stations across the country—because factories didn't have armatures going on their motors on Sundays, thus greatly reducing interference. "You could hear both coasts, everything," Anthony said. "You were getting every kind of music you could want. Sometimes you'd get the same songs, within a very short period of time. I wondered if they were calling back and forth: 'Play this song now.'"

Anthony got his start organizing Knights of Columbus teen record hops at Immaculate Conception Church in Columbia Heights, funded partly by Rose Totino of Totino's Pizza. She provided the $10 per week budget for Anthony to buy new records—five of which he gave away at the dances. "I had to buy a new copy of Chuck Berry's 'School Days' every week," he said.

By 1957 he had started booking bands and was doing business as D. A. Enterprises. He'd book a group for $60 a night, take his 10 percent, and bring most of it home to his mother, who'd been abandoned by his father and spent five years in a Rochester hospital because of a brain tumor. "I think that's why my dad left," Anthony said. "He just got tired of it. Christmas Day 1954, the man from the hospital came with a $153,000 bill and asked me how I was going to pay it. On Christmas Eve! I said to him, 'Just a minute.' I walked over to the refrigerator and there was a quart of milk in it. I said to him, 'As soon as I figure out how to pay for this, and fill that, I'll start working on that bill.' He said, 'You mean you can't pay it today?' I said, 'Hell, no, I can't pay it today. You know how we're heating the house? We got the oven open right here.'"

Anthony's drive to help his mother made him a worthy and effective advocate for the bands he booked. "I made way for people," he said. "I opened doors. I always told bands, 'I'll get you in the door the first time. If you go back, it's up to you. I can't make you go back. I can get you more money.' Hopefully, anyway."

By 1961, he came across Jim Thaxter and the Travelers and met Tony Andreason at one of their performances in the Camden neighborhood of Minneapolis. He knew he had to work with a band that talented. "I'm not a musician," he said. "I just watch how people use their fingers. Tony was a great player. When he played 'Malaguena,' he drove everybody nuts."

The Travelers made their first recording in May 1961, taping two original songs in the living room of Jim Thaxter's parents' house. There was a Link Wray–styled guitar instrumental called "Cyclon" (intended to be "Cyclone" but misspelled on the record label), written by Andreason and Winslow, and a rockabilly tune called "Sally Jo," written by Thaxter and Wahrer. Thaxter sang the verses ("Sally Jo, Sally Jo, sweetest little girl I know") while the band filled in with the response vocals "Sally Jo! Sally Jo!" The instrumental is the more professional-sounding track, while "Sally Jo" sounds more like a frat-house band. "It's just fraught with mistakes," Winslow said.

"I recall going to Thaxter's folks' house when they did that 'Cyclon' 45," said Jann, who was becoming increasingly interested in recording technology. "I had to be there for that. I thought, 'If they can make a record in the living room with a tape recorder they bring...' That was part of my education." Jann brought a tape recorder to a practice at Thaxter's house in Brooklyn Center a month later and recorded two songs, including "Johnny B. Goode," which ended up years later on a four-CD box set called *Bird Call* on the Sundazed label. "Too many people were coming to their practices, so they had to cut that off," Jann said. "Thaxter's father wouldn't allow people to come, because they weren't attending to business."

The band paid for five hundred copies of "Cyclon" / "Sally Jo" to be pressed on their own Ariel label and sold them at their gigs. They got a bit of airplay on KEVE, the country station where Dave Dudley worked as a deejay, and on WCCO, but "it didn't do anything,"

Winslow said. "It got played a couple of times, but it's actually more popular now than it ever was because of what happened later."

Had the record succeeded, The Trashmen's story might be significantly different, but the days when a Twin Cities rock 'n' roll band could score a hit record in their own home-town had not arrived yet. Shortly after recording their 45, the Travelers split up. Winslow got tired of the unpredictable schedule and the dictatorial nature of the Thaxters. "Thax-ter was a difficult guy to work with," Winslow said. "He was a nice guy, he had a good voice, and the band was pretty popular at the time, but his dad was a real pusher. He way overmanaged him. It got to be a problem. He'd call you on a Saturday morning and say, 'We're playing tonight.' Eventually he called one Friday and said, 'Yeah, we're playing over at Bill's Roller Rink in Anoka,' and I said, 'Jim, I can't go there. I've got a date tonight, and I'm not going to break it. You've got to let us know in advance.'"

"Well, if that's the way you feel about it, you're fired," Thaxter said.

The rest of the band played the job, and Winslow decided to attend as a spectator—just for spite. Thaxter was livid.

"You're fired!" he yelled at Winslow. "You're never playing in this band again."

"Yeah, we aren't, either," Andreason and Wahrer told Thaxter. "See ya."

"He lost his whole band that night," Winslow said. "We were all pretty much fed up with him."

Andreason, just out of high school and facing the likelihood of being drafted, entered the Army reserves. Enlistees younger than eighteen and a half had a three-year obligation—six months of active duty and three years of active reserves. With his band broken up, Thaxter decided to join the reserves, too. Andreason and Thaxter ended up spending the next six months together, moving from one training camp to another. "Guernsey, Wyoming, places like that," said Andreason, who ended up being an artillery and recon instructor. "I fired lots of big guns, but I never went anywhere," he said. "They brought us up and had us standing by to go to Vietnam—or someplace. They send a staff car to your house, and you're going. I was actually at the airport, and they stood us down. I just reported back to my reserve unit in downtown Robbinsdale. We just went to meet-ings and summer camps. I was so lucky with that."

While Andreason was away, Winslow went back to his bank job, and Wahrer looked for another band. He landed in the Trespassers with Butch Maness. "We were friends," Maness said. "He played with us for a couple of months. Steve was a very good drum-mer. I wish at that time we could have kept him, but he had his friends he wanted to play with. He was just doing this to keep in practice. He was always fun to be around. I always

THE TRASHMEN

DANCE

IN STYLE THE

TRASHMEN

The name *Trashmen*—and the band's original logo—came from a Tony Kai-Ray song called "Trashman's Blues." Courtesy of Tom Tourville.

thought he was a little more shy. He wasn't real outgoing, and he was pretty serious when it came to drumming. I do remember him singing a few songs."

"Really, we were just biding our time until Tony came back," Winslow said. "The three of us got along well together."

Andreason got out of the reserves in early 1962, enrolled at the University of Minnesota, and immediately reunited with Winslow and Wahrer, who were still living in the Lake Street duplex. They were starting fresh as a new band and needed a bass player and a name. After using a few fill-in bass players, including Maness, they gave the job to Don Woody. The name came soon thereafter. "We said we don't want to be This and That and the Stringalongs," Winslow said. "We started going through our records, saw Tony Kai-Ray's 'Trashman's Blues,' and came up with The Trashmen. Somebody, I think it was Steve, said, 'Let's call ourselves the Trashmen—ho ho ho, nobody's going to forget that name, no matter how bad you are.' So then we started using that. That's where it started."

Tony Kai-Ray's real name was Richard A. Caire. He was a lead guitar player, singer, and songwriter from Wichita, Kansas, who recorded his first single, "Trashman's Blues" / "I Want Some of That" in 1961 on Lodestar, a Bloomington-based label owned by Clarence Brown of New Ulm, Minnesota. Kai-Ray worked with several bands and recorded a half-dozen singles in the 1960s on various labels, including two owned by George Garrett. Garrett also owned Nic-O-Lake Record Shop at the corner of Lake Street and Nicollet Avenue in Minneapolis and had a small recording studio in the basement of his shop. Kai-Ray produced and played on a number of the tracks recorded there and sold used amplifiers in a shop a few doors down. Larry Wiegand remembers Kai-Ray as being the main engineer at the recording sessions he did at Kay Bank. "Tony was a nice guy," Wiegand said. "What I remember, he was older, a guitar player. He was kind of a country guy."

The Trashmen debuted their new lineup at a teen dance in Brooklyn Park in August 1962—and if there was any doubt about what name they would use, Wahrer eliminated that by painting *The Trashmen* on his bass drum head. They had renewed their acquaintance with David Anthony, who began booking them frequently, despite the fact that their personnel had not yet jelled. "Bob Reed was not with them," Anthony said. "I think there were a lot of people playing with the band. I think maybe they were trying out people." Woody soon decided to leave The Trashmen to play with his brother's band, the Star-Tones. "He played bass with us just a couple of times," Andreason said. "He thought the Star-Tones were going places and we weren't, so he left."

"I think our name was another reason Don Woody left," Winslow said. "The Trashmen? No, you can't do that." But they did, and they found a bass player to replace Woody—one who would be with them for the next fifty years.

Robert Allen Reed was born in 1942 in Oakes, North Dakota, a town of about 1,800 in the southeast corner of the state, about 115 miles from Fargo. His father was born in South Dakota, north of Aberdeen, and his mother came from eastern Montana. Reed's maternal grandfather escaped from Prussia when the First World War started, and the family made their way to Canada. Eventually they entered Montana, living in a settlement of Russian and German immigrants where they raised sheep. "They had a hole in the side of the hill for a house," Reed said. "My grandmother said, 'I've had enough of this,' and she went to California. Then my grandfather and the kids got blowed out of there in the Dust Bowl in the '30s, so they headed east—why, I'm not sure—into North Dakota. They started renting a farm about twenty miles west of Oakes. At that time my dad lived west of Oakes, so they kind of got together that way."

Reed and his younger brother Richard grew up on their parents' farm and attended a two-room country school for eight years—first through fourth grade in one room, fifth through eighth in the other. When he started high school at age fourteen, Reed drove himself the mile and a half into town. "If you were on the farm, you had to have a license, because you were driving trucks and everything else." Reed said the farm was "only a few hundred acres." They had two hundred chickens, a hundred hogs, and fifty to one hundred head of beef cattle, and they also grew grain. "I was on a tractor in the field at ten years old," Reed said. "I spent a lot of time going up and down those rows. There was not a lot of help." Nevertheless, he was not looking for a way to get off the farm. "It's a lifestyle you can't match anywhere with anything."

Yet music began to exert a pull on him, too. On Saturday nights the family would listen to the Grand Ole Opry from the Ryman Auditorium in Nashville; Reed's earliest musical influences were the stars of the Opry, including Webb Pierce and Hank Williams. His father had played guitar when he was young and still had it at the house. When Bob showed interest in it, his father taught him some chords. He also learned to play the baritone ukulele his parents bought for him. He eventually bought himself a Silvertone guitar and amp from a Sears catalog for $125. His 4-H Club would often ask him to play and sing before or after meetings.

That brought Reed to the attention of Joe Schroeder, the old farmer down the road who had a dance band with an accordion player. They were looking for a rhythm guitar player to replace a boy Reed knew named Dick Pfeiffer, who had decided to leave the band. "Joe comes up to our place and says to my dad, 'I want the kid to play the rhythm guitar with us—we'll take care of him,'" Reed said. "I'm twelve or thirteen." Reed played on and off with Schroeder's band, and when he went into town for high school, he joined the high school band. The band director asked Reed if he would play the tuba. "They could never get anybody to play the tuba or sousaphone," Reed said. "It was too big. Nobody wanted to monkey with it. But I always had this leaning: I listened to the bass. I can't remember words to songs, because all I hear is the bass." Reed started on tuba, then switched to the sousaphone and played it in the marching band, playing at games all over the state, "marching with that thing around my neck."

Reed got together with Pfeiffer and started a rock 'n' roll band called the Corvairs at Oakes High School. Pfeiffer was an Indian from a tribe on the Canadian border. He'd been adopted by a family in Oakes. "He was kind of a wild guy," Reed said. "He's a good musician. He had a country-rock band that was on the road for quite a few years, and he was a steel worker in his spare time. He still plays in East Lansing, Michigan."

The drummer was Keith Bymers, the lead guitar player was another farm boy, Dennis Pfutzenreuter, and Pfeiffer played rhythm. With two guitarists in the band, Reed tried tuning down the strings of his Silvertone guitar to play bass parts, the way Jim Thaxter had done in the Travelers, but they rattled too much, so he went to Fargo and swapped his guitar for a Danelectro Longhorn bass—the same one that can be seen on the cover of The Trashmen's *Surfin' Bird* album.

Like all fledgling bands, the Corvairs had to scratch for jobs at first, booking themselves at dances and events, making and distributing their own posters, and paying for their own advertising. After two years of this, the Corvairs encountered the man who was seemingly everywhere in North Dakota and Minnesota rock 'n' roll circles—Burnell "Bing" Bengtsson. "Bengtsson would get us some jobs," Reed said. "There were three or four groups he was booking besides Bobby Vee and us. We would have to go to the old KXJO radio studio in Fargo to see Charlie Boone, and we'd buy ten fifteen-second spots for five bucks for an upcoming job. Charlie was like the Bill Diehl of Fargo. At that time he did a lot of the sock hop and disc jockey things at dances and gymnasiums."

The Corvairs never cut a record. They did record some material at a radio station in Jamestown, but the tape has been lost. As Reed was nearing his 1960 high school graduation, he knew he had to make some decisions. Two of the Corvairs committed to the National Guard and reported to Fort Leonard Wood in Missouri. Reed found a couple of temporary replacements but realized the band's days were numbered. Meanwhile, his father had rented more land, and though Reed described them as "one of the little guys around there," they were farming about a thousand acres. "One day my dad comes to me and says, 'Well, I don't think there's going to be room enough here for the both of us,'" Reed said. "'You'd better see if you can find yourself a job.'"

Between the military and college, Reed had few friends left in Oakes. He and a couple of buddies moved to Minneapolis and enrolled in broadcasting school at Brown Institute with the intention of becoming deejays. Reed hadn't given up on playing music, however. According to David Anthony, the staff at Brown had not been encouraging about Reed's broadcasting future. "They told him, 'First of all, your voice sucks,'" Anthony said. "'Secondly, you can't read well.' He said, 'No, I'm a dyslexic.' 'We think you'd better try something else.'" Though he ultimately graduated, Reed did drop out of Brown for a while, because he couldn't afford it. He picked up odd jobs playing his bass, including a few gigs with Twin Cities bluesman Mojo Buford. He also played occasionally with eclectic folk and bluegrass musician Harold Streeter. "He was playing 'Unchained Melody,' all kinds of stuff," Reed said. "I didn't have a clue what I was doing. I was standing up there faking it."

He also worked for a year and a half at the fabled Porky's Drive-In on University Avenue in St. Paul. It was the epicenter of the east metro's *American Graffiti–Happy Days* teenage cruising scene. "That was an interesting place," Reed said. "The manager would say, 'I need you to open up on Sunday,' but they wouldn't give me a key. We knew how to get in there—basically, you'd slide the windows open for the carhops, then crawl in there ass-through, hoping you didn't have a cop tapping you on the shoulder. It was a big hangout for the St. Paul police, too. They'd park in the back, come in the back door, and walk down the line, patting the girls on the butt. Somebody would throw a hamburger in their hand, I'd give them a couple onion rings, and they'd hang around, shoot the breeze with the girls, and get free hamburgers. The good thing was, if they ever had any trouble and called the cops, they were there in thirty seconds."

While Reed was treading water at school and work, Anthony continued to book revolving versions of The Trashmen. During a conversation with one of the administrators at Brown, Anthony asked if he knew any bass players. "The guy says, 'Oh, I know this guy. I'll have him call you,'" Anthony said. "And it was Bob Reed. I needed him for The Trashmen." Reed went to the audition with a friend of his named Larry Best, who had spent some time singing with the Corvairs and had come to Minneapolis with Reed to go to broadcasting school.

"We went over there to Dal's place in Robbinsdale," Reed said. "We went downstairs, sat down, and started playing. It seemed like everybody's style sort of fit together. I had a totally different style than anybody, because I taught myself how to play. It all seemed to fit, so we said, 'Yeah, let's do this.'" That's when Larry Best asked the band what they were going to call themselves.

"I don't know if it was Steve, or who, said, 'We'll call ourselves The Trashmen,'" Reed said. "Larry and I looked at each other and said, 'Let's get out of here.'" Reed left a phone number, however, and the band called him to talk him into joining. "I said, 'Really? The

When Tony Andreason returned from a stint in the Army Reserves after high school, The Trashmen became a permanent quartet with the addition of bassist Bob Reed. Courtesy of Dal Winslow.

Trashmen? Are you shitting me?'" Reed said. "But I agreed to join. That's how we started. I guess it worked." As Andreason remembers, "He came over and he knew all the stuff at the time. He played a real different bass style. He fit right in with us because we were all pretty untrained. That's where it started."

"When Bob came in, we practiced at my folks' basement over at Robbinsdale all the time," Winslow said. "I don't think we hardly ever practiced in the garage, so when they say, 'You're the original garage band' . . . When Bob came, he sat down, and we went through a half-dozen songs, and you could just hear the music click. He fit in just perfect."

Teen dances were beginning to flourish at the time, so there was plenty of work to be had. "These teen dances that we don't have anymore were lucrative for the bands," Mike Jann said. "They played dance halls, the old ballrooms, high school dances, the whole list. The market was ripe. Kids wanted to get out and dance—or get out. The dance was the excuse."

There was an increased amount of fighting at the teen dances, sometimes between gangs like the Greasers and the Baldies, but Jann said the cops and bouncers didn't worry about things getting out of hand. "They said, 'Okay, they come out here, get a little rowdy, maybe they sneak off to the cars, open up a few beers, whatever they're drinking. It's okay. We won't keep them out because by the time they dance, they'll work it off.' It wasn't anything like nowadays. It was a physical workout—if they really went to the dance."

The first job Andreason, Reed, Wahrer, and Winslow played together as The Trashmen was at the city hall in Chisago City, thirty-five miles northeast of Minneapolis. "I think we got, probably, a hundred bucks to split," Andreason said. Soon they were making a lot more than that. "Bill Diehl heard us play, and he said, 'We'll get you in more places,'" Winslow said. "He was very influential in getting us bookings. We were going great guns, we were packing dances, we were packing roller rinks. I worked for Norwest for two and half years out of high school before I found out I was making more money in one weekend than in a month at the bank. So that's when I quit. My mother was very upset about that, of course. 'No future in that.' And then my parents become our strongest supporters."

"When I got together with these guys, I found out I could make as much in one night as working at Porky's for seven nights," Reed said. "Then I ended up leaving Porky's."

The band was in steady and growing demand, and they were starting to play farther from the Twin Cities. "I was booking The Trashmen out in Hatfield, Minnesota, for one, St. Cloud, maybe New Munich—I don't remember all those dates anymore," Anthony said. "But right off the bat, they were hot. They just had a driving beat that was basically because Bob played the bass one quarter note behind the beat, and it just hit."

While playing hard-rocking music for hundreds of kids in packed, sweaty dance halls, The Trashmen always wore suits and ties. Courtesy of Mike Jann.

Though revisionist history sometimes pegs them as a mere garage band or early punks, The Trashmen were a professional performing outfit with a unique style. They did cover songs, but not the way other groups did them. "We started doing something like 'Breathless' by Jerry Lee Lewis, and we'd go off," Andreason said. "Because, say your audience is dancing, really having a great time—'Breathless' is only two and half minutes long. So you'd want to make it five minutes long. You didn't want to do the same thing over again, so we started doing different leads, going different places with the songs. We started doing cover songs where you knew it was that song, but it wasn't just like the record—it was different. Everybody else was trying to copy note for note, and we'd do 'What'd I Say,' but we wouldn't do it like Ray Charles. We'd do it our own way. I think that's what made us different and made us kind of go off on our own. We found the sound we wanted, and it was simple, straight ahead, hard, fast rock 'n' roll."

As the band gained a following, Bill Diehl began calling Anthony more often to book The Trashmen for his ballroom jobs. "He got really mad at me one day," Anthony said. "I had a date that was firm, and I knew the posters were out. It was back in the day when the [promoters] used to put four or five dates on one poster. It was hard board, not a piece of paper. And I said, 'The [promoter's] been buying the band long before you bought them.'"

When Reed graduated from Brown Institute, he had to decide whether to go into broadcasting or stay with a band that truly looked like it had a future. He chose the band. "Have you got a job yet?" his father asked when Reed made a trip back to the farm. "Well, I had a couple offers from a couple radio stations, but [I said] I think I'm going to stick with this band for a while, because it's going pretty good," said Reed, whose father was not pleased.

"You went through school and now you're going to do this?" he said.

"Yeah. Yeah, I guess."

Andreason was still attending classes at the University of Minnesota, but it would have been difficult for any of the band members to turn their backs on the lucrative teen dance scene that was developing in 1962. Other new bands were jumping in and grabbing their share of the audiences, including the Underbeats, whom Anthony was also booking. The first night Anthony heard the Underbeats play, he invited them over to his house. "It was that party where we met The Trashmen," Jim Johnson said. "They played some songs, we played some songs. Tony and I locked right away. We were closet country. We'd go sit down in his basement and sing."

"They were close with the Underbeats," Jann said. "I remember after a gig, they'd get together at Dal's house. Jim Johnson would come there, and they'd continue jamming. I remember getting exposed to them. That's maybe the only other band I was aware of."

Jann and Anthony met during this time and quickly formed a friendship. Jann had started working as a layout artist in the advertising department of the *Minneapolis Star and Tribune* in 1961, but he had not lost his interest in the music business. The booking business was beginning to heat up; Anthony and Diehl would soon have more competition.

As good as The Trashmen were technically, there was little that set them overtly apart from the other bands working the same clubs and ballrooms. They wore suits and ties and played the familiar hits by Chuck Berry, Buddy Holly, and Jerry Lee Lewis, with Steve handling all the vocals and Tony dazzling the crowds with his lead guitar work. In November 1962, needing a break and seeking some inspiration, Steve, Tony, and Dal decided to drive to the West Coast and check out the scene. The Beach Boys had just had a Top 20 hit with "Surfin' Safari," their second single, and Dick Dale's early surf singles "Let's Go Trippin'" and "Miserlou" were becoming cult favorites with guitarists. Steve in particular was taken by the surf sound and urged the others to make a surfing safari of their own. "We didn't have anything else going, so we said, 'Let's just drive to California, out to Newport Beach, listen to the ocean, and listen to these bands,'" Winslow said.

Bob Reed turned down the proposal without a second thought: "I was not going to spend the money to do that." He was already married and raising a child and had moved out of the band's Lake Street duplex to a home in the Queen Ann Trailer Park. "He didn't have the money to make his $83-a-month payment," Andreason said. "We just gave him our paycheck. 'Here, you can have it, make your payment.' He said he knew he was one of the guys when we gave him the money."

Reed met his wife, Judy, through her cousin Larry Westveer—nicknamed Deacon because he was a deacon in the Presbyterian Church—who hung around with The Trashmen at their gigs and parties. Deacon accompanied the other three Trashmen on their California safari when Reed chose to stay home. "We all went out in one big car," Winslow said. "I think I drove a Grand Prix. Deacon was one of my best friends, but he was an enigma. He wasn't into music, but he thought he was Elvis with his slicked-back hair. He'd get out and dance and clear the floor."

The guys were intensely curious about the surfing culture that had developed in Southern California. They all tried surfing on longboards—"We didn't know any better—just headed into the ocean," Andreason recalled in the liner notes for the *Bird Call* box set. "The real surfers weren't even going out 'cause the waves were so big. I got washed in to shore like an old log." After several similar efforts, one of the local surfers told the guys that the surf was too dangerous that day. He offered them some basic instruction for when the waves calmed a bit.

The real reason for the trip, however, was to pick up some musical and cultural tips. "There wasn't that much difference in the kids out there, what they were wearing," Winslow said. "Tony had a friend out there, Ken Severson, who took us around to a couple of clubs. We were out there twice; in fact, Steve was probably out there three or four times.

Drummer Steve Wahrer *(center, front)* doubled as The Trashmen's lead singer. Courtesy of Mike Jann.

He would just drive out there all of a sudden, he and Larry, and come back. When you're just playing on the weekends, you can do things like that, I guess."

They didn't see the Beach Boys or Dick Dale on the trip, but they did listen to a lot of records that weren't being played in Minnesota, and they saw the Chantays play surf instrumentals at the Rendezvous Club in Balboa. They returned to Minnesota with a determination to start playing surf music. "I went to the record store in Robbinsdale and said, 'I'll take every surf album you can get,'" Winslow said. "We just sat down and started going over that stuff, 'Miserlou' and all the other stuff that was going on. Up here, there was nobody playing that. They had heard of the Beach Boys, but that was it."

"I liked playing surf, but they said we were primarily a surf band," Andreason said. "Well, we were for a period of time. We went to California and heard Dick Dale's records and brought them back. We were a landlocked surf band. But we went with that for a short period of time, then we really got away from that. We were doing a lot of other stuff."

They debuted their new sound and image at Big Reggie's Danceland at the Excelsior Amusement Park. Instead of their suits, ties, and black leather boots, they wore blue jeans, cut-off sweatshirts, and tennis shoes. "We said, 'We're going to shed the suits,'" Winslow said. "We were trying to be surfer guys. That lasted a couple of times, and then we said, 'Nah, let's go back to the suits.'"

The surf music remained in their set list, and as 1963 arrived, they were well positioned for success. The Beach Boys ruled the *Billboard* charts with hits like "Surfin' U.S.A." and "Surfer Girl," while also introducing hot rod songs like "Shut Down" and "Little Deuce Coupe." The Chantays made the Top 10 with their surf instrumental "Pipeline" in May, and Jan & Dean hit the top of the charts with "Surf City" in July. In August, the Surfari's two-sided hit "Wipe Out" / "Surfer Joe" reached Number 2. The sun, surf, and car culture of Southern California made a profound impact on American teens that year, and the Beach Boys would be a huge influence on many Minnesota bands.

Yet no one suspected that the last big surfin' hit of 1963—and of the surf era—would come from a band based twelve hundred miles from the nearest ocean.

CHAPTER 5

EVERYBODY'S HEARD ABOUT THE BIRD

FROM THE LAND OF 10,000 HITS

MONOPHONIC 33⅓ RPM

FOR PROMOTIONAL USE ONLY

HIGH FIDELITY SIDE ONE

THE BIRD IS THE WORD

"WE WERE PLAYING up at Woodley's Country Dam a lot," Dal Winslow said. "What a great place to play. That's kind of really where we honed our act. Steve used to spend all weekend up there. There's a little house by the dam site that you could crash in. It was beyond belief. But what a great place for music and unwinding."

Woodley's Country Dam was notorious in the 1960s as a place where eighteen-year-old kids (and younger, if they had a fake ID) could get a beer and find companionship. Located about six miles north of Amery, Wisconsin, and fifteen miles east of St. Croix Falls at Highway 8 and County Road H, the bar and restaurant had originally been known as Riddler's Mill until owner Fred Riddler sold the business to Jim Woodley, a former boxer who liked to serve as his own bouncer. Woodley saw the bar on the Apple River as an ideal location to draw underage teens from Minnesota over to Wisconsin, where the drinking age for beer was eighteen. Woodley's Country Dam was just sixty miles from Minneapolis, and what rock 'n' roll loving teen wouldn't drive an hour to see the area's best bands while downing a few brews?

"It was both famous and infamous," Mike Waggoner told Tom Campbell of the MinniepaulMusic Website. "It was Wisconsin, first of all. There was always plenty of beer. They had hard beer instead of soft (3.2) beer. There was an island behind the dam out in the Apple River

Woodley's Country Dam near Amery, Wisconsin, attracted kids from the Twin Cities because of its eighteen-year-old beer-drinking age and its great lineup of bands, including The Trashmen. Exterior photograph courtesy of Mike Jann/Sundazed Records; interior photograph courtesy of Tony Andreason.

that was also a recreational area for people, daylight and nighttime both. It was a crazy place—we had a ball up there. It was just a cool place; and if your band got to play up there, you must have been good. He had an open deck that hung out over the pond behind the dam. The deck was full of people, the dance hall was full of people—it was just a wonderful deal."

"I wanted to go to Woodley's to drink with the guys, so I needed a fake ID," said Jim Faragher, who later drummed for the Chancellors. "How do I do that? Make one. I went to Murphy's department store in the Midway and bought a wallet for two bucks. Inside was an official ID card. I glued on my yearbook photo, plastic coated it, showed it at Woodley's, and walked right in. Little did I know they didn't even look at it."

"That was unbelievable—wow," said David Anthony. "You'd get laid six times in a night. Unbelievable. Everybody would drive up there on the weekend, and they'd be sleeping in their cars because there were no hotel rooms—or if there were, you couldn't afford them. There was a little hotel there later. The first time I walked up there, Jim Woodley put a girl on each side of me. They had their hands on my thighs. I walked up there with a handful of contracts and, shit, they all got signed for half price. It was hysterical. He taught me a lesson; it never happened again."

Anthony's list of bands was expanding, but he tried to keep his relationships with the musicians to a minimum—for good reason. "At that time I tried to only remember the leader's name, because I didn't want everyone calling me—it just overloaded the frickin' single line," said Anthony, who still lived with his mother. "The worst thing was when I had my office and I had all these bands out, and I had all these girls calling and asking, 'Where are they playing?' I said, 'I'm sorry, I can't tell you. It's company policy not to give out schedules.' These chicks were calling, and she's pregnant. I don't want to deal with all this. It's not my jurisdiction. That was a big hassle—girlfriends calling.

"The other thing we kept telling the bands: don't call up and ask for a schedule. We'll give you the schedule on Monday for that reason.' Because dates back then would fall in and out for the stupidest reasons. The road going to the Parkway Ballroom is tore up. People can't get there—the band's canceled. Here I spent money sending out the contract, and for posters that didn't get used."

Just as Anthony's business was taking off, he received word from the government to report for his draft physical. "I got drafted on April 10, 1963. I got sent home because I didn't pass the background examination for some reason." But it was only a temporary reprieve. By early fall, he'd be on his way to Korea—just as The Trashmen were heading to unimagined heights.

The Trashmen were eager to record again but didn't have a particular song or style in mind. Jann attempted to help out by introducing them to a songwriter he'd met, fellow *Star and Tribune* advertising department artist Larry LaPole, who joined the paper in 1962. They talked about interests and hobbies, and when LaPole said he played the guitar, Jann suddenly got very interested—and even more interested when LaPole said his favorite style of music was country. "He had written songs, he'd been to Nashville, and placed some songs with the Wilburn Brothers, but nothing had happened," Jann said.

Larry LaPole was born in Minneapolis in 1934, to French-Canadian and Irish parents. His mother sent him to Belle Plaine each summer to sell vegetables at his cousin's roadside stand on Highway 169, mostly to keep him out of trouble. He started playing piano in his early teens, and then bought a Sears Roebuck acoustic guitar—the same model Mike Jann had owned. He was a big fan of Hank Williams, and—unlike his city friends—he listened to the National Barn Dance and the Grand Ole Opry on WSM radio from Nashville. He knew he could sing, but it took him a long time to develop enough confidence to do it in public.

He graduated from Washburn High School in 1952 and did a stint in the military from 1954 to 1957. In 1960, he began taking guitar and voice lessons at the MacPhail School of Music. Then he heard about a weekly talent contest at the Music Bar on Cedar Avenue. "I knew I had to get onstage sooner or later," LaPole said. He also knew he couldn't do it alone. He recruited hotshot guitarist Eddie Lovejoy from the Big M's to back him on three songs, including "Johnny B. Goode." Lovejoy, who lived in his parents' apartment on West Broadway in Minneapolis and did little else but play guitar, told LaPole he'd play lead guitar at the talent contest but warned him not to sing the turnaround too fast, or they'd never stay together. LaPole agreed and gave Lovejoy a ride to the Music Bar on the night of the contest. Forgetting his promise, LaPole pushed the tempo on "Johnny B. Goode," and Lovejoy fell behind and started glaring at LaPole. When the song was over, Lovejoy unplugged his guitar and stomped out of the bar. LaPole followed him out.

"He was already in the car," LaPole said. "I drove him back to West Broadway. He didn't say a word the whole way up. When we got there, he slammed the door and went into the apartment."

When LaPole walked into the Music Bar the following week, the bartender asked him why he and Lovejoy had left so quickly. "For crying out loud, you won the contest," the bartender said. "I've been holding your money all week." LaPole took the money to Lovejoy's apartment and split it with the stunned guitar player. With a successful live performance under his belt, LaPole started hanging out at the local rock 'n' roll clubs, watching bands like Mike Waggoner and the Bops to see what they were playing and how they were playing it. "I thought, 'That's not that difficult,'" LaPole said. "I could get into that if I really wanted to do that, but country music was still my thing."

LaPole was laid off from his job as an artist for Brown & Bigelow in 1961. Figuring this might be his last chance to get into the music business, he traveled to Nashville in December 1961 to try to sell some of the songs he'd been writing. A friend had directed him to the publishing office of Teddy and Doyle Wilburn, a country singing duo ("Trouble's Back in Town," "I'm Gonna Tie One on Tonight") that was branching into artist management. LaPole was excited when Teddy Wilburn agreed to take eight of the songs on his demo reel. "That was my introduction to Nashville and the business," LaPole said. "What I didn't know as he took the songs, I signed the writer's contract for twenty-eight years, and then shortly after that, Loretta Lynn came to Nashville and they stopped everything and started devoting everything to her career. So those songs sat on the shelf. They never did anything with them. I didn't realize they were gone for twenty-eight years, until years later. That was the first setback I had. But you learn from experience."

When LaPole returned from Nashville, word got around that he'd placed songs with the Wilburn Brothers, and it got blown out of proportion. "Everybody thought I had scored, and I was on my way to fame and fortune," LaPole said. "They didn't pay you for the songs. They only paid you if they gave it to a known artists and it took off." Nevertheless, Mike Jann was impressed when he heard LaPole's songs, and he got Tony Andreason to listen to them. Though The Trashmen were certainly not a country band, Andreason had honed his skills on country songs and had an open mind about the material. As the Underbeats' Jim Johnson correctly surmised, Andreason was "closet country."

"Tony said, 'Yeah, there's a couple there I like,'" Jann said. "By then The Trashmen were talking about wanting to make a record because it would boost their booking price. They had nothing in mind, but everybody was doing covers of national material. Tony knew they had to have something original." They recorded several of LaPole's songs on January 29, 1963, in a small basement studio in Columbia Heights built by one of David Anthony's neighbors. "He said, 'I need somebody to come over here to check it out,'" Anthony said. "Well, he wasn't ready for the volume that The Trashmen had, but he did make up some kind of a limiter so the thing didn't jump off the dial, and he patented it and made money off it. After a couple hours, I don't think they were real impressed, and he didn't know what he was up against. They were learning."

One of the songs they recorded was a LaPole original called "A Million Reasons,"

HERE COME

THE

EXCITING

TRASHMEN

TRASHMEN 3848-2nd St. N.E. Minneapolis 21, Minn. Phone 788-2040

PRESENTING
SENSATIONAL SOUNDS OF
PAST & PRESENT

The Trashmen were updating their sound in early 1963 but still used the original logo. That would soon change. Courtesy of Mike Jann.

which was an upbeat Elvis Presley–Ral Donner kind of rocker sung by Steve. "We were looking for original stuff," Andreason said. "He wanted us to play on 'A Million Reasons,' and so we did, and we got to know him."

Around this time, Jann started working on a demo tape of LaPole songs they could send out to national labels under the name The Trashmen. The Trashmen played the backing tracks while LaPole and Wahrer each did vocals and were joined on backup vocals by a trio of high school girls called the Arlyles that Anthony had found in Mounds View. "They had just the right sound, real nice," Jann said.

The demo sessions were done at Jann's parents' house in South Minneapolis, or at the home of one of the girls. Jann did the recording on his own machine, having learned from the "Sally Jo" session that you could make an acceptable tape in someone's living room. "Bathroom echo was good, too," Jann said.

It was becoming apparent to Jann, however, that LaPole's writing style was not a good fit for The Trashmen, and particularly for Steve's voice. "They went in a completely different direction," Jann said. "Larry's songs were like Ricky Nelson, Gary Lewis, maybe Pat Boone, with country overtones. We knew it had to be rock. We were pushing Steve for what he could sing, because his thing was Jerry Lee Lewis. That's not what Larry was bringing to the table. We weren't thinking surf. They weren't about to sign Larry singing with the band, I don't know what we were thinking there. They're playing behind Larry's singing on these demos. We were off in the wrong direction completely, in hindsight, but it was a direction."

While The Trashmen were looking for the right songs to record, they continued to play throughout the state to growing crowds. One night in 1963 they were at Woodley's Country Dam when they heard a band from Solvang, California, called the Sorensen Brothers. The five brothers had evolved from an earlier group called the Revels, who recorded the surf-styled instrumental "Church Key" in 1960. By 1963 they had expanded their repertoire to R&B, including a medley of two songs, "Papa Oom Mow Mow" and "The Bird's the Word," written and recorded by fellow Californians the Rivingtons.

The Rivingtons were a black singing group that traced its origins to Los Angeles high schooler Al Frazier in the late 1940s. His first group, the Mello-Moods, included future Platters vocalist Paul Robi but never recorded. After serving in the military in Korea, Frazier returned to L.A. and formed a vocal group called the Emanons ("No Names" spelled backwards—Amos Heilicher would have liked them). Frazier moved on to a group called the Lamplighters, which featured future "Little Bitty Pretty One" vocalist Thurston Harris. When Harris quit the group, Frazier teamed up with lead singer Carl White and tenor John "Sonny" Harris and went through a series of name changes and labels until adding bass singer Turner "Rocky" Wilson Jr. As the Sharps, they sang backup on "Little Bitty Pretty One" and did rebel yells on Duane Eddy's instrumental "Rebel Rouser." Eventually they settled on the name the Rivingtons (so named because producers Jack Levy and Adam Ross once lived on Rivington Avenue in New York City). It was Wilson who came up with the "Papa Oom Mow Mow" bass line that led to their first successful single in the summer of 1962—on Liberty Records, home of Bobby Vee. "Papa Oom Mow Mow" ("Funniest sound I ever heard, and I can't understand a single word") peaked at Number 48 on the *Billboard* singles chart but was a substantial hit in L.A., reaching Number 3 on KFWB in July.

Frazier, Harris, White, and Wilson wrote "Papa Oom Mow Mow," as well as the group's next hit, "The Bird's the Word," an ode to the dance that was gaining popularity across the country in the spring of 1963. "The Bird's the Word" peaked at Number 52 on the national charts but scraped into the Top 10 in L.A. in April 1963. Dee Dee Sharpe had a simultaneous hit with a song called "Do the Bird" on the Philadelphia label Cameo-Parkway.

The Bird began to fade away, as all dance crazes do, but the Sorensen Brothers kept the two Rivingtons' hits in their act by grafting them together in a goofy medley. During a summer 1963 tour of the Upper Midwest, the Sorensen Brothers played the medley at Woodley's Country Dam, with Alan Sorensen ad-libbing some gibberish during the breaks in the songs. The crowd loved it, but it held particular appeal for one crowd member: Steve Wahrer. "They did it kind of crazy, but not with that kind of voice or anything," Andreason said. "Evidently this was going through Steve's head."

At their next job, Chubb's Ballroom in Eagle Lake, Wahrer told the other Trashmen that he had an idea for the "Papa Oom Mow Mow" / "Bird" medley. "He was fooling around with that, and he said, 'Wouldn't it be kind of fun to do it like surf?'" Andreason said. "He came up with this kind of voice. We were laughing about it and fooled around with it in the dressing room. He said, 'I'm just going to do this: "Everybody's heard about the bird—bird, bird, bird, the bird is the word"—and then we're just going to do three chords, E-B-A, and I'll shake my head when I want you to change chords, because I don't know what I'm going to do with it.' We said okay.

"So he just started going. And when he hit the middle of it, he stopped. He had to do something, and so that's what he did, he just did 'Oommmhhh . . .' just fooled around, and the audience went crazy. He just started singing the song again. So the second time we did it, we changed it around a little bit. We did the 'Papa Oom Mow Mow' the second time instead of 'Everybody's heard about the bird . . .'"

The Rivingtons were all but unknown to Twin Cities audiences. Neither song had charted on WDGY or KDWB. And as far as The Trashmen knew, they had adapted a novelty tune by the Sorensen Brothers. Their trip to California had fallen between the time that "Papa Oom Mow Mow" and "The Bird's the Word" were hits in L.A. "We weren't really aware of the Rivingtons at the time," Andreason said. "I didn't have clue who the Rivingtons were," Reed said. "I'd never heard of them."

They played the song four times at Chubb's, due to audience request. It could vary in length or spontaneity, but Wahrer's deep-throated vocals, lung-depleting gibberish, and gasps for breath in the middle of the song never failed to bring down the house. When Bill Diehl heard The Trashmen play the song, he knew they had stumbled onto something special. "I think it's terrific," he told them. "Are you going to record it?"

It didn't even have a name yet. At first "Surfer Bird" was considered, to capitalize on the band's new style, but Diehl thought the title was too static. "Surfer Bird—there's no action," he said. "Surfer bird implies he's standing there. Give me some action—call him 'Surfin' Bird'—he's moving! He's a surfin' bird." Diehl said The Trashmen loved the idea and changed the title. They'd found their single, totally by accident. Instead of one of LaPole's pop- and country-oriented originals, they were going into the studio with a novelty number they'd practically pulled out of the air. The next decision was where to record.

LaPole had put together a country band called the Pole-Cats and was playing at the Black Forest Inn on Twenty-sixth Street and Nicollet Avenue with Ronnie Brown, who ran

NORTHWEST'S DOMINANT ENTERTAINMENT CENTER

1190 UNIVERSITY AVENUE • SAINT PAUL 4, MINNESOTA • MIdway 6-6121

June 6, 1963

To Whom It May Concern,

The men of the Trashmen band have asked that we go on record regarding the relative merit of their band. We have employed the band here once a month for over a year. It is our feeling that the TRASHMEN are a well organized, rehersed, talented band, and that they believe in their product, as all performers must.

The band has good potential for additional developement because the guys are aware of changing trends and styles in the music business.

In the rock and roll category, the band is among the leaders in this region.

Sincerely,

Richard D. Clay
Promotion Manager

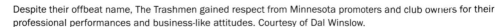

Despite their offbeat name, The Trashmen gained respect from Minnesota promoters and club owners for their professional performances and business-like attitudes. Courtesy of Dal Winslow.

the recording studio in the basement of George Garrett's Nic-O-Lake record store. Though the studio was nowhere near the quality of Kay Bank, which was across the street from the Black Forest Inn, Brown charged bands just $15 an hour to record. When Jann told LaPole that The Trashmen had decided to record a song called "Surfin' Bird," he offered some advice. "Don't go to Kay Bank and get charged $50–$60 an hour," he said. "I know this guy Ronnie Brown who'll only charge you fifteen bucks an hour." The Trashmen took his advice and went into George Garrett's basement studio to record "Surfin' Bird."

"I wasn't down there," LaPole said. "I was sitting in Hills Cafe across the street with George Garrett, waiting for them to finish the session. He didn't know The Trashmen from Mike Waggoner and the Bops. He'd never heard of them. He didn't go down to the sessions, Ronnie Brown did." The session lasted a couple of hours, and finally they spotted Brown crossing the street from Nic-O-Lake Records to Hills Cafe. "George looks up—I'll never forget it—and says, 'What have you got? Have they got anything?'" LaPole said. "Ronnie, in the understatement of his life, said, 'Oh, same old stuff.'"

LaPole later learned that Brown had an oral agreement with Garrett that the two would split any proceeds that came from recordings made in Garrett's basement studio. "Ronnie Brown regretted that all the rest of his life, until the day he died," LaPole said. "He never forgot it, and George never gave him a dime."

In fact, "Surfin' Bird" was not the same old stuff. It was very different stuff—so different, in fact, that Reed had not been in favor of recording it. "I wasn't real enthusiastic about that deal," he said. "I was worried about being labeled as a gimmick band." They took the tape made in Garrett's basement studio to the WDGY studios in Bloomington on a Saturday. Diehl was there, listened to the tape, and told the band, "You can do better than this." He said the three-and-a-half-minute song had to be cut down to two-and-a-half minutes to get airplay. It was the summer of Dave Dudley's "Six Days on the Road"; Soma Records and Kay Bank Studio were riding high. If the record was going to be produced locally, and produced right, there was only one place to go.

In the meantime, Amos Heilicher had heard about the song and the band and wanted in. In a vignette oddly reminiscent of the bank-run scene from *It's a Wonderful Life*, Heilicher called George Garrett. LaPole heard the story this way:

"George, I've got kids coming into my record stores asking for a song called 'Surfin' Bird,' and I don't know who released it," Heilicher said. "Have you heard of it?"

"Oh, yeah, that's my group. I'm managing them," Garrett replied.

At that point, Heilicher and Garrett began a business arrangement that would tie up The Trashmen for the next two years and siphon off royalties for decades. "Right there was where Mike Jann and I lost about thirty-five to forty thousand dollars," LaPole said. "Right there. That's the way George operated. He was nobody's dummy, and he wasn't afraid to take chances or risks. He wasn't always that honest about everything. That's what he told Heilicher."

"I really thought that was a horrible sounding recording," Amos Heilicher said in the liner notes to *The Soma Records Story, 1963–1967*, a two-disc compilation of the label's biggest hits. "George Garrett was an independent producer who brought the tune to our attention. We were the only outlet for him to get his product out."

George Garrett left many fingerprints on the Twin Cities music scene of the 1960s, but his background is hard to pin down. LaPole believes Garrett grew up at the St. Joseph's Catholic orphans' home at Forty-sixth Street and Chicago Avenue. "I don't know how old he was," LaPole said. "I'm guessing mid- to late-thirties. He was going by the seat of his pants all his adult life—anything he could to make a buck. I don't know how he got the record store. I know for sure he was purchasing used albums and rewrapping them in cellophane and selling them as new. Tony Kai-Ray told me about it. He wasn't musical. It was just a business to him."

Once he began producing and managing rock 'n' roll bands, Garrett created a series of record labels—Garrett, Bangar (from letters in the names Vern BANk and George GARrett), Twin Town, and Studio City—and, with local country singer Johnny Long, created a company called Willong that secured the publishing rights to many of the original songs recorded by Twin Cities bands. Garrett also ran Uncle George's Record Shop, a mail order company that advertised on Wolfman Jack's late-night radio show from Mexico.

Sam Sabean, program director at KDWB, was a good friend of Amos and Danny Heilicher, but he said he didn't know George Garrett. David Anthony didn't know him until after he returned from Korea and walked into Nic-O-Lake to buy some records. "I don't think I've said one hundred words to George Garrett," Anthony said. "I think he looked at me like a hell of a competitor. Because I came out of nowhere and all of a sudden I've got bands everywhere."

"George Garrett was a salt-of-the-earth kind of guy," said Dennis Libby, who would play in a later version of the Castaways. "There was a synergistic relationship between Amos and George. I can't speak firsthand what those meetings were like, but he loved to get anybody in there and record. He was a visionary. He had an innate quality and ability to recognize unique talent. He loved to cultivate that. He did it economically. He was your biggest fan. He just had a great nurturing spirit. He did take a lot of guys under his wing."

"He was very interested in our musical capabilities," said Jim Johnson of the Underbeats. "He had a little rehearsal thing in the basement with a couple-track recorder to see if you were worth a shit. He couldn't sing a note, but he had that kind of brain, like Colonel Tom Parker. That's the way I looked at it. I could get any record I wanted from his record store. He was a friend of the musicians."

Larry Wiegand met Garrett in 1964 when his band, the Rave-Ons, decided they wanted to cut a record. "George was a guy who had good ideas," Wiegand said. "He'd have a lot to say. We were kids, he was older, and he ran the session and lined up the engineer. He wanted to hear the songs before we recorded them. He wasn't a musician. He wasn't a player at all, but George was the kind of a guy who would hear a song and connect you with that song. When we wrote a song, or he heard a song, if he had anything to do with it, all of a sudden his name would be on that song. He was one of those kinds of operators. We didn't have anything to lose. We were kids. We never felt we were taken advantage of. If anything, he got our name around. When we started working with him, the records got around. We were better off than we were before."

The Trashmen, who found themselves managed by Garrett mostly by accident, came to a different conclusion. "He was a frickin' idiot, you know?" Winslow said. "A country boy out of the sticks with holes in his sweaters and everything else. I mean, jeez. I don't know anything about his background. I know that George had done some recording with some of the country people that you don't hear that much about. George was just an uncouth guy, but hell, he was going to make us stars. He said, 'Sign here, boy.' No cigar, but he smoked a lot of cigarettes. Garrett did nothing as a manager. He didn't get us anything as far as endorsements or things that we've seen since. He just wanted to sit back and collect money."

"George was an interesting character," Andreason said. "He didn't have any experience managing anybody. He had a hard time managing himself and didn't do a very good job of it. So he was our manager, but just in name only. If there's anything he ever did for us, I don't know what it is. He couldn't tell you where we were even playing, but he was getting a cut of what we were doing. He wasn't working for Amos, but years later I found out he and Amos were working together, trying to take full advantage of what they could take advantage of."

"He was a hustler," booking agent Jimmy Thomas told *Star-Tribune* reporter Jon Bream in 1989. At that time, Thomas had been searching fruitlessly for Garrett to resolve business issues regarding The Trashmen. "I've always felt the guy was one jump ahead of the law, so to speak." Garrett had moved to Washington State and died in 2006.

Garrett claimed ownership of The Trashmen, but he wasn't about to pay for a re-recording of 'Surfin' Bird.' They had to come up with their own money to record at Kay Bank, so Winslow borrowed $280 from his parents. "Of course, as a musician, you never had any money," Winslow said. "You're playing four-hour jobs and you're getting union scale, which was ninety-five bucks for the night. We weren't banking anything—we were spending it faster than we could make it." The Trashmen went into the Kay Bank Studio in September 1963 to cut the definitive version of "Surfin' Bird." This time it clocked in at two minutes and twenty seconds, with "Wahrer" listed as the composer.

"We basically did it live in the studio," Andreason said. "Except when we came to the middle part. We did that a couple of time until we liked it, and went on to the 'Papa Oom Mow Mow' part. Steve had his drum set here, and we were facing him with our amps. They had some baffles around them and some mics." Along with the bizarre vocals, the track's most prominent feature is Wahrer's ferocious drumming. "Steve would hit the

The Trashmen recorded exclusively at Kay Bank Studio in 1963–64. Courtesy of Mike Jann/Sundazed Records.

drums so hard sometimes he'd come right off the stool," Andreason said. "He really played hard, and he really had a heavy foot."

Engineer Tom Jung handled most of the recording sessions at Kay Bank, even though he had just gotten into the recording business earlier that year at age twenty. Jung started by cutting the 16-inch transcription discs that WCCO radio used for its commercials. He was also in charge of quality control at the Soma record-pressing plant. Away from the studio, Jung would take an Ampex 15 ips monophonic tape recorder to local schools to record bands and choirs. Jung got extremely busy after "Six Days on the Road" became a hit, sometimes recording, editing, and producing masters for three groups in a single day. On "Surfin' Bird," Garrett asked Jung to create an unusual effect for Wahrer's gasping interlude. Jung put a pencil behind the tape and wiggled it as it passed the heads to increase the wavering of Wahrer's vocals.

"[Jung] was brilliant," Mike Jann said. "He was just coming on the scene and knew what he was doing. He was working with a devised 3-track machine, and overdubbing. It was something they had rigged up at the studio. I remember Tony's amp being in repair. He borrowed my Gibson amp and didn't turn the reverb on. It was recorded dry."

Before a "Surfin' Bird" 45 could be released, the record needed a B-side. It had to be about surfing—everyone agreed on that. But where was the song going to come from? Jann asked his *Tribune* coworker LaPole if he would come to a Trashmen's practice session and listen to "Surfin' Bird," hoping that would help him write another surfing song to back it. LaPole knew nothing about surfing but agreed to go to the practice session to listen. The band played 'Surfin Bird' for LaPole, with Steve pouring on the vocal theatrics. Then he leaned back on his drum stool and asked LaPole what he thought of it.

"That's the worst damned thing I've ever heard in my whole life," LaPole said.

"We don't give a damn what you think," Wahrer replied. "All we want to know is can you write a surfing song for the other side of the record."

"Well, I'll try."

"Good. You've got two days."

All LaPole could think was, "Oh, my god." He returned to his drawing board at the *Tribune* and started thinking about writing a rock 'n' roll song with surf lyrics. "Once I had a good melody, then I would go back and make up the lyrics to fit the melody," LaPole said. "I'm thinking, 'What is the greatest rock song that all the bands play every night?' I'm thinking 'Johnny B. Goode.' I had the melody going around in my head."

Jann showed him a Sunday, July 28, 1963, piece written by *Tribune* entertainment columnist Will Jones that included a list of surfing terms, as a setup to an appearance by the Beach Boys at the Prom Ballroom the following Friday. "To prepare the uninitiated for the swell that is yet to come (and to help them translate the lyrics of some of the surfing tunes), a glossary of surfing terms is being circulated in the record business," Jones wrote. His column went on to define such terms as *heavies* (very big waves, eighteen to twenty feet high, found only in Hawaii); *ho-dad* (a greaser; sort of a hot rodder with long hair and sideburns); *cruncher* (a hard-breaking wave that folds over; almost impossible to ride); *gremmie* (a beginner or young hanger-on who is troublesome to surfmen); *wipeout* (being spilled by a wave); and *spinner* (a full 360-degree turn while riding a wave). It was not the most insightful piece ever written about the surfing culture, but it was enough to give LaPole some lyrical direction.

"I took those terms Mike gave me and incorporated them into 'King of the Surf,' which was as close to 'Johnny B. Goode' as I could get without getting sued," LaPole said. "I put it on tape. The song went together in less than a day. It was amazing. Once I had it going, it didn't take long to finish it. I made the two-day deadline." The finished chorus goes, "Well, I'm a high-ridin' surfer, and it takes three crunchers and a heavy to wipe me out. I can do a double spinner before you count to three. Whoa-oh, king of the surf, that's me."

The Trashmen went back to Kay Bank and cut "King of the Surf." When the record was finished, they brought the acetate back to Diehl, who told them, "You've got a hit." A few nights later, the acetate of "Surfin' Bird" was played on WDGY, pitted against other new songs to test it for listener appeal. Andreason never forgot that night. "We were practicing and Mike Jann was there," Andreason said. "I went out to his '62 Oldsmobile, because we knew they were going to play it, and turned the radio on. That was the first time I heard it. Bobby Vee told me he was in his '50 Mercury and he was going to Fargo when he heard 'Suzie Baby' on the air. He said he almost drove off the road. When you hear something of yours on the radio, it's mind-boggling. It was just amazing that they would play it."

"That was the 'a-ha' moment for me, when the record hit the airwaves," Jann said. "The night 'Surfin' Bird' came out, we were working on the demo tapes. There was a call-in vote for your favorite 'Pick to Click' for the night. We were trying to record in the house. Tony would say, 'Let me go out to listen to the car radio.' He'd come running in and say, 'They played it again, they played it again!' It disrupted our recording session, but by the end of the night, it was the Pick to Click. That was the night when it started to come together. Something's going on here. Larry, Tony, and I went over to some restaurant, where we talked about, 'Wow, what's going to happen now? We can't stay here all night drinking coffee. We've got to get to work in the morning.'"

LaPole was beginning to suspect that "Surfin' Bird" / "King of the Surf" was going to be hugely successful, and with the experience he'd had in the music business, he didn't trust Garrett or Heilicher to deal squarely with the band. He remembers standing in George Garrett's record store and suggesting to Tony Andreason that they ought to try to find another record label rather than Garrett's start-up Soma subsidiary. "Tony, we're going to get screwed," LaPole said. "He did it to Dudley, Jimmy Sundquist with 'Mule

Soma records wanted a suburban setting for The Trashmen's *Surfin' Bird* album cover, but Mike Jann and John Thule found a dump truck and shot the band in a downtown Minneapolis parking lot on a cold November afternoon. Courtesy of Denny Johnson of Minniepaulmusic.com.

Skinner Blues,' and every other artist who's come through here. I don't know about Bobby Vee, but we're going to get screwed. He's got that reputation."

LaPole sent a copy of the single to someone he knew in the Artists and Repertoire (A&R) department at Capitol Records in Los Angeles, saying Minnesota teens were going crazy for "Surfin' Bird." At the time, Capitol had rejected a series of singles by the Beatles, even though they were selling spectacularly in England for Capitol's sister label, Parlophone. The label simply didn't think the U.S. market would buy the Beatles. The Capitol A&R man liked "Surfin' Bird," however.

"You're right, it's a hit," the A&R man said when he called LaPole. "Who's got the publishing?"

"I don't know," LaPole said. "I assume George gave it to Amos."

"Well, that's too bad."

LaPole's warning to Andreason that they were going to get screwed was well founded, but as Andreason told him, "Well, this is our big chance. Don't screw it up for us. I'd rather get it in my own back yard than in California."

"I wasn't going to argue with him," LaPole said. "I was lucky to have 'King of the Surf' on the record. We let it go."

The record was the second single released on the new Garrett label: GA-4002. The first single on the label—GA-4001—was recorded by a country-rockabilly singer named Chuck Howard. The 45 had the misspelled "Johnny Be Good" on the A-side and the treacly Garrett-Howard composition "Don't Let Them Move" on the B-side. It was released in October 1963 and sank into obscurity while "Surfin' Bird" exploded.

The Trashmen appeared at an autograph session in the eighth floor auditorium of Dayton's department store immediately after "Surfin' Bird" was released and had to run down a hallway and across the street to escape the girls who were chasing them. That was the day Winslow found out that Columbia, RCA, and Liberty were also interested in signing the band. "Steve and I talked and said, 'Boy, we're finally going to get somewhere. We'll go to California, get into some of these big studios, etc.,'" said Winslow. "And George Garrett came up and said, 'We just sold your contract to Soma Records. They're going to produce everything and distribute it.' And Steve and I just looked at each other and said, 'Oh, f—.' We didn't like Soma to start with. So that was it. We figured our career in recording was pretty much toast."

But not initially. "Surfin' Bird" was released on November 13, 1963, and sold thirty-eight thousand copies in the first week. The impact of the record in the Twin Cities can't be overstated; no local group or artist had ever sold so many records so fast. Even Bob

'The Trashmen'

And Bill Diehl visit Dayton's
Varsity Shop, Saturday, Downtown

Bill Diehl, popular WDGY disc jockey, interviews 'The Trashmen', the Twin Cities boys who scored a national hit with their song, "Surfin' Bird." Get their autographs, hear Bill spin top new records. Register to win one of the portable transistor phonographs from Levi Strauss and Co. and records at the Varsity Shop, 1 to 2 p.m., Saturday, February 15.

†Varsity Shop—2nd Floor, Dayton's Downtown only

MEN'S STORE

†Reg. State of Minn.
Just say, "Charge it", with your Dayton's Shopping Card

For several years Bill Diehl hosted Dayton's Top 10 show in the department store's eighth floor auditorium. Courtesy of Mike Jann.

Reed, who'd been skeptical that they'd recorded and released the right song, was beginning to have second thoughts. "The first time I heard it [on the radio] I said, 'Are you kidding me?'" Reed said. "'You're actually playing this thing?' I couldn't believe it did what it did. I thought we were destined to be a gimmick band. But it took off, and all of a sudden we were on the road."

"When the Bird started, I left school," Andreason said. "The dean was really upset that I left. I was living at home in my parents' house. The other guys, as soon as it happened, they got themselves a Trashmen pad. I never bought a place. I stayed right with my parents. I might have been there only a couple months out of twelve. Believe it or not, my dad made me pay rent. I think I paid $60 a month."

The band's bookings—and the fee they could charge—rapidly increased as the song took off. They opened several ballroom shows for the Four Seasons, who were riding a wave of popularity after hits like "Sherry," "Big Girls Don't Cry," and "Walk Like a Man." The touring drummer for the Four Seasons was unavailable, so after playing The Trashmen's opening set, Wahrer sat in as drummer for the headliners, too. "They were the best guys," Winslow said. "Frankie Valli and those guys were just the nicest guys, especially the bass player [Nick Massi]. Except Bob Gaudio was just a little into himself. He had done stuff before and went on to do a lot of stuff afterward. He was nice, but you could tell his head was always elsewhere."

There was a shocking speed bump on the way to the top of the charts, however: the "Surfin' Bird" mania was interrupted on November 22, 1963, by the assassination of President John F. Kennedy. "Everything came to a stop," Winslow said. "Like the self-centered idiots we were, we were thinking, 'Oh, this is going to hurt our career.' Hey, the president's been shot—come on!"

A grieving nation—particularly its teenagers—seemed to need something silly, fun, and danceable in the aftermath of the Kennedy assassination. "Surfin' Bird" was facing some diverse—and not particularly rocking—competition for the top rungs of the *Billboard* singles chart: the countrified "I'm Leaving It Up to You" by Dale & Grace; a light-pop treatment of the standard "Deep Purple" by Nino Tempo & April Stevens; the folky "Dominique" by the Singing Nun; a cover of the Drifters' "Drip Drop" by Dion; an upbeat version of the standard "Fools Rush In" by Rick Nelson; the breathy "You Don't Have to Be a Baby to Cry" by the Caravelles; the moody ballad "In My Room" by the Beach Boys; the soft girl-group ballad "Popsicles and Icicles" by the Murmaids; the pop ditty "Sugar Shack" by Jimmy Gilmer and the Fireballs; and the Dixieland jazz tune "Washington Square" by the Village Stompers. Only the Kingsmen's "Louie Louie" bore any similarity to "Surfin' Bird"—and it, too, would go on to be a party-rock classic.

By December, "Surfin' Bird" was Number 1 on both the WDGY and KDWB charts; more surprisingly, it was headed for the Top 10 in New York, Chicago, San Francisco, Kansas City, St. Louis, Phoenix, Philadelphia, Miami, and other markets across the country. "We sold a thousand copies a day locally in stores that we owned," Amos Heilicher said in the *Soma Records Story* liner notes. "Again, I sent out promos to all my friends across the country, and we had an instantaneous hit on our hands before we knew what happened. We did sell over a million copies."

"Surfin' Bird" entered the *Billboard* singles chart on December 7, and by the end of the month it was a certified national smash. The question was, could the Heilichers capitalize on the obvious demand for product? Heilicher threw a party for The Trashmen at Kay Bank Studios to celebrate the national success of "Surfin' Bird," but distribution was always going to be a problem for Soma. "Amos Heilicher was not set up to do a mass distribution like this," Winslow said. "He'd had 'Mule Skinner Blues' and 'Six Days on the Road,' but other than that, they had so many advance orders for this that it created a rift. Heilicher provided all his music stores with the records first, and the other music stores kind of suffered because of that." The record store in Robbinsdale where

Winslow shopped was not part of the Musicland/Heilicher empire, which meant the store couldn't get the record. "That guy was pretty ticked off," Winslow said. "I said, 'It's out of my hands.'"

"The pressing plant just couldn't keep up with the listeners' demand," Jann said. He recalled a rumor that workers at the pressing plant on Washington Avenue North would go out and grab pieces of asphalt from the street to press into 45s. Somehow, Soma managed to press and ship enough records to propel "Surfin' Bird" toward the top of the *Billboard* singles chart.

The record was even having an impact on the other side of the world. David Anthony had been shipped overseas shortly before The Trashmen decided to record "Surfin' Bird." His parting move as a booking agent was to list The Trashmen, the Underbeats, and a couple of other bands he worked with in a *Billboard* publication of bands available for college parties. He included his name and his mother's telephone number in the listing. Then it was off to basic training, and finally Korea, where he was put in charge of telephone communications. He listened to the Army radio station while he was on duty, occasionally calling the deejay—Bob Mercer, grandson of songwriter and Capitol Records founder Johnny Mercer—to request songs.

"If you ever get anything by The Trashmen, let me know," Anthony mentioned to the deejay. "They're a really good band."

Mercer called him two months later. "Dave, didn't you ask me about a band called The Trashmen?"

"Yeah."

"I got a record."

It was "Surfin' Bird." Anthony had expected The Trashmen to record, but not that.

"I went, 'What? Steve, you couldn't do anything better?'" Anthony said. "I don't think I would have recognized them. I didn't hear them ever rehearse that beat or anything." Anthony soon realized "Surfin'

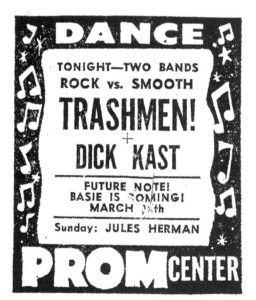

The Trashmen played St. Paul's Prom Center many times, initially alternating with big band orchestras to attract both teenagers and adults. Courtesy of Tom Tourville.

THE TRASHMEN *Garrett* RECORDS   Distributed by **soma** Recording Co.

Soma Records mounted a publicity campaign for The Trashmen but fell short on supplying product to distant markets. Steve Wahrer was billing himself as Steve Ward at the time. Courtesy of Mike Jann.

Bird" was a smash when he started receiving letters from his mother, asking what she was supposed to say to all the club owners who kept calling her number, asking how they could book The Trashmen. "The phone company called my mother when 'Surfin' Bird' hit to tell her she had to put in more telephone lines because she was jamming up the circuit," said Anthony, who had to serve almost two years in Korea before he could return to resume his booking activities. He'd asked a friend named Jack Martin to take over his bookings, but Martin was a musician, not a businessman. "He was not ready for the details, returning phone calls, and paying his phone bill because his mom and dad weren't going to let him call from home," Anthony said. "He apologized to me when I got home from the service. I said, 'Hey, lesson learned.'"

In the meantime, Soma rushed The Trashmen back to Kay Bank Studio to record an album. Once again, LaPole was enlisted to come up with material. "They had made the decision, based on the hit single, from George on down, everybody, that we need original material," Jann said. "'We're not going to do all covers. Larry, what else can you come up with?' By then it was a working relationship." LaPole worked furiously to write more songs for the band, somehow finding time to drop by the daytime sessions at Kay Bank while still holding down his full-time artist job at the newspaper.

"It was hell on wheels after that for Mike and me," LaPole said.

Not only did they have to fill out an album, but they had to create a follow-up single for "Surfin' Bird." The A-side chosen was a song called "Bird Dance Beat," very similar in style and substance to "Surfin' Bird," even including a "papa oom mow mow" chorus. The writing credit went solely to George Garrett. "I don't think he [Garrett] contributed one iota to 'Bird Dance,'" LaPole said. "He just put his name on there because he brought them in to Kay Bank to do the recording. I think The Trashmen wrote it. I don't know for sure. Things were happening so fast, it was all Mike and I could do to keep up with it. We'd leave the paper on our lunch hours to go to Kay Bank where The Trashmen were doing follow-up songs. I'd bring new ones down there and they'd work on them right in the studio. I can't believe I wrote all that in a short period of time."

LaPole had written the B-side of the band's massive hit single, their second B-side ("A-Bone," a hot rod song that used Wahrer's "Surfin' Bird" voice), and two album cuts—the surf tune "My Woodie" and another hot rod song called "The Sleeper." Despite risking getting fired from his full-time job for taking so much time away from the office, LaPole had not received any compensation from Garrett or Heilicher. "We hadn't received a penny," LaPole said. "I wrote this nasty letter to Amos, telling him I was going to pull the rights to the BMI royalties. I don't think he ever got a letter like that from any of the other recording artists he'd worked with."

Eventually, the situation became clear: Heilicher was paying Garrett, but Garrett wasn't paying LaPole or The Trashmen. "I didn't know that at the time," LaPole said. "I thought we should have been getting paid from Amos. When I wrote that letter, Vern Bank told me, 'You shouldn't have sent that letter to Mr. Heilicher.' I said, 'We haven't received a dime. We've done two songs, and we're into the album.' Then George showed up at the studio. I can still see the look on his face. He pulled out his checkbook and looked at me just like a little kid who got caught with his hand in the cookie jar. He didn't say a word, just looked at me, like, 'Well, here, maybe this will shut you up for a while.' He wrote a check for $3,000 to me, minus $500 for a service fee or some b.s. term. That was quite a bit of money in those days, but that was it—the only check I ever got from George."

LaPole estimated that Garrett owed The Trashmen about $56,000 for both singles and the album they were working on at the time, based on the assumption that "Surfin' Bird" had sold more than a million copies ("George had the gold record hanging in his record store"). "One million on the single would have been ten thousand in my pocket at a penny a record, and The Trashmen should have been receiving somewhere around a nickel a record. That's where I came up with the $56,000. They had that much coming, and I don't think they ever saw any of it."

"We don't know how many it sold," Andreason said. "We have no idea. It's all water under the bridge now—it's been a long, long time. But it was too bad that people in this town really didn't have a vision of what they could have done. It could really have been a big deal here in town. But it was just short-term greed on their part. But in that business, there's young people out there who love the music who don't know anything about it, and it's like taking candy away from a baby for them," Andreason said. "I remember Amos Heilicher's son-in-law— he's long gone, too—putting his arm around me and saying, 'We're going to take care of you boys.' They took care of us, all right."

At the height of the flight of the Bird, The Trashmen were too busy promoting the record and profiting from their increased touring revenue to complain, playing in Des Moines, Omaha, Milwaukee, Duluth, Fargo, and Chicago. "We got our first big check in Duluth," Andreason said. "The first time we went out and played the Duluth Armory, we took twenty-eight hundred bucks out of that place, in the beginning of '64. You could buy a brand new car for that. It was a really big check. We couldn't believe it."

Their most important promotional trip didn't even involve the entire band. In January 1964, Dick Clark's *American Bandstand* asked The Trashmen to do an appearance on the Philadelphia-based show. Soma would not pay to send the entire band to Philadelphia, and neither would *Bandstand,* so Wahrer went by himself to lip-sync the band's hit in front of the show's studio audience of teen dancers. "One of the biggest questions we get asked is, 'Why wasn't the whole band there?'" Winslow said. "They paid for one guy to go out there, go to the studio, do the song, get on a plane, and get out. Not going to stay the night. At that time, Dick Clark's studio was shutting down. They were getting ready to move to L.A., so they were cutting expenses. With Heilicher being the tight-ass that he was, they didn't want to send the whole band out there."

The result was one of the stranger episodes in television rock 'n' roll history. Dick Clark began the segment sitting behind his desk, with a telephone next to him, one arm leaning on the American Bandstand insignia. His full head of hair was slicked back in a pre-Beatles pomp, and he wore a skinny tie and narrow-lapelled dark jacket. Clark initially seemed a bit disdainful of his next guest. "If you were to review back and think of all the strange and unusual sounds of 1963, I guess this one would have to win an award

A publicity shot of The Trashmen from their first burst of fame: *(left to right)* Tony Andreason *(front)*, Bob Reed, Steve Wahrer, and Dal Winslow. Courtesy of Denny Johnson of Minniepaulmusic.com.

of some sort," Clark said. "One of the biggest novelties of late '63, still very big in early '64, and our guests are here to perform it for us. Ladies and gentlemen, the strange sounds of the 'Surfin' Bird'—let's greet The Trashmen!"

The audience in the bleachers—a mix of black and white teen boys and girls—applauded and cheered politely. The girls wore flouncy, church-like dresses with big, round collars, and the boys wore coats and ties. It was the last time the audience was shown until after the performance, so there was no way to judge how the song went over with the Philly teens.

The first thing visible once the record started was a large, fake, blinking bird with a painted bill that looked like the Froot Loops toucan, perched in a tree in the studio. The camera then panned down to Steve Wahrer, dressed in a light-colored, tight-fitting suit with tiny lapels, a thin dark tie, and a white shirt, lip-syncing to the song while doing his version of the Bird. He hopped on one leg and then the other, forward and backward while flapping his elbows at his side, looking something like Chuck Berry doing his duck-walk without his guitar. At the vocal break, Wahrer ran out of wind and lowered his head to take in another lungful as his blond hair dangled in front of his forehead. Then he pulled back and let loose another lip-synced blast of nonsense and began sliding back and forth like James Brown—great moves for a drummer who was always seated throughout the band's performances.

Dick Clark walked over to shake his hand as the music faded out.

"That's Steve Ward of The Trashmen," Clark said. (Wahrer tried using the stage name *Ward* for a brief time.) "Come over here and sit down."

Clark led Wahrer over to the American Bandstand desk, and they sat in front of it on the raised step. "Make yourself at home here," Clark said to the panting Wahrer. "I should explain that there are other members of the group who also play instruments. Are you the only singing member of The Trashmen?"

"Well, actually, Dick—" Wahrer started to say, then coughed.

"The poor man is out of breath," Clark said. "Catch your breath a second here. I'll ask you again, are you the only—and I hesitate here, I put quote, unquote, because there will be some cynics who listen to that and say, 'Singing? What kind of business—?' It's a strange sound. Did you create it?"

"Yes, I have to agree with you," Wahrer said with a grin. "It is a very strange sound, and we—the four of us in the group—did write the song."

"When did you do this thing, and what on earth inspired you to come up with that blblblblblb and all of that crazy stuff? I heard that record and fell in love with it. I said, that has gotta be a hit—and it was."

"Well, probably I've just been watching too many Tarzan movies," Wahrer laughed. "Anyway, we—well, let me explain. First of all, we hadn't even decided on recording this particular tune, and . . ."

"Was this by any chance your first recording?" Clark asked.

"Yes, it is."

"And it's your first—I don't know what you're going to do to follow this thing with. You have any ideas?"

"Well, we have a couple of things that are cooking right now. We are going to try to come out with something possibly that might just resemble this song a little bit. We don't know yet."

"Let me ask another question," Clark said. "Is The Trashmen—has that always been the name of this group?"

"Right from the beginning."

"It's the strangest combination of things I've ever heard of. Where did it all start, where did you, where did you meet?"

"Well, actually, three of us from the group had been playing together for six or seven years. We got a hold of our bass player, who comes from the wilds of North Dakota, and formed the group, and looked for the name. We just happened to come up with it one night while looking through a stack of records."

"This is going to be a funny thing if this goes on," Clark said, warming to the polite, breathless young man next to him, but still obviously skeptical of the band's long-term appeal. "Can you see now, ten years from now, 'The Copacabana presents The Trashmen!' There they are. I wish you all the very, very best of luck. I hope you can follow that. Would you join us at the autograph table?"

"Certainly. Be very happy to."

"Thank you, Steve, very nice to have you here. Steve Ward of The Trashmen."

They stood up and Dick shook Steve's hand, and the crowd applauded.

"It's nice that they gave Steve about fifteen seconds to catch his breath," Winslow said. "He couldn't talk. He was totally out of his element, for one thing. He always sang that behind the drums, and for him to stand there? He said, 'I was just petrified. What am I going to do?'"

Winslow said that he, Andreason, and Reed were "very, very" disappointed to not make that trip. "We were not envious of Steve in the slightest," Winslow said. "Good for him, and we supported him. But, yeah, it was stupid. I took Steve to the airport. When he came back, I picked him up, and we went straight to Matty's rib joint [where they frequently went to watch Mojo Buford play the blues] and had a few beers."

"Surfin' Bird" continued to dominate the Twin Cities charts, remaining at Number 1 on WDGY and KDWB through the month of January 1964. Their album *Surfin' Bird* was released on January 14 and sold thirty thousand copies almost immediately. That made the Trashmen the logical choice to headline WDGY's annual Winter Carnival Spectacular. There was no doubt about the identity of the top band in town. The Trashmen were now TV stars as well as chart toppers and had blown past all the old standard-bearers, including Mike Waggoner and the Bops. Waggoner admits to being surprised at how quickly The Trashmen shot to the top. "We all felt that we all had good bands here," Waggoner said. "The active bands were all good. The initial response from all of us might have been, 'Wow. I wonder how that came about?' But as the story unfolds, they had every right to be popular and unique, because the song is totally out of context from the stuff they'd

Soma co-owner Dan Heilicher posed with The Trashmen and their album *Surfin' Bird,* which was rushed out in 1964 after the single sold more than a million copies. Courtesy of Mike Jann/Sundazed Records.

been doing. Steve Wahrer could probably sing Jerry Lee Lewis better than anybody on the planet. All of a sudden the surf thing was like, 'What? Where did that come from?' They had a wonderful opportunity, they were qualified to carry it out, and they were talented way above the level of most of the bands in the region, because they had the pickers. They had the players. Of course, there was some envy. There's always a little when you're twenty-one years old and the guy across the street gets a cuter girl than you. 'Get a grip—we'll be all right.' Tony's a dear friend, and they were always such nice men—Bobby, Steve, Dal, and Tony, just gentlemen, gentlemen, gentlemen."

"Surfin' Bird" by The Trashmen reached the top spot on both Twin Cities singles charts and peaked at Number 4 nationally in early 1964. Courtesy of Richard Tvedten.

"We were all striving to be what The Trashmen were," said Owen Husney, who was just beginning his playing days with the High Spirits when "Surfin' Bird" hit the top of the local charts. "I saw The Trashmen at some packed place—phenomenal. They were really the real deal, a very professional unit. I always considered The Trashmen to be one step ahead of everybody else."

It appeared that every band in the country would soon aspire to be what The Trashmen were: the band with the Number 1 single in the nation. The frenzy of that Friday night Winter Carnival performance at the St. Paul Auditorium before twenty thousand fans seemed unprecedented for a four-piece band with no obvious front man. It was like Elvis times four. "They had the little old ribbon mics on the stage, and you couldn't hear what you were playing or singing or anything else," Winslow said. "There was a rumor of somebody in the balcony with a gun and they were going to shoot, or something. I think it was more b.s. than anything. But that was momentous. Especially when you had to try to get back to the dressing room. There was your typical rip, grab, and all of this type of thing. It was crazy."

Crazy, but it wasn't unprecedented—not in England. Another four-piece group—like The Trashmen, two guitars, drums, and bass—from Liverpool called the Beatles had been smashing attendance records in front of screaming, hysterical United Kingdom crowds throughout 1963. On January 18, 1964, the Beatles placed their first single on the U.S. *Billboard* charts: "I Want to Hold Your Hand" / "I Saw Her Standing There." Some thought the idea of four long-haired guys with British accents in a band named after an insect was some kind of a joke, but Ed Sullivan wasn't laughing. He'd already booked the Beatles for their first U.S. television appearance, to take place on February 9. The Trashmen had been issued no such invitation.

The morning after their triumphant performance at the WDGY Winter Carnival Spectacular, The Trashmen received a jolt: the Beatles had leap-frogged them to the Number 1 spot on the *Billboard* singles chart with "I Want to Hold Your Hand." No one could know it at the time, but the Beatles would go on to place nineteen records on the *Billboard* singles chart in 1964. Eleven would make the Top 10; six would go to Number 1. The new kings of rock 'n' roll had arrived, and they were not The Trashmen.

The young rock 'n' rollers in Minnesota paid close attention. "Being around when the Beatles first hit, that changed everything," said Bob Folschow of the Castaways. "It was a game changer, from the [music and clothing] styles to the way you wore your hair. I used to comb it back in a Pompadour, then all of a sudden I'm imitating the Beatles look."

"Yeah, we loved the Beatles," said Dave Maetzold, bass player for Gregory Dee and

The press party for The Trashmen at Kay Bank Studio on January 12, 1964, represented the Big Bang of Minnesota rock 'n' roll, bringing together everyone who was present at the creation of the phenomenon, including *(from left)* producer/manager George Garrett, Steve Wahrer, Tony Andreason, producer/engineer Tom Jung, Soma Records co-owner Amos Heilicher, Kay Bank co-owner Vern Bank, Dal Winslow, Soma Records co-owner Dan Heilicher, and Bob Reed. Courtesy of Tony Andreason.

the Avanties. "Their harmony was great. The songs were so different. That British sound captured everyone's interest."

"The Beatles changed everything," said Charles Schoen of the Del Counts. "When I replaced somebody, I made sure they could sing backup. We had to adapt to what was popular."

Phil Berdahl, drummer with the Stillroven, recalls sitting in a car one night with a friend, ready to go to a Lake Conference hockey game at the Golden Valley ice arena, when he heard a Beatles song on the radio for the first time. "That was it," Berdahl said. "We'd been hearing Elvis and doo-wop but never thought about playing until that night. We started getting together and found out we could kind of do it."

Jim Donna, keyboard player for the Castaways, said the Beatles influenced his band's clothes and haircuts, but he thought the British Invasion had a bigger impact on surf-oriented groups like The Trashmen. "Jimmy Lopes at B-Sharp Music had stacks and stacks of these reverb units for the surf sound," Donna said. "He was selling hundreds a year, but within six months of the Beatles arriving, they weren't selling anything."

"I remember I first saw the Beatles before 1964, pre–Ed Sullivan," said Lonnie Knight, who at the time was playing guitar with the Rave-Ons. "It was a news story—it might have been Walter Cronkite. I remember more clearly than Sullivan, seeing this clip. They didn't play an entire song, but I was mesmerized by the pandemonium around them. American rock 'n' roll was getting inundated by things like the Beach Boys, ticky, whiny little guitar sounds. After Bobby Vee did 'Suzie Baby'—a marvelous song—they started adding strings to sophomoric, pablum-y rock 'n' roll. American music hit a low point, and then the Beatles came out. 'I Want to Hold Your Hand' had a visceral, dirty-guitar sound, and harmonies that weren't choir-perfect. You went, 'My God, what is that?'"

The Trashmen could be excused for wondering the same thing. On the eve of gaining the Number 1 slot on the *Billboard* singles chart, they were run over by the biggest phenomenon in pop music history. Winslow acknowledges that The Trashmen were disappointed to be denied the top spot in the charts by an upstart British group that no one had heard of a month earlier. "I remember how it instilled a hate for the Beatles at the time because we didn't think—. Actually, I think some of their early stuff was pretty good," Winslow said. "But your ego suffered a big blow at that time. We didn't really think a lot of it, because we thought maybe it would go up and then they'd be gone, while we would just keep going."

"Sure, we were aware," Andreason

The relationship between The Trashmen and B-Sharp Music was mutually beneficial: free instruments for free publicity. Courtesy of Tom Tourville.

The Trashmen: "Everybody's heard about the Bird . . . and B-Sharp Music"

The Trashmen get all their Fender equipment at B-Sharp . . . because that's where the top deals are made. Dependable Fender guitars and amplifiers help the Trashmen get their distinct sound like on their new "Surfin' Bird" album. They play Jaguar guitars through two Showman piggy-back amps . . . plus a Fender Reverb echo unit. Stop in and see B-Sharp's wide selection of guitars and amps—make sure you get their price before you buy . . . Tell 'em the Trashmen sent you in!

● *Fender, Gibson, Ampeg & Martin* ● Guitars & Amps

B-SHARP MUSIC

4050 Central Ave., N.E. ● SU 8-9249
Open Every Night until 9 P.M., Saturdays until 6 P.M.

said. "Yeah, it would have been our Number 1. I don't think it would have made much of a difference [in our lives]. We didn't have any bad feelings about the Beatles." The feeling might not have been mutual. Andreason still remembers Ringo Starr being asked about The Trashmen when the Beatles arrived in New York. "He said he didn't like The Trashmen," Andreason said. "We'd never met him or anything. But, you know, take it for what it's worth. I thought, 'Gee—really? Okay.' But they were pretty outspoken. If they were asked a question by somebody, they would answer it. It's all right with me. I don't care. We didn't take a lot of that stuff seriously."

"Yeah, I heard they said, 'We're not very fond of that group'—like that kept me up all night," Winslow said. "Big deal. We weren't playing the same type of music they were doing. We weren't fond of them, either, but now I kind of thank them. God knows what would have happened if we'd just tried to keep playing and playing. Steve stayed in the music business after we quit, and it just drove him six feet under."

"It was disappointing to not be Number 1," Reed said. "The biggest disappointment was the first time I heard that record ['I Want to Hold Your Hand']. I was driving down Lake Street in my old Ford, and I stopped and I said, 'Are you kidding me? Those guys gotta get themselves some good guitars.' Then I got to the duplex there, and I told them other guys, 'You can't believe what I just heard on the radio.' It was a little disappointing, but it was the hype. It was a fantastic sales job. I gotta give them a lot of credit. They put a lot of advertising into that thing, and it worked. They wrote some pretty good stuff. There was one here and there that I liked, the content of it, the way it was constructed—a good song."

Over the next several years, the songwriting team of John Lennon and Paul McCartney would write one good song after another for the Beatles, while The Trashmen searched with little success for one more hit.

THE BRITISH ARRIVE

THE BEATLES visited the United States briefly in February 1964, playing the *Ed Sullivan Show* in New York and a week later from Miami, and also doing concerts in Washington, D.C., and New York's Carnegie Hall. By the time the Beatles returned to our shores in August 1964, they had sold eighty million records worldwide (including five Number 1 singles in the United States), had toured Australia and the Far East, and were starring in their first full-length motion picture, *A Hard Day's Night*. They performed thirty concerts in twenty-three North American cities, but the closest they got to Minnesota was Milwaukee on September 4.

The Beatles weren't the only British act, however, creating moments of hysteria. Their success opened the door for many bands from the United Kingdom that rushed to follow the Beatles into the lucrative American pop music market. Other acts that scored U.S.

THE 'a GO GO SPOTLIGHT

by Jim Karnstedt

Cool it! The Beatles are finally coming to Minneapolis. Their jet will land at the International Airport on Saturday, August 21. This seemed reason enough to interview the man who is responsible for the entire operation. Ray Colihan, better known as "Big Reggie" of Excelsior. The 37 year old promoter was quite congenial about being interviewed. It went like this.

Q. How did you ever get the name "Big Reggie"?

A. Well, about ten years ago, while some friends and I were socializing at Michael's, a Reginald Van Gleason skit appeared on the TV set. Just then the bartender yelled out, "Hey, there's Big Reggie over there!" The name has stuck ever since. At that time I weighed 275 pounds though I'm down to 200 now.

Q. What brought you into the promoting field?

A. I succeeded my father, who passed away, as promotion director. I've been at the Park since '43.

Q. My parents used to tell me about the good times they had at Danceland. Has it been there that long?

A. Sure, Danceland was opened in 1925. Such greats as Lawrence Welk, Perry Como, Glen Gray, and a host of others played there for an admission price of only 40¢.

Q. How long have you operated Danceland?

A. I leased it out about four years ago and have been running dances ever since.

Q. What is the difference between teenagers then and now?

A. Generally, kids aren't any differ-

ent today than they were 20 years ago. There are always going to be a few troublemakers in the crowd, and at the dances we try to weed them out, but as a whole teenagers are a pretty decent group.

Q. What is some of the major talent you have brought to the Twin Cities?

A. Well, let me see.... The Rolling Stones, The Dave Clark Five, The Beach Boys, Jan and Dean, Jerry Lee Lewis, Dick and DeDee, Bobby Vee, Roy Orbeson, ... you'd probably remember the rest of them better than I.

Q. Why did the Rolling Stones and the Dave Clark Five receive such a poor turnout?

A. I booked the Stones about a month too early.... before they became popular in the Twin Cities. As

continued on page 9

Ray "Big Reggie" Colihan booked the Beatles into Met Stadium on August 21, 1965. After meeting Paul McCartney and the other Beatles at an earlier stop in Chicago, he was interviewed in the August 1965 issue of *Twin City 'a Go Go* magazine. Courtesy of Robb Henry.

Beatles *continued from page 5*

far as the D. C. Five goes, all I can say is that I expected a much larger crowd because of the response they got in other cities, but Minneapolis has always been a slow show town.

Q. How did you get the Beatles to come to Minneapolis?

A. I made the booking with Brian Epstein and General Artists corporation, guaranteeing the Beatles $50,000 or 65% of the gate.

Q. How large of an audience do you expect when the Beatles appear?

A. I hope to fill two-thirds of the stadium or 25 to 30,000 seats. Right now we're already one-third sold out.

Q. In other words this will be quite a success?

A. Yes, in fact it will be the biggest musical attraction since Harry Belafonte appeared.

Q. Could you briefly tell me what the show consists of?

A. The Beatles bring with them a cast of top stars, but at this point I'm not certain who they are. The Beatles will perform for thirty minutes, and the show will last for two hours, beginning at 7:30 P. M. Also, there may be an after-Beatle party and dance.

Q. Do you have an antidote for the Beatlemania you're going to bring about?

A. Well, I've hired a number of doctors and over a hundred policemen. I hope that they will ease the confusion.

Don't miss the Beatle Concert Saturday, August 21, 7:30 to 9:30 P. M. at Met Stadium in Bloomington. Also don't miss next month's interview. I hope to have a few witty remarks from John, Paul, George, and Ringo!

hits during the so-called British Invasion of 1964 were the Dave Clark Five, the Animals, the Kinks, the Searchers, Peter & Gordon, Gerry and the Pacemakers, Billy J. Kramer and the Dakotas, the Swingin' Blue Jeans, Herman's Hermits, Chad & Jeremy, and the Rolling Stones.

To look at performance tapes today of the Rolling Stones in 1964, it is puzzling that they were considered the bad boys of British rock. Frontman Mick Jagger could have been described as baby-faced, almost like an older brother to Herman's Hermits' cherubic lead singer Peter Noone. But the music the Stones played was not light, frothy pop, but down-and-dirty Chicago/Memphis blues and R&B. Their set list consisted of songs by Jimmy Reed, Bo Diddley, Chuck Berry, Muddy Waters, Willie Dixon, Slim Harpo, Howlin' Wolf, and Rufus Thomas. The Beatles sang "I Want to Hold Your Hand"; the Stones sang "I Just Want to Make Love to You."

It was not at all clear in the spring of 1964 which, if any, of these new groups coming out of England were going to rival the Beatles in sustained popularity, but American promoters who couldn't land the Beatles were willing to gamble. Ray Colihan—aka Big Reggie, who ran Danceland in Excelsior—had made a killing by booking the Beach Boys in 1963 before "Surfin' U.S.A." made them big stars. He missed out on landing the Beatles

IN PERSON FRIDAY, MAY 8
AT EXCELSIOR AMUSEMENT PARK

THE **TRASHMEN**

WDGY HIGH SCHOOL NIGHT 6:30-7

ALL WEE GEE DJ'S WILL BE ON HAND

FREE STAGE SHOW

SINGING THEIR HIT RECORDS!

STAY FOR THE BIG DANCE AT DANCELAND 8:30-11:30

ALL RIDES ARE FREE 5-7 P.M.!

EXCELSIOR
◆◆◆AMUSEMENT PARK
HWY. 7   TEL. 474-5454

The Trashmen played frequently at Big Reggie's Danceland in Excelsior, where they were as big a draw as some of the national touring rock 'n' roll bands. Courtesy of Tom Tourville.

in 1964, but he did sign the Rolling Stones and the Dave Clark Five to Twin Cities appearances. The Stones played Danceland in June.

Big Reggie's Danceland was located across the road from the Excelsior Amusement Park, an operation modeled after New York's Coney Island and opened on the shores of Lake Minnetonka in 1923. The hemispherical wooden dance hall had originally been built as a roller rink but was transported across iced-over Lake Minnetonka in sections and rebuilt as a ballroom, with a capacity of two thousand. As described by writer Daniel Gabriel on the Lakeminnetonka.com Website, light bulbs hung from the huge wooden beams that supported the roof, and windows and booths were located between the arched support columns along the sides of the building.

Colihan had swept floors in the Danceland ballroom since he was fourteen years old, and when manager Rudy Shogran retired in the late 1950s, he passed the job on to Colihan, who had come to be known as Big Reggie, after Jackie Gleason's TV character Reginald Van Gleason III. Colihan embraced rock 'n' roll because the baby boom kids loved the music and supported it with their dollars. "Big Reggie had a tomato nose, like W. C. Fields, he drank, and he would book the local bands," said Bill Diehl. "He got ahold of me, got me out there one Saturday night, and the crowd was bigger than usual. He said, 'I could use you next Saturday night.' Then he said, 'What are you doing Thursday night?' And I said, 'Because I've got bookings on Saturday night already at the K.C. Hall in Bloomington, I'm not free.' He said, 'What if you went out there first and came here afterward?' Gradually it expanded to Saturday and Tuesday and Thursday, and we always had a crowd. He made a lot of money."

Beach Boys lead singer Mike Love told an interviewer that he remembered the exact moment that he knew the Beach Boys were a success: "It was when we played at a place called Danceland at Excelsior, in Minnesota. The cars were stacked up for miles, and I turned to the rest of the guys and told them that we were now bigger than Elvis." Along with the occasional national act, Big Reggie's Danceland featured the best local bands each week. Bill Diehl would emcee shows by The Trashmen, the Underbeats, the Gestures, the Castaways, the Accents, Gregory Dee and the Avanties, and others that often attracted a thousand or more dancers. "When you went to a place like Danceland, there was electricity in the air before the band went on," Tony Andreason said. "Once things kicked off, bands would feed off the intensity in the room, and [off of] the dancers' requests."

"Big Reggie—what a character," Jim Johnson said. "Every time we played Danceland, we played 'Cottonfields' because he wanted to sing it with us. We were playing 'Foot Stompin'' out there one night and all of a sudden there's a big cloud of dust. What the hell—the floor caved in. Big Reggie's yelling to stop. I imagine there were a couple of lawsuits."

Colihan did not sell alcohol at his dances, but the teens brought their own, often leading to brawls in the parking lot or even on the dance floor. Daniel Gabriel wrote that there were fights almost every night. Gangs such as the Suprees and the X-Boys, both of whom wore green letter jackets, would fight each other in the streets.

Colihan booked the Rolling Stones to play on Friday, June 12, a night that normally would have featured one of the top local bands. Colihan decided not to heavily promote the Stones on radio and jacked up the ticket prices, fearing that the hall would be overrun the way it was when the Beach Boys appeared. There was little chance of that, however. The Rolling Stones' first U.S. single, a cover of Buddy Holly's "Not Fade Away," had been released just a month earlier and had not made the Top 40 on either KDWB or WDGY. Few Twin Cities teens had any idea who the Rolling Stones were. When he realized the event was not creating a buzz, Colihan asked Mike Waggoner and the Bops to play an opening set, hoping that the local favorites would attract a few more kids. He even asked the Bops to be ready to play a second set if the Stones bombed.

The Rolling Stones had arrived in New York on June 1 and were greeted by five hundred screaming young fans at Kennedy Airport, but they also heard shouts of "Get your hair cut." They flew cross-country to tape Dean Martin's *Hollywood Palace* TV show, and though they performed well, they were treated like freaks by the host, who at one point turned to his audience and said, "Weren't they great?" and rolled his eyes, drawing big guffaws. (Stones bassist Bill Wyman wrote that the band got their revenge on a later tour, when guitarist Brian Jones had an affair with one of Martin's daughters.)

The following day, June 5, they played their first U.S. concert in San Bernardino, where a good crowd gave them a rousing reception. On June 6, they flew to San Antonio, Texas, for two days of shows at the state fair. They shared an outdoor stage with country singer George Jones and Minnesota's own Bobby Vee, whose string of hits was beginning to dry up. In fact, his most recent single, the obviously Beatles-inspired "I'll Make You Mine," had stalled outside the *Billboard* Top 40. Vee and his band all wore mohair suits, collared shirts, and silk ties, while the Rolling Stones wore an unmatched assortment of shirts and pants. None of the acts fared very well with the Texas crowd the first day; the second day, perhaps inspired by the casual attire of the Stones, Vee came out wearing Bermuda shorts. His Texas-born saxophone player, Bobby Keys, tried doing the same and was almost fired. But meeting and sharing the bill with the Rolling Stones proved a huge boost for Keys's career; he would play on many of their future albums.

The Stones then took a few days off to record at Chess Studios in Chicago; two of the songs, covers of the Valentinos' "It's All Over Now" and Irma Thomas's "Time Is on My Side," would be their breakthrough singles later in the year. Then it was off to the Twin Cities. "From the start we always had very good morale, but it did almost collapse during the first American tour, which was a disaster," wrote Bill Wyman years later. "When we arrived, we didn't have a hit record or anything going for us. All the other English groups that had ever been there had at least one or two big hits to their credit. We had nothing except that we were English."

An estimated crowd of just three hundred kids (there were 243, according to Mick Jagger at the Stones' 2015 concert at TCF Bank Stadium, "and none of them liked it very much") showed up at Big Reggie's Danceland for the Rolling Stones' first Minnesota show. By all accounts, the Minnesota teens weren't very impressed by the headliners, who played a set list that included "Route 66," "Not Fade Away," "I Wanna Be Your Man" (written by John Lennon and Paul McCartney and given to the Stones), "High Heel Sneakers," "I'm All Right," and "I Just Want to Make Love to You." "The reception was similar to our first English ballroom dates—one of curiosity and disbelief," Wyman recalled.

"It was the first time I'd heard a British group," Waggoner said. "In all honesty, it was the same old stuff. They were pretty much a blues band—John Lee Hooker, Jimmy Reed. The difference might be this: they really had taken more black music and made it white than we had done locally or regionally. Their influences were out of the same era and style. We'd all heard those songs—they were playing them note for note. Most of the songs they played the other bands played, too. It was not a new wrinkle—it was the presentation. I could anticipate everything they were going to do. In hindsight, after I

Mike Waggoner and the Bops were winding down their career in 1964 but were a big hit opening for the Rolling Stones at Big Reggie's Danceland. The Stones didn't fare as well. Courtesy of Denny Johnson of Minniepaul music.com.

thought about it, I felt a little sorry for the guys, because that type of music was not being played for teenagers in dance halls. People wanted to hear 'Little Latin Lupe Lu' or 'King of the Surf.' These guys were playing 'Little Red Rooster'—why would you play that here? They were just a bunch of kids like we were, just out visiting the world."

Butch Maness, who played bass that night for the Bops, is more blunt in his assessment of the Stones' performance. "Nobody liked them," Maness said. "I had never heard them or heard of them. They hadn't made their big boom here yet. When we played, everybody got up and danced. When they played, everybody sat down and had a Coke. When we were changing spots, I tried to get a conversation with the bass player [Wyman]. He mumbled a couple of words and went offstage. They wouldn't talk to us. They realized we were a better band than them. We were. They came out with their weird stuff and the kids didn't like it. I can't remember exactly the stuff we played, but whatever we played, the kids liked it. We had the beat that got them up and made them dance. From what I can remember, the Stones material was not real easy to dance to. Not like their stuff that came on later. They had one guy who set up the stage, the drums, everything. They didn't have a big entourage. Then the guy came and took down the stuff and they went their own way. The last set, the kids kind of ignored them. I don't remember if they booed them. I don't think they played the complete last set. I think they got pissed off and quit. We did the first, they did one, we did another set, and they did the last one. When we put on our second set, we hit a note and the kids were right back up dancing.

"The ironic part about that is a year later, they're millionaires, and we're starting to play their music and still getting five hundred bucks a night," Maness said. "Where's the fairness? We were just as good a band or better, talent-wise."

Bill Diehl, who emceed the show, has one overriding memory from the night: Mick Jagger's filthy collar. "Each little individual pore on the skin of his neck was dirty," Diehl said. "The kids didn't know who they were. I didn't fuss over them. The Trashmen would have caused more excitement, or the Underbeats."

"I wasn't crazy about the Stones," Jim Johnson of the Underbeats said. "They ripped us off. We were doing Chuck Berry and B. B. King, too. Big Reggie wouldn't let his daughter talk to them." Stories allege that the Stones were heckled and had rotten tomatoes thrown at them. Timothy D. Kehr, who worked for the Stones' record label, was in the band's limousine after the show and later said the car was egged as they departed Big Reggie's Danceland. Waggoner disputes those tales. "Where do you get tomatoes? There's no supermarket nearby that I know of," he told Minniepaulmusic.com. "The tomatoes incidents didn't happen, there was no riot, nobody yelled and screamed, and there weren't very many people there. No big deal."

The indifference—or hostility—shown to the Rolling Stones was a far cry from the reception the Beatles received when Colihan was able to book their only Minnesota appearance the following summer. Bill Diehl was the emcee of that show, too, and was deeply involved in the preparation for the Fab Four's visit. "Bill, I'm just signing the contracts to bring in the Beatles," Colihan told Diehl. "Of course, you'll be the emcee. They told me they have a local emcee wherever they go, but you're my emcee. They're down in

The Beatles arrived at Minneapolis–St. Paul Airport on August 21, 1965, to play their only Minnesota concert. They drew twenty-five thousand screaming fans to Metropolitan Stadium that night and left the next morning. Photograph by *St. Paul Dispatch and Pioneer Press.* Courtesy of Minnesota Historical Society.

Chicago the weekend after this one at the Stockyards, the big amphitheater. They want to meet you before they approve that you're the emcee."

"Wow," Diehl said. "Okay."

"I'll pay your way down," Colihan said. "And take Helen [Diehl's soon-to-be-wife] with you. I'll pay for that, too."

Diehl went to Chicago and shot film with his 16 mm camera outside the stockyards and then went upstairs to the Beatles' packed press conference. The Beatles were seated next to each other at a table, and Diehl asked Helen to move around the room to try to hear what they were saying and to take pictures. When the press conference ended, they were told that there were tickets waiting for them at the stockyards, arranged for by George Harrison. "The stage was here, and we were here, right below," Diehl said. "They came out, and there was just a ROAR. To make a long story short, I was approved as their emcee."

Back in the Twin Cities, Diehl got a phone call from Paul Goetz, branch manager from Capitol Records. Sam Sherwood of KDWB had called and wanted to be part of the Beatles promotion, including being onstage with the Beatles. "I'm sorry, Big Reggie hired me," Diehl said. "It's WDGY's promotion, too."

"Well, Sherwood is bound and determined," Goetz said.

Diehl, who belonged to five separate unions, including the American Guild of Variety Artists, thought of a way to keep Sherwood off the stage. "I was told I was lucky I belonged to AGVA, because I could appear with any union act," Diehl said. "If I didn't belong to AGVA, I couldn't go on the stage and perform or do anything. So I got an idea. I called Goetz back and said, 'Call Sherwood and ask him if he belonged to AGVA. Just ask him. If he doesn't belong to AGVA, he can't go on that stage.' And I knew he didn't."

Sherwood thought KDWB had an inside track to the Beatles because the station's corporate officers were in Hollywood, as was Capitol Records. "Capitol Records had the Beatles, and we had Capitol Records in our hip pocket," Sherwood said. "We had access to them all the time. We had an exclusive on every Beatles song except one—WDGY got some copy of them doing a German version of a Beatles song. They played that, but I got an exclusive on every album. Three of us program directors—Cleveland, New York, and me in Minneapolis—would all cooperate. We'd get the news when it was coming down. I would have the pilot who delivered the Beatles album come off the plane and hand it to me personally. I would rush to the station, and Lou Riegert would be on the air playing the whole album exclusively. It was nuts. It was crazy. When I heard the Beatles were coming, and they were tied in with WDGY with Big Reggie at Danceland, I was furious. I got on the plane and flew to Chicago. I wanted to get the other half of the promotion to talk to them. I said, 'If you don't give us the other half, I'll never put a Beatles record on the station, ever.'"

A short time later, Goetz called Diehl back.

"Aw, Bill, I'm calling you to save my job," he said. "Sherwood said if we won't let him be part of that show out there, he'll never play a Beatles song again. Please, Bill, as a favor to me, please, please. He just wants to step onstage for a moment and say, 'Here I am, from KDWB.'"

"And foolishly, I said, 'Okay,'" Diehl said.

"So they cut us in," Sherwood said. "I had limousines to pick up the Beatles, with telephones in the limos so they could talk to our disc jockeys on the air."

Sherwood said the preconcert press conference was his idea, but it was given to WDGY because of Diehl's friendship with George Harrison's sister. Diehl disputes that, saying that WDGY got the press conference through Colihan, the promoter. It was held in the Minnesota Room at Met Stadium in Bloomington, where the concert would be held

The Beatles were their usual irreverent, cheeky selves at a preconcert press conference at Met Center. Photograph by *St. Paul Dispatch and Pioneer Press*. Courtesy of Minnesota Historical Society.

later that night. The Beatles sat at a table, each with a WDGY microphone in front of them. John wore a cap and they all wore jackets, but only Paul wore a tie. They all smoked cigarettes at one point or another during the press conference.

"Here's the Beatles sitting at this table, and here we all are, running around," Diehl said. "Over here is a public phone booth, and I mean a booth, with a door that shut. KDWB—I thought they were pretty clever—they went over there and monopolized the phone. They kept putting nickels in, and they would hold the phone out when one of the Beatles was talking. We had a guy go over near the phone booth to listen to them. They would say 'KDWB covers the Beatles, and we'd stand right outside the phone booth and shout, 'WDGY brings you the Beatles! It's a WDGY exclusive!' That's the way radio was—it was great fun."

"Yeah, I had a telephone there," Sherwood said. "That's the only way we could get in there. It was edgy, but it was fun, because we were winning all the way. I had all our disc jockeys get out there and sit in the front seats," Sherwood said. "Every question, I said, say 'KDWB wants to know . . .' because DGY was broadcasting the press conference live. John Lennon picked up on it. He got a question from DGY. They said. 'WDGY wants to know,' and Lennon said, 'Does KDWB want to know that, too?'"

During the press conference, Randy Resnick and Ron Butwin of B-Sharp Music presented George Harrison with the latest model Rickenbacker 360 twelve-string guitar. Video of the press conference captures the moment when George accepts the guitar, and Lennon says, "That's great, that's fab, that's marvelous, that's fine. You got one for me?"

"John's pissed as hell that we gave a guitar to George," Butwin said. "George Harrison was like a little child, he's so excited. Why? He doesn't have one. A 360 twelve-string was not a common guitar. It was not in all the stores yet. He had other twelve-strings, but he didn't have this new hollow-body. This was the one the Byrds were using. This became *the* Rickenbacker."

Seventeen-year-old Lynn Krzmarcik received the thrill of a lifetime when she was allowed to meet and be photographed with the Beatles in the Met Stadium locker room before their August 1965 concert. She had photographs taken with *(from left)* John Lennon, George Harrison (playing the new Rickenbacker guitar he received from B-Sharp Music earlier in the day), and Ringo Starr. She ran out of flashbulbs before she could be photographed with her favorite, Paul McCartney. Courtesy of Lynn Krzmarcik Kordus.

That evening's concert was preceded by the Underbeats, the Accents, Gregory Dee and the Avanties, and T. C. Atlantic playing sets around the concourse of the stadium as the crowd of twenty-eight thousand filed in. Met Stadium had a musicians' union minimum, so Colihan was forced to hire enough musicians to meet the minimum. They could not set up on the field as part of the Beatles concert, so they had to play in the concourse. Jim Johnson of the Underbeats found the gig embarrassing. Frank Prout, the mop-topped bass player who'd replaced Dave Maetzold in Gregory Dee and the Avanties, bore a resemblance to Paul McCartney and was mobbed on his way out to the parking lot after the Avanties finished their set.

There were several official opening acts before the Beatles took the stage, including Brenda Holloway and the King Curtis Band, Cannibal and the Headhunters, and the Sounds Incorporated. "That night Bill Diehl was emceeing the show," Sherwood said. "I said, 'Man, I gotta get some visibility.' I hired a helicopter with a sign on the bottom— 'KDWB Welcomes The Beatles,' one of those turning Broadway signs. When it got dark,

141

I wondered where the heck the helicopter was, when all of a sudden I heard the thump-thump over the stadium. There it was, over the stage. It was great." Lennon pretended his guitar was a gun, aimed it at the helicopter, and took imaginary shots at it.

Neither the Beatles nor the audience members were able to hear much of the band's thirty-five-minute set over the crowd's screaming, thanks to less-than-adequate sound equipment. The Beatles played eleven songs: "She's a Woman," "I Feel Fine," "Dizzy Miss Lizzy," "Ticket to Ride," "Everybody's Trying to Be My Baby," "Can't Buy Me Love," "Baby's in Black," "I Wanna Be Your Man," "A Hard Day's Night," "Help!" and "I'm Down." Tickets cost $2.50, $3.50, $4.50, and $5.50. Colihan paid the Beatles $50,000, plus 65 percent of sales above 18,500 in attendance.

The Beatles stayed in the Leamington Motor Lodge in downtown Minneapolis. When word got out that they were staying there, the hotel was mobbed by girls who tried almost anything to get in, including climbing up drain spouts. City police claimed McCartney had an underaged girl in his room, but she turned out to be a twenty-one-year-old from Cleveland. The band left for Portland the next day at 11 A.M., with the hearty blessings of the Minneapolis police. Bill Diehl said all of the anti-Beatles statements made by the local police were blown out of proportion. "The Beatles were gentlemen," Diehl said.

ON THE MOVE

PERHAPS THE BEST THING that ever happened to The Trashmen—aside from recording "Surfin' Bird"—was meeting Jimmy Thomas.

Thomas was a big band drummer from Luverne, Minnesota, who'd played all of the Midwest ballrooms in the 1940s and had developed good relationships with almost everyone in the business. His own days as a musician were well behind him in the late 1950s, thanks to the rise of rock 'n' roll at the expense of big band music. Thomas initially couldn't stand rock 'n' roll music, but he wanted to stay involved in the music business— and he had eight kids to feed—so he began representing rock bands and booking them into the ballrooms he knew so well. His first act was Myron Lee and the Caddies from nearby Sioux Falls, South Dakota. He signed the band's leader, Myron Wachendorf, to a five-year contract in 1958 when Wachendorf was just seventeen years old. Thomas

After the success of "Surfin' Bird" in late 1963, The Trashmen adopted a new logo and began touring the country. Courtesy of Mike Jann.

assumed that the other members of the band were likely to come and go, so it was easier to deal with just the leader. Since neither Thomas nor Wachendorf had any idea whether there would be rock 'n' roll dances in five years, the length of the contract seemed immaterial. By the spring of his senior year, Myron Lee (his stage name) had quit high school because Thomas had his band working five nights a week.

As recounted in Jim Oldsberg's fanzine *Lost and Found #4*, Thomas offered the ballroom owners a contract either for a flat fee for the band, or a deal in which the band would get a smaller sum up front to cover their expenses plus a percentage of the door. Most of the operators paid the small fee, which turned out to be a great deal for the band, because they generally drew far more kids than the ballroom operators expected. Thomas's bands were clearing anywhere from $500 to $1,000 per night.

By the time The Trashmen made their breakthrough with "Surfin' Bird," Thomas owned the Showboat Ballroom in Lake Benton, forty-five miles north of Luverne on U.S. 75 and was looking for more bands to book. For their part, The Trashmen needed to work as much as possible to take advantage of their sudden fame, because they weren't seeing any record sales royalties. "We met Jimmy Thomas, and it was great, because he was such a positive influence on us when we were on the road," Andreason said. "He really looked after us. He was an honest guy. He put us into a situation where we were working a lot and getting what we should be paid. That was all because of him. You look back on it, and you sell a million records back then and you split $30,000, before taxes, between your manager and the four of you, there isn't a whole lot of money left over. Even though that happened, maybe it was a good learning experience. I'll tell you that because I was only twenty."

George Garrett was not interested in finding bookings for The Trashmen or handling their road schedule, so when Jimmy Thomas approached Garrett and offered to buy ten dates for the band, Garrett was only too happy to relinquish that part of the band's management. "Jimmy was like a second father to us," Winslow said. "He was the greatest guy in the world. The nicest guy. He gave us a lot of advice. He kicked our butts a lot, told us what to do, where to play." Thomas told the Trashmen that if they did well on those first ten dates, the band would get half the door. "That was pretty generous back in those days," Winslow said. "Well, we went out and just cleaned up. He came back and said, 'If you want, I can continue to do this.'"

Thomas booked the band in ballrooms all around the Midwest—his own Showboat, and ballrooms in Montevideo, Breckenridge, and Des Moines and Clear Lake in Iowa. "He knew all of these guys," Winslow said. "It was pretty easy for him to set all these dates up. After that, he did all our dates. He traveled with us on the road when we went down south, and up the West Coast, and booked us out east to colleges out there, which was a trip. Ithaca and Columbia. Toga parties."

Thomas was a balding, bespectacled man around sixty years old at the time—not exactly the kind of hipster you'd expect to see with a touring rock 'n' roll band. But Winslow said he actually liked rock 'n' roll by the time he'd been exposed to The Trashmen's stage show. "He didn't like some of the people who were doing it," Winslow said. "He said, 'I didn't know what to expect booking you guys, with the bands nowadays. They get onstage and they can't tie their shoes. You guys get up there and play four hours, and you come off.' He told somebody, 'If these guys come offstage and they're sweating like crazy, they worked their asses off up there. No bands are doing that anymore.' He had confidence in us, which you could see. We relied on him a lot. For him to go on the road with four young guys like us, that had to be a trip for him. He would always razz Steve on all his drinking, and Steve would end up throwing him in the pool. Good fun."

When The Trashmen toured Canada, Thomas and his oldest son Tommy accompanied the band and counted the door to make sure the band got their correct percentage. "Without him, we never would have made any money," Andreason said. "Jimmy was a real honest guy. We never had a contract with him. It was a handshake right from the start. What we'd do with Jimmy, we would go out and rent armories ourselves, and then we'd split it with him. He knew every place to go. We were exclusively with him, but he got us a lot of dates through GAC [General Artists Corporation] out of New York. But he was the one who set it up. He would then work the deals with them." As the band's traveling radius continued to expand, they bought a white heavy-duty Chevy van big enough to

The Trashmen toured constantly in their heavy-duty van in 1964–65. Courtesy of Mike Jann.

haul the band members and all the equipment. Mike Jann and Larry LaPole painted the sides with the band's new logo, a bird on a surfboard. "It was surprising we only had it vandalized twice," Winslow said. "Once in Chicago, somebody ripped the mirrors off, and we had some speakers in the back that somebody stole, which we didn't want anyway. Other than that, it was always fun to drive it into the small towns and drive up to the Dairy Queen. And everybody would go, 'Ooh, ooh!' It created a lot of notice."

The Trashmen's first national tour began in February 1964, as "Surfin' Bird" was beginning to slide down the charts and "Bird Dance Beat" was on its way up. The tour took them to Oklahoma City and Tulsa, then to Phoenix, California, and up the West Coast as far as Seattle. Bill Diehl arranged to have one of the band members call in to the WDGY studios every night while they were on the road. On Thursday, February 19, Bob Reed called Diehl from Phoenix:

DIEHL: How are the crowds reacting down in the Southwest part of the country?

REED: Fine, fine. As the other fellows have been saying, it varies from night to night which song they're going for the best.

DIEHL: What seems to be the story in Phoenix?

REED: Like I say, we haven't had a chance to find out yet, because we'll be playing tomor-row night. We have a two-day rest right now.

DIEHL: Oh, I see, you're right in the middle enjoying the sunshine. You get a little rest, a little sunshine, and you'll be very warm to go after them tomorrow night.

REED: Yeah, the other fellows are down at the pool right now.

DIEHL: Oh, crazy.

Two nights later, Diehl continued with WDGY's exclusive "Trashmen Report, on their first major tour of the United States." Andreason called in from Pismo Beach, California:

DIEHL: When did you get in there?

ANDREASON: Last night.

DIEHL: Are you playing tonight, or just getting settled in the area?

ANDREASON: We're going to drive to Los Angeles tonight, and we play in Los Angeles tomorrow night, Sacramento Wednesday.

DIEHL: Lot of the fellas and girls have been asking me, to ask The Trashmen as you travel across the country, do you notice whether the fellas and gals dance any differently in the areas where you've been on tour from what they dance here?

ANDREASON: Oh, yes. Every state varies. It's mostly the same. Of course, out here in Cali-fornia there's a lot of dances that we haven't got in Minnesota.

DIEHL: Such as what, Tony?

ANDREASON: Well, The Dog is real big here.

DIEHL: And surfing, too?

ANDREASON: Surfing isn't as big as it used to be—the music. Hot rod is in now. And blues is starting to come in a little bit down here, which surprises me.

DIEHL: Yes, that surprises me, too. How [are] the "Bird Dance Beat" and "Surfin' Bird" doing in the areas where you've been?

ANDREASON: "Bird Dance Beat" is the one that's taking off now. "Surfin' Bird" was here, of course that's what they know us for, but "Bird Dance Beat" is climbing up the charts out here. They're playing it a lot.

DIEHL: Well, just wonderful, and I notice on the national charts the album is way up there, too.

ANDREASON: I hope so. I haven't really—I haven't seen the charts.

DIEHL: Oh, you haven't? Well, the album is in the Top 50 sellers now in the United States, and as far as albums go, that is just tremendous. And "Bird Dance Beat" continues to climb in all the national charts, and they put those stars in front of it, and that means it's a real red-hot record. So, Tony, you be sure to tell the boys they're getting hotter all the time.

ANDREASON: I sure will.

DIEHL: Well, it's been a great tour for you so far, and I want you to continue to give us those exclusive reports here on WDGY.

ANDREASON: We surely will.

DIEHL: And Tony, I want to thank you very very much for being with us on the *Bill Diehl Show.*

ANDREASON: Thank you, Bill.

DIEHL: Now, will you hang on for just a minute? We're going to continue with the survey, because we're right in the middle of the survey report. I might as well tell you right now—I don't think I'm giving away a great big secret here, that your song is holding right up there, it's among the Top 5 on WDGY, the "Bird Dance Beat."

ANDREASON: Great.

The band was nervous when they got to San Luis Obispo, concerned that the local music fans on Dick Dale's sacred ground would have a tough time accepting a surf band from Minnesota. The band that opened for The Trashmen that night wasn't playing surf music, however. They were playing the blues. "We find out that nobody's playing surf anymore," Winslow said. "They're all playing blues, they're all playing James Brown. The band they had playing ahead of us was doing blues, and it was like a morgue. Before we went onstage, we thought, we're dead, so let's just get up there and do our gig, and we'll take off. We got up there and started doing our stuff, and they just went bananas. 'When are you guys coming back?'"

"That's when it kind of felt like, 'We're in Dick Dale's backyard now,'" Reed said. "And then you kind of felt like you had made it. You were on their turf, playing the same stuff with them."

Upon their return to the Midwest, the pace didn't slow. George Garrett brought the band back to Kay Bank Studios to

In the midsixties, the top Twin Cities rock 'n' roll bands had their own fan clubs. Courtesy of Tom Tourville.

begin work on another album. They recorded another batch of songs written by Larry LaPole, including "Think It Over," "Wildcat Loose in Town," and "Congratulations to Me." They also cut a new Tony Kai-Ray song called "True, True, Lovin'," and covers of songs by the Beach Boys ("Be True to Your School"), Booker T. and the M.G.'s ("Green Onions"), and Chuck Berry ("Roll Over Beethoven"). There was some thought that "Roll Over Beethoven" would be the band's next single, but when the Beatles included the song on their latest album, those plans were scrapped.

Depending on how "Bird Dance Beat" performed, Garrett and the Heilichers were prepared to rush another album into the stores immediately. It was common for record companies to pump out as much product as they thought the market would bear, since rock 'n' roll acts were not expected to have a long shelf life. In 1964 alone, Capitol released three Beach Boys and three Beatles albums, and a fourth album of the Beatles' earliest material was released on Vee-Jay. This formula ultimately was not applicable to The Trashmen, however; "Bird Dance Beat" peaked in March at a mildly disappointing Number 30 on the *Billboard* Hot 100, thanks in great part to the logjam of Beatles singles at the top of the chart (on April 5, the Beatles had the top five singles in the United States). "Bird Dance Beat," in fact, was The Trashmen's last nationally charted record.

It was also apparent that The Trashmen were groping for a direction, based on the material they cut for their second album. Surf music was clearly on the wane, and LaPole's songs still weren't the best fit for a versatile band with only one identifiable vocal sound: Wahrer's low growl on "Surfin' Bird" and "Bird Dance Beat." In addition, the Trashmen had run afoul of copyright laws with their biggest hit. As the band's first album was shipping, Garrett was contacted by lawyers representing the Rivingtons, who demanded that their clients receive sole writing credit for "Surfin' Bird." There was no question that the origin of The Trashmen's smash hit had been "The Bird's the Word" and "Papa Oom Mow Mow," but it could certainly have been argued that Wahrer and The Trashmen deserved partial credit for a totally different arrangement and new lyrics. The Rivingtons might have been willing to share writing credits on "Surfin' Bird" with The Trashmen, but Garrett apparently wanted to avoid conflict—and, after all, he did not have a writer's credit to lose. He dropped all claims to the song. "Our manager gave away the writing credit for that song," Andreason said. "We could have got at least half of that, because of what it was, but he just gave it away. He didn't do us any good."

"The way we did it was so much different, so much faster," Winslow told an interviewer. "And that shows you how naïve we were. We should have said, 'Look, we'll split it with you. That is not the same song that you guys did.'"

It was decided to hold back a second album until the band had released a third single in April, consisting of two surf instrumentals: "Bad News" (a slight rewrite of the Revel's "Church Key," an inferior version of which the band had already recorded, but not released, during the sessions for their first album in 1963); and "On the Move," a killer guitar tune written by the entire band. It was a very curious choice of songs to release, given that surf music was clearly in decline, blown out of the water by the vocal rock 'n' roll of the Beatles and the growing popularity of Motown-style soul music.

"We really never had anybody helping us along with that," Winslow said. "Jimmy Thomas was great as a booking agent, but he wasn't a producer. We became popular after Bobby Vee up here. And that's what should happen to somebody. They took Bobby Vee, signed him to Liberty Records, and they spent four years on him, building him up as the town heartthrob, doing the little cutesy songs, and it really made his career for him. Whereas with us, Heilicher wouldn't do anything. They didn't have any producer. The guys in Kay Bank Studio were good engineers, but they were learn-as-you-go types, too. What we didn't have behind us was somebody who knew music, like a producer, to say, 'Here's what you guys need to do. Here's some songs for you.'"

The "little cutesy songs" that made Vee a star were, in fact, being written by some of the best composers in New York's Brill Building songwriting stable: Carole King, Gerry Goffin, Jack Keller, Burt Bacharach, Howard Greenfield, Helen Miller, and Aaron Schroeder. Many of the new British rock bands were turning to that source for material, including the Searchers ("Needles and Pins" by Sonny Bono and Jack Nitzsche), Manfred Mann (Jeff Barry and Ellie Greenwich's "Do Wah Diddy Diddy"), and Herman's Hermits (King & Goffin's "I'm Into Something Good"). The Trashmen fully understood the importance of songwriting but had no equivalent writing stable providing songs for them. "Oh, we thought about it all the time," Winslow said. "Thank God we had Larry LaPole, who wrote a bucketful of songs for us. I couldn't write a song to save my life. Steve couldn't. Bob couldn't. Tony wrote a couple fairly good songs."

When "Bad News" failed to chart nationally and peaked at Number 20 on WDGY in May, Soma decided not to release the group's second album. Their fourth Garrett single, "Peppermint Man," a vocal tune previously recorded by Dick Dale, was released in July and did slightly better, stalling at Number 16 on WDGY and 17 on KDWB. The B-side of that single was "New Generation," an uptempo rocker written by Tony Kai-Ray. Garrett/ Soma continued to try to break another hit single for the band, but nothing seemed to click. In August 1964, the label released "Whoa, Dad," a teen lament written by Felice and Boudleaux Bryant, the composers who'd scored so many hits for the Everly Brothers in the late '50s, but whose well had apparently run dry. The B-side, "Walking My Baby," was a thinly disguised rewrite of Del Shannon's "Little Town Flirt." Both tracks featured Gary Nielsen on keyboards and the Arlyles on backing vocals, pushing the band further from their core sound. One last record came out on Garrett in December: the two-sided Christmas single "Dancin' with Santa" / "Real Live Doll," the A-side written by LaPole and the B-side by Wahrer.

With their Soma/Garrett sales declining, The Trashmen released a Christmas single in late 1964. Courtesy of Mike Jann.

The irony was that, even as The Trashmen's own chart success was waning, they had a noticeable impact on other recording groups. The October 1964 Swan single "Shaggy Dog" by Mickey Lee Lane opens with the line, "Do the Bird, pretty Bird, 'cause the Bird is the Word, Do the Dog, dirty dog, like a daddy frog . . ." In 1965, the Del Counts recorded their composition "Bird Dog," that starts, "Well now, everybody's heard about the Bird [growling voice]. Bird bird bird, bird is the word . . . and everybody knows all about the dog, I said the dog . . . well now, put 'em together and what do you get, you get the bird dog. . . ."

The Trashmen's own recording sessions had to be shoehorned between a breakneck touring schedule. In 1964 alone they played 292 dates and put 99,000 miles on their Chevy van. They did another 270 dates in 1965. The touring was endless, but it was lucrative, and it was fun. "We were playing two or three nights a week, and then it was four nights, five nights, and then it got to be seven nights," Andreason said. "We were going out farther and farther, and then we started really touring. We'd go out a month at a time, six weeks at a time."

Once the band was regularly touring outside of the Midwest, Wahrer would drive his Volkswagen and Winslow would ride with him to free up more space in the van. But initially, there would be five occupants in the van, plus suitcases and anything else that didn't fit into their equipment trailer. "There'd always be an extra person, somebody who could help get Steve's drums in there and help him get set up, and get [torn] down, and

Most audiences didn't get to see the casual side of The Trashmen, who nearly always wore suits and ties when they performed. This photograph from St. Cloud during the hectic early months of 1964 may have been taken during a sound check. Photograph by Ken Hagemeier. Courtesy of Dal Winslow.

count the door and whatever else," Winslow said. "That was our roadie. Whereas now you have forty-five of 'em with you."

The band's first roadie was Ken Severson, Andreason's California pal. After a few months, Severson was replaced by Paul France, an ex-Navy firefighter and Andreason's Patrick Henry classmate. Then they hired a tall, skinny, blond-haired guy named Tim

Rehberger, whom they'd befriended at Woodley's Country Dam. "We called him Cheese-burger," Andreason said. "He watched our back. He helped us drive and set up and help us count the door at places where we were on a percentage, because we were always getting beat at the door. Everybody was trying to cheat you out of everything. In that business, it's just a business of whores. The booking agent, he's going to sell you for a certain price, and he's going to tell you another price, and he's going to take 15 percent of the price that he told you on top of the other money you don't know about. It just goes on and on. Then you get to the venue. You go up to the ballroom and you're getting part of the door, and the guy at the ballroom is cheating you at the door, so you've got to have a guy there counting the door, and he doesn't like that: 'What's the matter, you don't trust me?' No, it's just good business. That's all it is. These guys would try to buy off the guy who worked for you—'Take twenty bucks and just don't count for a while.' But Tim was six foot nine, and he wasn't afraid of any living creature. He was just one of these fearless kind of guys. Very intimidating."

Rehberger was paid $15 a night plus hotel expenses but was expected to pay for his own food. He traveled with the band for several years, always keeping an eye out for their safety. "We were being threatened all the time," Andreason said. "You come into Pipestone, Minnesota, at the Hollyhock Ballroom, and there were fistfights all the time. We saw thousands of fistfights. You couldn't count the numbers that we saw—you know, morons who for whatever reason thought they wanted to do that. The girls would be smiling and winking at you—alcohol was always involved—and you'd just look down and smile, and these guys were waiting for you at the end of the night. It got to be kind of, 'Yeah, sure.'"

The band eventually got quite good at defusing such situations. Andreason recalled a night at Jimmy Thomas's Showboat Ballroom when some guys approached them while they were starting to pack up. "Say, remember those girls?" one of them said to Andreason. "They're our girls. We're going to be waiting for you."

"Just hang on for a second," Andreason said, pretending to be distracted by the load-out. "Yeah, let's put that amp in first. Now, what was that?"

"We're going to be waiting outside for you."

"Hang on a second—just wait for a second," Andreason said, attending to another piece of equipment. Then he turned back to the guy. "What was that again? You're going to be waiting outside for us and you're going to kick our ass? Hold on . . ." He went back to packing up equipment, and the guy eventually got tired of being ignored and walked away.

Winslow said Rehberger had "a mouth that wouldn't quit" and would sometimes get the band into more trouble than he prevented. In Salinas, Kansas, the band staged a mock wrestling match in a motel room. As they were checking out the next morning, the desk clerk said that a maid told him they'd broken a chair. Jimmy Thomas began to admonish the group, but Winslow said they had put the chair back together after it had come apart. "I don't think we did anything to it," Winslow said.

"The maid said it's broken," the clerk insisted.

Then Rehberger stepped up to the clerk.

"Are you calling me a fucking liar, you little shit?"

Winslow got between them quickly and said, "We'll pay whatever it is."

When it came to counting the door, Rehberger was incorruptible. "We had a lot of ballroom owners come up and say, 'Hey, go over there and buy yourself a beer. Get away from here for ten minutes,'" Winslow said. "He'd say, 'You can go fuck yourself.' He was a very good guy—a friend to the end. He worked his ass off, and we didn't pay him crap."

By the summer of 1964, the chart success of The Trashmen was declining, but their touring income was thriving, thanks in large part to booking agent Jimmy Thomas, who owned the Showboat Ballroom in Lake Benton, Minnesota, and had show business contacts across the country. Courtesy of Mike Jann.

Money was always a paramount concern on the road. The band was generally paid in cash—mostly ones, fives, and tens, often totaling $1,500 to $2,000. "We had a suitcase that we had onstage, right next to Steve's drums," Andreason said. "That was our money suitcase. There was the set list on it, and he might have the mixer on it, but it was full of cash. We had it with us at all times. What were [we] going to do with the money? We weren't going to be home for a while, and we didn't have time to wire it home."

In order to protect themselves and their loot, all four members of The Trashmen, and Rehberger, traveled with handguns. "We were in New Mexico when some guys tried to run us off the road and rob us," Andreason said. "We pulled out a .357 and stuck it out the window." Robbery attempt over.

"I carried a gun the whole time I was on the road," Andreason said. "Every day, seven days a week, I had one on me all the time."

A traveling band with cash and guns can create the wrong impression. Once the band members had all their cash spread out on top of a motel bed, with Winslow's .38 on the adjacent nightstand, when a cleaning woman walked in. She excused herself, backed out, and closed the door. A few minutes later the police knocked on their door. Fortunately, the first officer to walk in had worked security at the previous night's show and recognized them.

"It's okay, guys," the cop said. "It's the band. What are you guys doing?"

"We're counting our money."

"You're counting your money."

"Yeah, we had time. We only have a couple hundred miles to go. We get paid in cash every night, and we just haven't had time to go to the bank."

The cops made them wire most of the money to their Minneapolis bank. "But it cost money to do that, and we didn't want to spend the money," Andreason said.

Each year the band would buy a new van with the heaviest suspension they could find. They never had an accident, no one was ever hurt, and the vans never got dented. Neither did they indulge in any of the drink- or drug-fueled escapades that became synonymous with traveling rock 'n' roll bands in the next decade.

"Drugs? Nope, not at all," Winslow said. "We did a lot of booze, but we were pretty sedate. Roger Daltrey of The Who said something like rock 'n' roll has to be like chaos, where everybody fights and is throwing drums and smashing things. That's not rock 'n' roll to me. We really didn't do that much. None of us was really spoiled brats growing up. Our folks were all nose-to-the-grindstone, hard-working blue-collar workers. I think we all had that type of work ethic, so we're not going to go in and tear up a motel room."

The Trashmen's heyday preceded the era in which "sex, drugs, and rock 'n' roll" became a catch phrase. Andreason concedes that when the band was in the same location for several nights, quick relationships could develop, but most nights there wasn't time. "We never got in any trouble as far as women were concerned, because we were playing so many days, and traveling so much, and you had to get sleep," Andreason said. "You got done at midnight, one o'clock, and you were up all night, and then traveling the next day and had to play the next night. You really couldn't do that."

Both Winslow and Wahrer were married and quickly divorced. "When Kennedy came and said, 'We're not going to draft any married people,' Steve and I both went out and got married," Winslow said. "That didn't last very long." Winslow fathered a child with his first wife, who died from an aneurism at age twenty-three, and raised him with his second wife, whom he married in 1965. Andreason was single, had a girlfriend back in the Twin Cities, and worried about getting trapped into a marriage if he got a girl pregnant. "We were really paranoid about getting into that kind of trouble, because we knew other people who did," Andreason said. "I was with Bob all the time. Bob was married, straight-laced, and did not run around on his wife, ever."

"He had girls climbing over him, but he never strayed," Winslow said.

"I was with him, and that put a big crunch in my ability to do anything because I'm rooming with him," Andreason said. "Which was probably a good thing. I didn't want any kids running around. That was a big thing for me. I knew guys it had happened to. It was kind of financial suicide, and you marry somebody you don't want to marry. I just didn't participate."

Andreason and Reed once walked into their motel room and found two girls lying in bed waiting for them.

"Okay, time to go," Reed said.

"Now don't be hasty, Bob," Andreason said. "Don't be hasty."

Reed prevailed, and the girls left. At another motel, the manager and the local cops got a tip that there were underage girls in the room occupied by Rehberger, Wahrer, and Winslow. The cop opened their door at 3 A.M., flipped on the light, and said, "You got a girl in here?" They said no. Then the cop spotted long blond hair on a pillow. He shouted, "There she is! That one over there!" Tim Rehberger lifted his head and said, "What, you fucking talking to me?"

"I had a wife and kids, and payments to make," Reed said. "It was not all fun and games. I did most of the driving. I couldn't trust the other guys. I was coast to coast I don't know how many times. You'd pack up after a job, load out, and take off. You'd try to get at least halfway to the next destination, or all the way and check into a motel and sleep all day. I think we all had such a work ethic that we knew the pitfalls, and what best not to do. So we kept our noses pretty clean. It's not as though there weren't lots of opportunities. You just didn't dare participate."

Andreason was engaged to his Twin Cities girlfriend for a short time but broke it off after returning from a tour of California. His girlfriend had already made wedding plans and picked a date without having consulted with him. Andreason told her the date wouldn't work, because he had an East Coast tour coming up.

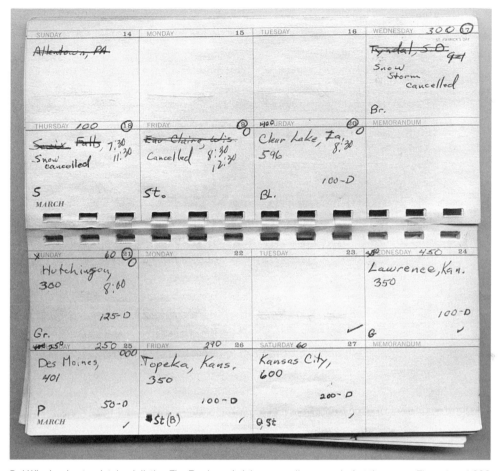

Dal Winslow kept a datebook listing The Trashmen's jobs, pay, mileage, and what they wore. They played 292 jobs in 1964 and 270 in 1965. Courtesy of Dal Winslow.

"Well, you've got to cancel it, because we're getting married," she said.

"Oh, no," Andreason said.

"Well, when do you think we should get married?"

"In a year."

"Why a year? We're either getting married in three months, or not at all."

"Well, I'm sorry you feel that way," Andreason said.

He was twenty years old at the time and had no intention of getting married that young.

"I thought that would have been the dumbest thing I could have done," he said. "So I didn't get married until I was twenty-eight. That was the right thing to do, it really was."

The Trashmen were never late for a job, but they did miss one. A fierce blizzard hit Fargo in 1965, shutting down all roads in and out of town. The band was stranded in a motel for three days. "It was the most unbelievable snowstorm I've ever seen," Andreason said. "We couldn't move, couldn't go outside, couldn't do anything. So we missed a show, and another one was called off after that because of the snow."

Even performing was grueling, as many of their jobs were four-hour dances rather than one-hour performances. Andreason called it a "cakewalk" when they got into some of the Caravan of Stars shows and had to play just one short set. The Trashmen made annual appearances at the Cornell and Columbia campuses when those colleges had their party weekends, usually playing two jobs in one day. "You'd play one o'clock in the afternoon for two hours, then you'd go over to fraternity XYZ and play five to seven," Winslow said. "Every year during that time, five or six kids would jump off the cliff and kill themselves, they'd get so drunk. It was just mayhem. There was a black group who all they wore onstage was jock straps. College kids liked stuff like that. *Animal House* was spot on. I can remember walking through beer up to my ankles in frat house basements."

The peak of The Trashmen's touring years was their trip to Venezuela in 1965. "We were bigger than the Beatles there," Andreason said. "A guy bought us for two weeks. Just a flat rate for two weeks. And boy, he had us busy. They'd come up with a car to pick us up and take us out with a different car to get us out of there. We played at the Hotel Tomanoco with Barbara McNair, a sweet person, really a talented singer and entertainer. We did TV shows during the day. The first TV show was called *The Rene Show*, I think, in Caracas, and it was like the *Ed Sullivan Show* here. It was in a big sound stage with a curtain. We had no clue what they were saying—the only thing we waited for was 'Los Trashmen!' and we started playing live. We would do two or three of those a day, and do the one at night. I think the promoters came out pretty well. But we got paid well, too."

Because the cost of shipping musical instruments and amps overseas was so expensive, when it was time to return to the United States, the band sold their sunburst-finish Fender Jaguar guitars and Dual Showman amps to a local group called the Supersonicos. "They couldn't get that equipment over there—couldn't buy it," Andreason said. "At the time it was like fifteen hundred bucks to ship our stuff. So they offered us a price we couldn't refuse."

While they were still in Venezuela, they called Jimmy Thomas and asked him to tell

Fender that they needed new equipment. When they returned to Minnesota, their new instruments and amps were waiting for them at B-Sharp Music, owned by Jimmy Lopes. "We put 'B-Sharp Music' on the amps, so his business escalated a thousand percent," Andreason said. "It really did—he sold a lot of stuff."

"Jim Lopes was pretty good," Winslow said. "But I think he owed his success to us, too. He would say the same thing. He used to have a little bootleg store, a hole in the wall up in Columbia Heights. A lot of the stuff he sold didn't have any serial numbers on it. We bought our stuff there, started going out to play, promoted him and his store. You just got such a better deal there than you did at Schmitt or any of the other music stores. He moved up to his new store and it took off like gangbusters. That store burned down a few years ago. We always called him José, but I don't think he was Hispanic. I think he was Italian, because his son was named Guido. He was a wheeler-dealer, short guy with a mustache and the black hair slicked down. He was a good guy."

After the Trashmen hit big, B-Sharp was the store where all Twin Cities rock musicians shopped, but nobody was ever completely sure whether they were getting a good deal. "When we got popular, Jimmy started treating us good," said Phil Berdahl of the Stillroven. "He put our picture on the wall. If a guitar was $200, we'd draw cards. You'd either get it for free or for $300."

"I'd have a Fender guitar, and he'd say, 'Why don't you play that Gretsch?'" said Chris Nelson of the More-Tishans. "I'd say, 'Yeah, I like that.' He'd say, 'Give me the Fender and $50 for the Gretsch.' He never had prices on anything. He'd ask, 'What do you want to pay for it?' I'd say, '$200.' He'd say, 'I got to have two and a quarter.' It was fun. I thought I had this old guy in the palm of my hand. I know I spent thousands of dollars there. He always made you think you got a deal."

Despite the pressure of traveling and performing, the four Trashmen remained steadfast friends. Even when the group came off the road, they'd generally hang around together. Winslow and Wahrer had their place on Lake Street, and Andreason would sometimes join them there overnight. "There'd be girls there sometimes, but we had kind of a core group of people that we hung around with—girls who we knew a long time, who we grew up with, and that was about it," Andreason said. "It was pretty much the same crowd. We didn't trust a lot of people. We became very distrusting of outsiders. People just wanted something from you."

During their years on the road, The Trashmen played on bills with Link Wray, the Crystals, Lou Christie, the Rip Chords, Terry Stafford, the Kinks, Frankie Avalon, Ronny and the Daytonas, the Hullaballoos, the Rivieras, Fabian, Roy Drusky, and Martha Reeves and the Vandellas. There was no way that The Trashmen could miss the changes in the musical landscape as they crisscrossed the country, performing with an eclectic array of groups, listening to both Top 40 radio and Wolfman Jack's all-night blues show from Mexico, while their singles sold in increasingly declining numbers. "I listened to some of it—some of it was great," Andreason said. "But when we were playing, we were in this kind of bubble, playing music that didn't have any political overtones or connotations. 'Peggy Sue Got Married,' 'Splish Splash, I Was Taking a Bath'—all those songs were just great songs to dance to, fun songs to play.

"Then we got to meet some of the people who really started getting into [drugs]," said Andreason. "There's Janis Joplin, people like that. They were a mess. A lot of these people have become idols now, but they were an absolute mess. Drugs started, and we just weren't doing it. We drank alcohol. I did a session here with Glen D. Hardin, the piano player for Elvis. They had some background singers—they were higher than a kite. They were smoking pot outside the studio, and they left. Two of them were killed. I'm sure it's because they were high." He recalls playing with Dion in Duluth when he was so high that he was stuffing toilet paper into his guitar and saying, "This is where it's at, man."

"You know, they say marijuana's okay, but I saw so many people get into smoking pot, then they'd do pills, then get into something else that wasn't good, so to this day I've never even tried pot. I never did drugs, and the guys in the group never did. We just saw too many people going down. They were 'circling the drain,' we'd call it at the time."

Nevertheless, drugs and psychedelic imagery were becoming increasingly influential on the pop music of the mid-1960s, and Bob Dylan's rule-breaking lyricism was at the center of the movement away from innocent party songs. Dylan had caught the ear of the nation by writing songs that challenged the status quo and railed against war and injustice. "Blowin' in the Wind" had been a Number 2 hit on the *Billboard* singles chart in August 1963 for folkies Peter, Paul, and Mary, and they followed that up in October with another Dylan cover that went Top 10, "Don't Think Twice, It's All Right." The troubadour from Hibbing seemed to have found his true voice in pointed protest folk rather than rock 'n' roll.

But just as he was being anointed the spokesperson of his generation, Dylan decided he didn't want that responsibility. His lyrics turned inward and became even more challenging and poetic, seeming at times to be free-association exercises that nevertheless held profound meaning, if one only looked hard enough for it. His work had a major impact on the Beatles, and John Lennon in particular, whose writing evolved from two-minute love songs to introspective folk-rock. Dylan also inspired the Byrds, who put the trippy lyrics of "Mr. Tambourine Man" to jangly twelve-string guitar rock. Then Dylan returned to his own Minnesota rock 'n' roll roots, releasing the full-blown rock song "Like a Rolling Stone" in the summer of 1965 and playing a Fender Stratocaster at that year's Newport Folk Festival. He was heckled by the purist crowd, but the marriage of meaningful lyrics and rock 'n' roll was complete and would permanently alter '60s pop music. "He changed the music, without a doubt," Winslow said. "When it got to be serious about 'Where's this country going?' and 'What are you doing with the rest of your life?' instead of 'Oh, I got a girlfriend, and we're going to go out and drink some beer and surf, and have a good time'—yeah, it definitely changed."

"I loved the stuff that Dylan was doing when he went electric," Andreason said. "His hardcore fans didn't like it, but I thought it was great. We did 'She's got everything she needs, she's an artist, she don't look back'—'She Belongs to Me.' We were doing stuff like that. We liked it because the audience liked it. It was cool to do those songs." In fact, Andreason wrote a couple of songs that bore strong resemblance to Bob Dylan's style—but after the band parted ways with the Garrett label. Winslow said the split was primarily over Soma's decision not to release The Trashmen's second album. The label was convinced it wouldn't sell due to the Beatles' influence on the record-buying public. "We said, 'Okay, we're not recording with you.'"

They first went to Amos Heilicher's local competitor, Harold Lieberman, who had run a music distribution company in Minneapolis for decades and had begun a record label called Bear. The Trashmen's sole release on Bear was recorded at Kay Bank Studio in January 1965: a cover of the 1963 Little Eva hit "Keep Your Hands Off My Baby," written by Carole King and Gerry Goffin and featuring Andreason singing the falsetto chorus. The production credit went to George Garrett, even though the band was no longer recording for his label. The flip, LaPole's "Lost Angel," was one of the demo songs the band had been working on prior to "Surfin' Bird." The basic track now featured the Arlyles on backing vocals, giving the stately ballad a Roy Orbison feel. Winslow said the record went to Number 1 in some Canadian markets, but it failed to chart in the Twin Cities or on *Billboard*. "It was squelched here because of Heilicher," Winslow said. "He didn't want it in his stores because it was a competitor."

They went back to Kay Bank one more time to try to recapture the past. The A-side, "Ubangi Stomp," was a '50s rockabilly standard that finally allowed Wahrer to display his uncanny Jerry Lee Lewis impression on record. In a move that suggested a certain amount of desperation, the B-side was an updated version of their biggest hit, "Bird '65,"

recorded in a slower tempo and with fuzz-tone guitar, changing the vibe from surf to hard rock. Wahrer came up with a new set of lyrics, too: "Well, everyone thought that it went away, but now the Bird's back and it's here to stay . . . whatever you like, we can make it work, 'cause now to the Surfin' Bird they're doin' the jerk. . . ." The

Steve Wahrer and The Trashmen cut four folk-rock tracks at Huey Meaux's recording studio near Houston, Texas, in January 1966. *(Below)* Courtesy of Dal Winslow; *(left)* courtesy of Mike Jann/Sundazed Records.

net impression, however, was that of a band that was still looking backward rather than forward. It was released in November 1965 on the Argo label, a mostly-jazz subsidiary of Chicago's Chess Records, and did not chart. During the same session, The Trashmen recorded a very Beatles/Searchers–sounding original by Andreason called "That I Love You." Hindsight suggests that this song would have fared much better with the public, which had fully embraced the British rock sound.

Jimmy Thomas arranged for the band to record with producer Huey P. Meaux at his studio outside Houston. Meaux, known as the Crazy Cajun, was a Louisiana native who'd been racking up successful singles with Roy Head ("Treat Her Right") and the Sir Douglas Quintet ("She's About a Mover") and would soon follow with B. J. Thomas ("I'm So Lonesome I Could Cry"). They arrived at Meaux's studio the first week of January 1966. "He was just, 'What do you guys want to do, what do you need?' all in this Cajun accent," Winslow said. "He was a record promoter, but he wasn't slick or anything like that. He said, 'Come in and do it, we'll put it out and see what happens.'"

The band cut four songs, two by songwriter Mark Charron, who also wrote "Billy and Sue" and "Mama" for B. J. Thomas. The other two, "Same Lines" and "Mind Your Own Business," were both written and sung by Andreason very much in the Bob Dylan style. "He went through a Dylan phase," Winslow said of Andreason. "He started singing 'Tambourine Man.' You can kind of see by looking at our pictures how we went through our various phases. In fact, that picture where we're sitting next to the amp with the beards, that's from the studio in Texas. That's where we're pissed at the world."

Charron's "Hanging on Me" was chosen for the A-side of the single on the Tribe label, while "Same Lines" was the B-side. Taken together, the four songs

Fashions changed with the arrival of the British Invasion, and The Trashmen changed their look to keep pace. Courtesy of Mike Jann.

were the strongest material the band had done in the studio, but they did not in any way sound like The Trashmen—or, at least, what The Trashmen were expected to sound like. "The problem is, we went in there and we got into this, 'Let's pull a tube out of the amp, and let's do this, let's do fourteen tracks of this,'" Winslow said. "We were playing 'Same Lines' before we went into the studio. In fact, we played it at Madison, and it was one of the most requested songs we had. We went into the studio and just butchered it. Just terrible. We'd go into a studio and we'd just fall apart. The best way to record us is to stick a mic in front of the stage and record us. That's us. Sort of like Jerry Lee Lewis, stick a mic and catch that ambiance. Put us in a studio and tell us to play this note and then play this note—that just wasn't our style."

The Tribe single fared no better than its predecessors, though some rock fans who profess to hate "Surfin' Bird" found it to be their favorite record by The Trashmen. The band's last studio effort took place on July 13, 1966, at the IGL Studio in Milford, Iowa. They recorded two Buddy Holly songs, "Well, All Right" and "Heartbeat," which again wasn't the most forward-thinking career move. "You think back—why did you do that?" Winslow said.

The Trashmen would find themselves doing a lot of self-examination in the coming months.

THE BIG THREE

WHILE THE TRASHMEN were chasing the Bird from coast to coast, the Minnesota rock 'n' roll scene had reached critical mass.

The arrival of the Beatles hadn't done the Trashmen much good, but it certainly pushed hundreds of other bands into overdrive. Rock music was becoming a way of life for the baby boomers who were in their teens; there were school dances, teen clubs, and armory, roller rink, and ballroom gigs everywhere, seemingly every night. The bands that had been playing '50s rock 'n' roll and Ventures/surf music suddenly were growing their hair long and learning how to sing harmony. Booking agent Dick Shapiro told the *Minneapolis Tribune* on October 17, 1965, that there were 350 bands in the Twin Cities area that were "good enough to get away with a dance job." And though there was good money to be made by the thousands of young guitar players, bass players, keyboard players, and

The first Underbeats lineup: Duke Duane, Doni Larson, Jim Johnson, and Russ Hagen in 1963 in Chisago Lakes, Minnesota. Courtesy of Doni Larson.

drummers, three bands clearly emerged from the scrum to inherit The Trashmen's place at the top of the Twin Cities heap: the Underbeats, the Accents, and Gregory Dee and the Avanties.

"The Underbeats were my favorites," Tony Andreason said. "The Underbeats were probably the best band that came out of Minneapolis in the '60s. Live, they couldn't be beat. Simply incredible. We'd play battles of the bands with the Underbeats, and it was amazing how on the radio we'd be depicted as adversaries, when we were the absolute best of friends. I mean, they made a big deal beforehand on KDWB and WDGY how 'The Bands are gonna be fightin' it out tonight!' But then we'd be hangin' out together after the battle every time."

Fans and musicians alike were astonished at Jim Johnson's ability to play anything on guitar. In the band's early days, he would play note for note Chuck Berry solos, and after the Beatles became the dominant band in pop music, he seamlessly picked up all of George Harrison's licks.

The Underbeats were initially booked by David Anthony, who impressed Johnson with his slick style. "He had a gift of gab," Johnson said. "He showed up in a red Thunderbird, and people were blown away." He was less impressed with the first gig Anthony got for the band. It was in Fairmont, Minnesota, near the Iowa border. "What the hell, what kind of a booking agent is that?" Johnson's father said.

The Underbeats never signed an exclusive arrangement with anyone, and after Anthony was drafted, they began working with Bill Diehl, Marsh Edelstein, Dick Shapiro, and anyone else who wanted to book them. Johnson remembers playing a job in Osseo on November 22, 1963, the night of President Kennedy's assassination. "It was a bummer," he said, but they played anyway.

Demand for the Underbeats soared after they went into Kay Bank Studio to record for the first time. Johnson said it wasn't the band's idea; he wasn't even aware that other bands were making records. George Garrett and Tony Kai-Ray, on the lookout for more local bands to add to their stable, approached the Underbeats and paid for the session. "There were people here in town talking about [how] George Garrett ripped you off. Bullshit," Johnson said. "If it wasn't for George Garrett, God knows what I'd be doing now."

They cut a rocked-up version of "Foot Stompin'," a 1961 R&B dance hit by an L.A. doo-wop group called the Flares. Johnson capped the infectious track with a tasty guitar solo as the record came to a close. On the B-side, Johnson showed off both his vocal chops and his guitar prowess on the jazz/R&B classic "Route 66." "I was the only one who could sing, so I got to learn how to sing," Johnson said. "I got to put my nose to the grindstone. I taught the other guys how to sing background. From high school band, I knew how to do harmony parts. I knew how to stack those harmonies."

The single was the fourth to be issued on the Garrett label, and though it did not make the national charts like its two predecessors, "Surfin' Bird" and "Bird Dance Beat," it was a hit in the Twin Cities. In the middle of the Beatles spring 1964 blitz on the charts, "Foot Stompin'" peaked at Number 16 on WDGY. "We were on the radio," Johnson said. "We were rock stars. My dad, he'd go to work, and they're all talking about me: 'We heard your kid on the radio.' This 'goddamn bum' thing was over. We played anywhere and everywhere in Minnesota and Wisconsin. One gig, we pulled into this town—absolutely nothing. There was a dog in the middle of the street that barked at our truck. But at night the place was packed. It was all teen dances. We never played a club. We played little towns. They came from five or six towns around. We were making plenty of dough. Two hundred dollars a week."

After playing some jobs at Bloomington's Knights of Columbus Hall, the Big Three decided to book themselves into the venue. The Underbeats, Avanties, and Accents each

After forming the Underbeats in 1962 with his North Minneapolis pal Russ Hagen, Jim Johnson led the group through a rapid evolution of both musical and fashion styles. Here he and drummer Rod Eaton *(with goatee)* sign autographs while sporting the berets and sunglasses they wore through much of 1964. Courtesy of Doni Larson.

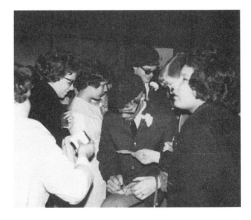

made $1,400; they were paid just $300 when they were booked into the same hall by a booking agent.

The Underbeats were one of the bands that could draw big enough crowds to headline at Big Reggie's Danceland with Bill Diehl. "I liked Bill Diehl," Johnson said. "Some kids thought he was square, but he was older—even a thirty-year-old guy was ancient. I remember that green Cadillac convertible. He never went home alone when he was single. Bill threw some parties. He took us to the World Theater to see *Goldfinger* before it was in the theater. *Behold a Pale Horse*, *Fail Safe*—we saw some good movies, just the band members, us and the Avanties."

Playing dance jobs was the way the Underbeats made money. They viewed recording as a way to keep their sound in front of the local teens and maintain a high profile in the competitive booking business. Through 1964 and 1965, the band recorded a series of singles on the Heilicher family of labels, including Garrett, Bangar, Twin Town, and Soma. The follow-up to "Foot Stompin'" was a Bangar 45 with two Johnson originals: "Annie Do

the Dog," a song Johnson "hates like poison" but was urged to write by Tony Kai-Ray to try to cash in on the current Dog dance fad, and "Sweet Words of Love," a midtempo tune that clearly seems to have been inspired by Buddy Holly. "Sweet Words of Love" was a local smash, reaching the Top 10 on both WDGY and KDWB in October 1964.

The last single the Underbeats recorded in 1964 proved to be controversial. The catchy Johnson original "Little Romance" featured terrific Chuck Berry–like solos between the verses, but the second verse—repeated for the third verse—was deemed to be risqué: "A little romance, from a girl like you; a little romance, a little [knock-knock], too." The knock-knock sound by drummer Rod Eaton was interpreted to be sexual; after debuting at Number 50 on the KDWB chart on January 2, 1965, the song was gone the following week. It never charted on WDGY. "We got a raw deal on 'Little Romance,'" Johnson said. "They wouldn't play it because it was sex. 'No, we can't put that on the radio.' What about Fats Domino?" Domino's 1958 hit "Whole Lotta Lovin'" had a verse that went "I got a whole lotta [clap-clap] to do." Censors didn't seem to have a problem with it. "I left it," Johnson said. "At that time it could have been a five-state regional hit. Little girls would have loved it."

Johnson received all the royalties he was entitled to from the songs he wrote for the Underbeats. Garrett got the publishing royalties through his Willong Corporation. "Why shouldn't he?" Johnson said. "He paid for the session, took us off the street, put us in the studio—why shouldn't he? Nobody knew anything about publishing then. It was not in the vocabulary of a musician. As long as I'm making $200 and getting laid, what do I care?" The Underbeats were living large. All bachelors, they rented a duplex, invited their girlfriends over, and didn't have to explain anything to anyone. Johnson had a Corvette, Rod Eaton had a Jaguar XK, and Doni Larson bought a TR6 Triumph. "We were living the dream," Larson said. "We were making stupid [loads of] money back then."

"The Underbeats played six nights a week," said James Walsh, who joined the band later as a keyboardist and singer. "When I was playing in a band in high school, I made more money than my father, who was a policeman in Minneapolis." "Quite honestly, local bands in the '60s were making roughly what local bands are making today," Lonnie Knight said. "We got paid three or four hundred bucks for a local gig. Back then, you made that kind of money, you got your rent paid."

The big bucks also enabled them to dress stylishly. Like The Trashmen, the Underbeats were having their suits custom made at Kieffers in Minneapolis. "The first time we're in there getting our clothes measured, the guy puts his thumb up to our balls and asks, 'Which side do you prefer?'" Johnson said. "They were the first outfits we had. It

Jim Johnson had the Underbeats wear berets for nearly a year because he saw Chuck Berry wear one in a photograph. Courtesy of Denny Johnson of Minniepaulmusic.com.

was so cool—thirteen-and-a-half-inch cuffs. You could barely get your feet through them. Later we got cranberry with satin." For almost a year, the Underbeats augmented their performing attire with berets and sunglasses. "I wore sunglasses ever since I found out about them," Johnson said. "The beret was my idea. I'd seen a picture of Chuck Berry with a beret, and I said, 'Okay, guys we gotta get those.'"

By 1965, the Underbeats were doing less Chuck Berry and far more Beatles. "I liked the Beatles," Johnson said. "When they first came out, we learned 'I Saw Her Standing There' and 'And I Love Her.' You had to do them, but I do respect them for a four-piece band coming up with those kinds of arrangements. We mostly did the flip sides or album cuts. Occasionally the hit, but I've always had a knack for picking songs to do."

The Underbeats were hanging out with the members of their two biggest rival bands, the Accents and the Avanties. Like The Trashmen, the Underbeats felt no ill will toward the other top bands. They had poker games with the other bands after every mutual gig.

They would party all night on the St. Croix with Doug "Froggy" Nelson of the Avanties, whose wealthy parents owned a boat that they kept at the river. Johnson recalls going to an actual St. Paul speakeasy with Avanties guitarist Bruce Madison.

The Avanties got their first big break when Dave Maetzold read in the paper that there was going to be a battle of the bands at the Silver Skate Roller Rink in North St. Paul. "It was one of the first times I ever saw the term *battle of the bands*," Maetzold said. "It was for truly amateur bands who were not performing in the clubs or ballrooms. We were still an amateur band, because we had no recordings."

The battles started in the morning and alternated between four stages. Each band was allowed to play three or four songs, and the winner would be signed to play two or three nights a week at the roller rink for the rest of the summer. The Avanties won, beating out Keith Zeller and the Starliners, with Zip Caplan's friend Bill Strandlof on guitar. "It was the first time I ever heard or saw them," Maetzold said. "They were really good, and really professional. Maybe they didn't fall in line with what the battle was all about. Eventually musicians changed and formed different groups. Whoever was there that day or that weekend, I'm sure many became popular groups in the future. We were just a small group. I don't know how we won."

Along with playing their own sets at the Silver Skate Roller Rink, the Avanties were used as the opening act for national entertainers who performed there. Their first opening gig was for the Ronettes. They also opened for Conway Twitty. "We couldn't believe it," Maetzold said. "Here we are, playing Top 40 songs, and we get to open for a national act. We had never seen anybody like that. We played the first set, they played maybe two sets. What was great was the free advertising. They'd say, 'Appearing with the Ronettes, the Avanties.' That finally got us some advertising. Before that, it was just word of mouth. We'd play at a party, and people would ask, 'Who are you guys?'"

Greg Maland was playing a rented electric Wurlitzer piano, but the first night the band set up at Silver Skate, he noticed the big Hammond organ that was used to play roller skating music. Maland asked the manager if the band could use the organ during their set, and the manager said, "Go ahead." "I didn't have very good equipment," Maetzold said. "I plugged my bass into the Leslie speaker with rotating horns on the organ. Greg played the organ and I was playing the cheap bass through the Leslie speaker. The sound was unbelievable. That was the first time Greg got to play an organ. It was a completely different sound. From then on, Greg said, 'I'm going to start renting an organ.'"

From that point on, the band had to get a U-Haul trailer to transport their equipment.

Gregory Dee and the Avanties became one of the Big Three rock 'n' roll bands in the Twin Cities after the release of their instrumental hit "The Grind" on Garrett Records: *(left to right)* Dave Maetzold, Doug "Froggy" Nelson *(kneeling),* Greg Maland, and Bruce Madison. Courtesy of Tom Tourville.

"Back then, there weren't chopped-down keyboards," Maetzold said. "It was a Hammond B-3. Every job, we had to carry that darn thing in, up onto the stage, and after three or four hours of playing, carry it back down and out to the U-Haul. What a pain." Yet it was the Hammond B-3 organ that gave the Avanties a sound like no other band in the Twin Cities.

"Most of the groups—the Underbeats, the Accents, and Mike Waggoner—they were all guitar groups," Maetzold said. "We had a distinct sound, playing Top 40 with a Hammond organ. There was Booker T., Bill Doggett, maybe some songs Ray Charles did. Those were the groups that Greg was listening to, besides piano players like Jerry Lee Lewis. He would take a song by any keyboard artist and play it on the organ, rearrange it, and make it his own. Greg did most of the singing, and I'd harmonize with him. He was a good singer."

After the Avanties won the battle of the bands, they put the word out that they were looking for a guitarist, because Bob Ohde had dropped out of the group. One the guitarists to try out was Bruce Madison, a St. Paul native who had just gotten out of the Marines. "He was fairly good," Maetzold. "Greg and I said, 'Let's try him out.' That became the true Avanties, with Bruce, Doug, myself, and Greg."

Maetzold believed the group needed to change its name to feature Maland as the lead singer and key instrumentalist in the group. "His middle name was Dean, so I said, 'Why don't we call the group Gregory Dee?' There was Bobby Vee and all these different names that ended in '-ee.' He said, 'I don't know,' but I said, 'Yeah, you've got the organ and the sound.' The name made it more distinct between the Accents and Avanties."

Now they had a name, a sound, and a growing reputation as one of the better bands in town, but the only way they could charge more money was to make a record. Maland and Maetzold used to go to the two local Top 40 radio stations at night to sit and schmooze with the deejays who were working when the most teens were listening. Often there would be only one person in the studio, spinning the records, dropping in the commercials, and engineering the broadcast. "We became friends with whoever the deejay was," Maetzold said. "My objective was, if we became friends with them, and if we had a record, we could ask, 'Would you play the record for us? Just give it a try.' They said, sure."

The first song the band recorded was an offbeat rockabilly novelty tune called "Olds-Mo-William," written and recorded in 1958 by Paul Peek, who had been a member of Gene Vincent's Blue Caps. The song frequently paused for the lead singer to answer the question, "Olds-Mo-William, whatcha gonna do?" In a voice lifted from Tweety Bird of the Looney Tunes cartoons, Peek answered, "I'm gonna wock and woll, if I can, if I can." The song never charted; Greg Maland came across it in a ten-cent bin and brought it to the band. "I changed the words to it because at the time, The Trashmen had 'Surfin' Bird' out," Maetzold said. "I changed the words to "I'm gonna do the bird if I can, if I can."

The band sped up the tempo and tried it out at the dances they were playing. The kids loved it and danced to it, so the band decided to record it. The Avanties didn't have an agent or a manager, but they knew most of the groups were recording at Kay Bank, and they knew about George Garrett and his Nic-O-Lake record store. Garrett agreed to get Gregory Dee and the Avanties into Kay Bank and to have their record released on his Bangar label. For the flip side, the band recorded Clarence "Frogman" Henry's "Ain't Got No Home," with Maland singing both the low vocals and the falsetto.

"If we signed a contract with Soma, I don't remember," Maetzold said. "Greg might have. He was the writer of some of the songs. I know George Garrett is on many of the songs, and to this day I don't know why. He had nothing to do with them. He didn't put any money up front. I guess since he got us in with the recording studio; he got some cut on that. We had to pay out of our own pocket, because George just got our foot in the door. Back then, it was a lot of money. We paid $400—$100 per band member—but they gave us four hundred copies so we could get our money back by selling copies for $1 at the dances. We dropped off a couple records at the radio stations. They started to play the record."

Maetzold called one of the stations and asked if they were going to play "Olds-Mo-William" that night. He was told when the record was going to be played. Maetzold immediately started calling family, friends, and anyone else he could think of. "As soon as you hear they're going to play this song by the Avanties, call in and say, 'I love this song. Play it some more,'" Maetzold told them. "As soon as the deejay played it, the phone rang off the hook. That's how we promoted ourselves with no money. It was all on our own, no agents or promoters. That week we got a lot of airplay."

At that time in the 1960s, WDGY and KDWB were actually eager to play records by Twin Cities bands.

"The local stations back then would just jump on records by local acts," said Lonnie Knight, whose band the Rave-Ons cut two singles in 1965. "They did an Instant Top 10 at night. We'd sit around our phones and call constantly, and get our record to Number 1. Initially, WDGY with Bill Diehl was a lot more involved, then KDWB started doing it to increase ratings and stay hip. I don't know that any of us ever made it very far on the official charts. There was still a lot of payola in those days. During business hours, the stations played what they were fed. Then at nighttime we made our mark."

The next step for the Avanties was to start playing the dances and ballrooms where

Bill Diehl was booking the bands. "That's how I got to know Bill—his appearances booking our group," Maetzold said. "I think he was working more exclusively with certain groups. In his eyes, I think we were just another band. But because we had a good relationship with him, we were able to get a lot of bookings. Bill Diehl would try to make three or four places in one night and give away records. That helped, too, because kids liked to see a deejay or someone they hear on the radio every day. He says, 'I'll be at Waconia arena or ballroom on Friday night, I'll be giving records away, and I'll be there with the Avanties.' That promotes the band, and he's playing our record. That increased the draw. He was really a dealer. We became good friends."

Once they hooked up with Diehl, Gregory Dee and the Avanties played everywhere—ballrooms in both the Cities and in small towns, hockey arenas, armories, and teen clubs like Mr. Lucky's and the Safari Club in South St. Paul. "People referred to the Big Three—the Accents, Underbeats, and Avanties," Maetzold said. "We were playing at the same places at the same time. Many times we'd play alternating sets. It was such a great time to experience that. The kids were so great. They went through different styles of dances, like

When Greg Maland switched from guitar to organ, the Avanties found their signature sound. Courtesy of Steve Kaplan.

the Bird and the Watusi. Every other month there was a new dance, and kids would go to the dances and try out the dance. It was a great time. They just had fun getting together, dancing, and hearing live bands. Today, kids are missing out."

Those were also the days of the Baldies, the Greasers, and the Animals—Twin Cities kids who dressed either like preps (short hair, Gant shirts, and wing-tip shoes) or like punks (greased-back hair, white socks, and black leather jackets) and fought each other whenever they met. Dayton's department store held hugely popular Top 10 Club dances each week in its eighth floor auditorium, but the dances were eventually canceled at least in part because of the fighting that would take place. "There were fights, but they weren't with guns," Maetzold said. "They'd have fist fights. Very seldom do I recall someone got stabbed. There were two main gangs, the Baldies and the Animals. I remember this one job, we were at the third floor of a bank in Camden, North Minneapolis, and after we got all set up, there were no girls. It was all guys. We thought, 'There's something strange here.' One group of guys on the right side of the dance floor, another group on the left side of the dance floor. All of a sudden, they ran together and there was a big massive fight. We all hid behind the Hammond organ."

The Del Counts' hit single "Let the Good Times Roll" was a song almost guaranteed to start a brawl. "Every time we got to 'Let it roll,' a fight would break out," said Charles Schoen. "I said to the guitar player one night, 'Let's just skip that part.' We definitely kept playing through the fights. We never stopped unless they were on the stage. That happened one time at the Marigold. [Bassist] Bill Soley took the mic stand and smacked him right in the head. I don't know who hit me, but the last guy hit me hard. He was the biggest guy in the group. We weren't very big people."

"There were always fights where we played, too," said Dave Rivkin of the Chancellors. "It was sort of a common thing—a lot more than you see now. The fighting ended when people started getting into flower children and smoking pot. It came to an end and everyone sort of relaxed, starting tripping, and listening to the music."

There was also a Highland Park gang called the Ptarmigans, named after a northern grouse with feathered feet. "I tried like crazy to get into the Ptarmigans," said Jim Faragher, who drummed for a St. Paul band called the VIPs before replacing original drummer John Hughes in the Chancellors. "They had the jackets, the whole deal. They weren't Greasers, they weren't Baldies. They were supposedly in the middle, on the river, stuck between the west side and Minneapolis."

It could get confusing—and expensive—for kids of that era who did not totally identify with one gang or style. "I remember shopping for clothes," Faragher said. "With the

VIPs, I played a lot of jobs on the east side of St. Paul. You bought your clothes at Nate's— sequined jackets and pointed-toed shoes. You looked like one of the cast of *West Side Story*. Then I joined the Chancellors. We shopped at Dayton's Varsity Shop—a completely different look. Then I joined Sunshine World, and we had bell-bottoms. I went through all three of those eras. When I was a senior in high school, I met seniors at [Minneapolis] Washburn. We hit it off. I would drive over there two or three times a week to hang out. They were really into the Baldie thing—short hair, button-down collars, Gant shirts. Then I'd go over to [keyboardist Bruce] Bartl's house, and it was the Mexican groups on the West Side. Latinos had the street dances, purple shirts, and pointed toes. I had different outfits depending on where I was going."

A St. Paul band called the Deacons, led by another one of Zip Caplan's old jamming buddies, Rick Youngberg, recorded a party song called "The Baldie Stomp," which peaked at Number 12 on the KDWB chart in September 1964, but the lyrics had nothing to do with fighting or clothing styles. Released on the Re-Car label, the song featured a Kingsmen/ Premiers–like sax and guitar riff and a lot of in-the-studio shouting and laughter while lead singer Jim Reiff sang, "Come on baby . . . shake and stomp" over and over again. Youngberg might have come up with the party-atmosphere idea from the second single by Gregory Dee and the Avanties. Following the modest success of "Olds-Mo-William"—it climbed as high as Number 23 on the WDGY survey in May 1964—the Avanties returned to Kay Bank Studio to record an instrumental that Maland had come up with during a frigid winter visit to northern Minnesota.

"We were playing someplace in the winter where it was ungodly cold," Maetzold said. "After driving three or four hours to this ballroom, when we unloaded, Greg tried to turn on the organ. The motor was frozen. There's a crowd building that wanted to dance. He kept trying, and eventually it started to thaw out. He'd play chords, and it had the weirdest sound. It started to waver. He'd play chords up and down, and finally it freed up. At the end of the night before we quit, he played the same sound, the instrumental chords wavering up and down. He was adjusting the Leslie speaker so it would waver. Next job we had, Greg tried it again because everyone liked the sound." Maland called the song "The Grind" because the motor was grinding at the beginning. The band decided to make it their next single. Maetzold called thirty friends and asked them to come to the studio and holler and cheer during the recording. The effect created is that of a live rock 'n' roll party. "That was the background—it wasn't dubbed in," Maetzold said. "Those were fans cheering when we were recording. A lot of people thought it was canned cheering."

"The Grind" was a midsummer anthem in 1964, reaching Number 4 on the WDGY chart and Number 6 on KDWB. Later on, Gregory Dee and the Avanties recorded another original song called "The Slide," written to capitalize on a dance by the same name in which the kids would take a step then slide to the side. At the peak of their popularity, the Avanties opened for both the Beach Boys and the Dave Clark Five at the Minneapolis Armory. Each show drew about five thousand people. "We opened for the Beach Boys just after 'The Grind' came out," Maetzold said. "There were not many places in Minneapolis for concerts. There was the Minneapolis Auditorium, then the Armory. There were a few national groups that performed at the Prom, but the Prom held maybe two thousand."

Maetzold was able to meet and talk to the Beach Boys backstage and formed an instant dislike for Dennis Wilson, the band's drummer ("arrogant, stuck up, in love with himself, didn't want to socialize—just seemed like a jerk") but got a completely different vibe from bandleader and songwriter Brian Wilson. "Brian was more mellow," Maetzold said. "Greg was backstage, sitting next to Brian. They were both playing piano together, sharing licks on the keys. I wish I'd had a camera, but all I have is the memory."

Maetzold had seen the Beach Boys at their 1963 appearance at Danceland and was somewhat tired of their surf sound, though he thought their harmonies were great. The Avanties loved the Beatles and the new British sound, however, and were enthralled by the Dave Clark Five at their November 17, 1964 concert at the Minneapolis Armory. "They were so good, and they were true gentlemen, dressed in three-piece suits," Maetzold said. "They just looked great. They looked more professional than the Beach Boys in their striped shirts. You're not there to see how they look, but I was just more impressed with Dave Clark Five. We were playing some of the DC5 songs in the Avanties—they had an organ, too." After the show, Avanties drummer Froggy Nelson was talking to the members of the Dave Clark Five and decided to make up the story that it was

A friendly "battle" among top Twin Cities bands, circa 1965: *(left to right)* Bill Miller (Accents), Frank Prout (Avanties), Skip Dahlin (Accents), Greg Maland (Avanties), Tom Nystrom (Accents), Bruce Madison (Avanties), David Rivkin (Chancellors), Mike Judge (Chancellors), John Hughes (Chancellors), and *(kneeling in front)* Doug "Froggy" Nelson (Avanties). Courtesy of Doni Larson.

his birthday. "He lived in a nice house in South Minneapolis, and his parents weren't home," Maetzold said. "Out of the blue he said, 'It's my birthday. Do you want to go to my birthday party?' Two or three of the DC5 members went. The word got out, and it was just mayhem. There were hundreds of people at the party."

Maetzold said the girls screamed for the Avanties while they played their opening sets for the Beach Boys and the Dave Clark Five, but they were used to being idolized by their local fans. "There were actually kids who followed us, no matter where we played," Maetzold said. "I can remember, they used to have Dayton's Top 10 show in the fall of the year before school started. They'd have bands play on the eighth floor of Dayton's. I think Bill Diehl booked all that. The crowds were unbelievable. They even chased us through the store. They treated us like we were the Beatles. They wanted our autographs. We thought, 'This is unbelievable, we're just musicians. We're no big deal.' But they were hungry for live entertainers who were local. These were teens who weren't even able to go to the dances yet. This Dayton's Top 10 show gave them the opportunity to hear and see live musicians, and hear songs they heard on the radio. They see them live and they just go crazy. I can understand how they felt."

It was a heady lifestyle for a twenty-one-year-old kid. The money was good and the jobs were there for the playing, especially in the summer months. "If you had a record playing on the radio, you could ask for more money because they'd sell more tickets," Maetzold said. "The Trashmen were going to make a lot more money than the Underbeats or Avanties. That's one of the reasons every group needed to get a record out and have their name played on the air. If you didn't have a record, you're just another local group. You want to get a good fan base and have everyone following the group around. Most groups had a following, because each group had a style of music. The Underbeats had Chuck Berry, the Chancellors had surf music, the Accents were a blues group. If everyone played the same song and didn't write their own songs, the kids would hear the same music."

With all the money they were making, most of the members of the Big Three bought expensive sports cars. Maetzold was no different. "I'd pull up to Danceland in a Corvette," Maetzold said. "The money was really easy to make. Most guys took advantage, they took it for granted. I was kind of thrifty, other than that Corvette, because the Avanties decided to get a checking account. We'd draw on a weekly salary, rather than just taking the money and blowing it. With the money that built up in the account, we bought a van and a PA system, rather than having to kick in out-of-pocket. We treated it like a business because we were a business. Any expenses that occurred, we documented it for tax purposes. The other groups weren't reporting their income, though I didn't hear about other groups getting in trouble."

Eventually, the shared bank account got to be a sore spot for Maetzold. He recalled going to a restaurant after a gig and Bruce Madison ordering a steak, Froggy Nelson ordering lobster, and both of them putting it on the band's account. Maetzold didn't think that was fair. "I'm not that hungry, and you guys are all buying expensive meals, and you're going to write out expensive checks from the band account," Maetzold said. "It's not fair to me."

"Majority rules," the others said, laughing.

They played an outdoor gig in the fall in the parking lot of Montgomery Ward's in the Midway and then walked into the store after the show.

"Let's get matching luggage," one of the Avanties suggested.

"I got luggage already," Maetzold said.

"We don't," the others replied.

"What if I don't want luggage?" Maetzold said.

"We're getting luggage out of our account."

"They just blew money on stuff that wasn't necessary," Maetzold said. "But we're all young, we've got the money, so we spend it. Some guys were buying expensive cars and not thinking ahead. They never thought about it. I don't blame them. They were just enjoying the times."

George Garrett arranged for the Avanties to do a five-state tour as the backing band for the Angels, who had a hit with "My Boyfriend's Back," and Jimmy Soul, whose hit single was "If You Wanna Be Happy." The tour lasted three or four weeks, which put a strain on Maetzold's studies at the University of Minnesota. It was now 1965, and the draft was beginning to be a major concern for men in their early twenties. "The draft affected a lot of us," said Lonnie Knight, then with the Rave-Ons. "I got my physical notice from Detroit, but if you were living somewhere else, you could apply for a deferment or an extension, so I could do my physical in Minneapolis. In the intervening six months, I found a psychiatrist and antiwar sympathizer. We met, I told him I liked to sit and look out my second floor window and imagine people bursting into flames. He wrote a letter that said I was not fit for military service. It was an attempt to snow the psychiatrist. I would make up whatever I could think of. He absolutely knew I was conning him, but he went along with it. 'Sure, here's a letter. Go plant flowers.' I got horrendously drunk the night before my physical and failed it. I had to go back in six months. During my second physical, they found the vision in my eye was twenty-four thousand, and I was unfit anyway."

Maetzold was down to the last of his three allowable deferments; if he didn't finish school, he'd be subject to the draft and in all likelihood be sent to Vietnam; even after graduating, he had to join the National Guard to avoid the draft. The other Avanties had no such worries: Maland had emphysema, among other health problems; Nelson had damaged fingers from his childhood pipe bomb accident; and Madison had already been in the Marines.

"When we came back after the tour, I said, 'Greg, I've got to finish school,'" Maetzold said. "That's when I dropped out of the group." Maland tried to talk Maetzold out of leaving the band, but his mind was made up. He was replaced on bass by Frank Prout. Within six months, Gregory Dee and the Avanties, the Accents, and the Underbeats would come together for their biggest hurrah: playing in the concourse at Met Stadium prior to the Beatles concert there in July 1965.

"Just my luck," Maetzold said. "I drop out and now they're opening for the Beatles."

The third band that comprised the Big Three—the Accents—was more blues- and R&B-oriented than the Avanties or the Underbeats. Yet they also jumped quickly on the Beatles, learning most of *Meet the Beatles* soon after it was released in February 1964. They even wore Beatles wigs a couple of times onstage. Something in their act caught Bill Diehl's attention, and Diehl started booking and promoting the band heavily. That in turn led to their landing steady work at Mr. Lucky's, which had become the premiere teen club in the Twin Cities metro area. George Garrett's record store was just around the corner from Mr. Lucky's, so Garrett often dropped by to scout for fresh talent. He was impressed by the Accents and asked them for a demo tape. After hearing the songs, which included some band originals and some blues tunes, Garrett brought the Accents to Kay Bank, where they recorded their first single on January 22, 1964. The A-side was "Howlin' for My Baby," a 1959 Willie Dixon composition written for and recorded by Chicago blues growler Howlin' Wolf (whose real name was Chester Burnett). Most Twin Cities teens weren't listening to Chicago blues, but the Accents had tapped into the same rich vein of American rhythm and blues that made the Rolling Stones and the Animals among the early stars of the British Invasion. The B-side of their first single was an impassioned Tom Nystrom delivery of "Wherever There's a Will," a Lee Williams–penned ballad that became popular among Minnesota musicians because it appeared on the hugely influential Lonnie Mack album *The Wham of That Memphis Man*. The single peaked at Number 29 on the WDGY survey in May 1964 but helped establish the Accents as a cutting-edge band that could compete with the British groups. Their second single, "Searchin'," was a cover of a Mike Leiber/Jerry Stoller–written Coasters' novelty tune from 1957. It was paired

The Accents rode their hit single "Why" to big success: *(left to right)* Skip Dahlin, Tom Nystrom, Bill Miller, Ken Sand. Courtesy of Tom Tourville.

EXCLUSIVE REPRESENTATION · CB · Central Booking alliance Agency
Area Code 612·
332-6666 OR 698-8653

Like the other Big Three bands, the Accents toured the area ballrooms as well as playing Twin Cities teen clubs. Courtesy of Tom Tourville.

with a Tom Nystrom original called "You Don't Love Me," a deft pop-rock song very much in the Beatles style. That record made it to Number 15 on the WDGY chart in September.

The Accents' third single cemented Nystrom's reputation as one of the great singers in Minnesota rock. Once again the band dipped into Lonnie Mack's album for his ballad "Why," sung by Nystrom with an almost desperate wail in his voice, and accompanied by a Ken Sand guitar solo that did not suffer by comparison to Lonnie Mack's original. For the B-side, the Accents covered Bo Diddley's "Road Runner," a popular song with many rock 'n' roll bands. The single reached the Top 10 on both the WDGY and KDWB surveys in December.

Garrett now had The Trashmen, the Underbeats, Gregory Dee and the Avanties, and the Accents recording for his record label. To maximize his profit, Garrett released a compilation album in the fall of 1964 that included four tracks from each of the Accents, Avanties, and Underbeats, and labeled it *The Big Hits of Mid-America*. The album cost little to produce and sold extremely well, but the bands weren't paid from the profits. The Accents weren't complaining, however; their income from their packed performing schedule enabled them to join the Underbeats and Avanties as sports car owners. Nystrom bought a Plymouth Barracuda, Sand a new MG, Dahlin bought a Thunderbird, and Miller an Austin-Healey. The Accents found working with George Garrett to be a rewarding experience. In 1994 interviews with Jim Oldsberg, Tom Nystrom described Garrett as a "real nice guy, laid back," who was always in the studio with the band. "He was noninterfering with our music, which I give him credit for being smart enough to realize," Sand told Oldsberg. "He wasn't a musician, but he did have a good ear for what sounded aesthetically pleasing and commercial. He provided us with the perfect medium to express ourselves."

"I liked Gregory Dee—they were really cool, and I really liked the Accents with Tom [Nystrom] on drums," said Jim Faragher, drummer for the Chancellors. "He had a voice that would make the hair on your neck stand up. The keyboard player and guitar player were good. The Underbeats were the number-one group we liked, but we were booked so much, at so many varied locations, we rarely ran into them."

The members of the Big Three were like a small fraternity, recording for the same label and producer, and performing in the same clubs and dance halls. It was inevitable that there would be both attraction and friction. The first schism occurred in early 1966 when Bill Miller and Tom Nystrom had a falling out and Miller left the Accents. That was just the opening Jim Johnson of the Underbeats had been looking for. Nystrom sat in for Rod Eaton with the Underbeats one night at Mr. Lucky's and opened Johnson's eyes to a more contemporary style of drumming, as opposed to the wide-open Chuck Berry shuffle the Underbeats had been employing. "When Tom got up and played, I looked at Doni and said, 'God, that's it,'" Johnson said. "And what a voice. I remember talking to him and said, 'Tom, we should be playing in the same band.' He was having the same kind of feelings."

One more piece of the puzzle had to fall in place, however, for Johnson to execute his Underbeats makeover.

THE GREAT DECEPTION

THOUGH MOST OF THE PROMINENT MINNESOTA ROCK BANDS had already formed before the Beatles hit the U.S. charts in 1964, it would be a mistake to underestimate the impact the Beatles had on all of them. Tom "Zippy" Caplan and Ron Butwin of the Uniques may have been impacted most of all.

After the Uniques had morphed from folk to surf rock in the early 1960s, second guitarist John Sklar quit the St. Paul band to play blues, so the band added guitarist Ken Blank and sax player Shel Gulinson and became a five-piece group. Up to that point, Caplan and Butwin had worked primarily with St. Paul booking agent Clarence Hajney, a retired actor and vaudeville hoofer. He had the time to offer help to a select number of groups if he decided they had enough talent to progress. "He was just doing it out of a love for the music," Butwin said. "He was honest and trustworthy. He was one of the

The Uniques from St. Paul were an acoustic trio until "Walk, Don't Run" by the Ventures caught their ear. The expanded band featured *(from left)* Ken Blank, Shel Gulinson, Ron Butwin, Larry "Red" Cable, and Zip Caplan *(kneeling)*. Courtesy of Tom Tourville.

few I ever met I felt really cared. We had had a couple guys who were going to handle our group and be our agent. We learned the industry was full of guys like that. We were young, we didn't know. Luckily we didn't get hurt; they just didn't come through with what they promised. It was a lesson for me."

Hajney booked the band into a Ray Farhner auto show with some other local bands, including the Corvets, Keith Zeller and the Starliners, and Tim McManus and the Galaxies. Bill Diehl emceed that show, passing out records and introducing the bands. After the Uniques' set, Diehl approached Butwin. "You know, I like the way you flip your sticks, Ron," Diehl said. "None of the other drummers do that. You're a showman. How would you feel about me doing some booking for you?"

"I have my calendar," Butwin said. "If you call me at home, we can talk if you've got some dates for us. We've got nobody exclusive."

"I like to be exclusive," Diehl replied. "You can't book with anyone else."

"Let's just see how it works," Butwin said.

The band was booking more jobs, more than half through Hajney. Everyone was making money and the band was improving. Then the top local groups started making records: "Surfin' Bird," then the Underbeats with "Foot Stompin'," followed by Gregory Dee and the Avanties and the Accents.

With vocal music becoming more popular than instrumentals, Caplan and Butwin realized they weren't happy with the Uniques and started talking about what to do next.

"Let's re-form the group," Butwin said. "People like us, and we're not arguing or fighting with anybody, but we're not going any further than we are now." Butwin and Caplan wanted to be nationally famous, and with the explosive success of The Trashmen, they had no doubts that it was possible. They started inviting dozens of musicians to rehearse with them on the side, without the other members of the Uniques knowing about it. They tried having Rick Youngberg of the Deacons trade lead solos with Caplan. They tried Bill Strandlof of the Starliners. They auditioned Lonnie Knight and Larry Wiegand of the Rave-Ons. "All these guys were playing the same way we were," Butwin said. "They were out there in some other band but hadn't gotten to the next level. Week after week we tried out lots of people. Not all these people knew they were trying out."

Eventually they found a bass player named Terry Bellows, and an accomplished jazz pianist named Pete Malajewski, who said he was willing and able to play rock 'n' roll. Ted Lamere became their new sax player when Gulinson left for college. The band had problems with Blank, who left for the service. Playing with a steadily revolving lineup of guitar players, the Uniques evolved into a new band called the Continentals. Hajney did most of their booking, and Diehl got a few jobs for them, too. Butwin liked the players, but he still wasn't happy. The Continentals were still doing Ventures tunes and sax solos, a sound that was rapidly becoming passé. "We were still rooted in going back to a sound that we were beyond already," Butwin said. "Not that the Ventures were out of place, but we needed a bigger sound than that. Tom and I were both together on the fact that we needed something different."

Then the Beatles appeared.

"By '64, it was the Beatles and the whole English thing," Caplan said. "Eventually the Continentals thing crapped out. Ron and I were so taken by the Beatles. I remember watching them on the *Ed Sullivan Show,* and they were so good. Ron said, 'We gotta switch over.' The surf and regular band music was getting crushed by all the British groups. We knew that was going to be huge. We decided to put together a group that would play English music—Stones, Beatles. To do that we had to get new guys."

"When the Beatles came out, Tom and I were thinking, 'This might be our chance,'" Butwin said. "Everybody's going crazy for this music, but nobody's really doing it yet. It's just happening right now. We're in the midst of changing our sound. Let's build it as an English sound right now while it's hot. The Continentals are not going to be able to play that sound."

They decided to keep Bellows on bass and start searching for another guitar player who could sing—this time, however, with a very specific sound in mind: British beat music. They went through a lot of the same guitar players again, but as it turned out, they didn't have to look any farther than a block or two away from Butwin's house in St. Paul. "A guy comes to me, a year older, a drummer named Skip Effress, who lives a block and a half from me," Butwin said. "He says, 'I got this band. You guys are far better than we are. How about coming to hear the band and giving us some suggestions or something?'" Butwin agreed to give the band a listen, and though the band itself wasn't good, the rhythm guitar player caught his attention. "I thought, 'This guy is potentially really good,'" Butwin said. "He's just playing with some guys. He isn't real good yet on rhythm. I sense that he's got a good voice, but in this group it almost doesn't matter, because it's just not good enough. But I keep looking at him and listening to him and thinking, 'Maybe I should pull him out and have him do a tryout.'"

The young rhythm guitarist's name was Enrico "Rico" Rosenbaum. He was a year or two older than Butwin, who recognized him from the neighborhood but knew nothing about him. "There was a Jewish community," Caplan said. "Ron's Jewish, so am I. We might have known Rico that way."

Butwin called Rosenbaum that night. "Enrico, I really enjoyed the way you played," Butwin said. "Would you like to come over and rehearse with us one night just for the fun of it?" Rosenbaum agreed and attended a rehearsal in the basement of Butwin's parents' house. "He sits in with us, and he clearly sounds far better, even on the first song," Butwin said. "Because he's got strong drums, a strong bass—everybody's strong enough to give him a good backing. Tom and I look at each other. Let's just say we're doing Jerry Lee Lewis, or something like that. He's got the sound down. He sounds a little like Jerry Lee Lewis, and yet that's not what his normal voice sounds like. So that means he's good at mimicking."

Rosenbaum sounded better on the next song than he did on the first, changing his vocal sound to fit the style. Then Caplan and Butwin decided to jump in and do a Beatles song. Once again, he sounded great. "He really did a job on the Beatles, and that's what we wanted to hear," Butwin said. "Then he says, 'Can we do it with the oohs and the ahhs parts?' Which he did. It wasn't perfect or anything, but we heard a sound that works. That's when Tom and I knew this might be the right person." The band continued to rehearse until Butwin's mother, Rita, came down with cookies for the band. During the break, Rita said, "You should hear it upstairs. It's really good." Butwin's mother had a discerning ear, able to notice such small details as a guitar not in rhythm—and she clearly liked what Rico brought to the band.

"I'll give you a call," Butwin told Rico after the rehearsal. "It was fun. Did you enjoy it?"

"Yeah, it was fun," Rosenbaum said. "It was way different with you as a drummer, and the bass player."

"He was really charming and he was really funny," Butwin said. "I knew him as kind of a fun guy." They brought him back for another rehearsal and started teaching him specific songs. Rosenbaum was a quick study; he could pick out the right harmonies, and if a Beatles song was a John Lennon song, he sounded like John, and if it was a Paul McCartney song, he sounded like Paul. He could sing soul numbers like James Brown, too. They invited him to join their band, which was to be called the Escapades.

"Rico was the best of everybody we tried," Caplan said. "Good singer, excellent player, plus he lived right by us, which helped." Gradually, they came to learn more about their unusual new band member. Enrico had been born in Italy, and his parents were Jewish Holocaust survivors. His mother, Ida, had a concentration camp number tattooed on her arm. She was fluent in six languages, had sung Tin Pan Alley tunes in cafés, and worked as a seamstress at a Sears store in St. Paul. His father, Hubert, had been a successful businessman before losing everything, including his health, when taken prisoner by the

When the Escapades emerged from their secret rehearsals in late 1964, they wore natural-looking long-haired wigs and spoke with English accents while playing hits of the British Invasion. Courtesy of Denny Johnson of Minniepaulmusic.com.

Nazis. He worked in real estate when he came to the United States but had not been particularly successful.

The Escapades went into secret rehearsal mode. They were going to play nothing but British Invasion music, and to complete the image, they decided to wear long-haired wigs and speak with British accents. "None of us had long hair," Caplan said. "We couldn't get up and look like '50s guys."

"We couldn't grow our hair fast enough," Butwin said. "So I said, 'Let's get wigs of human hair. Not the [Beatle wig] junk they're selling. Real human hair wigs. Let's dress the part.'" The band had been wearing blazers with a shirt and tie, or sometimes an open shirt with an ascot. It was still the era in which band members dressed alike on stage. Then the Beatles appeared, wearing suits. The Escapades knew they had to upgrade their look. "We went downtown to a clothing store that had all the latest stuff coming in from overseas and got uniforms—a combination of suede and velour," Caplan said. "They weren't even a shirt, not a jacket, more a sweatshirt thing, but fancy. We wore black pants and got black Italian boots like the Beatles were wearing."

"I knew the store's owner, because he sold Butwin jackets," Butwin said. "I said, 'Here's what we're looking for. This is an English group, wearing a very thin suede turtleneck, really tight pants, and boots.' It was based on the look of the Beatles without the suits. The plan was, I usually did the announcing for the group. We get up onstage, and it's [in Liverpool accent]: 'Well, I'd like to welcome you all here this afternoon, y'know. We're going to be playing for you four or five songs. . . .' And I could go the whole evening in an English voice. I don't do it that often anymore. Tom wasn't much into talking into the mic onstage, and Terry wasn't. Rico was fine with that. He could do a bit of an English accent, too, but I was the one who could carry it on."

"We wood-shedded that thing," Caplan said. "We worked really hard on getting the harmonies." Butwin had graduated from high school the previous spring and was work-ing at B-Sharp Music in Minneapolis, running the Teen Center, where local bands came in to play short sets. "I didn't want to have us play at the Teen Center," Butwin said. "We weren't ready for it. But I was seeing every band, hearing every sound, just taking it all in. Every forty-five minutes I would change bands. All day long, every local band would sign up. Everyone was there—The Trashmen were there one day. If there was a national band playing in town, they would come over, because we had so much equipment there that they got a chance to try out the guitars. Though I wasn't friends with these guys yet, we'd met, we knew each other. And I didn't want to tell any of them what we were doing. It was like a brand; I wanted to break the brand in the marketplace at the right time. We're all set. We got the thing nailed. We got a show that's killer for this town. There's no group in town doing what we're doing. They may do a Beatles song or Stones or something, but we got the Beatles, the Stones, the Dave Clark Five, we've got this stuff down cold. And then we've got the look."

Rico also liked to sing soul, R&B, and blues—much like some of the British bands at the time. By the end of 1964 they were tightly rehearsed and believed they were ready to spring their act on Twin Cities teens. Through Amos Heilicher, who was a friend of the family, Butwin knew the manager of the Musicland store in downtown St. Paul. He was aware of the Uniques and mentioned to Butwin that he did a little booking on the side. Butwin decided to tell him that he was rehearsing a faux-English band and showed him a picture of the group in their uniforms and wigs. "We're not used to wearing those clothes, those turtlenecks, and we didn't usually wear the wigs, because you had to glue them on in a certain way," Butwin said. "Each one of us picked a style that we liked. It's pretty cool for that era."

The Musicland manager landed the Escapades a job opening for Chuck Berry on New Year's Eve at the St. Paul National Guard Armory. "New Year's Eve, Chuck Berry—what a great way for a band to play its first job," Butwin said. "We were so excited to be onstage with Chuck Berry, but he'd just been touring with the Beatles. And we're doing this English thing, hoping he's going to like it. He might think we're a bunch of rank amateurs. But Zippy and I believed in this new sound. Rico loved it, too."

By the time the band took the stage in front of a full house at the St. Paul Armory, Berry had not arrived yet. He was notorious for walking in minutes before showtime, so Butwin went into his act: "Well, we'd like to welcome you all here this evening," he said in his English accent. "We're going to be playing some really fun songs. We hope you enjoy it. Our good friend Chuck Berry will be on shortly. Just sit back relax, clap your hands, whatever you want to do, and we're going to have fun with you all."

"They thought we were from fuckin' England," Caplan said.

"We had them right off the bat," Butwin said. "Some of the guys didn't like the long hair, and we did have trouble with that for a while. If their girlfriend was at the stage screaming, the boyfriend was not particularly happy. It led to some pretty interesting situations at first."

The first set was a big hit. Butwin recalls seeing a number of friends and acquaintances, including record company rep, producer, and booking agent Timothy D. Kehr, standing in front of the stage. Thanks to the wigs and sunglasses, nobody recognized the Escapades. "We did the first set, we come off, and we're so excited," Butwin said. "Can you believe this? It's working. We had played in front of fairly large audiences before, but we had never had this kind of reaction. We could tell right away that this was different."

Chuck Berry arrived minutes before he was to go on and walked over to the Escapades. "He was really nice to us," Butwin said. "He thinks we're from England. I'm thinking, 'What do I do with my character?' He came by me first and said, 'I'm Chuck Berry.' I say [in accent]: 'Hello, Chuck, we've been waiting a long time to meet you.' And the guys in the band are going, 'Oh, come on, Ron—Chuck Berry! Don't be doing the fake accent.' I said, 'No, we've got to stay in character.' We would not go out of our dressing room except to play, because we didn't want a friend coming up and saying, 'Tom?' or 'Ron?'"

Berry's days as a chart-topper were coming to an end, but he'd had a bit of a resurgence in 1964 with two Top 20 songs, "No Particular Place to Go" and "You Never Can Tell," and his catalog of rock 'n' roll classics—"Johnny B. Goode," "Maybellene," "Sweet Little Sixteen," "Roll Over Beethoven"—was unsurpassed. Berry could always bring a crowd to its feet with his patented duck-walk across the stage while playing one of his instantly familiar solos. Because every rock musician with any experience knew all of Berry's songs, he never traveled with his own band but, rather, had the local promoters hire a backing band for him at each stop. In St. Paul, the promoter had hired some guys Butwin and Caplan had never seen before.

"They were just terrible," Butwin said. "But Chuck Berry doesn't care what the group sounds like behind him, because he'll just forget about them and still do his thing. He could do that—he didn't care. I mean, he'd rather have a good group, but he wouldn't rehearse with anybody. Chuck Berry's band is up there, and they're all drunk. They were real bad musicians, they're out of rhythm—they got nothing. Shortly into the first song, the drummer literally falls off the stool. I'm looking at Tom and I said, 'Can you believe that?' Then I thought, 'Wait a minute. My drums are up there, set up for our band.' So I just jump up on the stage and start playing drums. Chuck turns around, looks at me, and goes, like this [the OK sign] while he's doing a song. I felt like a million bucks. Chuck Berry gave me the okay.

"So I play with him for a couple songs. The other guys were looking around— the bass player can't stay on beat, whatever. What I remember happening is that I motion to the other guys to come up. So Zippy came up and started to play rhythm guitar. Now Chuck's got strong rhythm behind him. Then Terry came up, and Rico, each guy came up, and now he's got a solid band behind him. We were just cooking. The first set this band ever

Rock 'n' roll legend Chuck Berry appeared in St. Paul on New Year's Eve, 1964. He posed here with Jerry Severs, a friend of many local rock 'n' roll musicians, and taught valuable business lessons to his opening act, the Escapades of St. Paul. Courtesy of Doni Larson.

played in public, we had this huge reaction; and the second set we're playing with Chuck Berry. What more could you ask for?"

When the set was over, Berry thanked the Escapades.

"That was really great," he said. "You guys really helped out and I appreciate it. I didn't have to do everything on my own. That was really nice. Will you sit in with me on the next set?"

The Escapades agreed to play but asked about the other band.

"Fuck 'em," Berry said. "Don't worry about them."

"This guy was a wild man," Caplan said of Berry. "I think he'd been drinking."

Butwin stayed near the stage to talk to Berry while the other Escapades went back to the dressing room, all the while reminding himself not to go out of character. Berry told Butwin that he'd been paid half his fee before arriving at the Armory and demanded to be paid the rest of his fee, in cash, before he would walk out onstage. The promoter had been reluctant, but he'd paid up.

"Did you get paid yet?" Berry then asked Butwin.

"No, we didn't get paid," Butwin said. "We'll get paid at the end of the job."

"Are you crazy?" Berry said.

"No, that's how we've always done business."

"This is a one-night thing they put on," Berry said. "I can tell you what's going to happen. At the end of the show the promoters will be nowhere to be found. You won't get paid. The police won't get paid. The concessions people won't get paid. They will just be gone. These aren't regular promoters or anything. They scraped the money together to get this bundle of money, and they're going to be gone."

"I don't think so," Butwin said. "A friend of mine who got us the job knows these guys."

"I don't care what you're telling me. Don't be a dumb shit. You gotta stay on top of this."

Butwin got more excited as the conversation went on and finally came to the conclusion that he couldn't stay in English character any longer.

"Chuck, I have to tell you something," Butwin said. "I hope you're not going to be upset, but we are actually not an English group."

"What do you mean, you're not an English group?"

"Well, I'm just using that voice for us to appear tonight. So I'd like to use my regular voice in talking to you because I can't keep this up."

"Are you kidding me?"

"No. My name is Ron Butwin and I'm in this group."

"So which one is really you?"

"This is me. I don't know how we get paid before we go on. I've never done that."

"You come with me," Berry said.

He picked up his guitar case, and he and Butwin walked from the back of the Armory down a long restricted hallway to the box office at the front of the Armory. At the door of the box office, they were stopped by two huge men. "Gotta be like six foot eight, arms crossed, look like something out of a movie," said Butwin. Berry walked right up to them.

"Tell Steve and Mike that Chuck Berry's out here, and he needs to see them immediately," Berry said.

"They're not going to talk to you right now," one of the men said. "They're busy."

"I don't give a shit what they're doing," Berry said. "You tell them I want to talk to them, or I'm not going back on."

Butwin was already squirming and wondering what he'd gotten himself into. One of the men went inside and returned quickly.

"Come back after the show."

"Tell them, go fuck themselves, and they'd better let me see them right now," Berry said.

"I'm not going to say that to them."

"Well, you better."

The man went back inside and came back out.

"Come in," he said to Berry. "Don't bring the kid with you. Just you come in."

"I'm only coming in if the kid comes in with me."

"I'm good out here," said the petrified Butwin.

The door opened and Berry brought Butwin in with him. The room was full of men with cigars, creating a smoky haze as they counted out stacks of cash on a huge table. Everybody had a bulge under their coat, and one of the men had his hand inside his coat. Butwin was in a world he'd never experienced. He was afraid they were all going to get shot.

"Chuck, what do you want?" said the promoter, who clearly was not one of Berry's friends.

"I understand that the guys who are backing me now, not the guys you hired, are the Escapades," Berry said. "I want them to get paid now."

"What do you care about an English group?" the promoter said.

"These guys came up and played for me, and they're really good, and I want them paid now."

"That's not going to happen."

They proceeded to call each motherfuckers, back and forth, and one of the huge guys put his hand on his belt, revealing the butt end of a handgun. Butwin was thinking, "Oh, no, this is like out of every bad TV show I've ever seen. I'm a musician. I'm not supposed to be here. This is too much."

"You think you want to fool around with us?" said the man with his hand on his gun. "You got paid already. Now just leave us alone."

Though Butwin was scared to death, Berry wasn't the least bit fazed by the tough talk. He reached back, opened up his guitar case, and pulled out the biggest gun in the room.

"I'm thinking, 'What did I just get myself into?'" Butwin said. "I don't want to be standing next to him, because if they're going to be shooting, honest to God, I'm looking for the first table I can hide under. I'm a kid, nineteen years old. This is not something I want to partake in."

Berry and the promoter continued to argue back and forth, until finally the enforcer took his hand off his gun—a very good sign, in Butwin's estimation.

"Ah, fuck, all right," the promoter finally said. He handed a pile of cash to Butwin, who was more than ready to leave.

"Count it," Berry said.

"No, I'm okay with it," Butwin said.

"Count it," Berry repeated.

Butwin counted the money and, not surprisingly, found he was short $300.

"Pay him the whole amount," Berry told the promoter.

"Well, they're not done yet."

"I'm not going through that shit with you again. You get him paid right now."

Butwin was given the rest of his money. As he and Berry were leaving, the promoter had a parting comment.

"You're awfully lucky, kid. That's all I can tell ya."

As they walked back down the hallway to the stage, Butwin didn't know whether to be grateful to Berry for saving his life or angry for being put in that situation.

"Kid, now this is your lesson," Berry said as they walked. "Don't ever play, don't ever go somewhere, a plane or a car, without getting your money up front."

"Nobody pays that way here," Butwin said.

"I don't give a shit. It's your money. You can't trust anybody. I've played everywhere, and I don't trust one of them. And you don't tell anyone you got paid. It doesn't matter who they are. Just say, 'No, not yet, why?'"

When Butwin got back to his group, they asked him what happened.

"You won't believe it, but Chuck Berry helped us get paid," Butwin told them.

The Escapades played their next set and everything went fine. Berry's original backing band gave the Escapades dirty looks and then left the building. The Escapades went back out to play behind Chuck Berry during his second set. When the show was over, Berry lingered backstage.

"I just wanted to be here with you so you could see," he said.

"See what?"

"Just watch for a few more minutes."

A couple of St. Paul cops who'd worked security came up to the stage and asked the band if they got paid. Butwin followed Berry's advice and told them they had not been paid.

"I'm looking over at Rico, and they're going, 'What? You said . . .' Because they didn't hear what Chuck said. But they went along with it. They were good about it."

"You telling us the truth?" the cops said. "You better be telling us the truth."

"I am."

A few minutes later, the head of concessions comes up and says, "Did you get paid?"

"Now I start to see what's going on," Butwin said. "Everybody got stiffed. Everybody except Chuck Berry, and us, because he did that. That was a lesson I'll never forget. Not only was it cool that we played with him, but look what happened."

The other lesson Butwin learned was that it was possible to fool all of the people some of the time. Butwin thought it might be difficult to keep their secret from the local musicians he saw frequently at his day job at B-Sharp. But a few days after the Chuck Berry show, Jim Johnson of the Underbeats and Greg Maland of Gregory Dee and the Avanties were at B-Sharp, and though Butwin had seen them at the St. Paul Armory on New Year's Eve, neither recognized him as being the English drummer for Chuck Berry's backing band. The Escapades decided to continue with the English ruse for as long as they could keep it going. The question was, how could they play often enough in the Twin Cities while maintaining the fiction that they were from England? Butwin wanted to get the Escapades into the Marigold Ballroom in downtown Minneapolis, but he needed to pull another deception.

Butwin had grown up next door to his "Uncle" Don Swartz, owner and president of KMSP Channel 9 television, and Swartz's son, Stuart, who would run the station after his father retired in 1983. Channel 9 aired *A Date with Dino*, a *Bandstand*-type weekday afternoon show where Twin Cities high school kids would dance to records and local rock bands. The show was hosted by a deejay named George Murphy, who went by the pseudonym Dino Day. Teen news was reported by Nancy Nelson, who would later do Saturday night weather on WCCO-TV, produce and host a talk show on WTCN-TV, and anchor the local news in Los Angeles. Butwin showed Uncle Don a picture of his band and asked if he could get the Escapades on *A Date with Dino*. Don agreed. Butwin's next move was to have lunch with his booking agent friend Marsh Edelstein, who knew Butwin was working on a new act but didn't know what it was.

"You know that group that played with Chuck Berry called the Escapades?" Butwin said to Edelstein when they met.

"Yeah."

"That was my group."

"Bullshit," Edelstein said. "They had long hair and English accents."

"No," Butwin said, switching into his accent. "Yer wrong, y'see, because it was really our group."

"Yeah, bullshit."

"No, I'm not kidding. Here's a picture, that's my group. Look at that picture really well." Edelstein studied the picture and looked at Butwin.

"Yeah, is that really you?"

"Yes. Here's what I want to do. I want to play the ballroom. But we don't have enough songs to get through a full evening. If we could come in like it was the Beatles coming in, and you, Marsh, could say you liked them so much at Chuck Berry that you brought them in special as a one-time thing at the Marigold Ballroom with whatever groups are there that night. You'll rent a limo to pick us up at my house. We'll call you when we're leaving my house. And you can make the announcement that the Escapades have just landed and they're coming directly from the airport down to the Marigold to do a few songs, because they're passing through."

Edelstein thought the idea would work. Butwin told him he was talking to Don and Stu Swartz about appearing on *A Date with Dino*, and Edelstein suggested they do the TV show the same week as the Marigold appearance to hype the event. Butwin agreed and explained the plan to the band. "We get there an hour and a half, two hours before the show," Butwin said. "Dino's normal thing is he'd bring the group out, sit down with them on a stool, and he'd interview them a little bit and then they'd play a song. It was kind of a cheap man's version of *Shindig* or *Hullabaloo* or *Bandstand*. George [Dino] was a really nice guy. Don or Stuart had told him that we were not in fact English, but we were playing that part, and it was important to go along with this." Dino was willing to participate in the ruse, but he wasn't clear on the logistics of doing the interview. Where was the band supposed to be? Butwin suggested they take a page from *Shindig* or *Hullabaloo* and pretend to cut away to England for a transatlantic interview. The band would be seated on stools behind a curtain where the kids couldn't see them, and Dino would stand out front to do the video interview. Dino agreed. "So we're never going to appear in front of all these kids," Butwin said. "We're behind the stage and back far enough that the lights are on us but you can't see that from the front. They've got this split-screen television. Dino never says our names. He says the band's name. He says to me, 'You're the spokesman of the group,' and I say, "Y'know, we're so excited that we're going to be coming to Minnesota. Y'know, we were just there with Chuck Berry not too long ago.' I did most of the talking."

Even though the Escapades brought their equipment, they decided not to play after the interview, because the studio audience would hear it coming from backstage. "So that's how we approached it," Butwin said. "Of course, Marsh was really excited because it added a whole new dimension for him trying to get an audience, and Stuart loved it because it made it look like Channel 9 had this whole thing going on. It went over real well. We had to wait about an hour or so to make sure all the kids were gone, because kids would wait outside to try to get Dino's autograph. We just stayed there back in the dressing room."

There were plenty of radio ads hyping the Escapades' appearance at the Marigold Ballroom a few nights later, generating an extra buzz and a big crowd. Butwin recalls that the Underbeats and the Accents were also on the bill that night. Edelstein worked the crowd, telling them that the Escapades had just landed at the airport and should be arriving at the ballroom in about twenty minutes. The plan was to have the music stop and the kids go out onto the sidewalk to welcome the Escapades when they pulled up. "Nobody was onto us yet," Butwin said. "Maybe our best friends, but we told very few people. I remember my dad saying, 'You're never going to pull this off. It will never work.' Well, we pulled it off the first time."

When the Escapades arrived at the Marigold in a limousine, Edelstein had girls standing outside screaming hysterically at the car. "We're thinking, 'Holy shit,'" Butwin said. "Of course, we felt like the Beatles at that point. He'd arranged to have police around us. We're guarded all the way up to the back of the stage. The bands are there, standing around. We get in the back, and the guys start coming up to introduce themselves. I saw a couple of these guys that afternoon at B-Sharp. The glasses, the long hair—they've got no clue. I said to Tom Nystrom, 'Excuse me, would y'be willing to lend me yer trap set? We're gonna do a few songs, y'know?' So then one of the guys said to Tom, 'Would you like to use my guitar?' Everybody was real nice about letting us use their instruments, because I think they were excited about us."

The Escapades took the stage and prepared to play. "We'd like to welcome y'all here," Butwin said in his English accent. Then he attempted to set up a plausible reason why Twin Cities teens might be seeing a lot of the Escapades in the future: "We were just here not too long ago and had such a great time that we've decided we're going to come back here as much as we can." They played three or four songs by the Beatles, the Rolling Stones, and the Kinks. The girls screamed, the boys thought it was cool, and the bands were watching. "I'm thinking Tom Nystrom is going to recognize my drumming style, something's going to give us away," Butwin said. "Nothing gave us away. The idea was, as soon as we got done playing, we thanked the musicians onstage: 'We'd like to thank the groups for letting us use their equipment, thanks to Marsh, thanks to Channel 9'—it was like a paid ad." The Escapades were escorted by police back out to the limo, and they drove off—to St. Paul. They didn't have to bring any equipment. All they had to do was play a few songs and not get exposed as fakes. "I still revel in that," Butwin said. "It was fun, but it was a bigger deal than just having fun."

Unlike most new or reorganized bands, the Escapades came onto the scene as stars. Butwin gave out his home phone number for bookings and answered in his regular voice, saying he was the Escapades' agent. He began getting calls from Bill Diehl, Dick Shapiro, and other booking agents. Tim Kehr called, telling Butwin he'd seen the band at the Chuck Berry show and wanted to book them. Their secret held for a few months, thanks in part to Edelstein, who began booking them into the Marigold on a regular basis. "He's not good at keeping quiet, but he was on this, because it would mean money for him," Butwin said.

"To make sure nobody discovered us, we wanted to keep the illusion going for a while," Caplan said. "It was kind of sneaky, actually. We didn't want to take a chance of getting too close to anybody. These girls were going nuts. When we started playing more intimate settings, the girls wanted to touch our hair. We were really worried somebody was going to yank our wigs off. We hired a couple of guys as bodyguards. At Mr. Lucky's, these guys would walk us from the back of the place to the stage. The reason we did it was the wigs, but it created the illusion that you can't get near these guys. People weren't used to that. We kept that going for quite a while. Even the Underbeats would come to see us at Lucky's."

"I think Jim Johnson had a pretty good idea," Butwin said. "I'd see him at B-Sharp, and I think it probably started to compute."

"We played someplace where this girl was coming on to me big-time," Caplan said. "I was outside talking to her. She grabbed my wig and pulled, but it was on pretty good and it didn't come off. I said, 'Ow!' and she said, 'My God, it's real!'"

When they played Dayton's Top 10 Club, hundreds of girls surrounded them and trapped them in their eighth floor dressing room. There was no use trying to make it down to the street level; security called up to say they'd be mobbed there, too. They simply waited it out in the dressing room. "We never made up names," Butwin said. "Rico was a total unknown. None of the other musicians knew him. So eventually we would talk about Rico. It was a unique name to be using. And we were safe with that for a while. This went on for a while, but we knew our days were going to be numbered as far as pulling it off."

The first time Bill Diehl booked the band was at the Marian K. C. Ballroom in Bloomington. "We were doing the English thing, and he took me aside because he knew I was the leader," Butwin said. "The sense was, 'How come you're here so much?' It was one thing for a couple months to say we liked being here. I would make sure to get us bookings out of town. We might be down in Rochester or down in Iowa. I'd book us away from here so that it would appear we were coming back. After a while that got tired, and the rumors had already started, so we finally let it be known that we were really a local group. But we continued to keep the look. Many people were like, 'Holy shit, why didn't you tell me? I see you all the time.' By that point we could get rid of the wigs, and we did."

"Our hair was longer," Caplan said. "It didn't look like the wigs, but it was longer. Then we didn't have the bodyguards. Eventually everybody knew." By then, most Minnesota rockers were letting their hair grow long, but the Escapades had jumped on the trend sooner than most, and it had paid off. They were playing regularly at Mr. Lucky's and Big Reggie's Danceland, having moved very close in status to the Big Three. "There were the Underbeats, the Accents, and the Avanties, and now we were coming in from a whole different direction than any of the other groups," Butwin said. "Everywhere we played, we were a big draw. In the summer of 1965, I think we had fifty-eight or fifty-nine dates out of sixty days. We were making good money. We really had our say of where we wanted to play, who we wanted to play with, how we wanted to play. Bill Diehl didn't have any hold on us like he did with the Underbeats, the Accents, and the Avanties. He had a grip on everybody. Me, he had no grip. I booked when I wanted, where I wanted. If we really had big crowds in Rochester and a guy was offering $500 more than anyone else, we'd probably do Rochester. I was looking for our benefit, because I knew we were now not the group we started. We played every bit as well, even better, but we weren't the group that everybody thought we were."

As the rock cliché goes, behind the scenes things were falling apart. Butwin believed the Escapades' increasing popularity coincided with the inflation of Rosenbaum's ego—apparently with good reason. "I remember Rico being one of the best-looking musicians I'd ever seen," said Chris Nelson of the More-Tishans. "We'd been around for a while, and I knew a little bit, though I never claimed to be a great guitar player. But the chords he was playing, I had no idea what he was doing. And he had a voice like an angel."

"It was the old story, 'a legend in his own mind,'" Butwin said. "He got to be very arrogant about it and made it hard. He didn't work well with a couple of guys in the group. I was always the peacemaker. He would terrorize one of the guys all the time, verbally. The candle burned too bright."

Butwin and Caplan believed at first that the personality clashes alone made it hard for the band to rehearse and eventually led to the demise of the Escapades. But there was another factor at work: Jim Johnson was reconfiguring the Underbeats into an all-star band, and he had his eyes on Rico. "I said, 'Have you heard the Escapades? Let's go to Lucky's,'" Johnson said. "That was Rico. I heard Rico, and I said, "Sorry, Ray [Berg], this kid is too good. I got to get him."

"All of a sudden, Jim Johnson started courting Rico, and I could see what that was going to lead to," Butwin said. "They had a good group, Johnson was a good singer, and there was a rumor that he wanted Nystrom, and Nystrom hinted to me one time when we were together that he might break away and start a group with Jim and Rico."

During a gig one night, Rosenbaum told the Escapades he was leaving the group. "I'll finish the dates that we have set," he said.

Butwin noticed Jim Johnson was standing out in the audience, looking at Rosenbaum.

"Are you leaving to go with Jim?" he asked.

"I don't know," Rosenbaum said. "Maybe."

The Escapades usually went out to eat together after a job, but that night Rosenbaum told the others he was leaving with Johnson rather than going out with the band. The rest of the Escapades gathered at a restaurant. "Look, this group, this persona we have in town, is going to be over," Butwin told Caplan and bassist Terry Bellows, who were upset about Rosenbaum's impending departure. "I don't think we can re-create it the same way. I don't know if it's necessary to re-create it. We'll try some people. We already know pretty much who's out there. And Rico is a whole different person now. Let's just play out our stuff and be on the watch for someone else to take his place, but I don't think we're going to be able to do it. Not locally."

"We thought we could replace him, but what for?" Caplan said. "It wouldn't be the same. It was one of those unique deals where you had the right guys together at the right

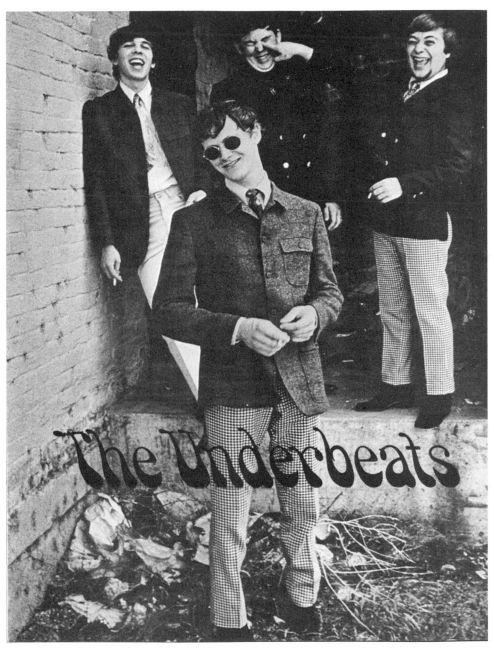

The new Underbeats lineup: *(from left)* Rico Rosenbaum, Jim Johnson, Tom Nystrom, and Doni Larson. Courtesy of Steve Kaplan.

time. There was no point in trying to replace him. We didn't know anybody who would replace him properly. Rico was purposely being an asshole to make it easier to get out. We knew that, but it wasn't a good scene. It kind of ended on a sour note, because of the way he chose to do it. We were pissed, but after a while, for me personally, I knew Jim Johnson and Doni Larson well. I was hanging out with Jim. I just blew it off."

"Zippy and I hung out, even after I took Rico out of the Escapades," Johnson said. "I still hear from Ron Butwin. We're still Laurel and Hardy freaks."

The Escapades accepted no more bookings and played their last job at the end of August. Rosenbaum jumped to the Underbeats before Nystrom did. "The deal was, 'Tom, you quit your band, and I'll get Rico,'" Johnson said. "Then Rico came first and said, 'I thought you were going to get Tom.'" Nystrom came over to the Underbeats shortly thereafter, giving Johnson his dream band. "When we got together, we had the voices, the harmonies," Johnson said. "I went out and chose the best of the crop. I ended up with the band that was just killer. I loved that band."

"I was always intimidated by seeing Jim Johnson and trying to talk to him," said Phil Berdahl of the Stillroven. "It was like talking to George Harrison. They were our idols, the band most bands in town wanted to sound like. When they got Rico from the Escapades and Tom Nystrom from the Accents, their singing was perfect. We went out to a ballroom in Plymouth one night to hear them. The *Rubber Soul* album had just come out. They did four songs from the album, and they sounded just like the Beatles. The singing, guitar tone, drumming [were] just perfect. They were so tight. People would dance, but most people would just stand and watch those guys. They were that good."

"I remember seeing them and being knocked out at how good these guys were," said Owen Husney, now in the music business in Los Angeles. "Jim Johnson was the real deal. They could still be touring today."

Larson said Johnson never picked a fight in the more than fifty years he's known him, yet he described him as a "bad ass—he don't take no shit." Shortly after Nystrom and Rosenbaum joined the Underbeats, Johnson got into a brawl at a Wisconsin gig. "A guy smashed a microphone into his mouth because the guy's girlfriend had been flirting with Jim while he was singing," Larson said. "He threw the guitar down and took off after the guy in the audience. I told Rico and Nystrom, 'Whatever you do, don't stop playing.' We saw the seas [the audience] part, and then we saw the guy's feet go over a railing. Jim came back to the stage while everybody applauded and finished 'Johnny B. Goode.' Tom and Rico were wondering what they'd gotten themselves into, but to me it was standard operating procedure, especially in Wisconsin. The only time he would do that was when something like that would happen. He's got a five-minute temper: five minutes go by, and it's over."

The new Underbeats created an almost seismic shift in the structure of the Twin Cities rock 'n' roll scene. The Accents had been molded around Tom Nystrom's voice, and now he was gone. Dave Maetzold had quit the Avanties, and Greg Maland would soon be looking for a new band. To create a fuller sound, Johnson would soon pluck keyboard player James Walsh from the Hot Half Dozen, who scored a local hit with a cover of Martha and the Vandellas' "Heat Wave." And just as they were closing the gap on the Big Three, the Escapades had lost Rico Rosenbaum and were breaking up. The big bang from the Big Three had further ramifications. Zip Caplan ended up playing lead guitar with the Accents for a while, Frank Prout moved to the High Spirits, and Bill Miller and Terry Bellows joined the Avanties (Bellows later joined the TaBS, a Tim Kehr–managed band with Bill Strandlof on guitar). Rod Eaton joined T. C. Atlantic, and Ron Butwin drummed with the Del Counts and the Chancellors. The times were changing, but there was no lack of

Jim Johnson of the Underbeats raided the Escapades and the Accents to put together his dream band in 1966. The Underbeats' lineup then was *(from left)* Rico Rosenbaum, Tom Nystrom, Jim Johnson, and *(seated)* Doni Larson. Courtesy of Doni Larson.

work if you were an established rocker. "In those days, if you played, you played all the time," Caplan said. "When I was in the Accents, we were playing five or six times a week, sometimes twice [a day]. We were cleaning up, making good money. The amount they paid us then was good dough, though it would be crap today. Guys were living large and buying new sports cars."

Opposite: Like most of the top Twin Cities bands, the Underbeats got their equipment from B-Sharp Music in Minneapolis. They used the back of the B-Sharp building for this promotional photo in 1966. From left: Rico Rosenbaum, Tom Nystrom, Jim Johnson, and Doni Larson. Courtesy of Doni Larson.

Going into 1966, there were more bands playing than ever, but the Underbeats were the undisputed kingpins. Butwin now believes none of this was accidental. "The true story, Tom Nystrom told me years and years later, is this," Butwin said. "Bill Diehl didn't like that he didn't have control of us. He was always very nice to us [the Escapades], and we booked a lot of jobs with him when he and Dick Shapiro were partners, but they had no hold. He wined and dined us, so to speak. The way that Nystrom said it was, there were the top three groups, and Bill Diehl had control of where they worked and how they worked, and made a pretty good income from all this. What's going to happen when we, number four, show up and start rocking that whole boat? Some of the other

The Underbeats were always a top draw at teen dance locations like the Bel Rae Ballroom. Courtesy Denny Johnson of Minniepaulmusic.com.

Jim Johnson was considered the Twin Cities' premiere lead guitarist when the Underbeats were at their peak in the mid-1960s. Courtesy of Denny Johnson of Minniepaulmusic.com.

groups are starting to do more English music because there's a group doing it, and they're so popular. We're new on the block and these guys are coming to see us play."

Diehl had combined forces with Dick Shapiro to form Central Booking Alliance, the most powerful booking agency in the state. David Anthony returned from Korea in 1965 to resume his booking agency, which represented the Rave-Ons, among others. And Marsh Edelstein had begun booking the Del Counts and other bands. "Bill Diehl went to Jim Johnson and said, 'We need to get the Escapades out of the picture,'" Butwin said. "'They're changing this Big Three concept we've got, where we have control over how much you get paid. They're changing the marketplace.' It's the old story that you either have to buy your competition or make them disappear. Then Tom said, 'Bill Diehl said to us, if we do form that group with Johnson and Nystrom and Rico and maybe Jim Walsh, it eliminates the Escapades as we know it, and I'm back to the Big Three. I'll book you guys.'"

Butwin said Diehl was not concerned about hurting the Accents by taking out Nystrom. "I think he figured he'd end up

Enrico "Rico" Rosenbaum *(right)* had been the missing element that gave the Escapades the musicality and stage appeal to move into the upper echelon of Twin Cities bands. Courtesy of Denny Johnson of Minniepaulmusic.com.

with something bigger," Butwin said. "And he'd still be able to handle the Accents. They'll get somebody else, and that'll be okay. Tom said, 'You know, Ron, that's the way it was. There was a campaign basically to bust you guys up as soon as possible, because you were affecting [the business].'"

Diehl's memory is remarkable at age eighty-eight, but he was so busy in those days that he can barely remember the bands, much less the individuals in them. "I wasn't with the bands," Diehl said. "I hardly knew the personnel. If you asked me to name five people from all the bands we worked with, I could name Rod Eaton, Mike Waggoner, Skip Dahlin, Tony Andreason—a dark-haired, good-looking kid—and Dal Winslow. I can see his face, but I can't tell you a thing about him."

Jim Johnson couldn't imagine doing anything else but play with his terrific new band.

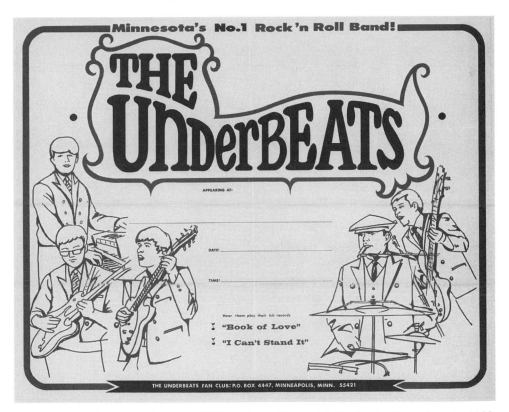

It was not hyperbole for the Underbeats to bill themselves as Minnesota's Number 1 rock 'n' roll band in 1966. With Rico Rosenbaum on guitar, Tom Nystrom on drums, and James Walsh on keyboards—all fine singers—the band could perform a dazzling variety of styles. Courtesy of Mike Jann.

Not only were they the most popular band in town: they often opened for top national touring acts. He had a special fondness for the gigs the Underbeats played with the Everly Brothers. "They were such nice people," Johnson said. "Don was so cordial. They had a five-piece band—the brothers, bass, lead guitar, and drummer. Jimmy Gordon played drums with them the first time I saw him, and Tony Love was the bass player. The second time I saw them it was Sonny Curtis on lead guitar. The last time we played with them was in Mankato. We were talking backstage. We'd released 'Sweet Words of Love,' and they wanted to know if they could do it. Sonny gave me a card and said, 'If you make it to L.A., call me.'"

It was clear that if any band in the Twin Cities was going places, it was the Underbeats. As it turned out, however, Johnson was the only one who was going someplace: Vietnam. "A few months later I got drafted."

"I had my first marijuana on account of Jim's draft status," Lonnie Knight said. "None of us had done any drugs whatsoever, and Jim brought home a little baggie with four or five prerolled joints he'd gotten from somewhere. He said, 'If I smoke this stuff, I'll be a junkie and they won't take me.' We each took one joint, went into a closet, put a towel under the door, and smoked it like a cigarette. We didn't inhale, so we couldn't figure out what the big deal was. I didn't [get high], that's for sure."

And Johnson didn't get out of the army. By late 1966, he was headed for basic training.

RUN, RUN, RUN

MANKATO, MINNESOTA, is actually two towns separated by the Minnesota River: Mankato proper, with forty thousand residents, and North Mankato, with thirteen thousand. The metropolitan area, a cultural hub in the middle of rich farm country, is located seventy-eight miles south of Lake Street and Nicollet Avenue in Minneapolis, the epicenter of Minnesota rock in the 1960s.

Dale Menten was born in Mankato in 1945, then moved across the river with his family.

"We were from North Mankato," Menten said. "Mankato was the elite side of the river, and the image of North Mankato was kind of like where the poor people go to live. Our family wasn't rich. Dad gave us what we needed and Mom got a job at the school lunchroom, so we were okay. Most of the people in North Mankato kind of resented that [image], because a lot of us weren't dirt poor. But we weren't like some of the people up on Sumner Hill, with millions."

His family was deeply musical: his father, Peter, was a drummer, and his aunts and uncles played fiddle, accordion, piano, and guitar. His grandfather was a German violin maker who sold most of his instruments to tourists from the United States, so he decided to leave Germany and move to where the customers were. They ended up in Lake Washington, Minnesota, a few miles northeast of Mankato, and soon came to realize that no one wanted to buy a violin made in Lake Washington, Minnesota. The Mentens turned to farming. "Which is a lot like if I were to turn to farming," Dale Menten said. "It wouldn't work well. And it didn't work well. What he was good at, though, was he had twenty-one kids. He had that part down. Two wives, twenty-one kids. The last wife had five kids, the first wife, all the rest. There's a lot of us all over the place."

Menten's mother played piano. When it came time for him to learn an instrument, it had to be the piano. "It was just required to stay in the family," Menten said. "Otherwise you'd be shipped away. I did that a while. I'm going back to that now because I'm playing more and more piano, and I have to get back to scales and things, which I was really fairly good at, as good as you can get when you're five or six years old. But back then it wasn't exciting."

What was exciting was the guitar, an instrument that was becoming prominent in the pop music of the mid-1950s. "No, we'd have none of that, because we had a piano in the house, and that's what you did," Menten said. "I did it until I was able to say, 'I can't do this anymore. Can I change?' Well, I could—to drums. Because dad was a drummer." Menten played drums in the marching band and in orchestra through junior high. "I was always the guy who had the big marching drum that has the bracket on your thigh so that when you're done, blood is running down your inner thigh. And sometimes you're marching at ten below—nothing works at ten below, except that blood still oozes, and now it's freezing. So I said, 'Mom, I can't do this anymore. I'm going to lose a leg—this is awful.'"

In the orchestra, Menten was supposed to do cymbal crashes but believes it was undiagnosed ADD that made it almost impossible for him to count bars patiently until the right moment. He would lose track of where the orchestra was, take a guess, and come in with a crash at the wrong time. "The orchestra leader looked at me, and I could tell in his eyes that if he could fire me, I was fired," Menten said. "So I fired myself. I quit."

A junior high substitute teacher named Jim Sharp invited Menten and his pal Arnie Marshall ("Arnie was worse than I was, he was just a troublemaker—I was the follower") to his house in North Mankato, where he gave them cookies and showed them his guitar.

"He sat down and started playing some stuff, and we went, 'Wow! Look at your fingers—that's cool!'" Menten said. "He was playing the things that worked then, a lot of little licks, southern-flavored things that we never heard on the radio. From that moment on, Arnie and I both just said, 'We're leaving this world of crime, and we're going to do this.'" Menten and Marshall both bought guitars at Backlund's Music Store in Mankato, the gathering place for musicians from around the area. "Up here [Minneapolis] it was B-Sharp, down there it was Backlund's," Menten said. "We'd go there after school every day. We'd go through their albums to see if they had the new Lonnie Mack album, or whatever. And over here on an amp was Jimmy McGuire, sitting there going like this, doodle-oodle-oodle-do, playing Kenny Burrell and doing Howard Roberts. We're sitting there saying, 'He's playing notes I don't have on my guitar.'"

All novice players have to decide whether it's worth the pain of sore, callused fingers to keep going, but Menten found that when he was writing songs, he kept playing the same chords over and over again because he was motivated to finish the song. "So I went through the callus thing quickly," Menten said. "When they broke open, it was, 'Just keep going.' I would try putting Band-Aids on them, and that didn't work, so I just kept writing. I got fairly proficient just because I was writing songs. Obviously, I stayed within a certain number of chords until I discovered that you could use your finger and do bar chords—wow. This opened up a whole new world of keys for me. Then when I discovered the capo, at first I thought it was cheating. Now I love it."

Menten and Marshall put a little band together with a drummer, but no bass player, and played for parties—the first time they were ever invited to parties. Though he lettered in baseball, Menten wasn't considered a cool kid at school—more of a class clown—and in crossing the river to attend Mankato High School, he felt as though he'd lost most of his friends. There were cliques in high school that Menten said survive in Mankato to this day. His guitar was the secret password that got him into parties and pushed him ahead socially. "Because Arnie and I continued to play, there was this little rumor that Menten is writing some stuff, he plays guitar," Menten said. "I got asked by some of the kids on the other side to just get together and play. We had little bands start and stop, and that was better than sports for me, because I got to keep playing. I got to keep writing, and throughout high school I did that."

Tom Klugherz was born in Mankato in 1946, the youngest of seven children. His father was a watchmaker for thirty-eight years at Stan A. Smith Jewelry, and his mother was the head of the cafeteria at Loyola High School. Neither of Klugherz's parents was musical, but he got the bug from watching Ricky Nelson on the *Adventures of Ozzie and Harriet*. "I wanted to be Rick Nelson," Klugherz said. "That's all I cared about—I wanted to do that."

He was further motivated by watching his neighbor, Bob Drengler, and Drengler's friend Jim McGuire—both in local bands—play their guitars. When he was thirteen years old, Klugherz walked into Backlund's Music Store with $5 in his pocket and walked out with a brand-new acoustic guitar that cost $23. Owner Dave Boyce had never seen Klugherz in his life but simply asked for his father's name, address, and phone number. Klugherz paid the rest on time, using money from his paper route. A year later, when Klugherz told Boyce he wanted to start a band, Boyce told him he knew a twelve-year-old kid in North Mankato named Bruce Waterston who was a really good drummer. Klugherz called Waterston, and they ended up assembling a band that also included Steve Nitke on bass, Pat Reagan, and Dan Coughlin.

"I was the only Mankato boy," Klugherz said. "I was from the wrong side of the river. We thought North Mankato was the wrong side of the river. All I know is that if you were from Mankato and you went over there, you got beat up. But I didn't because I was in a band. We practiced at my house a lot, too. Bruce would ride over with his cymbals on the handlebars. At that time, we'd either practice at Bruce's house or my house. I supposedly played lead guitar, but I was never any good at it."

Waterston, on the other hand, was very good. "Bruce would play a half-hour drum solo because we didn't have enough songs," Klugherz said. "For being twelve years old, he was one of the best drummers I ever heard. Just incredible. He was small, a cocky little guy, and very smart. He was never wrong. If he said something, you could take it to the bank."

They called themselves the Mark V and played at the YWCA for $15 a night, then went to Pizza Kato and spent all their earnings. They played together for a couple of years, until 1961, performing songs like Sandy Nelson's "Let There Be Drums," "Wild Weekend," ("That was the only song I could play," Klugherz said), and "Bonie Maronie." Then they met Gus Dewey.

Daniel Gregg "Gus" Dewey was from North Mankato. Dale Menten knew him because Dewey played a four-string Stella tenor guitar in a little group called the Nairobi Trio that would dress up in gorilla suits and play for class functions. "Gus was a brilliant guy," Menten said. "He was my first real sad guy. I always thought during school I was sad. I was kind of introverted, and in Gus I'd found my counterpart. I thought, 'Wow, you're as dreary as I can be, that's really great.' We both loved Roy Orbison, especially all

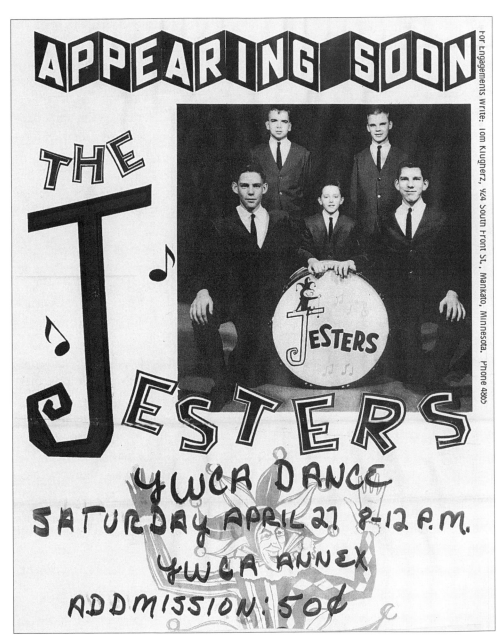

APPEARING SOON

THE JESTERS

For engagements write: Tom Klughertz, 924 South Front St., Mankato, Minnesota. Phone 4865

YWCA DANCE
SATURDAY APRIL 27 8-12 P.M.
YWCA ANNEX
ADDMISSION: 50¢

The Mark V evolved into the Jesters. The name (and personnel) would change again. Courtesy of Mike Gretz.

the dreary ones like 'Only the Lonely.' It was so great, we can just wallow in this grief. We became really good friends."

Dewey also had a car, which was a big deal for a band because he could pull an equipment trailer. The Mark V started practicing in Dewey's garage, and as far as Klugherz knew, Dewey was merely the group's roadie/manager. "Then I come to find out they're practicing without me," Klugherz said. "One day they said, 'We don't need you in the band anymore.' It was my band!" Menten was asked to come in and play lead guitar with the group that was now calling itself the Jesters, and Dewey was learning to play rhythm on a six-string guitar. "Some weeks later Gus called me," Klugherz said. "He said, 'We're getting rid of Steve Nitke. Do you want to play bass?' I didn't know anything about playing bass. So I ended up going over there and practicing playing Steve's bass. They didn't tell him we were practicing without him."

"We forced Tom to learn how to play bass," Menten said. "'You go play bass.' 'I don't even own a bass.' 'We'll get you a bass.' So he became a bass player. The little drummer [Waterston] was about this big, and he had to be [only about] thirteen years old. He had a full set, but it was kind of rigged up differently because he couldn't reach the pedals. He was young, but he was good." They played high school dances through the winter and spring of Menten's senior year in 1963. "Dale was a bag boy at Madsen's grocery store in Mankato," Klugherz said. "We learned a bunch of songs with Dale, and we had some gigs. Some nights we would play a teen dance that started at 8 or 9, and Dale couldn't be there for the first set because he was working at Madsen's until 9 o'clock."

The Jesters continued to perform through 1963 and into 1964, and Menten continued to write songs. Like so many guitarists of that era, he was influenced by Lonnie Mack. "That, to me, was quick fingers," Menten said. "On the Gestures [as the band came to be called] stuff you could tell I was trying to mimic a lot of those double-stop things, because Lonnie Mack did it." He was also influenced by Roy Orbison, the Everly Brothers, and Buddy Holly, but the more he wrote, the less he listened to other artists. "I was becoming prolific," he said. "I was just annoying. Maybe I turned off the influence faucets a little bit."

Sometime during that period he came up with a near-perfect two minutes and twenty seconds of guitar-driven teen urgency called "Run, Run, Run," a song referred to by All-Music's Richie Unterberger as "a stone classic." The song began with an ascending staccato guitar riff and is then pounded forward by Waterston's propulsive drumming. The lyric is the usual teenage lament—"There I was all alone, waiting for you to phone, but you were out with another guy, why, oh, why, oh why?"—and yet each syllable seems to fit

The Jesters played a number of dances at Mankato High School. Courtesy of Dale Menten.

perfectly into the tight pocket created by the band. "Maybe I wrote because it was easier to sing my own tunes than to learn someone else's, because they were harder," Menten said. "And back then, the vinyl we had to go off of, you could not hear a word."

Menten wrote the opening guitar lick on "Run, Run, Run" and played it on his Fender Stratocaster, a guitar he no longer has. "It probably came from something we'd all heard, or something I was playing before," Menten said. "Because it was pretty basic—maybe one of those East Coast vocal groups with three guys. I know I ripped it [off], because it

Northside's Own Beatles

IT HAD to come sooner or later. Now North Mankato has its own Beatle band, a largely Mankato high group known as The Jesters. The gathering at which they're performing, above, started out as a warm weather rehearsal but ended up as an open air concert for the 900 Block Nicollet ave. neighborhood. The Jesters, left to right above, are Tom Klugherz, Gus Dewey, Dale Menten and Bruce Waterston. Leader Dewey does a vocal in inset at left. The little girl pointing at far right seems to notice Jester drummer Waterston is a ringer for Beatle beater Ringo. (Free Press Photos)

The Jesters were big news in Mankato even before they hit the national charts. Courtesy of Dale Menten.

was a rip-able thing. If I were to do that again today, I don't think I'd do that. But I'd have to do something. Whether I thought it was going to be a hit—I don't know, I was writing a lot of things. I don't know if this one was the hippest, but it seemed to be kind of more commercial. It kind of has a driving thing. We were listening to stuff that had that kind of thing going on. People try to figure out what makes a hit. I don't think you can. It's a whole series of things that have to be aligned just perfectly."

Everything was in alignment on "Run, Run, Run." The Jesters taped that song and a few other Menten originals on a little Wollensak recorder and took the tape to deejay Bob Sparrow at KYSM, Mankato's rock radio station. "It's like, 'Okay, how do we get it out of Mankato?'" Menten said. "Minneapolis to me was the place that I wanted to be. Whenever I knew Mom and Dad were sleeping, I would sneak out the bedroom window. A couple of guys from my class would pick me up in a Volkswagen, and we'd come up and we'd go to the

Dale Menten *(left)* and Gus Dewey *(center)* teamed with Waterston *(rear)* and Klugherz to form the final version of the Jesters. Courtesy of Dale Menten.

Embers [all-night restaurant] on 494 and have a huge Emberger Royal and fries. They'd drive me home and I'd climb back in the window. That was Minneapolis to me. We realized this was the music mecca. 'How do we get into this?'"

Sparrow listened to the Jesters' tape and thought it was good, but said he couldn't do much with it. Sparrow contacted Jim Madison, the owner of Golden Wing Records who'd recorded and released Dave Dudley's "Six Days on the Road." "He was a big part of Dave Dudley, and he was feeling good," Menten said. "We come in there, and we're not country. He's ready to diversify, and he hears us, and he thinks, 'Yeah.'" Madison put together a recording session for the Jesters at Kay Bank Studio on August 16, 1964, and brought in KDWB deejay Lou Riegert to help with the session. Riegert was not necessarily a fan of all the local rock bands—he hated "Surfin' Bird"—but when he heard the Jesters, he knew they had something.

"When Jim Madison brought 'Run, Run, Run' to me, I said, 'It sounds pretty good, but it's missing something,'" Riegert said. "He introduced me to the group, I went into the session, and he had me produce this thing. I had no piece of the group, the record, or the publishing. It was just fun for me. I was in my midtwenties, the fun phase of my life, and those guys were all adorable, not too much younger than me. Bruce Waterston, the tousle-headed blond kid, made that group. When they went out on the road, the girls all fell in love with Bruce Waterston."

In the studio with the Jesters, Riegert told the band the beat of the song had to be punched up. "Why don't you have Bruce pound on the bass drum on the beat?" he suggested. Waterston did as he was asked, even though he had to stand up behind the bass drum to do it. The effect of doubling the pace of the bass drum beat on the "Run, run, run, run baby" lyric worked like magic, however, turning a good song into a great rock 'n' roll record.

"I'm not sure if he [Riegert] was the one who decided 'Run, Run, Run' was going to be the A-side," Klugherz said. "When we sent it to Bob Sparrow, we had 'It Seems to Me' as the A-side, and we had this 'Run, Run, Run' song on the other side. Somebody decided, 'No, it's "Run, Run, Run" for the A-side.' 'It Seems to Me' was just so unique. All the Minneapolis bands were doing copies, and our stuff was original. Everybody said we were, like, British, but we were pre-Beatles. It wasn't the Minneapolis sound either, because we didn't sound like any of the other bands. We all recorded at Kay Bank, but if you listen to *Big Hits of Mid-America*, our stuff sounds way better than that stuff. Even the quality of the recording of 'It Seems to Me'—somehow ours sounds better."

"The day we recorded 'Olds-Mo-William,' the Jesters were waiting in line to record 'Run, Run, Run,'" said Dave Maetzold of Gregory Dee and the Avanties. "That's when I met Dale. When they started singing, I looked at Greg and said, 'Man, is that good. I don't know, comparing our song with "Run, Run, Run," I don't know.' Greg said, 'Well, it's a different style.'"

Menten doesn't think much of the sound quality that the band achieved at Kay Bank or the quality of the pressing of the record. "Most people don't realize this, but 'Run, Run, Run' was in the key of B minor," Menten said. "On the recording, Tom Klugherz's bass line is in B major. So there's not a minor third in there; he's going to a straight third, a real third. And yet, the recording quality is so horrible, you can't even hear it. Well, you can a little bit. He's just so embarrassed by it now. But who cares? There may have been a bass player in the front row who laughed or thought, 'That's really cool how they're combining two modes like that.' Thankfully, the recording quality is just horrible, so you couldn't tell."

The Kay Bank/Soma connection was at work again; the single "Run, Run, Run" / "It Seems to Me" was being prepared for release on the Soma label in September 1964 when somebody discovered that there was a band called Troy Seals and the Jesters playing out of Shreveport, Louisiana. There was also a California band called the Jesters—a surf-rock group fronted by lead guitarist Jim Messina, later of Buffalo Springfield, and Loggins and Messina. The Minnesota Jesters had to come up with a new name even as their records were being pressed. "So it was like, 'Who do we want to be, the Boomerangs or something?'" Menten said. "I said, 'How about just get close, like the Gestures?'" Dewey was afraid it would be interpreted as an obscene gesture, but Menten disagreed. "On the other hand, I thought, 'Why is that bad?'" Menten said. "So we went with that. A lot of people

After recording their national hit "Run, Run, Run," the Jesters were forced to change their name and became the Gestures. Courtesy of Dale Menten.

scratched their heads—'The Gestures?' Whatever. Nobody had time to think, because it was ready to go, the contract was signed."

As KDWB's music director, Riegert was able to get the record into the hands of deejays and music directors he knew around the country, including tastemakers Bobby Dale—formerly of KDWB—in Los Angeles and Tom Donahue in San Francisco. "I got them to include this record on their record sheets," Riegert said. "I was instrumental only in that I helped with the producing and got the record to guys I knew, and I'll be damned if it didn't make it to [Number] 44 on the *Billboard* charts." It did a lot better than that in specific markets. Of course, it was a smash in both Mankato and the Twin Cities, where it received its first airplay. Menten didn't recall exactly where he was when he first heard "Run, Run, Run" played on the radio but said it was a kick. Klugherz remembered hearing it at the A&W Drive-In in Mankato. "The radio station in town played it every ten minutes," he said. "Everybody would point to us and say, 'That's those guys.' We were pretty proud about that. Locally, regionally, it took off right away. We started doing gigs in South Dakota, Iowa, and we started opening for other acts."

Menten was attending Mankato State College when "Run, Run, Run" was released. Because the school did not offer a music major in guitar, Menten became a psychology major—something that probably came in handy during the following year as a touring musician.

"Run, Run, Run" eventually went Top 10 in San Jose, Seattle, Phoenix, Des Moines, Buffalo, Providence, Tucson, San Bernardino, and Calgary, and Top 20 in Miami, Los Angeles, San Francisco, Salem, Vancouver, Columbus, Boise, San Diego, and Akron. If anything, the record took off too fast. It was often unavailable when fans around the country went to their local record stores to buy it. "We had no idea that Amos would be that lame on getting product out," Menten said. "Soma gave us no support at all. When they weren't able to get distribution, they put all of us in a van, and we drove to Detroit to talk to the people at a big distributor. [Soma] was begging them to distribute to the East Coast. It was Number 3 or Number 5 in New York City, but there wasn't one record there. It was called a turntable hit back then. We found out that people didn't like Amos—'We're not working with that guy.' I think it was because he wouldn't give them things."

Whether the record was available or not, the Gestures had to get out on the road and support it. For lack of anyone else to take on the job, Lou Riegert assumed the role of the band's manager. Riegert and Madison formed a company called Dawn Enterprises, which essentially owned the band. "If Soma had distributed them properly, they would have sold more records and gotten more support for follow-ups," Riegert said. "I wasn't a producer. I just helped them. You gotta get professional help. I was just doing my radio career."

Amos Heilicher was a personable man who seemed more concerned about his artists' physical welfare than their financial success. "I remember one time in the winter we went into Amos's office," Klugherz said. "He said, 'Where are your overshoes? You kids should not be out there walking around without overshoes.' That's the only thing about him I really remember. We bought clothing, including Mohair suits, and charged everything to Soma Records. They paid for it."

"Before the record came out, we weren't playing very much—dumb little things, and not for much money," Menten said. "We'd play a lot at the North Mankato Armory, Olivia, Lamberton, stuff like that. You go there for $125, and oh, God, back then that was big-time money. When the record came out, it was charting real high here, and it was breaking out in Oklahoma City. At that time, Gus was keeping the books, because his

Soma Recording Company conducted a promotional campaign for "Run, Run, Run," but the single stalled just outside the national Top 40 because many markets could not get copies of the record. Courtesy of Dale Menten.

mom owned the van. So we said, 'Well, since we're using your mom's van, you can keep the books.' So he was kind of a quasi-leader. We were all such prima donnas in a way, we all wanted to lead. But we said, 'No, Gus, it's your van, it's your football, it's your game.'"

Each member drew a $125 a week salary from the band's bank account whether they were playing or not. Then Dewey got a call from two bookers from Minneapolis who wanted to talk business. When Dewey met with the rest of the band members the next day, he was elated.

"We're there," he exulted. "We have ninety jobs booked over the next year. Ninety jobs!"

"How much per job, Gus?" they asked.

"A hundred-fifty dollars."

"Gus, are you crazy? We have a Number 1 record in Minneapolis. These guys sat you down and gave you a burger and some fries, and you do that for a hundred-fifty bucks, on dates and places they can fill in whenever they want?" The band asked Jim Madison to bring in a lawyer to help them break the contract, which was in fact legal. At that point, Riegert and Madison decided to book the band themselves. "It wasn't a lot better, because Lou wasn't a booker, and Madison was a part-time butcher at a grocery store in North Minneapolis," Menten said.

Before "Run, Run, Run," the Gestures' biggest shows were at the Municipal Building in North Mankato, where two friends would hire them to play once a month to ever-increasing crowds. After "Run, Run, Run" became a smash, they were scheduled to play at the Municipal Building on Sunday, November 22, 1964. Promoter Herb Martinka called the band and offered them $500 not to play, because he had the Everly Brothers at the Kato Ballroom and was afraid the Gestures' gig would kill his attendance. "We're playing, unless you want to pay us to open for the Everly Brothers," Dewey told him. A couple of hours later, Martinka called back and booked them as the Everly Brothers' opening act. The show drew 2,400 fans, breaking the Kato's previous attendance record, set in 1959 when Buddy Holly headlined the Winter Dance Party.

The Gestures quickly moved up to the top of the local circuit, playing Big Reggie's Danceland in Excelsior, Mr. Lucky's, and all the clubs and ballrooms Bill Diehl booked. "Wherever The Trashmen, Avanties, Chancellors, and the Underbeats were playing, we were playing," Klugherz said. "The same places for the same money. We looked up to those bands, especially the Underbeats. Doni's bass sound—I loved it. He played a Gibson EBO, and what a neat sound he had."

After the band got out of the ninety-job contract Dewey had signed, Riegert and Madison started booking them out of state. Jimmy Thomas, who had been such a big help to The Trashmen, also booked some dates for the Gestures. The band had a small white Chevy van with *The Gestures* painted on the side. It was barely big enough to hold them and their equipment. It didn't take long for Menten to come to dislike life in a national touring band with one poorly distributed hit and little professional direction. "The first tour was just incredibly horrible," Menten said. "We had to get down to Oklahoma City within a day and play the Ray Farhner Auto Show, and then three nights from then we were playing in Toppenish, Washington. This was the dead of winter. There was snow in the panhandle of Texas." The van's engine was located between and behind the front

MEMBERS OF THE GESTURES, popular teen age rock and roll group, put aside their guitars for sandbags in dike duty while their band bus was converted temporarily into a civil defense vehicle for communications and evacuation. Above, band manager John Olscheid, 18, of Southvi Heights gets instructions for the bus' next assignment walkie talkie. (Free Press Photos)

When floods threatened Mankato, Gestures manager John Olscheid used the band's van as a communications and evacuation vehicle for the Red Cross. Courtesy of Dale Menten.

seats. As they motored through the Texas panhandle, Waterston was sitting on top of the engine for warmth, Klugherz was driving, Dewey was sleeping in the front passenger seat, and Menten was sprawled on top of their clothes and musical gear in the back. At two A.M. they smelled something burning.

"All of a sudden Bruce gets up and says, 'Geez!'" Menten said. "There's smoke coming from his pants. So we pull over and Tom lifts up the thing. The entire motor was glowing red like when they do welding. Tom looked at Gus and said, 'Have you been putting oil in this?' Gus said, 'No, I thought you did the last time.' We waited to have the thing towed in and that just put us back."

Because weather forced them to take the southern route through California and back up the coast, the Gestures did not have time to stop at motels. Instead, they kept switching drivers and taking turns sleeping in the back of the van. For meals, they pulled over at truck stops, which proved to be unwise. "It was like the movies—we'd go into a truck stop, and cops would hassle us and the locals would hassle us, because we had longer hair," Menten said. "Things like, 'Hey, a Beatle! You got a Beatle haircut.' We got all that classic stuff, because we'd get to those places after midnight. That was when a lot of the drunk crowd came in, and they'd look at us, and they'd either want to beat us up or run us out of town. We just wanted to get our fries and be left alone. We're not going to fight. We're not fighters. God, it was just horrible."

They also got pulled over by cops on the highways, primarily because the fifteen-year-old Waterston, who took his turns behind the wheel, looked like a runaway from a boy's home.

"How old is this kid?" the cops would ask. "Is he nine? Ten?"

"No, he's not. We got a slip from his parents."

Life on the road for the Gestures was a series of endless drives and one-night stands, with occasional mistakes and confrontations. The music sustained them. Courtesy of Dale Menten.

"We don't care. Where are his parents?"

Then Menten would have to call Waterston's parents and have them speak with the cops before the band could get back on the road. When they finally got to their destination in Washington, it turned out they were in the wrong city. They were supposed to be at a place with a different name in a different state. "A total screwup," Menten said. "So we missed that one. We had to send our apologies and do a make-do and all that kind of crap. We played in one place that was like a fabric plant or something, and they would put big wooden slats on top of the rolls of cloth. You're up there and all of a sudden the rolls start moving, and you're like, 'Oh, my God!' It was just dumb, you know? And in almost all those places it was hostile crowds, because they would come and say, 'Where do I get the record?' I mean, we got that all the time. We finally started giving them paper and said, 'Call this number. It's Minneapolis.' 'You call them. It's your band. I can't buy this record.' It got really bad. Amos got no product out."

"Distribution—that's what ruined it," Klugherz said. "They couldn't get the product in the stores. It was disappointing. It was kind of fun to watch it ["Run, Run, Run"] at first, moving up the charts with a bullet—yahoo! But it stopped just short of heaven: the national Top 40. I think we still sold almost a quarter-million copies. All I know is it bought me my first Corvette in 1964."

They enjoyed their next tour—staying in Toronto and working smaller Canadian towns within a hundred-mile radius as the opening act and backing band for the Orlons and Ronnie Dove. "That one was fun, because the Orlons were terrific to work with," Menten said. "The whole Canadian attitude—these were like big venues, lots of seats, lots of people, klieg lights, everything. Then you felt it wasn't like being on the big rolls of cloth that moved every time you moved. This was actually in a theater or on a big stage."

Klugherz said the girls screamed for the Gestures on the Canadian tour, but he doesn't recall that happening in the United States. "In Canada they went nuts," he said. "Those girls up there, they wanted to touch you, grab you—it was kind of cool."

Unfortunately, some of those shows were in hockey arenas, and the Gestures' equipment was not adequate to fill up that kind of space. "I hated hockey arenas," Klugherz said. "We had Fender Showman amp bottoms with some horns stacked on them. That was the P.A. There was no such thing as monitors."

They appeared on the same bill with other national acts, including Paul Revere and the Raiders, Roy Orbison, and a battle of the bands with the Hondells at the Marigold Ballroom. "We could play 'Little Honda' better than they did, because they weren't the Hondells," Klugherz said. The single had actually been recorded by L.A. studio musicians, including Glen Campbell and Hal Blaine, and the group that went on the road as the Hondells was four guys recruited by producer Gary Usher. "These guys who were touring didn't record that. They didn't play it for shit."

But the Gestures never toured the East Coast because there was no product available to promote. "There wasn't even a hint of that," Menten said. "They had a little product in Washington and Oregon, but not enough to make the people happy. The product distribution was here in Minneapolis. They sold in the five-state area. They had product in Oklahoma. It was what Amos could carve out of the center. But he didn't have that reach, or people didn't like him."

"It was also very interesting how you got your record played on the radio, too—payola," Klugherz said. "I'm not saying the Minnesota deejays. I'm saying, when we were on the road, we'd stop at KOMA in Oklahoma City, and they were playing it, the same as WDGY. Why? Because they were a sister station. When we stopped at WLS in Chicago, we said, 'Hi, we're the Gestures. Why aren't you guys playing our record?' The deejay says, 'You didn't give us $400. If you'd given us $400, we'd be playing it.' Well, we didn't know that. We were just punk kids, eighteen years old. That should have been Lou Riegert or somebody else's job to deal with that."

"They asked me to manage them when they went on the road when the record took off, and I reluctantly did," said Riegert, who himself was just twenty-six at the time. "They'd call and whine about how the rooms were too small, they didn't pay us on time, or didn't pay the right amount. I hated every minute of that. They were out there trying to make it, but they were just too young. They didn't have close-in management. Jim Madison was just in it to make a few bucks. I guess he made some money, but he didn't take care of them after their record became a hit. I never managed a band before. I was more a big brother to them—'Don't worry about it, I'll get the money for you.' It's rough on the road. They were great kids, but they were doing stuff they weren't ready for."

Bruce Waterston's mother looked to Menten to take care of her son and, by extension, the rest of the band members. Primarily, he tried to keep their drinking to a minimum while they were on the road. "I don't think I ever saw those guys drunk, but they always had a bottle in their suitcase," Menten said. When he found a liquor bottle, he poured it out, and when the other guys found the empty bottle, they complained that Menten was spoiling their fun. "Call your mom," Menten would say to Waterston. "If she releases me from this duty, I'll go buy you a bottle." He knew they were sneaking in booze, and he was certain they were often getting around him. "It wasn't fun," he said. "And we were young. My god, I was seventeen, eighteen. That's too young. Bruce was fifteen—that's too

young. And you're on the road. We had no
adult supervision except us. Now I hear
all these stories about entertainers, Justin
Bieber and stuff like that—I mean, I can
see where they just crash and burn. It's
too much, way too fast. Nothing is real.
And they even [have] people around them
trying to control them."

Menten and Klugherz both said
Waterston was the Gesture who had the
most girls on the road. "We used to keep
track on the wall of the van who got laid,"
Klugherz said. "Bruce had like a gazillion
of them compared to the rest of us—that
was none, or hardly any. Every band I've
been in, the drummer got all the women.
I don't know why. His personality was
very much outgoing, and mine isn't."
Whatever sex did occur, it usually wasn't
after a gig. As the Trashmen also discovered, the demands of getting to the next
city precluded hanging around with the
local groupies. "I'm trying to think back if
we had any time, because of the way we
were booked," Menten said. "In Mankato,
it was probably a different thing. When
they were hanging out in Mankato, I'm
sure that was wide open. But on the road,
we were trying to get to someplace we
weren't sure where it was, and we knew
we'd probably miss it and be yelled at.
Playing real late, and party? No."

Another problem for the Gestures was
that Minneapolis-area bands were beginning to get the reputation as novelty acts.

As the (barely) oldest member of the Gestures, Dale
Menten took on the role of authority figure while the
group toured the country in their Chevy van. Courtesy of Dale Menten.

That image might have begun with "Mule Skinner Blues," but it certainly took hold with "Surfin' Bird" by The Trashmen. Then an Edina band called the Novas walked into the cramped, recently opened Dove Studio in St. Louis Park in late 1964 and recorded a goofy pro wrestling satire called "The Crusher" (with a terrific surf-style instrumental B-side called "Take 7" that was just the right sound—for 1963). Released on the national Parrot label, "The Crusher" eked into the *Billboard* singles chart for three weeks, peaking at Number 88 in January 1965, just as "Run, Run, Run" was at the height of its popularity. The Castaways' "Liar, Liar" would add to Minneapolis's novelty tune reputation the following summer.

"Now, 'Run, Run, Run'—I don't think that was a novelty tune," Menten said. "'Liar, Liar' was, 'Surfin' Bird' was. 'The Crusher' was. But those were the ones that broke out of here. Actually, it was what could be recorded and sound good. Because sonically, we were so far behind what you could get in Chicago at Chess/Checker. The sound was so much better than this. These little novelty things, you couldn't compare them to anything else. They stood on their own as being fun, flippant little things. People bought it. The time was right. People wanted that. I don't know what they were all escaping from—probably the stuff that Gus and I worried about all the time. We were escaping from it."

When "Run, Run, Run" ran out of steam, the Gestures went back to Kay Bank and cut another fine two-sided single, "Candlelight" / "Don't Mess Around," both of which were written by Menten. The band actually recorded enough Menten originals to release an album, but that would not happen for another thirty years. Menten was demonstrating strong melodic and lyrical skills, something that separated one-hit wonders from bands with staying power. But once again, business mismanagement and bad luck undermined the band's possible success. The record stalled at Number 14 on the KDWB chart in April 1965; nationally, it didn't make a dent. "That got all messed up because KOMA was on 'Candlelight,' a station in Chicago was on 'Don't Mess Around,' everybody was confused, and I was in the meantime the babysitter of the band," Menten said. "My job on the road was going through suitcases and pouring out Jack Daniels. So I wasn't revered. I wasn't looked up to in the band." Klugherz said the failure of "Don't Mess Around" was tied to the band's falling out with Amos Heilicher. They believed Soma had turned down offers from bigger record companies to buy the Gestures' contract, and they wanted to go with RCA or Decca. "Amos wouldn't sell," Klugherz said. "We got upset about that. He just ditched 'Don't Mess Around.' I don't think it got distributed at all, or if it did, very little. 'Candlelight' was on our song list, but nobody had heard it. That's when Dale started thinking about leaving."

"The whole thing was just crashing," Menten said. "I was married in November 1965, and my wife wasn't nuts about rock 'n' roll, wasn't nuts about the band. She was more into religion and everything. So that kind of helped steer me, not away from music, but I can't do this band. Nobody wanted to rehearse."

Between tours, playing teen clubs and ballrooms was a far different challenge. Instead of playing their hit and a few other songs over the course of a half-hour to forty minutes, they were booked to play full, four-hour jobs. They simply didn't know enough songs. To stretch their material, they'd play extra-long instrumentals, just as the Mark V had at the very beginning. It made Menten feel amateurish. "I said, 'Guys, I'm not liking this,'" Menten said. "We're the Gestures, and we're playing 'Exodus' for twenty-five

By the end of his run with the Gestures, Menten found that being responsible for a teenage rock 'n' roll band didn't pay enough or hold his interest. Courtesy of Dale Menten.

minutes. I'm sorry, there are no good solos in that. That's just nuts."

In early 1966, Menten played with the Gestures for the last time. "I guess I don't regret moving on, because what I moved on to, I still like to do," said Menten, who went into studio music production. "But once in a while, you wonder what would have happened. Would we have been able to go back in the studio and finally get the one, the follow-up? I don't know. Chasing the second hit, that's the road you don't want to go down. Although it is fun. It keeps you in it."

Klugherz said there were no hard feelings when Menten quit the Gestures. "I don't recall any," he said. "Dale's obviously been the most successful at it, he's made a good career, made a lot of money. He made a lot of money on "Run," more than we did. He kept the publishing. I owned the band name. I started the Mark Vs, the Jesters, the Gestures. The Gestures' name was copyrighted in my name."

The rest of the group wanted to keep playing, so on they went. To replace Menten, they brought in Bill Miller, the former keyboard player with the Accents, and Klugherz began singing lead on Menten's songs. They were able to sustain their popularity on the strength of "Run, Run, Run," landing an opening gig for the Mamas and the Papas at the Civic Auditorium in Omaha in 1966. They discovered that even the biggest national acts had internal personnel issues: Michelle Phillips had been fired by the group prior to that tour and was replaced (temporarily, as it turned out) by Jill Gibson, who cowrote a half-dozen songs for Jan & Dean and had been Jan Berry's girlfriend. "She was beautiful," Klugherz said of Gibson. "She sang just like Michelle. It looked and sounded just like the Mamas and the Papas, but it wasn't Michelle. We had a really good time at the hotel-motel afterward. We did some serious partying. I still have a Crown Royal bottle somewhere signed by those guys. Mama Cass was just a riot. She was crawling on the floor of their suite, 'Bluebird One to Bluebird Two, over!' She was funny—a great lady."

One of Klugherz's favorite experiences with the Gestures was hosting the Turtles when they played the Kato Ballroom. They weren't due back in California for two weeks, so they crashed at the Gestures' band house. "They never left town after the gig," Klugherz said. "We partied for two weeks." Turtles bass player Chuck Portz admired the cutouts on the body of Klugherz's bass, so they went to Klugherz's father's basement and made similar cutouts on Portz's bass with a band saw. "Two weeks later he's playing it on *Ed Sullivan*," Klugherz said. "I said, 'Hey, I did that to his bass.' That was kind of cool."

By 1967, the Gestures were beginning to feel passé. The music that the kids were listening to had become more drug-oriented and lyrically complex, and the kids at the ballrooms and teen clubs were listening more than dancing. "We weren't a drug-oriented band," Klugherz said. "Everything got psychedelic. Vietnam was going on, and everything changed." Waterston's life changed the most. He entered the Army and was sent to Vietnam. Klugherz and Dewey were both drafted when they were eighteen and decided to wait until the last minute before joining the Navy Reserve. Putting off their induction for two years, they had both just gotten out of boot camp—complete with shaved heads—when they opened for the Mamas and the Papas. Klugherz was scheduled for active duty, but because he was married and had a child, he wasn't called. "We got by with just meetings and one cruise, on some destroyer escort they had on the Great Lakes," Klugherz said. "They gave me an honorable discharge."

Waterston wasn't so lucky. Though he refused to blame his Vietnam stint, he would eventually succumb to throat cancer in 1996, an illness his friends are convinced was caused by exposure to Agent Orange.

Menten's first band after leaving the Gestures comprised the remnants of a group from Hutchinson, Minnesota, called Mike Glieden and the Rhythm Kings. Menten had written and produced two songs for the band, "With This Kiss" and "The Party's Over," recorded at Kay Bank and released as a single in 1965 under the name the Only Ones on the Sight label. "With This Kiss" starts out as a straightforward 4/4 folk-rock tune with a prominent bass line but builds to a powerful crescendo with horns and backing vocals. "The Party's Over" is a three-part vocal ballad in the style of the Flamingos' "I Only Have Eyes for You." By 1966, Menten replaced Glieden and the group changed its name to the Best Things. The band recorded two more of Menten's songs, the poppy, near-bubblegum tune "Chicks Are for Kids" and a moody, beautiful ballad called "You May See Me Cry," released on United Artists. "I was really close to that song," Menten said. "It was a real sensitive tune. We were sitting around listening to KOMA in Oklahoma City, back in the time when you could get those stations here. And all of a sudden, it comes on. Up here, we kinda knew we'd hear it. Lou said, 'I'm gonna play it tonight,' and that was great. But on KOMA, that's like, I can't believe we're hearing this. We just heard the Beach Boys and the Beatles before that. And this is our tune. This isn't coming out of Minneapolis. This is Oklahoma City, and on United Artists."

Throughout 1966, Menten's band would change its name whenever it had a deal with a new record label, so they wouldn't have to learn more songs. "We'd just change the name of the band, put on a different outfit, and then go play," Menten said. "That was fun."

The height of this identity swapping came in August 1966, when booking agent Dick Shapiro put on a battle of the bands at the Minnesota State Fair. The winner would receive new equipment and stage outfits in return for changing its group name to the USAs. "So the Only Ones/Best Things decided, we'll do that," Menten said. "We won that, so now we're the USAs, dressing in red, white, and blue. We did that for a couple of months and then thought, 'Ish.' So I called Shapiro and asked, 'Do we have to give the stuff back?' And he said, 'Nah, that's okay.'"

The band added twelve-string guitar player Ross Ingram from St. Paul and became the Madhatters, releasing "You May See Me Cry" once again, this time on the Cardinal label. Neither release of the song became a hit, so Menten moved on again, joining Ron Butwin in a new version of the Escapades, along with Michael Flaherty on bass, Bruce Edwards on organ, and Michael O'Gara on vocals, all formerly of the Bad Omens from Columbia Heights.

"Dale was the lead guitar player when I re-formed the Escapades," Butwin said. "Tom Caplan wasn't in this one. This was an unbelievable group—a really special group. We would do songs by Jay and the Americans—Flaherty and O'Gara had the whole range, and then Dale's voice, and Edwards and me. O'Gara could boom it out so strong. We would do those songs right-on perfect, and then Dale would say, 'I'm going to write a different chorus to go with this.' And he'd write and arrange a whole new section of the song, and it would be just as good or better than what was there, and it would be unique. And the audience would always go, 'Oh, my God, where did that come from?' He wasn't Brian Wilson, but he had that same ear for harmonies. He was orchestrating while we were playing a song. We'd be doing the Temptations, we did the Association, then we'd do the Beatles. We nailed everything. If it was an old song—let's say a Jerry Lee Lewis song—we were thinking, 'How can we make it fit now?' No problem—Dale would just write a whole new way to approach it that was still tremendous."

Butwin estimates that this version of the Escapades stayed together about six months. Their demise resulted from a strong collection of egos and abilities that began pulling in different directions. "There's an example of a group where, in our minds, we all felt we were the main reason that the group existed," Butwin said. "The response was so big, everybody had their mind in a different place—what they wanted to be and what they wanted to be doing. There were a couple of the guys who made their career offstage arguing. We'd get in bad arguments with each other, then argue with everyone else in the group, and then finally it fell apart. I remember saying one night, 'Guys, I'm done with this group. I might have started the group, but I'm done with it. I can't put up with this anymore.' It was a really good group, but it was burning so hot that it fell apart, unfortunately."

From the ashes of that version of the Escapades came a group called the Seraphic Street Sounds, which Menten called "undoubtedly the best vocal group I was ever in." Butwin and Edwards were out, and they picked up David Steineck from Michael's Mystics on drums. "David Steineck had one of the most incredible high tenor voices I've ever had the pleasure of working with," Menten said. "The Seraphic Street Sounds were truly one of those bands that had a real chance of breaking out of here. They were unbelievable. That was the band—and we did so little recording. Flaherty, Steineck, and O'Gara—those three were the best voices in town."

Menten was moving more and more into production, and one of the ideas he was developing was to add a Swingle Singers/Mamas and Papas vocal sound to basic rock 'n' roll songs. For example, the Seraphic Street Sounds did a version of Sam & Dave's soul classic "Hold On, I'm Coming" with an intricate vocal opening. "Those guys could pull it off," Menten said. "I did all the high parts. We dressed up in Elizabethan outfits, all these old clothes, with the swords and everything. We bought them from the Guthrie Theater shop. We'd just come onstage looking like something out of *Macbeth,* and do 'Hold On, I'm

Coming' starting with a Swingle Singers' thing. It took this town by surprise. Everybody else was doing something totally different, and we walk out and do this. It was my fault for not keeping that one together."

In truth, Menten had discovered something he loved more than making music onstage: making music in the studio. "I never really had a good time playing," Menten said. "Back then, you had the front row—two guitar players, the drummer, and beyond that was all hell. Just the dregs. There were fights, and things going on sexually over there, and yelling and screaming. You could have been—and later it did turn out to be— just a disc jockey playing records, because they didn't care. And so, somehow I wasn't able to care. I'm trying to care, but I don't care. Why do we even practice? There, people don't care. Why do we try to play perfect, because they wouldn't even notice. It was awful. And you didn't improve. Actually, you just kept getting worse and worse, and the drives kept getting longer and longer.

"And then I got a bunch of studio work. I loved the studio thing. Because it was more personal to me. I could control it, and I could redo. Onstage, I also discovered that if you messed up, you messed up. You couldn't go back for take two. And you couldn't go for perfection. Not that I'm a perfectionist, but I'm probably close. I like that whole illusion. I always thought the reality was playing live. The illusion is recording. I love that world. It's an illusion until it's put out on a disc or CD, and even then it's still an illusion. I'm not in the room playing for you. But I like that. I like the fact that I can stop and go, 'Punch in there.' I can do that better."

Menten also liked the fact that, unlike touring and performing, all his studio jobs had a beginning and an end. As a performer, each night was a continuation of the same old grind, with no end in sight. In the studio, whether he started scoring a film or writing a jingle last week, yesterday or this morning, at some specific point, it would be done. He'd put his bill in the mail, and thirty days later he'd have a check and have done five or six other things in the meantime.

"I love that world," he said. "This is civilized."

Which is not to say that he was ungrateful for or dismissive of the brief burst of success of the Gestures and "Run, Run, Run." He said he would not be in the music business without it. After a year of attending classes at the University of Minnesota, he decided to drop out of school. He would pick up David Rivkin of the Chancellors, and they'd drive to the campus together but couldn't find parking spaces. "I got towed three or four times," Menten said. "The day that I quit was the day I was sitting way up on top in Northrop Hall in a psychology class with over two thousand people. The place was packed. The guy was way down there, just a little guy who looked this big. He had an overhead projector, and he was talking and he said something, and I raised my hand because I had a question, and about forty people around me started laughing. I got so embarrassed. The guy said, 'If you have any questions, why don't you come see me after the class.' I went from that class to the car. That was it. I said, 'It's too big, and you can't hardly park there anyway. What am I doing?'"

Because of the opened doors resulting from "Run, Run, Run," Menten was able to walk away from college and commit his life to music. "I let this business continue to push me down the road," he said. It would continue to push him to places he couldn't have imagined.

LIAR, LIAR

When Lonnie Knight left the Castaways after a few gigs in 1963 to play with Dick and Larry Wiegand in the Rave-Ons, the Richfield-based Castaways were left with original members Denny Craswell on drums, Dick Roby on bass, and Roy Hensley on guitar.

Roby was born in San Diego in 1946. His father was a pharmacist's mate during World War II, stationed in San Diego; his mother, whose father ran the accounting department for the Cargill Corporation, decided to accept an offer to work at a San Diego bank during the war. The two met at a big band dance in an old San Diego ballroom. Roby's father mustered out of the navy, went to college on the G.I. Bill, studied mortuary science, and got a degree to be a mortician. "He didn't like it," Roby said. "It made him depressed to be around people who were grieving. Then mom got sick and wanted to be back here with her folks. My father and I lived with my maternal grandparents here for a while until she was better. Then we bought a house out in Richfield."

Roby's father went into sales, peddling several different products door to door, including Petco knives, potty chairs, and freezers. "He'd bring a signed contract home, stand on the front porch, and hold it up like a dog that just caught a dead rat," Roby said. "I saw that scene a lot. 'Look what I've got!' A lot of times he would barter with people. If they didn't have money for a down payment, he would take a motorcycle, a used car, or whatever." Roby's dad took a Sears Silvertone guitar and amp as a down payment to close one of his deals. He told Dick that he'd provide him with lessons if he wanted to learn how to play the guitar; otherwise, he'd put an ad in the paper and sell it. "I was ten years old in 1956," Roby said. "I was rather enamored with the prospect of being a rock star. I said, 'Sure, let's keep it.' I learned how to play."

Though he wasn't a musician, Roby's father was a big fan of Frank Sinatra's music, always playing Billy May and Tommy Dorsey records at their home. Roby's mother was a singer, and his uncle played trumpet in his own big band in high school. His maternal grandfather played the clarinet and the bagpipes. Despite having somewhat of a musical ancestry, Roby came to realize he wasn't as gifted as his friend Lonnie Knight. After he and Knight met on the baseball field across the street from Roby's house, they began to teach each other songs they knew, especially Ventures instrumentals. Roby had been playing for two years and was impressed with Knight's skill.

"How long have you been playing?" Roby asked Knight. "You're really good."

"Two weeks."

"This guy's really something—a prodigy," Roby thought. "He's already better than me."

They hung out together the rest of the summer and jammed at each other's houses. When school started, Knight told Roby he had a friend named Denny Craswell who played drums in the school band and was so good that the band leader taped him playing drum rudiments, because he was better than the recording supplied by the Ludwig drum company.

Craswell was just thirteen at the time. His father, Wally, was an excellent singer and comic who played ukulele and sang at cocktail parties with friends. He also worked as a caricature artist in the lobby of the Orpheum Theater in downtown Minneapolis and was a qualified pastel artist who eventually opened a photography, framing, and art supply store. Craswell's mother played piano without having taken formal training. He began playing the drums when he was eleven or twelve years old. "My earliest memory is I always wanted to play drums, and I wanted to be the best at it," Craswell said. "I practiced hours and hours. I don't know how dad put up with me. We used to live in our studio where we had the store. I was upstairs pounding the drums. When we had a customer, they'd pound on the walls to have me stop."

Craswell sometimes played with the Knights, who later became the Rave-Ons, but the Knights were playing mostly instrumentals, and Craswell wanted to be in a vocal band. Lonnie Knight was the singer in the original Castaways lineup, but the band didn't have a microphone. Someone said that they knew a guy who had a mic—Roy Hensley. Craswell and Knight went to Hensley's house.

"Do you have a mic?" they asked him.

"Yes," Hensley replied.

"Can we borrow it?"

"Yes, on one condition—I go with it." Hensley thus became a member of the band that Roby and Knight had dubbed the Castaways, so named when the two were watching TV one night and saw an ad for the Castaway Inn in Florida. Hensley played bass and sang a majority of the lead vocals.

After a year or so with the Castaways, playing mostly school dances, Knight left to join the Wiegand brothers. He was replaced by Bob Folschow. "It's hard to say why I left," Knight said. "I don't remember. I remained friends with Denny. There was something that happened, but I do recall one night, Dick and Larry Wiegand and I were sitting around. We had a childhood vendetta against Bob Folschow. We called the Fire Department, called seven or eight pizza places, and sent them all to his house. I think Fol and I have come to terms with that. Whatever—we're Facebook friends, anyway."

Robert Folschow was born in Detroit Lakes in 1947 and moved to Minneapolis when he was five years old. His father was an auto mechanic who had played guitar, harmonica, keyboards, banjo, and Hawaiian lap steel guitar in bands around the Detroit Lakes area. "I have a picture of him with his sister, who also was a musician," Folschow said. "When they were teenagers, they actually traveled with a medicine show in the Upper Midwest. They used to hit the towns that didn't have drug stores. It wasn't a horse-drawn thing, but an old truck with the sign. There's a picture of my dad with a cowboy hat and a guitar, and my aunt dressed up like a gypsy. They were just teenagers. They played the popular songs of the day, like 'Red River Valley' and old-time stuff. His sister could do ragtime like Jo Ann Castle on Lawrence Welk."

Folschow remembers his dad getting out the guitar at home, strapping on a home-made harmonica holder, and belting out a tune like Bob Dylan would do later on. Sometimes he would sit at the piano and play. He had a disc-cutting machine with which he made records of his performances.

Folschow began playing music in kindergarten, shortly after moving to Minneapolis.

"There was a guy going door to door signing up people for accordion lessons," Folschow said. "I did six years on the accordion until puberty, then I wanted to play guitar. I stopped accordion, but I kept messing with my dad's three guitars. Finally, we went to Sears and he got me my guitar, a Silvertone, with a little amp."

Folschow's mother died when he was eight; in his early teens, his father was going through a divorce from his second wife. "My teenage years were getting kind of flaky," he said. He moved to his aunt's farm outside Enderlin, North Dakota, for two years. He learned to play guitar with his favorite cousin, who played piano. They would take his guitar and amp to the silo and play it as loud as possible, enjoying the echo. They played guitar instrumentals like "Raunchy" by Bill Justis, "Rumble" by Link Wray, and even "Torture," the flip side of the Fendermen's "Mule Skinner Blues." Years later, Folschow had a chance to back Jim Sundquist of the Fendermen at an induction ceremony to the Minnesota Rock 'n' Roll Hall of Fame. As the thrown-together band was practicing, Folschow started playing "Torture." "I got the weird look—'Where do you know that from?'" Folschow said. "I was into it, back in the day."

When he returned to the Twin Cities, Folschow joined a band called Mike and the Shadows, fronted by Mike Judge, who would later join the Chancellors. Beginning with instrumentals, they progressed to vocal rock by Buddy Holly, Elvis, Buddy Knox, Carl Perkins, Gene Vincent, and the Everly Brothers. "My sister had the records," Folschow said. "I pretty much learned music by learning to sing both harmonies to every Everly Brothers tune. It was all such an exciting adventure back then, discovering new people and just being in awe of it all."

In fact, Folschow was going through the same musical education as the Beatles, who loved the same groups and songs—and in turn influenced so many bands on both sides of the Atlantic. "I read about their roots—pretty much the same as ours," Folschow said of the Beatles. "They were big into the American stuff. Their invasion opened up [America] for a lot of English groups, like the Kinks and the Stones."

Bob Dylan was another early influence on Folschow, partly because he played guitar and used a harmonica rack. "The time I saw him was on some TV show—I think it was Steve Allen. I can't remember the song, but I knew right away he was a big deal, and the sound of his guitar and harmonica sounded like my dad." Folschow recalls spending a night at his father's house while the furniture was being moved to the house of his father's new wife. The electricity was still on so he could listen to his Dylan albums on his record player while he lay on the couch. "It was like going to Dylan school," he said. "I was listening while I was sleeping. He had a big influence on me."

Folschow was attending Minneapolis Southwest High School when he was recruited to join the Castaways in 1963. They rehearsed in Roy's or Denny's garage and then started playing gigs. The sound didn't seem full enough, so they began auditioning keyboard players. They ended up hiring Jim Donna, who had graduated from DeLaSalle High School that spring.

James Joseph Donna was born in 1945 in Minneapolis. His father was an engineer at Honeywell, as well as a professional musician who played saxophone, clarinet, accordion, and organ. Donna took piano lessons from the nuns at St. Charles grade school in Northeast Minneapolis. "They said, 'James, you're jazzing that up too much,'" he said. "Little did they know."

He was a big fan of Jerry Lee Lewis and went out to see the Killer at Big Reggie's Danceland in 1962. Bill Diehl—"the Deacon of the Discs" as Donna remembered him ("I owe him a lot, a lot of bands owed him a lot")—was emceeing the show that night and introduced Donna to Lewis. "He was behind the ballroom, smoking a cigar, and he had a bottle of whiskey," Donna said. "He offered me some. I said no thanks. We sat down after the concert, and he showed me how to play 'Great Balls of Fire.' I went home at two in the morning, pounding on the piano. I must have [woken] my parents up, but I was bound and determined to learn those chords. That was the start of my career." Donna needed a band and nearly started out at the top with The Trashmen, who were considering adding a keyboard player. "I didn't know them at the time, but some friend put me in touch with them," Donna said. "I auditioned with them, but they went with all guitars."

Shortly thereafter, Donna auditioned for the Castaways. He doesn't remember how that connection came about. "I just remember hauling my dad's organ from his living room over there," he said. "That was all we had, a console organ. It was no small feat to bring it over to Richfield to jam with the guys. During the audition I got a good feeling. They were pretty good musicians, as I recall, although they're better now."

"We decided we needed a keyboard player, because a lot of the bands were having them," Craswell said. "I don't know how we located Jim Donna. We auditioned him, he set up his piano, and he became a member of the band. We took the first one." Donna was studying business at the University of Minnesota when he joined the Castaways and suggested to the others, who were still in high school, that he become the band's manager and booker. "We acquiesced," Roby said. "He was the leader."

"I have pictures of us playing before Jim and after Jim," Folschow said. "Jim was in the group, and then we elected him to be our leader to handle the booking and distribute checks, so he kind of took care of the business side."

After Donna joined, Roby and Hensley swapped instruments. "I sang, but it was more important to Roy than it was to me," Roby said. "Bob was writing some little tunes, and he was a good singer. It became apparent if Roy was going to be lead singer, he'd rather play rhythm guitar than bass. Bob knew how to play rudimentary bass from his dad, who had a band, so Bob got me started on the bass. Roy played my guitar and I played his old early '60s Fender bass."

Folschow lined up a job for the band at the original Medina Ballroom, but the Castaways were mostly doing pizza places and teen dances until April 10, 1964, when the St. Louis Park dance team (and volunteer Minnesota Vikings cheerleaders) the Parkettes hosted the River City Talent Tournament at the Minneapolis Auditorium. There were several categories, including professional acts, which included pop singer Jimmie Rodgers and Greenwich Village folksingers the Big Three, consisting of Cass Elliot, Tim Rose, and Jim Hendricks. The Castaways played the Bobby "Blue" Bland staple "Turn On Your Lovelight" and won first prize, worth $50, in the rock 'n' roll category. The band also won a gig at Jerry's Bar on Highway 35.

The Castaways found their signature sound when Jim Donna (center) joined the band on keyboards in 1964. Courtesy of Jim Donna.

"We were too young to go in there, but they let us play as long as we were downstairs where the liquor wasn't served," Craswell said. "That broke the band into Minnesota regional-type status, playing all the top ballrooms and dances," Donna said. "We had broken into the big circuit and were one of the big bands in the Twin Cities. We were pretty polished by that time. The money was decent, but we didn't get rich. I was trying to go to the university, and that was hard to do when you're playing in a band."

The Castaways were undergoing a style change at the time, too. The Beatles had drawn a sharp line between the high school kids who greased their hair and the kids who were growing their hair out. "I was into Brylcreem until 1963, then I got myself some wingtips and did the Ivy League–Baldy look with V-neck sweaters, Gant shirts, bleeding madras, that kind of thing," Roby said. "I adapted more to the collegiate look. Not necessarily all of us. When I look at pictures of us back then, there's one picture that appeared in the *Richfield News*. I've got pre-Beatles hair, as does Roy, and Denny. When the Beatles came along, I started wearing my hair more in that style, but Roy still had the pompadour."

Bill Diehl began booking the Castaways on a regular basis, and Donna filled in the schedule with bookings of his own. The Castaways were playing all covers, making use of Donna's Wurlitzer piano to do songs like "Peppermint Twist" and Jerry Lee Lewis numbers. Hensley sang the rock 'n' roll songs while Folschow sang the more pop-oriented tunes by artists like Bobby Vee. The two harmonized on many Everly Brothers songs—which led to an embarrassing incident at the Prom Ballroom in St. Paul, when the Castaways opened for the Everlys. "All our best stuff was the Everly Brothers, so we did all their hits, thinking they would be proud of us," Craswell said. "They were so gracious. They said, 'Boys, that's the best we've heard. Good job.' We didn't know any better—we were just little kids, and they probably thought we were cute." Don Everly probably didn't think they were terribly cute after Roby, a high school junior at the time, went backstage with a senior girl he wanted to impress.

"Mary, come on, I'm going to introduce you to the Everly Brothers," Roby said to her.

"Let's not," she said. "I don't want to intrude."

But Roby insisted, practically dragging her into the dressing room.

"There's Don Everly with nothing on but his underpants, talking to his road manager," Roby said. "The road manger saw us, grabbed us, and pulled us out of the dressing room and read the riot act to me. I never did talk to him. I would have been surprised if they wanted to talk to me after that."

The Castaways practiced incessantly, according to Craswell, becoming an expert cover band. "We covered everything, right off the charts, whatever was hot," Craswell said. "Whatever made them dance. We were a dance band."

Still, they were not on equal footing with the Big Three. One of the big thrills of Craswell's early career was being asked to sit in with the Avanties at Danceland in Excelsior on a night when Froggy Nelson was unavailable. "They were really big, and we hadn't had our hit record yet," Craswell said. "The place is packed, and a gal comes up and says, 'Denny, are you playing with these guys now?' I thought I was really on top of the world that night."

The Castaways realized they were never going to reach Big Three status if they didn't cut a record. "The other groups in town—the Accents, Underbeats, and Avanties—all had records that were getting airplay on WDGY and KDWB," Folschow said. "They could charge a little more money at Mr. Lucky's and whatnot. Our reason to record was, 'Let's make the big bucks like the Accents.'" "Our actual goal was try to make $50 more a night," Craswell said. "We were making $50 a night for the whole band for frat parties. We just wanted to get into a little better moneymaking position."

What to record? The Accents and the Underbeats went with lesser-known cover songs; the Chancellors were currently enjoying a Number 1 hit on WDGY with "Little Latin Lupe Lu" by the Righteous Brothers. But Donna wanted to write an original, and prior to a band rehearsal at his parents' house in North Minneapolis, he began experimenting with a chord progression on the living room organ. "Denny came over, and we started collaborating," Donna said. "I had written part of it ahead of time and showed it to him. We did some more, and he started throwing out some words, some ideas, and we put the thing together." The "thing" would come to be known as "Liar, Liar."

Craswell said Donna played him the basic chord progression, but when he got to the signature "Liar, Liar" riff, Craswell asked him to play the part again. "He played those chords over and over," Craswell said. "They were his chord progressions, but I picked the best chords out of a group. They had what I call the magic change. He said, 'What are we going to call it?' I said, 'Liar, Liar, pants on fire—a kid's rhyme.' He said, 'What's it about?' I said, 'It's about love gone bad.' We sat and thought up all the rhymes we could think of. This all happened in about ten minutes."

"We went downstairs, showed it to the band, and they thought it was pretty cool," Donna said. "The band started arranging it, doing our parts, vocals and all that. That was the genesis. It was amazing—it all just came together in my parents' basement."

"That falsetto part, which came to be the title of the song, that was Denny's idea," Folschow said. "We used to cover 'Bread and Butter' by the Newbeats. I sang the falsetto. Somehow it was decided, 'Yeah, let's do it like that.' At that time I could rough up the falsetto like that. When we went into the studio to do it, I sang it kind of straight. I didn't do the 'Bread and Butter' thing. Thank God—I had enough trouble with my falsetto over the years after smoking."

The Castaways had the A-side of their record. They fine-tuned "Liar, Liar" in front of crowds at ballrooms around the area and practiced it hundreds of times in Jim Donna's basement in preparation for recording it. "If anybody made a mistake, we stopped and played it again," Craswell said. "We had to play it flawlessly because we only had a little bit of money [for studio time]." For the B-side, they chose a song Folschow had written called "Sam," inspired by a girl named Samantha who was the girlfriend of a guy who worked for the band as a roadie. They asked Timothy D. Kehr to produce the session, which was held at Kay Bank in late 1964 with engineer Tom Jung. Donna also invited Ira Heilicher—who had never heard of him—to come to the studio. Because the Castaways scraped up their own money to pay for the session, they asked how much one hour of time cost and when the hour would begin. They were told the clock started ticking the minute they stepped into the studio, not when the tape started running. "So we set up everything outside the studio door," Craswell said. "When they opened the door, we ran everything in, put it down, and said, 'We're ready.' We knew we'd go through that song one time. It wasn't too many takes."

Jung was working with a three-track recorder—one track for the band, two for the vocals. Donna played his keyboard part on Kay Bank's Hammond organ, and Roby sang the lead vocal. "Bob and I sang on one track, and I sang harmony with myself on another track," Roby said. "When Bob went falsetto, Ira said, 'Wait, what's that? I don't think it fits. That doesn't make sense.' Tim said, 'Ira, that's the hook, man! You don't understand.' Ira wasn't very insightful. Tim was on the cutting edge."

It was Craswell's decision to have Roby take the lead vocal, even though he never sang leads for the Castaways. "Bob and Roy were exclusively our onstage lead singers," Craswell said. "They drove the crowds wild. They were not great singers, but great performers. I recognized Dick's voice would be best for this record. I did that because Dick had the best intonation. He was on key all the time. In recording, you had to have perfect pitch. I never told the other guys, but I knew Dick would do it best and had the most blue-eyed soul to give it a funky sound. That worked out good. Here's two lead singers in the band allowing Dick to do the lead—that was courageous of those guys."

Though Kehr has always been credited as the song's producer, Craswell recalled him being a friend and adviser more than a producer. "Back in [those] days the engineer was the producer," Craswell said. "When Dick Roby was singing 'Liar, Liar,' he came to the middle of that solo and went 'Waaaaaw!' [Jung] said, 'Hold on, run back there, he blew it.' I said, 'No, let it go, that's impromptu, and it's Dick. That's cool.'"

The four Castaways play one of their earliest jobs, a battle of the bands at the Silver Skate Roller Rink in North St. Paul in 1962: *(left to right)* Dennis Craswell (drums, vocals), Roy Hensley (rhythm guitar, vocals), Dick Roby (bass, vocals), and Bob Folschow (lead guitar, vocals). Courtesy of Bob Folschow.

In the liner notes to *The Soma Records Story, 1963–1967,* released in 1998, Ira Heilicher said he told Donna that he really wanted "Liar, Liar" after hearing the final mix. "I was standing on my father's doorstep at 6 A.M. with the rough-mixed tape in my sweaty hands boldly stating 'This is a winner, Dad. We've got to put this one out!'" Heilicher said. "Luckily, he agreed after listening to it. One of the things my father really liked was novelty tunes."

Tim Kehr was also working his contacts to find a record deal for the Castaways and secured an offer from London Records, home of the Rolling Stones, Marianne Faithfull, and the Moody Blues. "We were either going to be on Parrot or London, but Tim said they didn't want to release 'Liar, Liar' until the spring," Roby said. "We just wanted a song to play on the radio to compete with other bands like Gregory Dee and the Avanties. Our aspirations weren't of that magnitude. Ira said, 'Dad will put it out right away. He can get it on the radio.' But they lied. They didn't put it out until the spring. We couldn't get it out in time for Christmas sales."

No one will ever know whether the Castaways would have had a more successful career had they signed with London, but there is no doubt that signing with Soma worked out in the short term. "The advantage was he was the record distributor for the Midwest and had an easier time hyping it up with distributors and radio stations," Craswell said. "They were in a position to give the record a good local start."

"Liar, Liar" was released in late spring 1965. It entered the WDGY singles chart on June 5 at Number 22, and by June 26 it was Number 1. Those were heady times for a bunch of high school kids. "When you're young like that, you take everything in stride," Craswell said. "It seems like it was meant to be. I do remember driving around Lake Calhoun when 'Liar' was Number 1, listening to it played on the radio. That's a moment right there. You realize you're on top, you're in your own hometown, riding around the lake in a convertible, and your song is Number 1."

Meanwhile, Lonnie Knight and the Rave-Ons had connected with George Garrett, who took them into Kay Bank to record their first single, "I Want You to Love Me" / "Everybody Tells Me," both cowritten by Knight. The record got some local airplay, but nothing like his Richfield High School classmates and former band members were getting with "Liar, Liar." "Did I envy the Castaways?" Knight said. "I think there was a lot of teenage angst, you know. I think we all thought it was simply a matter of getting something recorded, and we would immediately be hits."

"Liar, Liar" had the desired effect: it elevated the Castaways' status to the top rung of Twin Cities bands. But it would take a bit longer before they could raise their asking fee. They had already signed a number of contracts to play venues in Minnesota for what Donna called "local money." "It was decent for the times, but certainly not the kind of money we were going to make touring," Donna said. Nevertheless, the Castaways honored those contracts, despite drawing huge crowds to such venues as the Kato Ballroom in Mankato, where the kids lined up for three blocks to see Minnesota's newest superstars. "It was the biggest crowd they ever had," Donna said. "They made so much money that night, and they wanted us to come back. I said, 'You aren't going to get us for a hundred-fifty bucks anymore.' He never booked us back."

The Castaways began charging a guarantee against 50 percent of the door, which resulted in much bigger paydays. They also turned to Ira Heilicher and Dick Shapiro for management; they in turn connected the band with General Artists Corporation—the same firm that handled the Beatles and The Trashmen—to line up high-profile gigs.

"The Castaways were a democracy," Craswell said. "We voted on everything. I loved that about the band. We had rules and regulations in the band that we agreed upon and we all had to follow. We didn't have any rules about booze or drugs. Back in those days, nobody drank. We were too young. We had no problem with that. But we did have a rule that no physical violence was allowed—to each other. You could kill somebody else, but not within the band. That was a rule that got broke."

"Things were going a little nuts, and at the time you could say our bass player Dick Roby was going a little nuts," Folschow said. The Castaways were playing a job at Mr. Lucky's on a Friday night while "Liar, Liar" was at its local peak and the band members were feeling like celebrities. In the middle of a song, Roby stepped on his cord and pulled it out of his Mosrite bass. Some of the kids leaning against the stage saw Roby's bass get unplugged and started laughing and pointing. It happened twice more that night, and in frustration Roby threw his bass onto the stage floor, and the neck snapped off the

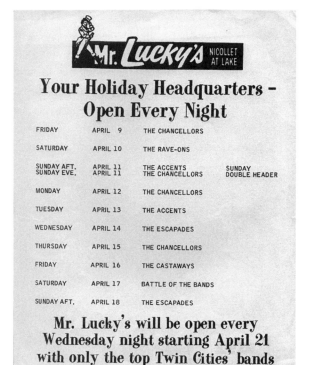

After the success of "Liar, Liar," the Castaways moved into the top rank of Twin Cities bands, featured frequently at Mr. Lucky's. Courtesy of Jim Donna.

body. The band took a break while Donna called Jim Lopes at B-Sharp and asked to have a replacement bass brought to Mr. Lucky's. "The place is packed, we're waiting, and I'm looking at the busted guitar," Folschow said. "I pick it up. It's my nature to think, 'Well, if we get a little baling wire and duct tape, maybe we can fix it.' Dick sees me messing with his guitar, which I shouldn't have done, and he comes out and says, 'I'm going to hit you'—which he did. He smacks me, a sucker punch, and now I'm fighting back."

The two wrestled onstage, knocking over a mic that started feeding back as a security guard ran up to the stage and separated the bandmates. Once backstage, Roby and Folschow were assessed fines of $25 each by the rest of the band. Folschow apologized, they shook hands, a new bass arrived, and the Castaways returned to the stage to finish their gig.

The band played again on Saturday night with no incident. On Sunday night they had another gig; everyone was going to ride together in the band's hearse, which had very little room for all five band members and their equipment. When they got to Roby's house that afternoon, Jim Donna brought the broken bass and its case inside to clear a little more space. "I was driving the hearse," Folschow said. "We hadn't picked up Denny yet. Jim goes to Roby's door and says, 'Here's your bass, Dick.' I didn't think he said much else. Dick goes berserk, does a sucker punch karate thing on Jim's mouth, and knocks some teeth out. The next thing I see, Jim has got a handkerchief up to his mouth, spitting blood. Dick's dad is holding him at the door because he wants to tear into Jim."

Roby concurred with Folschow's account of the incident, with some additional detail. "I punched him out," Roby said. "I had a habit of punching people out when I was about nineteen. It was my bad. I allowed a situation to develop that could have been avoided, but I let it go to the point where Jim got me in a lot of trouble with my folks." Roby said it was the weekend of his high school graduation, and his whole family was sitting around the table when Donna arrived with the broken bass—which Roby's father had bought for him. "Jim, you outed me, you son of bitch," Roby said. "It was like he was telling on me. I got mad and smacked him in the head—knocked him out. He bled all over my folks' living room carpet. He had to get oral surgery. I guess I threw quite a scare into him. I didn't see him for quite a while after that."

Folschow said in hindsight that he believed Roby was having "a meltdown." At the time he wasn't aware of Roby's embarrassment over the broken bass, but he, Donna, and Hensley decided on the spot that Roby was out of the band. "We go over to Denny's house nearby and tell him what happened," Folschow said. "Next to Denny's house lives a dentist who did a quick fix to Jim's mouth so we could play the gig. Roy, who played rhythm, said he always wanted to play bass. We decided we don't need a rhythm guitar. Dick is out—Jim, Denny, Roy, and myself were the Castaways. When the record hit big nationally, when we went out to California, it was the four of us, without Dick."

"It was unfortunate that Dick left the band," Donna said. "Bands have fallings-out sometimes. He left the band, and we became a four-piece very suddenly. I said, 'Roy, you're our new bass player. Start practicing.' We were on the way to a gig that very day. It was quite an adjustment. This was when we were still playing locally. It was just as the record was breaking in the Twin Cities." It would soon be breaking big everywhere. Unbeknownst to the Castaways, "Liar, Liar" was racing up the charts in markets all over the United States in the summer of 1965. Meanwhile, however, the band was going about its business, trying to get used to playing as a four-piece.

"So Dick is out of the group," Folschow said. "He had his issues. I remember we played at the Kato Ballroom, and Dick Roby was at the gig, in the audience, being a nice guy. He was the old Dick, no problem. He wanted a ride back to the Twin Cities. At that time Jim and Roy and Denny all had previous plans, so I had to drive the hearse back. I said, 'I'll give you a ride.' That's when the gun incident happened."

The remaining Castaways had heard rumors from other musicians that Roby was pissed off at them—understandable, Folschow said, since "Liar, Liar" was becoming a smash. Roby was asking to be paid his share of the royalties for the record, even though the rest of the band hadn't seen any. There were even rumors that Roby wanted to kill the Castaways— rumors that Folschow dismissed until Roby pulled out a gun on the drive home from Mankato and started shooting at highway signs in the middle of the night. "You're in a vehicle hearing that first shot go off, and you kind of pee a little bit," Folschow said. "Now I'm fast-talking to

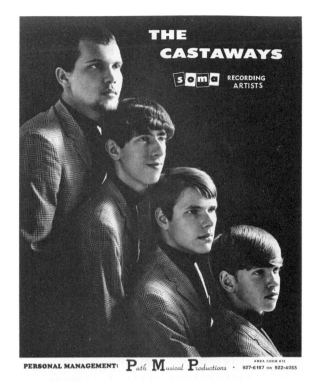

PERSONAL MANAGEMENT: Path Musical Productions · AREA CODE 612 927-6187 OR 922-4055

Dick Shapiro and Ira Heilicher, partners in the Path Musical Productions agency, managed the careers of the Castaways. Courtesy of Tom Tourville.

Roby, and we're just talking about whatever, I can't remember, but 'Keep talking, Bob, keep talking.' Pretty soon we're there at his house. I drop him off and say, 'Okay, Dick, see ya.' I go home and change my underwear."

The scope of the success of "Liar, Liar" was revealed to the Castaways toward the end of the summer when they were summoned to a meeting with Ira Heilicher at Soma Records. When the band walked in, they saw a large table covered with record charts from all over the country and even overseas. Each chart indicated that "Liar, Liar" was a big hit in that particular market. "We were totally astounded," Craswell said. "We knew it was Number 1 on Weegee, but we didn't know it was Number 1 in Holland, and all over the place. We didn't know, unless Jim knew and didn't tell us."

"You guys gotta tour, you gotta chase this down," Heilicher told them. "Your record's going to be Number 1 next week in Hollywood, California, and you're up there playing International Falls and all these crazy places."

"All of a sudden we get on a plane with our equipment," Folschow said. "Ira Heilicher was like an acting manager for us. He went with us." The band stayed at the Hollywood Landmark Motel and toured L.A. with some of the top deejays in the city. They went to Tiny Naylor's drive-in, a storied hangout right out of *Happy Days.* When they arrived, a deejay put them on the air. "Hey, guess who we've got in the back seat—the Castaways!" the deejay said. "Their song 'Liar, Liar' is going to be Number 1 next week!" In fact, "Liar, Liar" hit Number 1 on the KRLA singles chart on September 5, 1965, while the band was in town getting the star treatment. Heilicher booked the Castaways on a number of television shows, including Dick Clark's *Where the Action Is, Shivaree, The Lloyd Thaxton Show, Hollywood A-Go-Go,* and *Shebang* hosted by Casey Kasem. "We were on those shows multiple times," Folschow said. "It was all really thrilling. 'Gee, here's Andy Williams, we're on the same show with Andy Williams, and Paul Revere and the Raiders.'"

It also created the exceedingly odd television-viewing experience for Dick Roby. "I had to sit at home and watch them do half a dozen nationally televised shows, lip-syncing to my voice," Roby said.

The Castaways rode with host Dick Clark—wearing blue jeans—to the Old West set where they filmed their segment of *Where the Action Is.* Then they got an invitation to appear in a beach party film called *It's a Bikini World,* featuring Deborah Walley, Tommy Kirk, and pop groups the Toys, the Gentrys, and Eric Burdon and the Animals. "They didn't have the title at the time," Folschow said. "It was one of those low-budget bikini flicks. They wanted to record us along with the Animals at the same time. We're at this nightclub called the Haunted House, on a stage with fangs and teeth like an open mouth. They put the movie together and got the groups recorded."

"It all happened in one tour, one trip out, over a week or two," Craswell said. "We did all that stuff at one time. We played some gigs, too, and some clubs."

Still a senior at Richfield High School, Craswell had to get back to class, but Heilicher was not through exploiting the label's biggest hit since "Surfin' Bird." He booked the Castaways on another trip to the West Coast in October. The problem was getting their drummer out of school again. "A couple of us band members went to talk to the principal to see if we could get him out of school for a couple of months that fall," Donna said. "We showed the principal the gigs we had booked. He said, 'Yeah, by all means.' I remember that vividly. I was amazed they agreed to it."

So it was back to the Hollywood Landmark Motel, where Craswell found himself doing homework a couple of rooms away from the freshly formed Mamas and the Papas, who would not release their first single, "California Dreamin'," till January of the following year. Leader John Phillips had been a member of a folk trio called the Journeymen but had relocated to the West Coast for a fresh start. "They didn't even have the name of the group yet," Folschow said. "We're Number 1 on the charts, and we've got both John Phillips and Denny Doherty hanging out in our rooms, showing them my Rickenbacker twelve-string. You've got the fat chick [Cass Elliot] and the pretty chick [Michelle Phillips] down by the pool in bikinis."

"When Mama Cass jumped into that pool, what a splash she made," Craswell said. "I remember going, 'There's a band over there.' They opened up their door—'Yeah, we just changed our name to the Mamas and the Papas. We're doing some recording down there in L.A.'"

"It was not till sometime later on I saw them on TV," Folschow said. "'That's the group from the motel—hey, "Monday, Monday."' It was kind of neat to see."

That trip gave the Castaways their biggest moment, playing a fifteen-minute opening set before eighteen thousand fans at the Cow Palace in San Francisco on a Fall Spectacular package show that included Sonny and Cher, the Byrds, the Lovin' Spoonful, Roy Head, the Shangri-Las, the Beau Brummels, Little Anthony and the Imperials, Glen Campbell, Bobby Freeman, Charlie Rich, the Mojo Men, the Vejtables, the Sunrays, the Tikis, and the Toys.

"Eighteen thousand people screaming—that's when you start thinking, 'It's looking good,'" Craswell said. "We didn't have enough hits, so we did a version of 'Louie Louie,' and Bob did his Preacher Bob routine. He told people, 'At the count of three, I want everybody to clap your hands. At the count of three, jump up and scream, at the count of three, shout, clap your hands. . . .' People would go nuts to his preacher routine. We had some interactive things that worked really well in concert."

"It's the only time I've ever been scared onstage," Donna said. "I'd never seen a crowd that big in my life. It all settled down after we started playing."

Folschow recalled Glen Campbell performing the Beatles' "Norwegian Wood" on guitar as a solo act at the Cow Palace and sharing a dressing room with the Beau Brummels. "They were onstage when we were down in the dressing room," Folschow said. "Their guitar cases were on the floor. I remember nosing around in one of the guitar cases. There were business letters—musicians are an eclectic bunch. One of their producers was asking for folk-rock songs, kind of Dylan-esque, and I was on the same page at that point."

Present

1965 FALL SPECTACULAR

The Cow Palace
SATURDAY, OCTOBER 2, 1965
8:30 P.M.

Master of Ceremonies—Johnny Holiday of KYA

Featuring America's Top Recording Stars

Little Anthony & The Imperials	Bobby Freeman	The Sunrays
The Beau Brummels	The Lovin' Spoonful	The Tikis
The Byrds	The Mojo Men	The Toys
Glenn Campbell	Charlie Rich	The Vejtables
The Castaways	The Shangri Las	Roy Head
	● Sonny & Cher ●	

AN ATTRACTION OF TEMPO PRODUCTIONS, INC.
SAN FRANCISCO, CALIF.

Many of the biggest acts in rock 'n' roll shared the stage with the Castaways at the 1965 Fall Spectacular at the Cow Palace in San Francisco. Courtesy of Jim Donna.

Sonny and Cher were the king and queen of folk-rock in the fall of 1965 and were chosen to close the show. "By the time Sonny and Cher came on, the crowd was pretty worked up and a riot broke out," Donna said. "Sonny and Cher had a big orchestra. I'm behind stage. Somebody threw a bra onstage. Sonny picks it up, kisses it, and says, 'For me? Oh, thank you,' and throws it back to the girl. Then hundreds of kids, mostly girls, storm the stage. They had him pinned against the wall, ripping his shirt off. Everybody ran for their lives. Even the orchestra abandoned the stage. I guess it was something he'd done before but didn't expect that kind of reaction. I wish I'd had a picture."

The Castaways also opened a half-dozen shows for the Beach Boys on that trip. The two bands first met on a flight from L.A. to Vancouver to play a daytime show. "We partied with them all the way up," Folschow said. "The little airline booze bottles were flowing. Even though we weren't old enough to drink, we're on an airplane flying to a gig—'Gimme another one of those Lord Calverts.' We opened the show and didn't have to bring our PA. There was an amplifier supplied, so all we had to do was bring our guitars and plug in."

The Castaways never saw the Beach Boys play that gig. After their opening performance, the Castaways were rushed off onto a much smaller charter plane to go to Seattle, where they were given a motorcycle escort from the airport to the arena where they opened for the Animals. "We remembered them and they remembered us, because they were in the movie with us," Folschow said. "They always dressed in the same scruffy clothes." Craswell said Burdon wore a jean jacket with a big stain on it during the shooting of *It's a Bikini World*. In Seattle, Burdon was wearing the same jacket with the same stain on the back. "Oh, you poor guys," Craswell thought. "Your agent must be working you guys to death."

The Castaways were not into the scruffy look the Animals favored. Instead, they were wearing red jackets, white turtlenecks, and black pants. By the time they returned from their second tour of the coast, their look had become noticeably mod, and they were being studied by the other Minnesota bands. "'Liar, Liar' blew my mind," said Owen Husney, then playing guitar with the High Spirits. "It had distinctive moments, it became a huge hit, and they were on national TV shows. We were doing *Date with Dino*, and they had just come back from California. I remember Denny Craswell wearing love beads around his neck, their hair was all fluffed out, all California, and I thought, 'Oh, shit, this is big time. I want to be big time.' I was so jealous. 'Oh, my God, they had experienced and touched the other side.' My jealousy always turned into 'I've got to work harder. I've got to figure out a way to jump beyond this.' I understood why 'Liar, Liar' was so good. I was picking those songs apart in my brain. Much like Prince—he had the ability to take somebody's whole thing apart and analyze it. I was impressed with them."

In fact, the High Spirits had made the local charts—and some regional surveys—with their cover of "Turn On Your Lovelight" on Soma, which peaked at Number 5 on WDGY in August 1965. Like the Castaways, the High Spirits didn't realize how many records they were selling. "Unbeknownst to us, our record was starting to get airplay around the U.S.," Husney said. "I was hearing that in California, Colorado, Kansas City, we were like Number 1. We went down there and toured with the Chancellors. We had expanded beyond the five-state area and went west on many tours. I saw Amos before he died, and I'd say, 'Amos, where are my royalties?' And he'd say, 'Aahh, you don't know how much it costs to promote that shit. It all went into marketing. There were no royalties.'"

It certainly wasn't uncommon for any of Soma's breakout artists to be in the dark about their record sales. The Del Counts had a huge local hit with their cover version of the Rascals' "What Is the Reason" in 1967, reaching Number 4 on KDWB. Frank Venapole, regional manager for Musicland stores, told Charles Schoen he

At the height of their fame, the Castaways opened for the Beach Boys at the Minneapolis Auditorium. Courtesy of Tom Tourville.

had a big hit going. "I didn't realize how well it was doing," said Schoen. "I was just a young kid having fun playing. I didn't have any business mind then, and I still don't. I didn't have any relationship with the Heilichers. When my dad found out what was going on, he said, 'You guys have to find out how many records you've sold.'"

Schoen and Marsh Edelstein went to Heilicher's office and asked to see the books. Amos had his feet up on his desk.

"Which books do you want to see?" he asked them.

"I'd like to see the real ones," Schoen said.

"The real ones aren't here," Amos replied. "My bookkeeper's got them."

"This is going nowhere," Schoen said to Edelstein.

"It wasn't funny," Schoen said. "They did that with all the bands."

Acting with their usual sense of frugality, the Heilichers put out *The Big Hits of Mid-America, Volume Two,* packaging the label's latest string of hits: "Run, Run, Run," "Little Latin Lupe Lu," "Turn On Your Lovelight," and "Liar, Liar," plus the B-sides and the Gestures' second single. The label made more money; the bands kept working.

The Castaways continued to tour through the fall in support of "Liar, Liar," but a staggered release schedule meant it would stall at Number 12 on *Billboard*'s singles chart. "The song went Number 1 in every market, but because it broke slow, it didn't go to the top of the charts right away," Craswell said. "It was released in different markets at different times. It was supposed to be slow breaking."

A new complication arose: Dick Roby had put together his own version of the Castaways and was touring the country playing "Liar, Liar." Roby's bookings were set up by Jimmy Thomas of Luverne. "We appeared as the Castaways everywhere from Denver to New York," Roby said. "They were good players." The two bands actually met at a TV station in Pittsburgh, both booked to play the same show. "I remember the host of the local TV show wanted a battle of the bands," Folschow said. "There's no way. We are the Castaways. We got the writers and the singer, although Dick Roby did sing the low voice on 'Liar, Liar.' We ended up doing the show."

"We were about to do the interview when Jim Donna came in from the other end of the sound stage, demanding we not appear on that station, that he was the legitimate band from the record," Roby said. "He went on to do the interview, but I think he just made himself look bad, ranting and raving about us. That was the first time I'd seen him since I punched him out."

When the Castaways returned to Minneapolis, Roby sued them for royalties, which

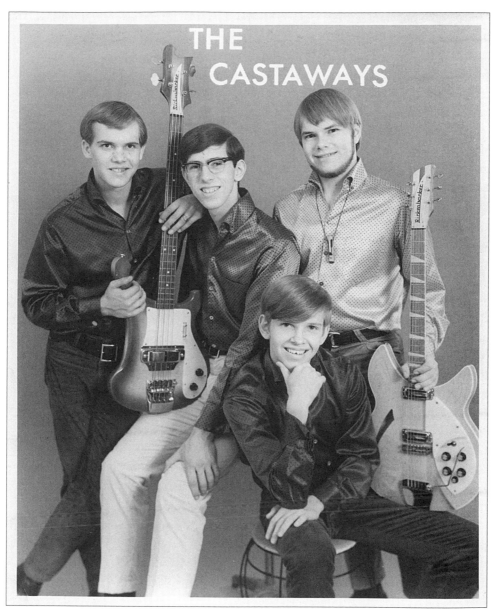

The Castaways recorded "Liar, Liar" as a five-piece, but by the time they traveled to the West Coast to promote their hit, bassist Dick Roby was out of the band, leaving *(from left)* Roy Hensley, Jim Donna, Denny Craswell, and Bob Folschow. Courtesy of Jim Donna.

typically did not start getting paid out until six months after a song was recorded. The band countersued Roby for fraudulent use of the name *Castaways*, despite the fact that Roby and Lonnie Knight had come up with the name. The two sides settled out of court, with Roby agreeing to cease and desist any Castaways activities and forfeit any royalties. "It's too bad that it ended that way," Folschow said. "He was a good guy, a great musician, and a good singer. He totally missed out on that fame thing."

Royalties would be an issue for the Castaways for years. When "Liar, Liar" was released, the only writing credit on the label was James Donna. Craswell didn't complain at first but eventually had to go to court to get his name restored as cowriter. "Me and Lonnie [Knight] were at that session," said Larry Wiegand. "I saw the whole thing. Jim Donna was cowriter." Craswell's name now appears as cowriter of "Liar, Liar," and he said he doesn't want any further hurt feelings over things that happened fifty years ago. "Let's put it in the past," Craswell said. "The money is being split now. What's done is done and was made right. We wrote it together."

The Castaways needed a follow-up single. Folschow was writing lots of songs, among them "A Man's Gotta Be a Man," which featured his Rickenbacker twelve-string guitar and Craswell's harmonica—a perfect sound for the folk-rock tastes of 1965. "I wanted to be the A-side guy," Folschow said. Instead, "A Man's Gotta Be a Man" was relegated to the B-side. For the A-side, the Castaways chose a song called "Goodbye, Babe," written by Hensley. It started with Hensley uttering an evil laugh, then singing "I'm leavin' you, babe, on the midnight train," in a low, gruff voice. The song was structured similarly to "Liar, Liar" but lacked that song's breezy, innocent charm. "Totally gimmicky, which I hated," Folschow said. "There was no thought-out decision I was aware of to stay with the gimmicky thing." It peaked at Number 9 on WDGY in November and didn't make the *Billboard* chart. "By that time, we were written off as another gimmicky thing out of Minneapolis," Folschow said.

"We should have tried the high voice, but that's hindsight," Craswell said. "It sounded pretty good to me, but it didn't sound like 'Liar, Liar.' I didn't think we went back and tried to use the same formula. It ended up sounding like a different band. 'Liar, Liar' was a combination of everything coming together." "Goodbye, Babe" was the sound of a band that had missed its opportunity. What none of the Castaways realized was that they were free to sign with any record label after their one-record deal with Soma for "Liar, Liar." "In hindsight we could have signed with any big-time label in Hollywood," Folschow said. "I'm surprised Ira didn't pick up on that. Our record was Number 1 out there, and breaking out all over the country. Once we got the TV exposure, we're getting on the charts in New York, Pittsburgh, everywhere."

"Nobody lets you have a Number 1 song before tying you up," Craswell said. "We were in a unique position. We could have talked to any label we wanted, but we didn't know it. Tim [Kehr] was giving us advice, and we made the mistake of not taking it. After we signed the first deal, we didn't ask him what to do after that."

They recorded more songs with Soma, mostly Folschow originals, which were of high quality, but Soma—and the record-buying public—had apparently lost interest. "We didn't really keep up with the recording as much as we should have," Craswell said. "We probably should have switched to a major label and let other people write for us and take over our career, but hindsight is twenty-twenty."

The band returned to California again in November, got on some of the same TV shows, and lip-synced to "Liar, Liar," "Sam," or "Goodbye, Babe." Then Folschow came down with laryngitis and Hensley got sick, too. They could continue to lip-sync, but they couldn't perform live, so they returned to Minneapolis to get healthy.

In the meantime, Dick Roby and Tim Kehr tried to start a record company. Roby recorded a single at Dove with Dale Hawkins's "Suzy Q" on one side and Nat Adderley's "The Work Song" on the other. Roby said it was horrible, partly because he had a cold, but he'd heard that the Castaways were going to cut a version of "The Work Song," and he wanted to scoop them. Kehr thought they could get the record distributed, but Amos Heilicher wanted Roby to return to the Castaways. "He held it against me that the second one ['Goodbye, Babe'] was a bomb," Roby said. Heilicher asked Roby to rejoin the band. "He said, 'You've got to apologize to Jim Donna before they accept you back.' I said, 'No, I'm not ready to apologize. I had a reason for doing that, and I don't want to apologize.' [Amos] had a lot of leverage in this town. He told me, 'You'll never work in this town again.' He certainly shut our record company down. I went to Marsh Edelstein and told him, 'I've got a band. I want you to book it.' He said, 'No, I can't help you with that. There are people who are preventing me from helping you.'"

Roby and Rick Youngberg, who'd played in the Deacons and the Paisleys, flew out to California together in 1968 to form a band, but after a few years in California, Roby returned and took a series of short-lived jobs with Minnesota groups. The Castaways, meanwhile, had come to the end of their initial run. "In 1966, we were still touring a lot, but we were making less money after the 'Goodbye' thing," Folschow said. "Now we're not flying to gigs, we're driving. We traded our old hearse in and were driving to gigs in a Ford Econoline van."

When the Castaways' first single, "Liar, Liar," took off up the local and national charts, Soma Records hustled to take advantage of the hit. Courtesy of Tom Tourville.

Then Folschow's draft notice arrived, and Donna decided to leave the band. "When Bob got drafted, I decided to go back to the university and get an education," Donna said. "It was a hard decision—it broke my heart—but I wanted to go on to something else." Rather than sever his ties with the Castaways, Donna lined up replacements for himself and Folschow, bringing in keyboard players Dennis Libby from Dudley and the Doo-Rytes, and Greg Maland from Gregory Dee and the Avanties. Donna continued to book the band while going to college. He would eventually put together a new version of the Castaways that continues to play occasional parties and events. Donna and Dick Roby have mended fences; Roby has played bass with Donna's Castaways on several occasions. "Dick Roby and I are good friends," Donna said. "We were pretty young kids back then. It was so long ago. It's all in the past."

The Castaways settled their financial differences in 1986. A few years later, Roby went to see Donna. "They were playing a job in a Minneapolis park," said Roby. "I approached him and told him I was really sorry that I hit him and wanted to make amends and tell him how sorry I was. We've been friendly ever since. We don't hang out, but when my mom died at the age of ninety, Jim showed up at the funeral to express his condolences. I thought that was really nice."

The original Castaways played their last show together at the Safari Club in 1966. The Castaways played upstairs while the Underbeats—with Jim Johnson, also soon to ship

Opposite: The Castaways continued to play regional venues after "Liar, Liar," but they were in demand all over the country. Courtesy of Jim Donna.

IN PERSON
THE
CASTAWAYS

★ ☆ ★ ☆ ★ ☆ ★ ☆

THE CASTAWAYS   soma RECORDING ARTISTS

PLAYING ALL THEIR HITS
INCLUDING
LIAR, LIAR
AND
GOODBYE BABE

APPEARING AT:
STARLIGHT ballroom
CHIPPEWA FALLS wis
SAT. APRIL 2 ND.
8:30 - 11:30 P.M.

off to Vietnam—played in the downstairs room. "Jim Donna's last night was the same as mine," Folschow said. "I think that was Jim Johnson's last night, too." Though each would get back onstage with future versions of the Castaways, Jim Donna and Bob Folschow were bidding farewell to their dreams of rock 'n' roll stardom. For Jim Johnson and Denny Craswell, even greater peaks were yet to come.

On the record label:

EVERYBODY'S HEARD
ABOUT THE BIRD

HIGH FIDELITY
SIDE ONE

MONOPHONIC
33⅓ RPM

FOR PROMOTIONAL USE ONLY

FROM THE LAND OF 10,000 HITS

CHAPTER
12

WE GOTTA GET OUT OF THIS PLACE

JIM JOHNSON wasn't about to let the Vietnam War ruin his ambitions as a rock musician. He'd put together the best rock 'n' roll band the Twin Cities had ever known. Now his plan was to make the Underbeats strong enough to survive without him until he returned from the war. "I knew we would keep going after Jim left for Vietnam," Doni Larson said. "We had too big [of a] momentum going. All any of us ever talked about was making it, and 'making it' meant we knew we had to leave."

Johnson's first choice on guitar was Bob Goffstein, who played with the band for a few months before receiving a draft notice of his own. Johnson replaced him with Loren "Wally" Walstad, who played in a band called the Defiants out of Clara City, Minnesota, twenty minutes southwest of Wilmar. In 1966, the Defiants released a dead-on version of Bob Dylan's "Maggie's Farm" on Studio City Records, with Walstad driving the song along with guitar licks that could have been played by Mike Bloomfield himself. "Loren Walstad was the best guitar player around," Johnson said. "Right after Jim got the draft notice, we started conspiring to pick up Wally," Larson said. "In Willmar, he'd always show up and ask to play Jim's guitars. He'd be bullshitting next to the stage while we were setting up, flying through these jazz exercises. We could tell him once, and he had it. Wally was told it was only a two-year gig, and at the end, you will have busted out of Willmar. It worked out just like that."

Walstad wasn't a singer, however, and the Underbeats were known for their power-house vocals. Johnson heard the Hot Half Dozen, who had a local hit with their cover of "Heat Wave," and was particularly impressed with James "Owl" Walsh, who sang lead and played keyboards. Walsh "could sing his ass off," Johnson said. "He was seventeen. I figured, 'Yeah, it could work.'"

Horn-rock by bands like the Hot Half Dozen became a popular style in Minnesota by the mid-1960s. Courtesy of Tom Tourville.

Walsh was born in Northeast Minneapolis in 1948 and attended Edison High School. He was into music from a very young age; when he was seven, his father bought him a tape recorder on which Walsh would record himself talking and singing. His mother sang and played piano, but the rock 'n' roll music Walsh listened to on WDGY inspired him to take up the drums first. He started a summer band as a drummer when he was in sixth grade and began teaching himself piano by ear on the side. His first professional band was Jerry Zelazny and the Polka All-Stars, whom he met through a drum and bugle corps. They would pick him up on Friday, drive north, play polka in ballrooms, and drop him off at home on Sunday. He'd play many of those same ballrooms a few years later with the Underbeats.

After a year and a half with the Polka All-Stars, he auditioned for a rock band called the Coronados at the Silver Skate Roller Rink in North St. Paul. "I'd hire you in a minute if you were a keyboard player," the leader said. "Let me take a crack at it," Walsh replied. Walsh said he had no idea what he was doing, but he was good enough for the Coronados, which consisted of Rick Ballot, Jeff Brenda, Fred Draper, and John Kaminsky. That band turned into the Hot Half Dozen, who added a couple of horns to their lineup and began to embrace the R&B sounds of Motown, James Brown, and Memphis. The Twin Cities rock 'n' roll scene had progressed from rockabilly to instrumental surf rock to British-influenced rock in the short span of just five years, and by 1966 it was being pulled in yet another direction: soul music. While most of the established bands were adding selected soul tunes to their sets, there were bands with horn sections that played it full-time, including Dave Brady and the Stars, Michael's Mystics, the Marauders, and the Hot Half Dozen.

Dave Brady and the Stars got their start when Minneapolis R&B legend Jimmy Hill put together Washburn High School guitarist Bill Lubov—a white fan of black music—with black singers Dave Brady, Wally Lockhart, and Rockie Robbins from Central High. They added black keyboard and sax player Carl Bradley and white bassist Bill Brisley and drummer Tom Hoth to form the city's first overtly integrated band. Their first gig was at Magoo's, the pizza place next door to Mr. Lucky's. "It was a Wednesday night when we knew there were not going to be lot of people there," Lubov said. "There were six people in the place. We played a few songs, and all those people disappeared. We didn't mind; we just practiced." Those six people had gone to tell their friends about the hot new R&B band at Magoo's. "Within forty-five minutes, the place was packed," Lubov said. "That was a heady beginning."

Dave Brady and the Stars played at many of the same clubs the white rock 'n' roll

Dave Brady fronted the first successful mixed-race band in the Twin Cities. Courtesy of Carl Bradley.

bands played—the Marigold, the Marian, the Prom, the Barn, Someplace Else in Rob-binsdale, the Prison in Burnsville—but there were clubs where they couldn't get booked. "There was a very clear divide between black clubs and white clubs," Lubov said. "White clubs very rarely permitted any black players at all, let alone a black band. The black clubs were not welcoming at all to white bands, except maybe one musician."

Like the white rock 'n' roll bands, Dave Brady and the Stars toured the greater Min-nesota ballroom circuit to appreciative crowds but also faced some hostility. "We were the first mixed-race band actively performing in the Midwest," Lubov said. "We went to a lot of small communities where we had to be escorted out by police due to racial issues. It was a growing experience for me. There were definitely two different communities, and R&B was the outlier. White musicians didn't know black musicians. That's just the way it was. I didn't care what they [white musicians] were doing—I wasn't interested in

The Mystics were a mixed-race horn band that helped push musical and social boundaries in Minnesota. Courtesy of Tom Tourville.

their music. The biggest agents had very little interest in the black groups. There was no market for it."

Brothers Michael Stokes and Hyland "Butch" Stokes, founders of the Mystics, did not play up the fact that they were part African American. Their seven-piece horn-rock band, founded at Harding High School in St. Paul in 1961, drew dance-oriented crowds to the usual circuit of clubs. "Because of the fact that we looked like we were all white, we appealed to everybody," keyboardist Butch Stokes said. "The only time we ran into any negativity was when we played some of the clubs. We attracted a lot of black people, and that was kind of a no-no. But it wasn't a big thing, because it didn't keep us from playing all the popular places in town. The only place we did not play was predominantly black clubs like King Solomon's Mines and the Ebony Lounge."

The Marauders, from Fairmont, Minnesota, had a near-hit in 1965 with an original

With Jim Johnson serving in Vietnam, the Under-beats carried on with *(from left)* Tom Nystrom, Rico Rosenbaum, Doni Larson, Wally Walstad, and James Walsh. Courtesy of Denny Johnson of Minniepaul-music.com.

song called "She Threw My Love Away" on the Studio City label, written by guitarist Dick Schreier. Just as WDGY and KDWB were beginning to play the record, however, the Marauders received notice that area stores had sold out their meager stock of the record. They called Soma, Studio City's parent company, but were told that Amos Heilicher had decided to throw all of his company's resources behind the Castaways' "Liar, Liar." Soma essentially threw away "She Threw My Love Away," but the Marauders continued to progress, adding horns and choreography to a stage show that leaned increasingly toward R&B. "You were either R&B or rock," said drummer Phil Berdahl of the Stillroven, a band that was definitely rock. "There was quite a division between the two in the Cities."

The Hot Half Dozen's horn-soaked cover of "Heat Wave" on Soma cracked the Top 30 on KDWB in May 1966. James Walsh's vocal was energetic and elastic, similar to the blue-eyed soul of Felix Cavaliere of the Rascals—though Walsh did not change the pronouns in the lyric from Martha and the Vandellas' original, singing "Whenever he's near me. . . ." "That was an idiot decision, just me being young and stupid," Walsh said. "Little did I know I was on the cutting edge. I was thirteen or fourteen, and so thrilled to be in this dream, that I never gave it a second thought."

When Jim Johnson of the Underbeats heard Walsh sing, he knew he'd found the other missing element to take his place in the Underbeats. "They had to get two guys to replace me," Johnson said. "I prided myself about that."

The new Underbeats jelled quickly, showcasing the blended three-part harmonies of Rosenbaum, Nystrom, and Walsh. The band wasn't interested in artificial stylistic divides either. Their set list included heavy doses of soul and R&B music, including "Back in My

Arms Again" by the Supremes, "Hold On, I'm Coming" by Sam & Dave, Arthur Conley's "Sweet Soul Music," and a Memphis medley of "Knock on Wood," "Midnight Hour," and "634-5789." In 1967 the Underbeats went into Kay Bank and cut a single that demonstrated their new direction. The A-Side was a remarkably fresh and vibrant original written and sung by Rosenbaum called "It's Gonna Rain Today"; the B-side featured Walsh singing lead on an obscure Holland-Dozier-Holland composition called "The Sweetest Girl in the World."

Johnson, meanwhile, had reported to Fort Leonard Wood in the Missouri Ozarks and was reluctantly learning how to be a soldier. He had Rosenbaum ship him a Gibson guitar and was still writing songs. Before shipping off to Vietnam, he returned to Minneapolis on leave and took the Underbeats into Dove recording studio, which had relocated to a bigger facility in Bloomington and hired Dale Menten as a staff producer. Johnson had a terrific original he wanted to record called "Footsteps," a big echoey ballad in the style of the Walker Brothers. To avoid confusing the Underbeats fans, Johnson left Walstad off the recording session, bringing in only Rosenbaum, Nystrom, Walsh, and Larson, and released the record on the local Stature label as Calvin James (his first and middle names) and the Haymarket Riot. Despite the excellence of the recording, "Footsteps" sank without a trace. "Coming back here, the worst thing I could have done was change my name to Calvin James," Johnson said. "If I had left the name, I would have done a lot. I thought Calvin James sound[ed] more showy. There are so many Jimmy Johnsons—car racing, football—all over

When their outstanding original song "It's Gonna Rain Today" failed to become a hit in 1967, the Underbeats could see that their future lay outside Minnesota. Courtesy of Mike Jann.

269

the planet. What the hell. Doesn't make any difference now. But 'Footsteps,' it turned out, might have saved my life in Vietnam."

He was receiving advanced training at Fort Polk, Louisiana, when his sergeant walked into his barracks one night and ordered him to report to the commissioned officer's room with his guitar and amp. Johnson was convinced that they were going to take his guitar away from him before shipping him overseas.

"Here we go," Johnson thought. "If the guitar don't go, I don't go."

He found Sergeant Jackson ("The baddest guy you can imagine") sitting at his desk. He looked at Johnson and held up a copy of the "Footsteps" 45.

"Is this you? Calvin James and the Haymarket Riot?" Jackson asked.

"Yes, sir."

"Bring that shit in the other room."

They sat up together until 4 A.M., with Johnson singing and playing for the sergeant. Jackson explained to Johnson that at twenty-three he was four years older than most of the other draftees. The kids looked up to him as a musician, but his snide attitude about training and military life was hurting the morale of the younger soldiers. The officers wanted him to set a positive example. "Look, Johnson, you got to help us here," Jackson said. "You can't be laughing. You boys are going over, you know that. We don't want to see you come home in a bag. You gotta help us." Johnson's relations with his superiors marginally improved for the rest of training. He bought a Stratocaster and put it in his duffel bag when his unit flew to Oakland, enjoyed a few days off, and then flew to Saigon. "I get off the plane, and it's like a heat monkey jumps on your back," Johnson said. "The guys getting on the plane are telling you, 'Charlie's waiting.'"

He found Vietnam to be tents with no sides, brown dust, helicopters, heat, and sleeping mats they unrolled every night. Johnson had brought a transistor radio and rewired it to serve as a tiny amplifier through which to play his Strat. "I remember doing that with a crowd of guys around me," Johnson said. "They were so entertained, it did my heart good. I know they're fighting a fucking war, but when I was singing, they forgot where they were."

When Johnson reported for duty at Fourth Infantry headquarters, he turned his guitar into supply. "You play professionally?" he was asked. He was told there was a Special Services band that went into forward areas to play for the troops, and he was asked if he wanted to audition. Johnson filled out a form and then went out into the field for three months with his infantry unit, seeing some of the worst of the war. He was made a commander of his unit but quickly learned that you did not outwardly display your rank in the field, because that made you a target. His elevated status only created problems for him. "I'm thinking, 'I wonder if they heard anything about that audition,'" Johnson said. "I'd sure like to get the fuck out of here."

Johnson discovered it was common practice among U.S. soldiers in the worst of the fighting to stop taking their malaria pills in order to get out of the field for a couple of weeks with an illness. "I did as everyone did," Johnson said. "When I got to the hospital, I asked, 'Are there any orders for me?'"

"Yeah, they've been there for a quite a while."

"Why didn't they tell me?"

He went from the hospital to Saigon for his audition. They told him they liked him a lot and sent him back to his unit. Again, he kept waiting to be called and heard nothing, so he intentionally broke his glasses and got sent back to base camp for new ones. His orders were waiting there for him: put a band together. He found drummer Rich Hensley, bass player Clovis Woodard, and a rhythm guitar player, and they played all over Saigon and most other cities in South Vietnam—even at the mansion in Hue where John Wayne and Miss America stayed. On a second tour of the country, Johnson met and performed with actress/singer Martha Raye, then fifty years old. Raye and Johnson's band were staying at the Myercord Hotel in Saigon when the Tet Offensive began in 1968. "We were all sent back to our units, but Martha kept me and Rich," Johnson said. "She was a real lieutenant colonel. We were in an officers' club, and somebody asked us, 'What are you guys doing in the officers' club?' Then we heard, 'Ten-hut! These boys are with me!' She was a wonderful woman."

Back in Minnesota, Dove was supplanting Kay Bank as the top studio in the metro area for rock bands. The studio began operating in 1964 in St. Louis Park; owner Don Peterson and engineer Darold "Arv" Arvidson moved to a new studio space at 98th and Bloomington in 1965 and bought most of the recording equipment owned by David Hersk, who had decided to fold his Gaity label. Bands paid $40 an hour for studio time at Dove, and for an extra $10 they could work with a staff producer/arranger. One such producer was Warren Kendrick, a guitar player who had attended Minnetonka High School and then the University of Minnesota, studying math and physical sciences while simultaneously owning and operating "an obscure little restaurant" called the Round-Up Drive-In on County Road 19 outside of Excelsior. "Like any other aspiring kid, I worked my buns off in seventh, eighth, and ninth grades, mowing lawns and washing cars," Kendrick said. "I had accumulated a little money at the end of my senior year. Of all things, I bought a drive-in restaurant, which was kind of popular in the late '50s. There was not much to it, just a shack by the side of the road with a parking lot. At the time, everybody knew me by Dudley. I hated the name, but it was my middle name, and I was stuck with it all my life. One of my customers was a kid that was just coming out of his junior or senior year—Jim Kane. He knew I played the guitar. He got himself a guitar and was learning a little bit. He asked my opinion, and I had to be a little tactful. I told him, 'Hey, why don't you pick up the bass?' The bass is not the easiest instrument in the world, but he was determined. He had the fire in the belly."

Kendrick had become proficient on guitar by gigging in piano bars with an African American keyboard player named Ralph Primm. "I couldn't drink—I was just sixteen or seventeen—but I'd play guitar with him," Kendrick said. "We made $400 to $500 a week plus tips, an incredible amount back then. I was like an intern learning the ropes, getting comfortable playing with somebody else, whatever the customer asked for. We sounded just great together."

Running the drive-in, Kendrick was exposed from open until close to the Top 40 music the carhops and customers listened to on KDWB and WDGY. Kendrick found himself thinking, "God, it's so rudimentary. With the little bit of composing I've been doing, I should be able to do something with that."

He had developed a crush on one of his young carhops—though being an excessively shy guy, he never made a move on her. One day she came into the restaurant and told Kendrick he ought to meet her new boyfriend, who also played guitar and wrote songs. Feeling deflated, Kendrick went back to his apartment and started writing a lovelorn ballad. Three weeks later he finished a song he was proud of, named after the carhop.

Bone-tired from working eighteen-hour days, seven days a week, Kendrick sold the drive-in in 1965 and decided to dip into his newfound cash to do some recording at a local studio. He knew about Kay Bank's rates—beginning at $40 an hour and going up to $60—and decided that was too pricey. "And I thought I'd feel uncomfortable there as an amateur musician in the presence of people who knew a heck of a lot more than I did," Kendrick said. He looked for other options in the Yellow Pages and found Dove Studio, which offered a producer package: ten hours or more for $20 an hour, plus mixing for an additional $15 an hour. Kendrick soon realized that it took hours and hours to perfect a three-minute song, so Dove was the ideal place for him to learn. "I grew with Dove," he said. "It was just two guys, Don Peterson and Darold Arvidson, not a receptionist sitting out there, phones buzzing, 'One minute please,' a layer of bureaucracy. It was a laid-back place, and I'm a laid-back person."

Kendrick had stayed in touch with Jim Kane, who had formed a group called the Victors. He brought them into Dove to record two Kendrick originals, "Beer Bust Blues" and an instrumental called "Scotch Mist." Kendrick put the record out under the name the Scotsmen on his own label, Scotty Records ("It happened to be a name I liked—I said to myself, 'If I ever had a little boy, one of the names would be Scott"). The record didn't get much airplay, but "Beer Bust Blues"—very much in the style of "The Crusher"—became a popular party song wherever the Victors played.

Kendrick's next production at Dove was for one of his carhops, a singer named Barbara Hess. He wrote several ballads for Hess, including "Once in a Lifetime Boy," "Summertime Girl," and "(Can't Drown This) Torch," clearly inspired by the drama-drenched ballads of the Shangri-Las. Jim Kane played on those recordings, which were also released

Members of the Batch (Gary Paulak, Barry Thomas Goldberg, and Whip Lane) endure Minnesota winter outside Dove Studio with singer-songwriter Michael Yonkers. Courtesy of Barry Thomas Goldberg.

on Scotty. "I was acting as my own ORM—original record manufacturer," Kendrick said. "By setting up your own business as a record label, there are all sorts of places you could get them custom made, including Kay Bank. I would send the acetates to Chicago to be done by RCA."

Kendrick had no trouble creating a label and pressing records; the problem was marketing them. "We were our own marketers," Kendrick said. "We found out that was like a stone wall. We never got anywhere. It was back to square one. I spent a decent piece of change on this." He was discouraged but not defeated. He was fascinated by the recording industry, so he kept driving out to Dove to do basic intern duties. One afternoon Petersen and Arvidson went to lunch and asked Kendrick to answer the phone while they were out. A call came in from Chuck Novak, the manager of a band in the northern Minnesota canoeing outpost of Ely. Novak's group, the Electras, had formed in 1962 after brothers Earl and Bill Bulinski moved to Ely from Chicago. They had evolved from a dance-variety band to a hard-driving rock group that was ready to make a record, and they were looking for a producer. "I'm thinking, this is a good deal," Kendrick said. "I'm telling them $40 an hour to do their recordings, knowing full well I could buy the time and resell it to them. I was just like a guy rubbing his hands together."

Kendrick drove 250 miles north to Ely to check out the band and came away impressed with their songs and their ability. When they came to Dove to record, Kendrick changed some of the chord progressions to their original song "'Bout My Love" and added a new wrinkle to their sound—a fuzz-tone guitar. "There were no stomp boxes or gadgets available to anybody at that time," Kendrick said. "'Satisfaction' was really the first use of the chainsaw fuzz-tone guitar. I accidentally came on that one day when I joined a cheap little amp and plugged it into the input of a big amplifier. It was that simple—there's a fuzz tone."

"'Bout My Love" got airplay on WEBC in Duluth in the fall of 1965 but didn't make the charts in the Twin Cities. Kendrick began writing new songs for the band, beginning with "Soul Searchin'" / "This Week's Children," released in January 1966. Kendrick loaded "Soul Searchin'" with female backup vocals, Farfisa organ, and heavily reverbed percussive effects. On "This Week's Children," Kendrick had lead guitarist Bill Bulinski play through two Showman amps to create an overloaded tone. "Man, that thing went through so many metamorphoses, the things I did to that song," Kendrick said. "It seemed as though there was no end to his bag of tricks," Bill Bulinski told Jim Oldsberg and Mark Prellberg in *Lost and Found, # 1*.

Despite making great-sounding records, the Electras were still looking for a breakthrough hit. Kendrick came up with the idea for their next song while rehearsing Jim

Kane's new group, the Litter, at his house. A fourteen-year-old girl, the daughter of a friend of Kendrick's mother, came by for an audition. She wasn't much of a singer, so Kendrick tactfully told her he wouldn't want to ruin such a beautiful operatic voice by having her sing rock 'n' roll. When she left, the guys descended to some locker room–type comments about her physical attributes. "Denny Waite, the singer for the Litter, looked at me with a little smile and said, 'You hairy old man, you,'" Kendrick said. "Of course, I'm constantly looking for something different to write about. I'm thinking, 'Nobody had ever put out a song about age difference.' It was starting to bother me, too. I'd been working with all these fifteen-year-olds in the restaurant. Every year you're one year older, and they're still fifteen. I had to deal with mothers and fathers letting their kids work there, so I maintained this hands-off policy. Here I am thinking, 'What a perfect idea for the song.' That's how 'Dirty Old Man' was born."

Ely's Electras began in 1962 as a band that could play rock 'n' roll or polka music, depending on the audience. Courtesy of Denny Johnson of Minniepaul-music.com.

Behind a menacing guitar and organ riff that sounded like "I'm Not Your Stepping Stone" by the Monkees and the Raiders, Electras lead singer Tim Elfving pleaded with a young girl to reject the attention of an older playboy: "He's nothing but a free-wheelin', girl-stealin' dirty old man." "I could just see the little smile on his face," Kendrick said. "Tim was one of these people who sang the best when you put a couple of beers down him. He smiled at the words. I had worked with Tim enough to know to get him to do a little cooling with his voice. It worked with him on stage, too—a half-whisper, sort of a throaty sound. I taught Tim about how girls react to things. They like a rasp in the voice, cooling, and they like the primal scream. I literally trained him in a lot of it that night. The Electras were so talented, it didn't take long to put this together."

Kendrick recalled the many times he'd seen hormone-fueled boys "peel out" of his

The Electras from Ely *(from left to right)*: Bill Bulinski, Earl Bulinski, Gary Omerza, Tim Elfving, and Jerry Fink. Courtesy of Denny Johnson of Minniepaulmusic.com.

drive-in in their hot cars and decided to add that sound effect to the record. They strung three or four microphones down the length of the Dove studio parking lot on a nice fall Minnesota evening. Kendrick's friend Bob Colombo got into bassist Earl Bulinski's '63 Corvette convertible and burned rubber down the length of the lot, with every screech and squeal picked up by the mics. That sound was punched directly into the song's rough mix.

"Dirty Old Man" is a raw, aggressive song, and it matched Kendrick's mood. In 1966 he was devastated by a diagnosis that he'd contracted polio—the only such victim in the state that year. It cost him the use of his right arm. "I had to overcompensate," Kendrick said. "If I was going to stay in the music business, I could no longer play guitar. I had my left arm, so I could plunk out chords on the keyboard, and I could train other people on the guitar by remembering what I did. When I was writing this song, I was angry at the world and anything in my way, so there was anger in that song. It was like saying, 'This is the way I'm going to have to get back to have any kind of standing with anybody: throw it right in the song.' I'm thinking I've got to put everything I can do into what's going to sell this record, what's going to make people want to hear it and buy it. Of course, your principal buyer in 1966–67 was a thirteen-year-old girl."

Local playlists were tightening considerably by then. WDGY and KDWB had both told Kendrick that if a local record had any chance of getting airplay now, it had to be hard rock—"no ballads, no surfing crap." Fortunately, Kendrick had developed a rapport with some of the KDWB disc jockeys, who were willing to put "Dirty Old Man" on the air. A week later, Dove owner Don Peterson called Kendrick.

"Warren, your record is not a hit . . . ," Peterson said.

Kendrick was crushed.

". . . it's a smash," Peterson continued. "We need more records."

The thirteen-year-old girls were buying "Dirty Old Man." Dove had to call RCA in Chicago and have more records airlifted to the Twin Cities to meet the demand. The record finally broke the Electras into the Twin Cities market, topping out at Number 20 on the KDWB singles chart in November 1966. Unfortunately, guitarist Bill Bulinski was drafted that summer and wasn't even available to play lead guitar on the recording of "Dirty Old Man."

Kendrick's next project—the Litter— would rock even harder than the Electras. The Litter consisted of Jim Kane on bass, his former Victors bandmate Denny Waite on lead vocals, Bill Strandlof on lead guitar, Dan Rinaldi on rhythm guitar, and Tom Murray on drums. Both the Litter and the newly constituted Electras—with Ely native Harvey Korkki now on lead guitar—recorded Kendrick's next and perhaps greatest composition, "Action Woman." Strandlof created a wah-wah sound on the Litter's version of

The Electras traveled from Ely to record at Dove Studio in Bloomington with producer/songwriter Warren Kendrick (seated on amp with guitar). Courtesy ARF! ARF! Records.

"Action Woman" just using the tone controls on the guitar, switching from mellow to bright. "Remember, we don't have any fuzz or stomp boxes, no wah-wah pedals," Kendrick said. "By then we were well into using the two amps put together in series to create the fuzz tone. By then, just about the time I would come out with a chord progression, Paul Revere and the Raiders would come out with the same one. Neither of us was hearing each other—this happened independently."

Kendrick was "ready to throw up" listening to and using the I-IV-V progression—C to F to G, the tonic to the subdominant to the dominant. "Isn't there something I can do to get rid of this?" he wondered. "I'm trying to think of the way chords work together. I decided for 'Action Woman' to start off on the flatted third. That would have been B flat, drop down to an F, then it would have gone to the G, the tonic or root note. Most of the time people would try to put four chords together; this one was only going to use three. I just held the root down a little longer, and it worked. 'Action Woman' was an interesting hit."

It came at a key time in Kendrick's life. Despite all of his studio work at Dove, he was working full time as a mathematics teacher in the little town of Rose Creek, outside of Austin, Minnesota. He was out sick one day, but an executive from Columbia Records managed to track him down and call him at the private home where he was renting a room. Columbia wanted to buy the Electras' recordings of "Dirty Old Men" and "This Week's Children" and put them out on a two-sided single on their Date subsidiary label—and they were not insisting on owning the publishing rights. Kendrick had already turned down several offers for the record from labels that insisted on acquiring his publishing. He agreed to the Columbia deal over the phone. Because there was another U.S. band using the name the Electras, Columbia released the "Dirty Old Man" single under the name 'Twas Brillig (from Lewis Carroll's poem "Jabberwocky")—a move that deeply upset the Electras and did nothing to help the record's sales.

"By then, I was also working with the Litter on 'Action Woman,'" Kendrick said. Both the Electras and the Litter released "Action Woman" on Scotty, but the Electras' version was quickly withdrawn and now sells for $750 on the collector's market. "I cleaned up the label," Kendrick said. "It used to be kind of homemade looking, but I put a little Scotty dog with a plaid suit on it—cute as all get-out."

Kendrick brought an acetate pressing of the Litter's version of "Action Woman" to KDWB, where deejay Tac Hammer at first was reluctant to listen to it. "Warren, haven't you heard?" Hammer said. "We're a tight playlist. No local bands, nothing. We're restricted to thirty songs." But Hammer did listen to the record, and Kendrick got a call later that night telling him that the station was playing "Action Woman" as a KDWB exclusive. It never went into heavy rotation, however; at that time, rival WDGY was airing its newscasts at twenty minutes before and after the hour, calling it "20–20 News." If KDWB had a record it wasn't sure about, the jocks would play it at the same time WDGY was doing its newscast, reasoning that even listeners who didn't like the record would switch back to KDWB rather than listen to news on the other rock station. That's where KDWB slotted "Action Woman"—and the single bombed.

"It had to do with demographics and marketing," Kendrick said. "The thirteen-year-old girls were able to step up from 89 cents for two songs to $2.99 for twelve songs on an album. I was starting to recognize that."

Kendrick wanted to get as far away as possible from the bubblegum music that the other producers at Dove were trying to create. Dove Studio had gone into high gear in 1966 with the arrival of Peter Steinberg and Dale Menten, who created a production company called Candy Floss. Steinberg asked Menten to come in and arrange a string quartet for a record he was producing for the band T. C. Atlantic. At that point, all Menten knew about string quartets was that a quartet was four. But he needed the money, so he went to the library and got a book by Hector Berlioz called *Treatise on Instrumentation and Orchestration*. He stayed up all night, learned that a string quartet was composed of two violins, a viola, and a cello, imagined the string parts, wrote them out on a chart, and brought it into the studio.

"I was just shaking," Menten said. "They're going to pay me—but only once, because if I flunk this class, I won't be asked to come back." Fortunately, the first violin player was a friend of his who took him aside and offered some subtle suggestions to improve the arrangement ("You know, ah, you may want to take this voicing up here—it's a little more brilliant. The part's right, but the illusion is wrong"). Menten learned a valuable lesson: "On a pencil, if you turn it over, there's a thing called an eraser, and you shouldn't be afraid of using that."

Soon thereafter, Menten and Steinberg became partners, writing and producing records for a variety of acts and trying to sell the songs to major labels. In the meantime, they were also representing bands that worked with Bill Diehl and Dick Shapiro at Central Booking. "We're booking, they're booking, we're trying to stay friendly," Menten said. "And Bobby Vee is sending us all his bands from North Dakota, and [booking agent and manager] Ken Mills is sending us all his bands from South Dakota, and we're churning out music."

Steinberg's background is murky, but most who knew him at the time describe him as more of a showman than a music man. Songwriter Barry Thomas Goldberg, whose band the Shambles was one of the first acts to work with Steinberg at Dove, called him a "Colonel Parker guy. He was good with lyrics, but he was all bluster. He didn't really do things above board."

Arne Fogel, who came to Dove Studio in 1966 with his singing partner Steve Long-man as a would-be Simon and Garfunkel duo and ended up joining the Shambles, said Steinberg was terribly unmusical. "Not to say he didn't deserve some of his songwriting credits," Fogel said. "One time he played me a song he'd written, accompanied himself on piano, and it wasn't too bad, but he had no sense of pitch, no sense of time, and couldn't carry a tune. Pete was a controversial guy. He was not untalented, but his talent was more in the hype and the salesmanship aspect of things rather than music." Steinberg's musical deficiencies are clearly evident when one compares his performance of his own composition "Find This Woman" on the Candy Floss compilation CD with the version recorded by the Underbeats in 1967. Jim Johnson's vocal cops a delightful Bob Dylan attitude while expertly navigating the melody; Steinberg's shaky, off-key vocal sounds as though he'd never heard the song before.

The Shambles became the Puddle—and later, the Batch—with Goldberg on vocals and rhythm guitar, Fogel on vocals and keyboards, Gary Paulak on vocals and lead guitar, Jay Lee on bass, and Whip Lane on drums. Initially, Steinberg was going to be in the band, too. "It was very difficult to deal with that," Fogel said. "Remember Howard Kaylan and Mark Volman of the Turtles? The bigger, fatter of the two [Volman] didn't play anything, just ran around and did stuff while the others were playing, except he could sing. But Pete couldn't do that. One time he was swinging a sound cable around his head on stage and it clipped me. I threatened to quit at one time."

Menten, on the other hand, carried cachet with aspiring rock musicians, who fondly remembered the Gestures. "He was a celebrity to me," Fogel said. "I grew up with 'Run, Run, Run.' All the local groups were great—'Little Latin Lupe Lu,' 'What Is the Reason'— and they were fun to dance to. But 'Run, Run, Run' was the one that was like the Beatles. It had harmonies, it was a little bit more progressive vocally than anything coming out of here. I was quite in awe of him for the first ten years I worked with him, quite honestly."

Despite his misgivings about Steinberg, Goldberg stayed with Candy Floss because of Menten. "He was a great guy and a fantastic musician," Goldberg said. "But he wasn't very hip. He was kind of a square."

In fact, it was Menten's ambition at this point in his career to produce songs for the radio. Production teams like Jerry Kasenetz–Jeff Katz were cranking out hits for groups like the Ohio Express, the 1910 Fruitgum Company, and the Music Explosion. They were simple, catchy, and dumb—and Menten and Steinberg saw no reason why the same couldn't be done out of the Twin Cities. Thus the name Candy Floss.

The first Menten–Steinberg project was the heavily orchestrated T. C. Atlantic recording of "Twenty Years Ago in Speedy's Kitchen," written by Goldberg, Gary Paulak, Menten, and Steinberg about some shady characters Goldberg had grown up with. The lead vocal was sung by T. C. Atlantic's Freddie Freeman, but the record was a studio collaboration. Then the four wrote songs for Goldberg and Paulak's band, the Shambles: "Lights of Rome," "World War II in Cincinnati," both in the light pop style of the Bee Gees, and "Flannigan's Circus," a straight shot of juvenile escapism.

"It was just like I was in heaven," Menten said. "I'm in a writing combine. Peter and I hopped in a plane with the Shambles, and we fly off to Buddha Records in New York." The plan was to sell a Shambles record to one of the major New York labels. Menten had never been to New York. As he and Steinberg walked down a Manhattan street, he actually used the line, "Wow, you could sure store a lot of corn in those buildings." Then a man with an attaché case bumped into him, spun him around, and said, "Fuck you"—something no one had ever said to him before. Menten looked at Steinberg with alarm.

"Keep walking," Steinberg said.

"I don't like this town," Menten said. "This town is aggressive."

"Oh, shut up," Steinberg said. "It's going to be fine."

They ultimately made a deal to place the record on the Atlantic subsidiary Atco, but there was a vibe of negativity to New York City that Menten wanted no part of.

The Shambles record went nowhere, but the fact that it got placed with Atco elevated Dove and Candy Floss beyond anything that was happening at Soma. George Garrett had moved his label to an office in Los Angeles; in 1966, he released his final record on Garrett, a frantic blue-eyed soul workout called "The Perfect Combination" by Lance and the Spirits, fronted by Hollywood bit player Lance LeGault. Soma's final hit single was the Del Counts' "What Is the Reason" in 1967, and the following year the Heilichers merged their Musicland business with Pickwick International, which acquired the Soma catalog. The days of Soma trying to go head-to-head with national record labels was over. It was another signal that Twin Cities bands with ambitions to follow in the footsteps of The Trashmen, Gestures, and Castaways had to get out of town—or at least make a record good enough to be placed with a major label. That continued to be Menten's focus through 1967.

"For a while it was a kick," Menten said. "There were some really neat ideas there. It was a writer/songwriter/production company, with no label affiliation. But those were the days when you couldn't get any local airplay, and even if you got Parrot Records to put it out, where did they put it? Looking back, it was during the time that people were doing scammy shelters and things like that. New guys in California would start a movie, never finish it, but they could turn in all kinds of receipts and get a big write-off. [A label] could show the IRS that they spent $200,000 in promotion and merchandizing trying to get this Shambles thing off the ground. I think it was that, because other than a little product that came to us in a box, it didn't appear anywhere. It got no airplay."

A few Candy Floss productions did get airplay. In 1967, KDWB disc jockey Peter Huntington May brought in a band from Maplewood called the C. A. Quintet and had Menten produce their cover of "Mickey's Monkey"—actually a mash-up of the Miracles' "Mickey's

The C. A. Quintet released a cover of "Mickey's Monkey" before recording one of the most collectible albums in rock, the psychedelic *Trip Thru Hell*. Courtesy of Denny Johnson of Minniepaulmusic.com.

Monkey," Bobby Bland's "Turn On Your Lovelight," and Gary U. S. Bonds's 1960 hit "New Orleans." Released on May's own Falcon label, the song peaked in the 20s at the end of August on both the WDGY and KDWB charts.

"Peter Steinberg asked me to help him manage the company," said Ken Erwin, the leader and songwriter of the C. A. Quintet. "I was always pretty good at organizing and so forth. The bands that Peter managed were supposed to pay a percentage of their gross from playing jobs, and in return they would get studio recording time. The only groups I can remember paying were T. C. Atlantic and the C. A. Quintet. It was a very disorganized, dysfunctional business, if you could call it that. However, the C. A. Quintet as a result built up a lot of studio time that we could use. And as a result I planned to use it to record an album." In 1969, the C. A. Quintet cashed in that studio time to record a psychedelic album that is now one of rock's most cherished collector's items, *Trip Thru Hell*, vinyl copies of which have sold at auctions for more than $5,000.

Duluth's Soul Seekers—an unusual band for the era in that they had a woman lead vocalist, Bonnie Matheson—recorded a pair of singles produced by Menten, "Boom Boom" and "New Directions," that were sizable hits in Duluth in 1967. "Boom Boom," a John Lee Hooker blues standard that was given a modern pop sound, eked into the KDWB chart for two weeks in December 1967, peaking at Number 28. "That was my best gig there, because I got to take that tune and give it a little Swingle Singers, Mamas and Papas thing, and they went with it," Menten said. "That was fun. It was a good band, and they actually were players. I wouldn't have been able to pull it off with many people, because they would have been, 'No, no, we're going to do it our way.' But they were open to it. I said, 'Let's just do something else with it.' That could have sucked if nobody could sing. That could have been a real train wreck. But the idea's only part of it. The execution is important, and they pulled it off."

Candy Floss nearly cracked the Top 10 on KDWB in November 1968 with a bubblegum song called "Oscar Crunch," written by Goldberg, Paulak, and Steinberg and recorded by Nickel Revolution (Ron Hort on keyboards and vocals; Keith Luer on lead guitar and vocals; Louie Lenz on rhythm guitar; Scott Jeffy on bass guitar; and Jerry Lenz on drums and vocals; Paulak sang lead on the record). Released on the Philips label (Four Seasons, Dusty Springfield, Blue Cheer), it was every bit as perky and disposable as anything coming out of the bubblegum factories on either coast: "Oscar Crunch is going to join the zoo, yes, he's trying to be a kangaroo. . . ." It was even given a spin on Dick Clark's *American Bandstand*.

By that point, however, Menten had grown weary of producing novelty tunes. "I wasn't going to get out," he said. "Instead of leaving, I thought 'What I'll do is I'll try to change the direction. I'll try to modify what we've been doing.' All this stuff was really what we then called bubblegum." Menten took his concerns to Steinberg and the rest of the Candy Floss writers. "We keep trying to write the same song—'Twenty Years Ago,' 'Oscar Crunch went to the zoo,' we're doing 'Hang on Sloopy's,'" Menten said. "Now let's do something else—some music. You guys all have writing talent. Let's put our heads together and let's try something."

"We're not going to change," Steinberg said.

"I understand," Menten said. "Then I'll just leave.'"

Yet the lure of Dove Studios continued to bring in ambitious bands that had already taken a crack at the George Garrett–Kay Bank route and decided to go elsewhere—like the Stillroven, a band from Robbinsdale that began as the Syndicate in 1965. "We knew The Trashmen were from our area, and the Underbeats' drummer [Rod Eaton] was from Robbinsdale," said Phil Berdahl, drummer for the band. "When you look back on it, there were a lot of bands and musicians that came out of the North Side area. I can't tell you why."

The Syndicate changed its name in 1966 after keyboard player Dave Dean took a drive north of Stillwater and saw a sign for the Dunrovin Christian Retreat Center. "We're not done rovin', we're still rovin'," Dean said.

"We thought Stillroven was kind of cool, so we went with it," Berdahl said.

The band's fortunes improved markedly when they auditioned at Mr. Lucky's for an agency called Stagefinders, run by Bill Roslansky—who was also managing Dave Brady and the Stars—and Peter Huntington May. "They were our first booking agents," Berdahl said. "Two weeks later we had new clothes and we were busy all the time." May took them to George Garrett's basement studio at Nic-O-Lake Records in 1966 to record "She's My Woman," an original by Dean and guitarist John Howarth. Released on May's Falcon label, the record attracted little attention, so the following spring the Stillroven went to Dove Studios and cut a cover version of "Hey Joe" by the Leaves. That record made the Top 25 on WDGY.

One afternoon after practice the band piled into their Econoline van, with *Stillroven* painted on the side, and drove to the Robins Nest, a popular A&W drive-in on Highway 100 across from Robbinsdale High School. "The place was packed as always," Berdahl said. "All of a sudden our song 'Hey Joe' came on the radio. It was the first time we had heard it. Everyone was looking at us. We jacked up the volume and others did, too. We finally had a song on the radio. It was the coolest thing ever."

The Stillroven came from Robbinsdale, beginning their existence under the name the Syndicate. Courtesy of Denny Johnson of Minniepaulmusic.com.

"Hey Joe" changed everything for the Stillroven. Their record was being played throughout Minnesota, as well as in Fargo, Sioux Falls, and La Crosse, and the band was in heavy demand for bookings. That summer the Stillroven and the Del Counts opened for Sonny Bono (minus an ill Cher) at the Minneapolis Auditorium. "The first band was the Del Counts, wearing their outfits, then we came out in our cool English suits and did Yardbirds songs," Berdahl said. "Cher had [had] a miscarriage, so they trained people to do her part. After the show, we had a picture taken with Sonny. Peter May said, 'Sonny was really stoned.' I said, 'Pete, I didn't think he looked drunk to me.' 'No—stoned.' I didn't know what the term even meant. We were pretty simple—naïve. Then we started smoking pot, too."

The Stillroven returned to Dove Studios to record a follow-up to "Hey Joe" and scored another regional hit with "Little Picture Playhouse," sung by new guitarist Jim Larkin. Larkin and guitarist Dave Berget left the band in the spring of 1968 and were replaced by Mike O'Gara and Michael Flaherty of Dale Menten's aborted dream group, the Seraphic Street Sounds. With their records getting wider airplay and May working his radio

The Stillroven was one of many bands to play all-ages shows at Dayton's eighth floor auditorium. Courtesy of Denny Johnson of Minniepaulmusic.com.

contacts, the Stillroven were booked to play an outdoor concert in Tucson with the Sunshine Company, Brenton Wood, and—in their last week together—Buffalo Springfield, a group that was splintering due to the egos within their multitalented lineup of Neil Young, Stephen Stills, Richie Furay, and Jim Messina.

"Buffalo Springfield was our favorite band; to play onstage with them was a big, big deal," Berdahl said. "It was a beautiful spring evening at a baseball stadium. We shared one locker room. Neil Young was having a falling-out with those guys. He's sitting in the visitors' locker room with us, in the corner playing his guitar. We tried to talk to him, but he was in a bad mood. He said, 'I don't want to talk. I'm pissed off with those guys.'"

The Stillroven's repertoire included many Buffalo Springfield songs, which featured strong vocals and intricate guitar parts. "We had multiple lead singers and harmonies," Berdahl said. "A lot of bands didn't try to do that. They'd have one guy. All of us sang lead at some point during the night."

Later that summer, Dave Rivkin joined the Stillroven, having already moved from the Chancellors to the High Spirits. "The High Spirits were a competitor, but Owen [Husney] was a good friend of mine, and Cliff [Siegel] was my cousin," Rivkin said. "They invited me to join just after they put out the record 'Turn On Your Lovelight.' I decided to give that a try. I wasn't with them for very long. I skipped from there to the Stillroven. I was really getting into the hippie-dippie days. They were all singers and all players and superb musicians."

It was time for the Stillroven to take a shot at the big time. "I remember for the longest time we were all saying, 'We got to get a national hit,'" Rivkin said. "But no one could really do it. Willie Weeks [briefly with the Mystics and, later, Gypsy] moved out, Bob Dylan moved out, everybody who was successful had to move away. There was no artist consistency. It was a one-hit thing for most of those groups. They were novelty records. Everyone was going in individual directions. It wasn't the sound of Minneapolis yet."

Peter May connected with a manager/booker in Kansas City named James Reardon, who in turn was connected to L.A. music mogul Mike Curb. The Stillroven had a sudden wealth of gigs, so they bought a Cadillac and a new van and traveled the country in luxury. The band still needed a hit single, however, and Rivkin didn't think they had a breakthrough song. "The day of album rock was just starting, and people didn't think of singles so much as self-expression," Rivkin said. "In those days, they'd sign a group and give them three albums before they expected a hit."

The band was sent to Norman Petty's studio in Clovis, New Mexico—Buddy Holly's starting place—to record a few songs with Michael Lloyd, who would later produce Barry

Manilow. They were then signed to A&M Records, moved to Los Angeles, rented a house, and recorded an album there. "Peter May wrote himself in as the producer," Rivkin said. "It sounded horrible. We learned what not to do. He wanted to quit his job at the station and go out on the road with us. He made a good day-to-day manager, but he wasn't a producer. He didn't know how to record. He promoted himself over his head. That kind of thing is what drove me to get three-dimensional depth on my records. I never wanted to sound like that. That was the Minneapolis sound then—shallow, no bass. I love Tom Jung, but I think at the time the technology was limited. On 'Little Latin Lupe Lu,' we used a three-track machine, did the band on two tracks, and put the vocal in the middle. Maybe it was a lack of e.q., or not knowing how to mic, I don't know. It was all a learning curve."

Perhaps because of the inferior sound, A&M did not release the Stillroven album. Mike O'Gara's girlfriend, Bonnie Diamond, then invited the band to come to Washington, D.C. She arranged an audition in New York City with Phil Ramone, a recording engineer who would go on to produce albums for Paul Simon and Billy Joel. Ramone told the Stillroven that he really liked them, but he wanted them to record a song called "Everybody's Talkin'," which was going to be in a movie called *Midnight Cowboy*. The song, written by Fred Neil, became a Top 10 *Billboard* hit in October 1969 for Harry Nilsson. The Stillroven hated it. "We listened to it, and it wasn't our style at all," Rivkin said. "I think a couple guys just quit right there: 'We didn't join the band for this. We're not going to go through with this.' We were on the verge of potentially something good, but the tension broke everything up. Sometimes I think the nervous tension of doing something successful can tear you up faster than not doing anything. So that was the end of that."

Not quite. On the drive back from New York, the roadie who was driving their equipment truck fell asleep and crashed. He was not injured, but all their guitars, amps, and sound equipment were gone. "We couldn't afford to replace them, so fuck it, we decided to call it a day," Rivkin said.

Berdahl believed that drugs also played some part in the Stillroven's demise. "It freed up a lot of people's minds and spirits for taking chances, but a lot of good practice time got spent sitting around smoking pot and talking," Berdahl said. "I don't think it helped. It's hard to practice too much. If you're not as good as you want to be, the only way to get better is to practice. We'd be practicing sometimes and start jamming for a while. Sometimes it was great, but we weren't trying to make Grateful Dead albums."

The changing times were getting to The Trashmen as well. The fun had gone out of the business; kids weren't dancing to rock 'n' roll anymore. "We were out East on a tour again

As the sixties progressed, the Stillroven's stage outfits became more psychedelic and colorful. Courtesy of Denny Johnson of Minniepaulmusic.com.

with clubs and ballrooms when Jimmy [Thomas] calls and says, 'The guy canceled your gig,'" Dal Winslow said. "We had played at a place in New Jersey and were supposed to play at Allentown, Pennsylvania. It was supposed to be a two-night gig. This guy said he canceled because his club had burned down, and Jimmy told us later the reason was he had a chance to get Herman's Hermits. They were the more popular group."

Winslow missed the days when The Trashmen would play roller rinks where the kids drank pop and danced on the bare wooden floors for four hours straight. "Take that a few years later, and nobody was dancing," he said. "They were sitting in the middle of the floor and meditating. They wanted to hear James Brown and stuff, and we weren't doing hardly any of that. The crowds weren't dancing at all."

"When we first started, we were doing ballrooms and teen dances, but now two, three, four years later, these kids are in bars," Reed said. "Now you're getting more and more club dates, and they want you to do a three-to-four-night deal in a club. That's when the fun started going out of it. I enjoyed the one-nighters. If you don't like where you're at, don't worry about it, you're gone tomorrow. Sitting in a motel in Madison, Wisconsin, or wherever, for three or four nights doing four-to-five-hour club jobs, the fun's gone."

"We knew it was going to come to an end, and we didn't want to ride it down," Tony Andreason said. "A lot of the groups that we knew were playing clubs after that, and we'd see them play, and we just made a conscious decision to stop. We were going to go on with our lives. It was quite a party, and we're out of here."

They had a job scheduled for Woodley's Country Dam at the end of summer in 1967, and Winslow, Reed, and Andreason agreed to make it their last. Steve Wahrer wanted to keep playing and asked the rest of The Trashmen if they minded him putting together a band called The New Trashmen. They said, Go ahead. After their last job together, The Trashmen didn't see or talk to each other for months but eventually decided to go out for a holiday dinner together at the end of 1967 to catch up with each others' lives. They went out to see Steve Wahrer's band, which Winslow thought was pretty good, but according to Andreason, "It just lasted for about ten minutes."

Andreason didn't totally check out of the music business. He, Mike Jann, and David Anthony had reunited to start a record label called Metrobeat, using the old Kay Bank Studio, which was renamed Universal Audio after Vern Bank sold it in 1968. The Trashmen had released their final single, an uncharacteristic country novelty outing called "Green, Green Backs Back Home" / "Address Enclosed," both written by Larry LaPole, as Metrobeat's second single in July 1967. The Underbeats' splendid "It's Gonna Rain Today" was also released on Metrobeat that summer, as was "All I See Is You," the first single by Lonnie Knight's new band, the Jokers Wild. Andreason produced the second Jokers Wild single, "Because I'm Free" / "Sunshine" for the Peak label, a subsidiary of Metrobeat. The More-Tishans also released their only single, "(I've Got) Nowhere to Run," on Peak.

Lonnie Knight's career had taken an odd twist when he was forced to leave the Rave-Ons in 1965. He was temporarily replaced by Jim Larkin of the Gremmies. "My dad was transferred to Detroit at the beginning of my senior year," Knight said. "They got another guitar player to fill in for me while I was gone. The day I graduated in 1966, they all flew to Warren, Michigan, attended my graduation, and we all got on a plane the next day and flew to Minneapolis."

Larkin moved on to the He-Toos and then to the Stillroven, while Knight moved back in to his spot as lead singer and guitarist with the Rave-Ons. The band had a heavy workload and made good money. They recorded their third single with George Garrett at Kay

The Trashmen eventually began working at adult clubs, including this stand at St. Paul's Whiskey A Go-Go in August 1966. Courtesy of Mike Jann.

THE RAVE-ONS

CONTACT: David Anthony Productions, Inc.
4150 Central Avenue, N. E., Mpls.

After leaving the Castaways, Lonnie Knight joined another Richfield band, the Rave-Ons *(left to right)*: Harry Nehls, Lonnie Knight, Dick Wiegand, Larry Wiegand. Courtesy of Denny Johnson of Minniepaulmusic.com.

Bank, a Beatle-esque Knight–Larry Wiegand original called "Baby Don't Love Me," with a B-side called "The Line" credited to Garrett, Tony Kai-Ray, and drummer Harry Nehls. "I think Harry and me and Tony wrote that," Knight said. "Garrett didn't have anything to do with it. He says he did." Then Garrett inexplicably brought Knight to his basement studio at Nic-O-Lake Records and had him record Nat King Cole's "Too Young" as a solo singer. Knight had no idea why. "He just brought me in and said, 'Do this song.'"

The Rave-Ons continued to work with Garrett until 1967, though there was no exclusive contract with him. They also cut some songs with Peter Steinberg at Dove, but they were never released. By then they were working with David Anthony, who was becoming increasingly prominent in the Twin Cities music scene. Anthony was counting the door for Jimmy Thomas at Schlief's Little City on a night when the Sir Douglas Quintet was headlining there. He handed out his card to several local musicians who had come to see the show—including members of the Rave-Ons. Anthony told them he had all kinds of work available for them. "They called me the next day, and I gave them six jobs on the first phone call," Anthony said. "I hadn't heard them, but I heard about them. I figured if they were playing around, they're doing something."

Before leaving for Korea, Anthony had worked with a band from Brooklyn Center called the Aardvarks, which included Dave Waggoner (Mike's cousin) on bass and vocals. When he returned from the service, Anthony changed the band's name to the He-Toos. They released one single, covers of Fats Domino's "Josephine" and Buddy Holly's "Reminiscing," but broke up after shifting their set list to primarily British Invasion material. Waggoner (who changed the spelling of his name to Wagner), guitarist Gene Balabon, and bassist Denny Johnson then put together a band called the New Gremmies, after meeting original Gremmies drummer Pete Huber at the Ritz Theater in Northeast Minneapolis. The Ritz was a practice/audition space Anthony maintained for bands to work in a simulated live setting. The New Gremmies added Kink Middlemist on keyboards and changed their name to Jokers Wild—a name Doni Larson of the Underbeats came up with during a poker game with Dave Wagner.

Perhaps influenced by Jim Johnson's remaking of the new Underbeats as a super group, Anthony did some mixing and matching of his own to create a band with a white R&B sound like Mitch Ryder and the Detroit Wheels. He and his assistant booking agent Bruce Brantseg took Larry and Dick Wiegand and Harry Nehls from the Rave-Ons and put them together with Wagner and Middlemist of the Jokers Wild to form a new band called South 40. They cut their first single, "The Penny Song" / "Good Lovin'" at Kay Bank and released it on Metrobeat in 1967. The remains of the Rave-Ons and Jokers Wild meanwhile—"Those of us who didn't make the cut," in Knight's words—decided to join up and retain the name Jokers Wild. "I wanted to be lead singer [of South 40], but David Wagner was a much stronger singer," Knight said. Jokers Wild's new lineup was Knight on lead vocals, Denny Johnson on bass, Peter Huber on drums, Bill Jordan on guitar, and Greg Springer on keyboards.

"After a period of time I was showing Bill all the guitar parts," Knight said. "He got fed up and quit. I took over on guitar." They played rhythm and blues by artists like Joe Tex and Wilson Pickett, as well as Beatles songs, but the band was rapidly moving in yet another new direction: psychedelia. "We were incredibly psychedelic," Knight said. "We had overhead projectors, smoke machines, the whole nine yards. You had to have a song twenty minutes long, or you weren't anywhere. It was great. I've unearthed songs from

Following the demise of the Rave-Ons, Lonnie Knight joined Jokers Wild *(left to right)*: Bill Jordan, Pete Huber, Knight, Denny Johnson, Greg Springer. Courtesy of Denny Johnson of Minniepaulmusic.com.

that era that I wrote that I forgot about. It was psychedelic babbling, but interesting chord progressions I would still use. We didn't know enough about music theory to know why things would happen. We would just throw things against the wall to see what would stick."

The band hit a brief bump in the road after the recording of "Because I'm Free" and "Sunshine." Knight and Springer left Jokers Wild to play in the Litter after that band's lead guitarist, Zippy Caplan, left to form White Lightning. "It was a bad decision, so we came back to Jokers Wild," Knight told *It's Psychedelic Baby* web magazine.

Jokers Wild eventually stripped down to a psychedelic power trio featuring Pete Huber, Lonnie Knight, and Denny Johnson. Courtesy of Denny Johnson of Minniepaulmusic.com.

In November 1968, Jokers Wild was rehearsing new songs at the temporarily closed Someplace Else teen club in Robbinsdale. They were going to record an album that would be produced by Warren Kendrick, but a midweek fire at the club destroyed $20,000 worth of uninsured musical equipment. The band plowed forward, however, opening for Credence Clearwater Revival at the Minneapolis Armory in May 1969. They were invited to open for Credence on a nationwide tour, and for several weeks they rehearsed in Albuquerque, where the tour was to begin. But Credence leader John Fogerty became ill, the tour was canceled, and Jokers Wild returned to the Twin Cities. Heavily influenced by

Cream and Jimi Hendrix, the group stripped down to a power trio with Knight, Johnson, and Huber. Their clothes were as stylish and colorful as any hard rock band of the day—striped bell-bottoms, paisley jackets, suede boots—and their music was as psychedelic as their light show.

Huber had to stop playing the drums due to physical problems in August 1969 and was replaced by Bill Gent. Johnson and Knight didn't feel right about playing as Jokers Wild without Huber, so they decided to change the band's name to Flash Tuesday in January 1970. That band lasted just a few months into 1970, however. Knight had become enthralled with the singer-songwriter genre that included James Taylor, Joni Mitchell, and John Martyn. He abruptly made the leap from earache–inducing psychedelic rock to soft acoustic sounds. "It was an entire new world," Knight said. "There was so much freedom in playing solo. I started out doing local venues like 1 Groveland—in the basement of a church—and the Coffee House Extempore on the West Bank. I got involved with the Bitter End college coffeehouse circuit. I drove or rode by Greyhound and played colleges all over the Midwest and up and down the East Coast."

The Castaways continued to be a big draw in Minnesota into the later 1960s, despite having just two original members, Denny Craswell and Roy Hensley. When Donna dropped out of the Castaways in 1967, he tapped Dennis Libby and guitarist Tom Husting from the Doo-Rytes and Greg Maland of Gregory Dee and the Avanties to replace him and Bob Folschow. Libby got his start in a St. Louis Park band called the Treble Men, because he could sing "Surfin' Bird." He was later replaced by Rick Beresford of the High Spirits but joined up with Dudley and the Doo-Rytes, who put out a 1966 single on Soma called "U.F.O.," cowritten by Jim Donna, who also booked the band. With two strong keyboard players, the Castaways became more versatile. They landed a deal with Fontana Records and cut a psychedelic pop tune called "Lavender Popcorn," written by professional songwriters Scott English and Eddie Reeves. "They shipped us to Sparta, Michigan, to record the song," Libby said. "The studio was an old vaudeville theater with the seats ripped out. In the corner was a gigantic pipe organ. Greg said, 'I want to play it.'" Maland got such an immense orchestral sound from the pipe organ that it had to be mixed back in the recording of the record's flip side, "What Kind of Face." To promote the A-side, the band ordered 150 pounds of lavender popcorn to be delivered to radio stations. Unfortunately, only the outside hulls of the kernels were dyed lavender. When the corn was popped, it was the usual white. Like the popcorn gimmick, the single stiffed, but the recordings the Castaways made during this period, particularly the Roy Hensley–written Who imitation "Just on High," were excellent.

"That was a pretty powerful version of the band," Craswell said. "In some ways it might have been a little better than the original. Libby had a great low voice, and we had an organ and a piano. We used to do a version of 'A Day in the Life' with huge strobe lights. We went through the psychedelic age and embraced it all—the Beatles, Yardbirds, English rock, and stuff. If it was good, we put it on the list. If they danced to it, we played it."

The Castaways once again traveled all around the Upper Midwest. In 1968, they were booked to open a double bill with the Beau Brummels at the Dane County Fairgrounds in Madison, Wisconsin. They made the drive to Madison at night in bad weather, and their bamboo-sided Castaways van left the road. "It was a terrible accident," Libby said. "The van rolled over numerous times at seventy-five miles per hour and wrapped around a tree. It completely demolished our equipment and the van. We were so fortunate that nobody died."

"Libby, me, and Kent Stearns, the roadie, were in that truck," Craswell said. "I'll never forget when we started rolling. The song playing on the radio was 'Walk Away Renee.' They said the van rolled over five times at least. Four sides of the van hit. Multiply times five, that's a lot of rolling. Then we were on the roof, bobsledding down that ditch. It was all snow 'till we wrapped around the tree. The van was literally cut in half, folded up like the Oscar Meyer wiener truck. Our equipment was scattered over two acres. I had a mic stand through my leg." It would have been worse had Jim Donna not had a screen welded to the inside roof rack of the van to hold the mic stands in case of an accident. "Thank God Jim Donna did that," Craswell said. "But they could get through the top. I'm lying on the snow after the wreck. Libby thought I was dead, and I thought he was dying. Then they came and picked us up with a hearse from the town of Mauston. They couldn't afford both an ambulance and a hearse."

Neither the equipment nor the van was insured, so the Castaways had to start over. Despite their injuries, they had to resume playing as soon as they could. "I ended up with two broken knees," Libby said. "B-Sharp helped us with some equipment. We went up and got another truck. I can't say we never recovered; we did a thing where we wore period costumes. You really had to keep reinventing yourself, and we were not averse to stealing other peoples' ideas."

At this point, the Castaways' path crossed with Dale Menten's. "The Castaways came to me back in 1968," Menten said. "They said Dunwich Productions out of Chicago wanted the Castaways to do an album. I said, 'Well, I'll play the tunes that I have.' Because I used to just go up into the attic in my house in Richfield and write tunes. I had five tunes, the names of which are all gone—I think the tapes are gone, too. And I had a longer tune probably, twelve to fifteen minutes long, called 'The House of Leather.'" It was an extended piece about the American South during the Civil War. It featured a teacher named Mama Grim who made rifles and handguns in the basement of her school to sell to either side. Though The Who's rock opera *Tommy* had been released to much fanfare by then, Menten was not a fan of the form and had not originally intended to write a rock opera. He brought the Castaways into Universal Audio, with Bob Schultz engineering, and recorded "House of Leather" and the other five songs he had written. They were submitted to Dunwich.

"Love it," the Dunwich people said. "Skip the five other tunes. This 'House of Leather'—that's the album."

Unfortunately for the Castaways, it couldn't be a Castaways album. The labels to which Dunwich was shopping the band wanted bubblegum music in the style of the American Breed ("Bend Me, Shape Me"). Fontana Records wanted Menten to put a band together and go on the road to promote "House of Leather." The band Menten assembled included Libby; bassist Dik Hedlund; organist Bruce Pedalty, who had played in a later version of the Accents; and drummer Joey Piazza, who had played on "Hang on Sloopy" with the McCoys and was now drumming with the Mystics. Menten named the band Blackwood Apology.

In the meantime, there was still a Castaways project to complete. "It started out dicey right away," Menten said. "Roy Hensley was the bass player, and he was the weakest link in the group. We'd start rehearsing, and he just couldn't get any of the tunes. So I sat down with both Dennys and Greg, and just said, 'Would you mind if I brought in a studio bass player? Because this is not going to happen. It's going to take forever. He's not getting it.' Since they came to me, I wasn't quick to put studio players in, if they're paying for it. But they could all realize this wasn't happening. It wasn't a happy time." Menten brought in bassist Ron Beckman from Mankato, who had played with the Best Things/Only Ones and could read charts. Libby decided he'd rather go with Blackwood Apology than stay with the Castaways, which angered the rest of the band. Without Libby, Dunwich wasn't interested in the Castaways anymore.

Blackwood Apology prepared for its tour at Dania Hall near the University of Minnesota campus, a former Scandinavian cultural center that had an auditorium on the third and fourth floors that smelled like marijuana and patchouli, according to Menten. After three weeks learning the songs and incorporating a slide show that included images of both the Civil War and the Vietnam War, the band drove to Chicago and played on bills with hard-rock bands Baby Huey and Aorta. In the Twin Cities, they opened for the Grateful Dead at the Labor Temple in Minneapolis, a show promoted by David Anthony.

Owsley Stanley, the Dead's sound engineer and LSD chemist, accompanied the band. "That was quite an experience," Libby said. "They were very late to show up at the Labor Temple. They had to drag these gigantic cable reels and all their tube amps upstairs. They fired up a cone-drive PA. The Grateful Dead got their shit set up, and then big trays of Coca-Cola came around. Everybody drank one."

"That was going to be our life now," Menten said. "You don't get any sleep. I tried smoking dope and had a real bad experience, so I couldn't be with the guys smoking dope. Once again it was, 'God, I can't do this.' And 'How much fun is this?' But I liked the process that got us to this point. So we go back to Minneapolis, and I'm wondering what I'm going to do." Menten's career then took yet another unexpected direction. Dick Shapiro introduced him to Wisconsin playwright Fred Gaines, who collaborated with Menten to turn "House of Leather" into a theatrical musical at the Cricket Theater in Minneapolis. Blackwood Apology performed the songs each night. The play received rave reviews and played to packed houses for months, then moved to the 2,300-seat Crawford-Livingston Theater in St. Paul. And then to New York. "It was sort of like when I moved from North Mankato across the bridge to Mankato," Menten said. "You lose things."

In New York, *House of Leather* got a new director and new cast—including Barry Bostwick in his first off-Broadway leading role. The producer hired different musicians, but Menten was musical director and stayed in New York for a couple of months to help stage the play. "We were in awe—probably too much in awe—and not fighting enough for what we thought was going to work," Menten said. "The director tried to fight, but the producer was in charge. It was his money. So we just kind of watched this little Midwestern play go to New York. They added dancing and five more tunes."

Everything went well during the show's eight previews, but on opening night everything went wrong. A police call with yelling and screaming interrupted one of the tenderest scenes, confusing the audience. Then during Bostwick's big song, the person running the spotlight couldn't find him on the otherwise darkened stage, and the audience began to laugh each time the spot turned on and off with no actor in it. After the performance, everyone went to Sardi's to await the reviews. The producers were upstairs watching a Teletype as the early reviews came in. "We're downstairs with all of our new friends, people I'd never met," Menten said. "They're having the shrimp and the hors d'oeuvres and the little meatballs and everything. God, it's great."

The cast from New York told Menten that good reviews were great, and bad reviews they'd just throw away—except for Clive Barnes of the *New York Times*, who could make or break a play. The initial reviews were mixed—some thought the music was a little to rock-y, while some thought it was brilliant. Then someone got his hands on Barnes's review—a pan. "It dribbled in slowly," Menten said. "It started at the end of the room. And by the time it got to me, there were only four or five of us standing alone in this place. As people got it, all of our new friends are just gone. The people remaining were the two people from the Minneapolis cast. They said, 'Screw it, let's just stay on another week. We can do this. That's just one guy who says this. It's got a chance. We'll change it.' They're ready to dig in."

Libby said the other reviews were mostly positive. The headline in the *Village Voice* review read, "A small Minneapolis Company shows us how to do it." The New York cast, however, left immediately to look for their next job. "We ended up the next few days trying to get money to fly out," Menten said. "Everybody was gone."

Menten returned to Minneapolis, bought Bob Schultz's half of the former Kay Bank/Universal Audio (now named Micside), and began running his own recording studio. Many of the other 1960s-era Minnesota rockers were moving into the business world, too, but a few clung to their dreams of rock 'n' roll stardom.

EVERYBODY'S HEARD
ABOUT THE BIRD

FROM THE LAND OF 10,000 HITS

MONOPHONIC
33⅓ RPM

HIGH FIDELITY
SIDE ONE

FOR PROMOTIONAL USE ONLY

CHAPTER
13

DREAM IF YOU CAN

"I DON'T THINK ANYBODY EXPECTED ME TO COME HOME."

There must have been times when Jim Johnson himself didn't expect to make it home from Vietnam. Though his base camp wasn't getting hit, they sent platoons out into the jungle to protect the area. Johnson said he saw "terrible combat"—a stark contrast to the times he was asked to play guitar for his company, the Fourth Infantry Division. "I had such a glory job, I felt guilty," he said. "After we played, these guys were so happy. They'd say, 'Johnson, this is what you should be doing.'" And in September 1968, he went back to doing it. He was mustered out of the army, returned to Minneapolis, and rejoined the Underbeats, just as he had promised. "I don't think [the war] had a long-lasting effect on him," keyboardist James Walsh said. "He was lucky enough to play music with the [Special Services]. He came back relatively unscathed."

Johnson's return gave the Underbeats a vocal lineup—Johnson, Tom Nystrom, Rico Rosenbaum, and Walsh—of unprecedented riches. As far as Johnson was considered, the band was too good to play the same old Twin Cities clubs. "When I came home, I was so tickled to be alive," Johnson said. "But I was not bound to stay in Minnesota anymore. I'd seen the tropics. I was going to California to see Sonny Curtis. As soon as I got back, I was going to Los Angeles."

First, some housekeeping was in order. Despite his superior guitar skills, Wally Walstad was now an unnecessary fifth wheel. "I had to tell Wally, 'That's it for you,'" Johnson said. "I said, 'Let's keep Walsh. We can use that voice, and he knows all these songs.'"

Johnson did feel as though he'd lost his leadership qualities while in Vietnam, where it usually didn't pay to take command. In the interim, the Underbeats had acquired a manager named Steve Freeman, who was an old Highland Park buddy of Rico Rosenbaum's. Freeman had plenty of money; his wealthy father owned Freeman's Lighting Concepts in St. Paul. The band now deferred to Freeman's decisions, but fortunately for Johnson, Freeman was all for relocating to the West Coast. It was time. "We'd gone as far as we could and wanted to focus on original music," Walsh said. "I knew there weren't any avenues here. We had decided to wait for Jim Johnson to come back from the service, and we had plans to leave for California upon his return. The plan was to look for a label, but we needed to get established first."

Everybody was ready to go—even Rosenbaum, who was very close to his mother, Ida. "Ida loved her boy—gosh, she loved her boy," Johnson said. Rosenbaum's relationship with his father, however, had always been complicated. "Rico was kind of rude to his father," Johnson said. "His father was very nice, very cordial, but never seemed well, like an old guy walking on eggshells. He pretty much stayed in his room. Rico felt he embarrassed him. He'd tell him to speak English."

The Underbeats got a school bus to haul themselves and their gear out to Los Angeles. On the trip west, however, Rosenbaum learned that his father had died suddenly. "That broke his heart," Johnson said. "He didn't come out to L.A. until a week later."

Johnson had taken Rosenbaum under his wing, teaching him to play harmony leads on the guitar and to stand in the right place next to his amp to create feedback. The two shared a sense of humor unique among the members of the band. Johnson also considered Rosenbaum an exceptional songwriter. The two collaborated on the band's parting shot in Minnesota, the single "You're Losing Me" / "Darkness," recorded at Dove in the fall of '68 and released on Ira Heilicher's P.I.P. label. Both songs were cowritten by Johnson and Rosenbaum. "You're Losing Me," featuring a tasteful horn section and lush group vocals backing Rosenbaum's lead singing, could have fit on Al Kooper's first Blood, Sweat & Tears album. Walsh sang lead on "Darkness," a heavy rock tune that sounded a bit like Cream.

By Thanksgiving 1968, the Underbeats were in Los Angeles. They lived in a house out in the Valley with bunk beds and a pool, financed by Steve Freeman, and got a gig at a club on the Sunset Strip called Gazzarri's, which was known as a place where new bands could break into the scene. The club's management changed the Underbeats' name to the Groovy People at the suggestion of some of their new fans. During this time, however, Tom Nystrom decided life in an L.A. rock 'n' roll band wasn't for him, so he moved back to Minnesota. "Tom was kind of a weenie—he wasn't a courageous guy, let's put it that way," Larson said. "But he figured if he were going to leave town, it was going to be with us. He was with us for the first six months. Tom was always afraid of earthquakes. It was a subject that was always in the media, how California was going to break off and fall into the ocean."

Nystrom was replaced by Jay Epstein, another Minnesotan. But soon other tensions began to surface. Larson was not happy with Freeman's management decisions or with Rosenbaum's ego trips. "At Gazzarri's, Rico was having one of his hissy fits," Larson said. "He was a narcissistic mama's boy, not getting his way, and he was embarrassing himself and the band. I told him to stop it, and he didn't, so I walked over and told him, 'Take your guitar off.' Then I knocked him on his ass. That was the last time he threatened me physically. Johnson looked at him and said, 'I told you.' I can handle myself. It did calm things down."

Larson also believes that was the point at which some of the other band members began discussing replacing him (Larson) with Willie Weeks, who had become one of the top bass players in the Twin Cities with Michael's Mystics. "Elmer Valentine came down from the Whisky a Go Go to see us after hearing about us," Walsh said. "Chicago was playing at the Whisky. Their *Chicago Transit Authority* album broke out, and he asked us to take their place as house band at the Whisky for a year." It was the break they'd been waiting for. Fortunately, the new gig coincided with another name change, this one inspired by a comment bassist Doni Larson made that they were living like gypsies. And so Gypsy was born. "We met everybody," Walsh said. "The guys from the Doors. Jimi Hendrix came to see us, Buddy Miles, King Crimson. As house band, we opened for everybody. That was the place."

Johnson liked Los Angeles. Because he'd been out of the country in 1967–68, he felt he was a year behind all the music trends and was playing catch-up while Woodstock was

The Underbeats moved to Los Angeles in 1968, landed a job as house band at a club on the Sunset Strip, and changed the band's name to Gypsy. Courtesy of Denny Johnson of Minniepaulmusic.com.

showing the way to the future. Rosenbaum had emerged as Gypsy's primary songwriter, with Walsh and Johnson contributing a song apiece to the material that would make up their first album. It was a strange period for Johnson, who got married after returning from Vietnam and didn't do much writing. "I wrote one song I'm not really proud of, 'Man of Reason,'" Johnson said. "I did a lot of arranging on the Gypsy things, but nobody got credit for that in those days."

Atlantic Records president Ahmet Ertegun saw the band at the Whisky and asked for some tapes, which he gave to several producers. One of the producers suggested they record "He Ain't Heavy, He's My Brother," a song that became a huge hit later that year for the Hollies. "We had the original shot at that but passed on it, and we shouldn't have," Walsh said. "Unfortunately, that's where our ego didn't match our business sense."

At the time it didn't seem like such a huge mistake, however. Gypsy had two contract offers, one from Atlantic—home of Crosby, Stills, Nash and Young, Aretha Franklin, and Led Zeppelin—and one from Metromedia, a fledgling label whose one star was teeny-bopper heartthrob Bobby Sherman. "We thought we'd be lost in the shuffle at Atlantic, so we went with Metromedia," Walsh said. "We thought the individual treatment would be better. Little did we know they didn't really know what to do." Nevertheless, the debut album *Gypsy* did "wonderfully well," in Walsh's words. Metromedia gave Gypsy more artistic freedom than they would have received at Atlantic, and Rosenbaum had written so much quality material that it was released as a double album—a rare leap of faith for a debut group. The first single, "Gypsy Queen," spent eight weeks on the *Billboard* singles charts, peaking at Number 62, and "Dead and Gone" was an FM radio favorite in an era in which album cuts were becoming as important as singles.

Larson hated the decision to go with Metromedia. "There were arguments between me, Rico, Walsh, and our manager, Steve Freeman," Larson said. "I'm not a shy person—I disagreed about the business end, the recording contract, and the band musically. I did not think we should have put out a double album. If the first one was a success, we had another one ready to go right away. We were a tax break for Bobby Sherman. It was time to leave, or I'm going to be fired."

Metromedia sent them back to the studio to record a second album, this one titled *In the Garden*, on which Rosenbaum wrote six tracks and Walsh one. By then, Larson and Epstein had left the band, replaced by bassist Willie Weeks and drummer Bill Lordan, both of whom had played with the Twin Cities R&B group the Amazers before moving to the Mystics. The band did most of its rehearsing in a house in Laurel Canyon, directly below a house owned by Mickey Dolenz of the Monkees. *In the Garden* was also well received, and Gypsy became a concert favorite with progressive rock fans across the country, particularly in St. Louis.

Weeks left the band to do studio work and tour with Chaka Khan's band Ask Rufus and was replaced by Randy Cates.

Gypsy's first release was a double album, almost unprecedented for a debut band. Courtesy of Richard Tvedten.

Gypsy eventually became the house band at the famed Whisky a Go Go club on the Sunset Strip, where bassist Doni Larson posed for this photograph. Courtesy of Doni Larson.

Unhappy with the inexperience of Metromedia's management, Gypsy signed a two-album deal with RCA Records, but sales were not as strong for their third album, *Antithesis*, all but two of its songs written by Rosenbaum. They remained a terrific performing quintet, however, and after playing with the Guess Who, Mason Proffit, and the Chambers Brothers at the Winterland Ballroom in San Francisco, Gypsy was signed by Don Hunter, the Winnipeg-based manager of the Guess Who. "We opened for the Guess Who for two and half years," Walsh said. "We went everywhere they went—Europe, Canada, and Hawaii. It was great exposure. We got about $1,500 to $2,500 a night with the Guess Who. We were on salary all the time, each making $175 a week. It was all right. We were able to eat and smoke. We were fine."

"We were their tax write-off, it felt to me," Johnson said. "My wife was ready to have her baby, so they moved us back to Minneapolis. When we were touring, it was cheaper to fly us back to Minneapolis. But Rico didn't want to go to Minneapolis. Neither did Bill, and if I wasn't married, I wouldn't either."

Lordan left Gypsy to play with Sly and the Family Stone and, later, Robin Trower. Walsh, however, was ready to leave the West Coast and come home. "I hated every minute of living in L.A." Walsh said. "I went to California for one reason: that's where the record companies were. I didn't like living away from home. Even the climate was bad. Jim eventually came home, and Doni came home. Rico liked it and stayed."

Johnson replaced Lordan with drummer Stan Kipper and began rehearsing Gypsy in Minneapolis, without Rosenbaum. "I said, 'I can't do this without him,'" Johnson said. "I told him, 'You either come back and rehearse, or you're not going to be in the band.'" Rico wasn't budging, so Johnson decided to head back to the coast. He had to play a few Gypsy gigs in Minneapolis to be able to afford to return to Los Angeles—a move that cost him his marriage. At that point in his life, however, he wasn't willing to abandon his dreams of reaching the top of the music world. "I can't stay here," he told himself in Minneapolis. "If I do, it's just over."

Once he got back to Los Angeles, he tried to put together a new Gypsy. He and Kipper found a bass player named Lewis Derrey, a six-four African American who, Johnson said, was "the best conditioned guy—he played basketball every day." But during a stop in Minneapolis, the twenty-four-year-old Derrey came down with a sore throat that turned into meningococcal meningitis. Three days later he was dead. "We couldn't believe it—he had a cold," Johnson said. "Now what?"

Johnson then found bassist Bradley Palmer, who went on to play with America, but Walsh decided he no longer wanted to try to make a go of it in Los Angeles and moved back to the Twin Cities for good. Gypsy's fate—and Johnson's—depended on luring Rosenbaum back to the band. He recorded some songs with Johnson and played a concert with Gypsy in St. Louis in 1977, but he would not stay. "Rico was gone, making money doing other things," Johnson said. "I really couldn't get him back."

Rosenbaum's old partner in the Escapades, Zippy Caplan, was harboring similar dreams of making it big in rock music, and he was ready to go anywhere to do it. After the first version of the Escapades folded, Caplan went through a swift succession of bands. He played with Froggy and His Friends, the band formed by former Gregory Dee and the Avanties drummer Doug Nelson. Bass player Charlie Lindley hung the sarcastic nickname Zippy on Caplan during this period, because Caplan was frequently late to gigs.

Froggy and His Friends recorded a single at Dove that was picked up by Chess but apparently never released; Caplan left the band because they played primarily covers, and he didn't see them going anywhere. He briefly put together a band called Weekdays, a mixed-race group including three female singers, a drummer, and a bass player. He played in a four-piece band with singer Jimmy Hill called the Intruders, with bassist Mark Brown and drummer Warren Lester. Jimmy Hill and the Intruders played ballrooms and clubs all over Minnesota. "I didn't remember ever having a problem because Jimmy and the bass player were black," Caplan said. "For me that was a transition period, a stopgap to what I was trying to do: get in a situation where I could go somewhere."

That was when Caplan first met Larry Loofbourrow, another guy who was trying to go somewhere. Loofbourrow and his friend Ted Dooley were a vocal duo called Bockeye who made trips to California to try to get a record deal. Loofbourrow had written songs with melodies and chord progressions similar to songs the Monkees were doing, and he hired Caplan to write and record guitar and bass parts for the songs at Kay Bank Studio.

Caplan then took a job with the Accents—Skip Dahlin on bass, Bruce Pedalty on keyboard, Bob Ramsey on drums, and Lorenzo Whitemarsh on vocals—when original guitarist Kenny Sand went into the service. Caplan was playing at Mr. Lucky's with the Accents when Larry Loofbourrow approached him again. "I want to move this thing to California, and I want you to come with," Loofbourrow said. "If we go, I'm going to shop my songs. I'm going to record there, too. We'll drive out. I'll put you up. You'll have a place to live. If we get the deal, I'll pay you $25,000 a year to write the parts."

Loofbourrow didn't want Caplan on stage, however. "He had kind of a Milli Vanilli idea—he wanted guys who looked a certain way to back them up," Caplan said. "It was weird, but I said, 'Yeah, sure, I'll go out with you.'" Caplan left the Accents and stayed in California for more than a year. They recorded all of Loofbourrow's material at the famous Gold Star Studios in Los Angeles, home to Phil Spector, Brian Wilson, Buffalo Springfield, the Monkees, and dozens of other hitmakers. After hearing the tracks, Tower Records told Loofbourrow they wanted to sign him to a songwriting contract but not as a performer. "He didn't like that idea," Caplan said. "It went against everything he wanted. He had a backer here in town who'd put up $10,000 for him to do all this stuff. He really did have some good stuff, and here he had this big chance, and the fucking guy said no. They wanted his songs, but they were going to give them to other people. He said, 'Forget it.' Now he regrets it, but we all made those kinds of mistakes back them. We were young and stupid—some of us."

While Caplan was on the coast, friends in the Twin Cities were telling him about the heavy sounds of the Stillroven and the Litter. Meanwhile, he was being exposed to the new psychedelic rock. "I saw the Seeds on the Strip, and I thought, 'I'd love to play this stuff,'" Caplan said. "The Larry thing was falling apart, so I came back here." He got in touch with Litter bassist Jim Kane, with whom Caplan had shared some bills when Kane was in the Victors. Kane was having problems with Caplan's old St. Paul friend Bill Strandlof, who wanted to do harmony pop like the Hollies, whereas Kane had the Litter positioned as a hardcore psychedelic rock band. Kane asked Caplan if he'd consider taking Strandlof's place in the band. "Do me a favor and come listen to us play," Kane said. "Come to some gigs so you can get a handle on what we do." After seeing them play several times, Caplan knew they were going to be successful and wanted to be a part of it, but he wouldn't take the job unless Strandlof quit on his own.

One night in Rochester, the Litter was playing with the Stillroven. Caplan and Stillroven drummer Phil Berdahl were standing backstage while the Litter was onstage. "Then there's some commotion in front of the curtain," Caplan said. "Strandlof had gone nuts. He was screaming, hollering, kicking stuff, and all of a sudden an amp came flying back and misses us by an inch. That was his last gig. Kane comes running back and says, 'You should have seen it. That's it. He's out.' Something must have happened up there. I don't know what the trigger was, but it brought it all to a head on the spot."

Strandlof had no hard feelings when Caplan replaced him on lead guitar in the Litter. The band had already begun recording their album *Distortions* at Dove Studio, using Strandlof's leads on Warren Kendrick's "Action Woman," "Soul Searching," and The Who's "A Legal Matter." Kendrick asked Caplan to come in and finish playing on the rest of the album. "Kendrick was a genius with music and math," said Caplan. "He had the phasing thing going before 'Itchycoo Park' [by England's Small Faces]. He was just one of those kind of guys, just a genius, but unfortunately his right arm went dead and he couldn't play anymore."

Caplan contributed "The Mummy," a song he'd been playing from the old Boris Karloff monster movie. The band thought it was cool and tacked it onto the end of their cover of The Who's "Substitute." The album also included Larry Loofbourrow's "The Egyptian," and the single "Somebody Help Me" / "I'm a Man," a pair of songs originally sung by Stevie Winwood with the Spencer Davis Group. The album was released on Kendrick's Warick label (*Warick* came from WAR-ren + Kendr-ICK). "They couldn't keep that one in stock, either," Kendrick said. "We had to have that one re-pressed. People had graduated from singles to albums. The single bombed, but the album, whoa. And albums were much more profitable."

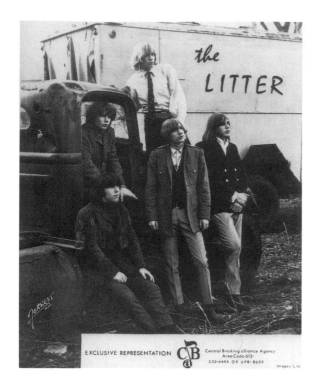

EXCLUSIVE REPRESENTATION C|B Central Booking alliance Agency
Area Code 612:
232-6666 OR 698-8653

Zip Caplan replaced Bill Strandlof as lead guitarist for the Litter, who were produced by Warren Kendrick. Courtesy of Denny Johnson of Minniepaulmusic.com.

"We went on to play all the big shows in Chicago," Caplan said. "We were bigger there than here. We were a cult phenomenon." In Chicago, they were the favorite band of Aaron Russo, the twenty-four-year-old promoter who ran a club called the Electric Theater. "Aaron Russo really wanted bad to manage the Litter," Caplan said. "He later managed Bette Midler [and the Manhattan Transfer]. He was not a schlocky guy; he was a hip guy with good business sense." The Litter was also now being booked into the Cheetah Club in California and the Peppermint Lounge in New York.

Larry Loofbourrow wanted to take another stab at getting a record deal, so he flew the Litter and Roy Hensley of the Castaways ("I wanted an actual bass player," Caplan said) to California to record some of his new songs. Back in the Twin Cities, Caplan brought Denny Waite and Dave Rivkin to Kay Bank to add harmony vocals to some of the tracks. Two of Loofbourrow's songs—"Morning Sun" and "Confessions of a Traveler through Time"—were used on the Litter's second album, *$100 Fine*, recorded and produced by Kendrick at Dove Studio.

"Now it's 1968, and we're really getting into Cream," Caplan said. "We'd put out our version of 'I'm So Glad,' we opened for Cream at New City Opera House, *Disraeli Gears* is out." The Litter was getting a jump on the newest English songs by The Who, Spencer Davis, Cream, the Small Faces, and the Yardbirds because Kane had a friend in the UK who sent him the latest records. "Nobody had these songs," Caplan said. "They thought all these songs were original material. They'd send over a Spencer Davis record, 'Somebody Help Me'—they thought that was a Litter song. Rinaldi started the smashing-the-equipment thing before anybody saw The Who live over here. By 1968, the show finished with strobe lights and wrecking the equipment. That's what got us to the second-to-the-top rung. That's why they loved us in Chicago."

The Litter were regulars at Chicago's two biggest clubs, the Electric Theater and the Aragon Ballroom. They opened for Iron Butterfly, Genesis, and Mountain. They played an outdoor festival in Grant Park for fifty thousand people. When Haskell Wexler was filming his movie *Medium Cool* about the street fighting at the 1968 Democratic Convention, he chose the Litter to be onstage at the Electric Theater for one of the scenes. The band went to Chicago and spent all day shooting, playing six or seven songs over and over. They're seen in the movie, but the sound track actually uses a song by Frank Zappa and the Mothers of Invention.

"Probably the biggest mistake I and the group ever made was when we were at the Cheetah in California with Gary Puckett and Genesis, and Elektra wanted to sign the group," Caplan said. "They wanted us to stay in California, put us up on a ranch, and write music, but we said no. It was a big, huge mistake. The reason we said no was there were so many problems in the group I didn't think we could do it. We thought we'd kill each other. We turned it down. That was the end. It was unfortunate. Looking back, in retrospect I would have really pushed hard to sign that deal and take my chances. We've all made mistakes, but that's not only the biggest but the one that haunts me to this day. But I can't do anything about it."

After the Litter shot their scene in *Medium Cool* in August 1968, Caplan knew the band was on the verge of falling apart. Lead singer Denny Waite was losing his voice trying to compete with the loud PA systems of the late '60s. Caplan knew Waite was going to quit, so he began looking for his own exit plan. "Everybody was having problems with everybody else, management was fucked up—they were doing a decent job, but making some mistakes with how money was handled—and there was dissent in which direction we were going. Half of me said Aaron Russo is a guy who can get us somewhere. It was getting sticky on all fronts."

Caplan was infatuated with Cream and wanted to put together a power trio. He'd already acquired a stack of Marshall amps like Eric Clapton's. "I was so loud, I think I had two stacks side by side," Caplan said. "The last gig I played at the Electric Theater, I was so loud I was drowning out the whole band. A guy said, 'You gotta turn that thing down. They can hear you out in the street.' I didn't know how loud they could get."

He wanted to find out. "We were all living in a big, huge, honking band house around Lake of the Isles—me, Rinaldi, Kane, our road manager, and Larry Loofbourrow, who by that point couldn't get anywhere as a writer and became our road manager. Down the block was Woody Woodrich, who started out as a lead player in a group called the Reactions, but who could also play bass. He would come over, and he and I started jamming." Woodrich accompanied the band to a gig in Chicago, and on the drive back he and Caplan formed their plans for their next band, a power trio called White Lightning, named after a variety of LSD. "All we needed was a drummer," Caplan said. "We talked to Gar Johnson. It wasn't his thing. If you talk to him today, he'd say he was sorry. He said yes to trying it, but we got two or three weeks into it, and it wasn't right, so he quit." Ronn Roberts, a friend of Woodrich's who was working for the Litter in Chicago, recommended Mickey Stanhope, a singer and drummer from Joliet, Illinois. Stanhope came to the Twin Cities, auditioned, and was hired to fill out the power trio.

The departure of Caplan and Waite from the Litter did not spell the end of that band. They brought in Lonnie Knight for a short-lived stint on lead guitar and lead vocals. Nor did it spell the end of Caplan's living arrangement. "We were still living in the same house with the Litter," Caplan said. "I didn't move out; they weren't going to shoot me or anything. Everything kind of evolved on its own. No big problem."

Caplan asked Warren Kendrick for a new song, because he didn't want to do cover songs in White Lightning. Kendrick came to the house and showed Caplan a song called "Of Paupers and Poets." "It sounded like a bubblegum group, like that kind of shit," Caplan said. "What the hell is this? He said, 'It's got a good melody and chords.' We took that thing and turned it more into a psychedelic Cream type of thing. We totally changed the feel and how it played." The song was recorded and released on Kendrick's Hexagon label. For the flip side, White Lightning recorded an unnamed hardcore tune they'd been working on and named it "William" after Bill Pluta, who worked for the band as an equipment guy. "Pluta was a wild man, a loose cannon, but loveable," Caplan said. "When we were recording it, I said to Pluta, 'Do this scream that goes into the solo.' It comes up to the solo, he screams, and Kendrick goes, 'Stop, stop! That's horrible, we're not using it.' We pulled it out."

Kendrick took the single to KDWB and told the music director he had to hear this new 45, without telling him who it was. "The guy thinks it's Cream," Caplan said. "He got them to play it, and it goes to Number 5 in a period of weeks." It peaked at Number 5 on KDWB on February 3, 1969; the last local song to make the singles chart on either KDWB or WDGY had been the insipid "Oscar Crunch" by Nickel Revolution back in November 1968.

Caplan wanted to come out big with White Lightning, so he asked to debut at the New City Opera House—the former Mr. Lucky's. Caplan had suggested the new name to his friends who owned and ran the place because Mr. Lucky's no longer seemed to fit with the more psychedelic times. "You know, I'm not with the Litter," he told them. "I've got a new three-piece, like Cream. A lot of originals." The New City Opera House was packed for the debut, which White Lightning concluded with an extended version of "The William

Tell Overture," a piece that Caplan and his friend Bernie Bomberg had arranged years earlier. Caplan told Woodrich, who announced their songs, to tell the audience before "William Tell" that a lot of groups were closing their shows with "Toad," a twenty-minute song by Cream that featured an extended Ginger Baker drum solo. Then he instructed Woodrich to say, "Well, fuck it, we're not going to do it," before launching into "William Tell." "Back then, in '68, if you said that into the mic, the crowd would go ooooohhh!" Caplan said. "It blows the fucking roof off the place. From there on, we didn't have no trouble getting gigs."

White Lightning was playing all over Minnesota, Wisconsin, and Iowa. When Ira Heilicher saw where "Of Paupers and Poets" was on the charts, he worked out a deal with Atco to re-release it. The song did not chart nationally, however, and copies of the song on both Hexagon and Atco are considered rare and collectible.

Zippy Caplan left the Litter to form the power trio White Lightning, which made its debut at New City Opera House, formerly Mr. Lucky's. Courtesy of Denny Johnson of Minniepaulmusic.com.

The band went into Kendrick's Lake Street studio to record some originals and some Larry Loofbourrow songs, but they were never released. Then Ira Heilicher asked the band to do an album for Pickwick International. The band added guitarist Ronn Roberts, who was writing songs that wouldn't work well in a power trio format. Then Stanhope, who had sung lead on "Of Paupers and Poets," became ill and asked to be relieved of his drumming duties so he could become the band's frontman. To replace Stanhope on drums, the group hired his friend Bernie Purshey from Joliet. Now the band was a five-piece, and they changed their name to simply Lightning. "When Bernie came up, Heilicher wanted to do the album, but I wish we'd had a different label," Caplan said. "We went into Sound 80, recorded the album, and Pickwick put it out. By then we are as big as the Litter in Chicago and huge in Iowa, playing to overflowing crowds every time we played there. They wanted us to do an East Coast tour to promote the album. We went to Philadelphia and opened for the Amboy Dukes. Guess what? No albums. Distribution problems."

It was the same old story with the Heilichers. On top of the scarcity of product, the company had used a new mastering process from Germany that resulted in poor sound because it wouldn't track properly on some turntables. Plus, there was supposed to be an insert to the album with song lyrics, but there was no insert. "We've got all these tours, gigs, people, crowds, but we're not able to follow it up," Caplan said. "They took the album out to radio stations, but they couldn't get the goddamn records. I never forgave Heilicher for that. In spite of themselves, the goddamn thing still sold twenty-five thousand copies, which wasn't bad for a record that was all screwed up."

Lightning lasted just a couple of years, breaking up in 1971. Caplan wanted to play more hard rock; Woodrich was into Emerson, Lake, and Palmer; Roberts was leaning toward CSNY and Poco, and lead singer Stanhope didn't know where the band was going. "It was a mess," Caplan said. "Finally, I quit."

Years later, the reissue market had rediscovered both the Litter and Lightning, and demand for the old songs and albums became intense. Caplan was asked to work on a reissue of the Lightning album, but he didn't want to do it without the original master tapes, so he called Amos Heilicher.

"Can I get the master tapes?" Caplan asked.

"Yeah, for ten grand," Heilicher said.

"Ten grand? Do you think this group was the fucking Rolling Stones?"

"If you want them," Heilicher said, "I know you're going to do something with them that's going to make money."

Larry Wiegand, who had split with Lonnie Knight when South 40 was formed, said the breakup was "pretty civil, but it was an awkward thing." He was surprised when Knight ended up going with the Hendrix-Cream sound of Jokers Wild, because he thought Knight was moving in a more country-Dylan direction. Wiegand's new band was not conflicted about its own direction. "We wanted white guys playing rockin' blues," Wiegand said. South 40 was playing songs by Otis Redding, Mitch Ryder, Wilson Pickett, and even some Rolling Stones. They were not into psychedelic music; they much preferred the R&B coming out of Muscle Shoals and Memphis. "The idea when we formed this band was we were going to try to make a dent," Wiegand said. "We were going to do everything we could, work-wise, practice-wise, to take a serious approach, instead of just high school kids being popular."

South 40, composed of members of the Rave-Ons and Jokers Wild, won a regional contest to record tracks for Columbia Records. Courtesy of Denny Johnson of Minniepaulmusic.com.

Unlike Gypsy and the Litter, however, they were not initially talking about relocating. "We were just trying to develop as players," Wiegand said. Beginning in the summer of 1967, South 40 cut a pair of singles and an album, *Live at Someplace Else,* on Metrobeat. The album was roughly split between originals and R&B songs by Joe Tex, Allen Toussaint, Lee Dorsey, and Holland-Dozier-Holland. They got airplay in Duluth and Fargo, as well as some in the Twin Cities, and started working constantly. "The money wasn't bad, but it wasn't the Underbeats," Wiegand said. "I wouldn't say we were terribly successful. After the top three, there was the next five, including us. We were working quite a bit. Later on, that changed drastically with our records coming out. We started making decent money. In the summer of 1968 when the [live] record came out, we only had two days off. That lasted until sometime in 1969. We knew we were at a point where we had conquered Mount Minnesota, if you want to call it that. Now we had to make a move."

They entered a contest among bands that had played the Midwest ballroom circuit and emerged as the winner among the fifty bands that entered. The finals, between South 40 and the Fabulous Flippers, were held at the Bel Air Ballroom in Des Moines. By winning, South 40 received a trip to Chicago to cut a demo with Columbia Records. The label passed on the five songs South 40 recorded, but they caught the ear of an executive at Dunwich Productions, the company behind the Buckinghams, the Cryan' Shames, and the Shadows of Knight. "Dunwich was also a management company," Wiegand said. "They were going to invest time and money into recording us. They thought they heard a couple of hits on their hands with the first five songs."

At this point, South 40 had to replace drummer Harry Nehls, who had accepted an offer to join T. C. Atlantic. "We picked up another guy named Mike Melascar," Wiegand said. "The guy we wanted was Denny Craswell, our old friend from Richfield, but he was still touring with the Castaways. Then they broke up, and he became available. We wanted him all along. We tried to get him before we had Harry Nehls, but the Castaways had such a huge hit." Dennis Libby's departure to Blackwood Apology had effectively brought an end to the Castaways, and Craswell was not ready to put away his sticks. "I just jumped on their bandwagon for another ride," Craswell said. "Luckily it went to the top again. It was a lucky deal to get."

A South 40 album was scheduled, but before it came out, the band members knew their name did not fit their sound. "We were not country," Wiegand said. "We decided on the name Crow. My recollection is Craswell came up with the name Mother Crow. There were a lot of mother bands [Motherlode, Mother Earth, and so on]. We kept the idea, and the name Crow came out."

The band had formed a corporation called South 40 Inc. Each member drew a salary, and all the money they made went into the corporation. "If we were smart, we would have put away some money, but it turns out there were more expenses than income," Wiegand said. "It caught up with us later on, but at that point we were on a pretty good salary, making quite a bit of money for our age." Crow signed with Amaret, a small subsidiary of Mercury Records run by president Kenny Myers. "He was hard-headed," Wiegand said. "He thought he knew everything." The first single Amaret issued from the album, "Time to Make a Turn," didn't get much airplay. The flip side was a song written by the Wiegands and Dave Wagner called "Evil Woman." "We wanted that out, but we didn't have any horsepower to change anything," Wiegand said. "The radio stations were playing 'Time to Make a Turn,' but a station in Seattle flipped it over and started playing 'Evil Woman,' and it just took off. Everybody started playing it. That's the one we tried to push in the first place."

Looking for a more hard-edged sound and image, South 40 hired Denny Craswell on drums and changed its name to Crow. They had a Top 20 hit with "Evil Woman" in late 1969. Courtesy of Larry Wiegand.

"Evil Woman" was a national smash, cracking the *Billboard* Top 20 in December 1969. The song also holds the distinction of being Black Sabbath's first single: Ozzy Osbourne sang a cover version of "Evil Woman" on the British version of Black Sabbath's 1970 debut album. "Evil Woman" set Crow up for a three-year run during which they would share stages with virtually every big-name act, including two tours with Janis Joplin. They appeared with Neil Diamond, Eric Burdon, Three Dog Night, Chicago, Johnny Winter, Blood, Sweat & Tears, the Allman Brothers, Iron Butterfly, Grand Funk Railroad, Steppenwolf, Fleetwood Mac, Savoy Brown, Jefferson Airplane, the Steve Miller Band, and Vanilla Fudge at arenas and outdoor festivals across North America.

"We were road dogs," Wiegand said.

Craswell even got a come-on from Joplin. When Crow opened for Joplin's Kozmik

Blues Band in Minneapolis, her baritone sax player, Cornelius "Snooky" Flowers, came into the dressing room and said, "Janis wants to talk to Dennis, the drummer."

"I'm not exactly comfortable going to her dressing room," Craswell said.

Undeterred, Joplin called Craswell later that night.

"Hey, sugar babe, what ya doing?" she said. "We're going out somewhere. You want to meet us?"

"We're locked in for the night," Craswell said.

"She was hitting on me," said Craswell, who perhaps disingenuously ascribed Joplin's interest to the brass drum kit he played at the time. "I didn't want to go with Janis. Her agent had told me in private she can claw you up on your back. It was just hearsay, but I didn't want to find out."

There were the usual shady characters on the road, particularly at festivals. Craswell said one of the festivals was short of cash, so their agent went to the promoter's office—much like Chuck Berry in St. Paul on New Year's Eve 1964—and collected Crow's fee with a gun. "He was going to make sure we got our money before it ran out," Craswell said. Craswell said Crow was a democracy, like the Castaways, but more of a brotherhood. "There was never a cross word I can remember in all the time I played with Crow," he said. "It was fun. We just got along great. It was a real privilege to be in that band."

Craswell recalls playing before crowds of people as far as the eye could see at the major rock festivals that were common during the era, but he said that was not much different from playing indoor concerts. It was the same songs and the same energy level no matter the venue. "We always made it a rule, no matter how big the stage was, to set up next to each other like you're on a small stage," Craswell said. "We wanted to hear and see each other."

Many times after a Crow concert, Craswell would retch with the dry heaves because he was so spent from the effort. "I don't know what it was, but it would wind us up to incredible peaks of energy," he said. "We developed this thing like a machine, winding up and up so tight. The way the Wiegand brothers played and the way Dave drove the band, I can't describe it. It was way different than playing with the Castaways. We were good players and we sounded good, but in Crow we got on a super plane of energy I've never been on before. We got standing ovations everywhere we played in the United States. We got multiple encores against every band we played. I felt sorry for Credence Clearwater after we got done with them. You wouldn't want to be Credence after Crow."

Crow followed "Evil Woman" with two more minor hits, "Don't Try to Lay No Boogie Woogie on the King of Rock and Roll" and "Cottage Cheese," both of which stalled out in the 50s on the *Billboard* chart. Wiegand voiced the same complaint about Amaret that many bands had with Amos Heilicher's labels: fans couldn't find the product in the record stores. "It was frustrating," Wiegand said. "All the promoting we were doing didn't help. When people can't find your record, they'll move on to their next favorite band. Before we signed with Amaret, we got an offer from Atlantic. We desperately wanted to be on Atlantic Records—that's where Wilson Pickett, Aretha, and all the people we'd been playing for years were. They [management] decided otherwise. They thought at Amaret we'd be bigger fish in a small pond. It came back to bite us."

In 1971, Crow was contacted by Jac Holzman of Elektra Records, who'd signed the Doors. He wanted to work with Crow, but Amaret president Myers wouldn't let it happen. "Our label owned the rights to our name," Wiegand said. "Myers told us, 'If you go with him, I'm going to keep the name.' Holzman didn't want us without the name. That didn't do him any good."

Amaret kept pitching songs to the band that the label thought would be hits, but Crow's biggest hits were the songs they'd written themselves. Finally, the band had had enough; when the contract expired in the third year, Crow left Amaret. Then they discovered that their accountants hadn't been withholding income tax from their pay, and they were in trouble with the IRS. "We had a band vote about what to do with our money," Craswell said. "I voted we should split our money after every job. In the Castaways, that was the best way. They decided to put the money in an account and draw on it while we're on the road to let it build up. I was not in favor of that. I don't think it's a good idea. It was the only difference we ever had."

All the money was sent back to the Minneapolis bank account of their manager, Bruce Brantseg. "He had us on the road a long time, making good money every job," Craswell said. "We come back, go to the band's offices, and all our band contracts have been piled up alongside our manager's desk and lit on fire. It was a pile of ashes. We had no idea how much we made or where we played. He emptied the bank account and left for L.A. I heard he used that money to buy into Peavey instruments. The last I heard, he owed $35,000 to the IRS. He left us with the bill, and we had to go out of business. And in order to go out of business, we had to stop playing. We were forced to break up. We never had an argument or a fight. We always loved playing together, but we didn't know we were playing for free."

Even without the business woes, the band members' tastes were starting to drift apart, just as audiences were starting to segment into fans of specific genres. The Wiegands were interested in getting deeper into R&B, while Wagner was becoming a fan of Waylon

Jennings and outlaw country-western. Wagner was first to quit. He was tired of being away from his children for such long stretches. Sometimes he brought his six-year-old daughter on tour with the band, but that led to funny looks from people when she was standing at the airport in the middle of the band's road crew, who were rough-looking bikers.

"We were all young men, we'd been on the road for five or six years, and it was time to do the family thing," Wiegand said. "We put a screeching halt to it in 1972. I didn't want to continue down that road. We were just kind of spent. We spent the whole 1960s trying to get to this point, and it was frustrating that this happened to us. We had a lot of great times, a lot of success, but it would have taken another superhuman effort to keep it going."

That's what Jim Johnson was trying to do in Los Angeles. He'd met a woman and brought her back to Los Angeles with him, where he was determined to establish a career. He wrote a couple of songs recorded by the 5th Dimension, "Magic in My Life" and "Don't Stop for Nothing," which appeared on their 1975 album *Earthbound*. The group sang "Magic in My Life" on the *Tonight Show with Johnny Carson, Merv Griffin Show,* and *Dinah Shore.* "I was on my way," Johnson said. "I took my girlfriend to Las Vegas. We had a great time there. We came back, and two weeks later the 5th Dimension had broken up. They stiffed the record."

Johnson moved to a house in Encino, where he built an eight-track studio in the garage. He and Kipper wrote and recorded filler music for movies. A friend of Johnson's had gotten to know Ray Charles and played some of Johnson's music for him, including a song called "Too Hard to Love You." Then one day, Johnson got a phone call from Charles.

"Hello—ah, ahh, ah, Jim?" Charles said. "I heard this song. Would it be okay if I recorded it? I like the way you play. Will you come down and play on it for me?"

"On one condition," Johnson said. "That you don't be hollering at me. I heard about you."

Charles cracked up over the phone and told Johnson to come to the session.

"I got down there and had a great time, all day and night," Johnson said. "Me and Ray Charles. He's dressed impeccably in crimson and gray, cowboy cut. That whole day, I got along with him so well, and he didn't holler at me. I felt very comfortable around Ray. I didn't feel like a stranger. He never gave me that feeling at all. When I left, I went to shake hands, and he grabbed a hold of my wrist. He said, 'Johnson—attack. Attack. Attack.' I was shivering. I promised, I'd attack. It still gives me the shiver. What a guy."

Johnson still hadn't given up on getting Rico Rosenbaum back into music. Johnson stayed with Rosenbaum for a while, and they recorded three or four songs together. During one of their sessions, they got word that Elvis Presley had died. "That put the kibosh on that day of recording," Johnson said. "That was crushing. I don't know if we ever really finished those tunes."

Rosenbaum's friends were beginning to worry that he might meet a similar fate to Elvis's. According to James Walsh, Rosenbaum had met a girl in New York who'd introduced him to heroin, and his drug problems were getting the best of him. "He was doing drugs, not music," Walsh said. "He was stealing his mother's money and lying."

For James Walsh *(left)*, there would be decades' more work with various versions of Gypsy, but for Rico Rosenbaum *(right)*, writing, recording, and touring with Gypsy in the early 1970s would be the apex of his career. Courtesy of Denny Johnson of Minnie-paulmusic.com.

"My relationship with Rico didn't get back on track till a little later," Caplan said. "Eventually we became close friends. Whenever he was in town while he was with Gypsy, we'd hang out and play. The very last time I saw him, after Gypsy corroded, they were having problems. He was writing stuff on his own. It was the late '70s. He came to town and hung out with me. We went to some movies, and he was telling me what was going on out there, telling me what he was going to do."

"Rico had problems," Johnson said. "I was trying to put a band back together when all that happened. I was going this way into music, and he was going the other way into another thing. He'd never call and ask to be back."

On September 10, 1979, Johnson and Kipper were at a friend's house rehearsing a song when Johnson received the terrible news by phone. He put the phone down and looked over at Kipper, sitting at his drum kit.

"Rico just killed himself," Johnson said.

Kipper's drumsticks went flying.

"That was the end of that rehearsal," Johnson said. "Sad times. After that, I floundered."

It was reported that Rosenbaum had put a shotgun to his head and pulled the trigger, bringing a tragic end to a career that had been as promising as that of any Minnesota rocker. It had been a painful spiral downward, but the ending still surprised his friends. "I didn't see it coming," Caplan said. "I didn't know what was going on out there. I heard stuff—Don Forte worked for White Lightning before he went out and worked for Gypsy as their road manager—but I didn't know the hardcore details."

"It was a tragedy," Larson said. "I heard some of the things that were going on out there. I know there was more to it. I still have my doubts that it was suicide. It could very well have been suicide—it was Hollywood—but I talked to him a couple of weeks before he passed away, and he didn't seem that way at all. Not suicidal. But Hollywood was a wide-open town at that time, and that's when the band was falling apart."

Seemingly every '60s rock 'n' roll musician in the Twin Cities attended Rosenbaum's Highland Park funeral. The chapel was packed—just like dance halls, teen clubs, and ballrooms had been packed wherever Rosenbaum's bands had played. "I went to his service," said Phil Berdahl of Stillroven. "It was crowded. I probably knew three-fourths of them. I didn't know him well, but he was a nice guy and a great singer. It was sad that he got into the drug thing. Nobody was happy that day."

"Rico's funeral was really depressing, especially when we got to the gravesite, and his mother tried to jump in the hole," Caplan said. "We had to restrain her. It was really sad."

"I didn't come back for the funeral," Johnson said. "I couldn't afford to. Times have been tough now and then." Larson missed the funeral, too. "Nobody let me know about Rico's funeral," he said. "I heard it was a horrific spectacle. I got invited by Rico's mom to a memorial service a year later at the big synagogue in St. Paul. We all made peace with each other."

Larson was deeply disappointed that things had not worked out with Gypsy but not surprised. "I told everybody it was going to happen," he said. "The closeness of the band we put together here was gone. I compare it to the Allman Brothers—after fights and tragedy, they kept it together. We didn't."

The label reads: FROM THE LAND OF 10 000 HITS • EVERYBODY'S HEARD ABOUT THE BIRD • HIGH FIDELITY SIDE ONE • MONOPHONIC 33⅓ RPM • FOR PROMOTIONAL USE ONLY • EPILOGUE

BRINGING IT ALL BACK HOME

ANOTHER MEMORIAL EVENT was held on Sunday, December 2, 2012, at Famous Dave's barbecue restaurant in Uptown Minneapolis. Greg Maland had died that September. Though he had moved to Washington State and lived there for many years, he and his former Castaway bandmate, Dennis Libby, had remained very close. Following a series of strokes, Maland was in bad shape when Libby flew out to visit him shortly before he died.

"He knew I was there," Libby said. "There was a light on, but nobody home. Coming back, I determined Greg was such an influential member of the scene, I would not let him disappear in obscurity." After Maland died, Libby organized a memorial show featuring many of the surviving members of the top local bands of Maland's era. There were forty-nine musicians and nine bands at the show, including Tony Andreason of The Trashmen, Dale Menten and Tom Klugherz of the Gestures (Gus Dewey died of an aneurism while being treated for cancer at age fifty-seven in 2004), and all the original members of the Castaways except Roy Hensley, who died in 2005. The benefit raised $2,800 for Guitars for Vets.

"Greg was a guy who really believed in the healing power of music," Libby said. "He had plenty of demons, but he would have been just delighted that this memorial raised money to teach people to play music. It was an amazing experience to stand onstage with the original members of the Castaways. We didn't even sound too bad."

Andreason sang and played "Surfin' Bird," backed by Zippy Caplan's latest band, the Surf Dawgs, a Ventures-style guitar instrumental band that brings Caplan full circle back to his roots as a guitarist. Even Jim Johnson gave it a try, though his declining health did not allow him to finish the one song he played. To take Twin Cities rock almost all the way back to the beginning, Mike Waggoner performed rockabilly with his group the Roadhouse Band. The last group to perform represented the Avanties, with Dave Maetzold on bass, Denny Craswell on drums, and Charles Schoen of the Del Counts playing Maland's keyboard parts. "Charles did such a great job," Maetzold said. "He had Greg's style down perfectly with a Hammond organ and a Leslie speaker. That night was so great. I'll remember it forever. All these guys were friends. I hadn't seen most of them for thirty years or so—some for fifty years. Some of them were missing. I wish that we could do an annual reunion of the '60s groups, but eventually you won't have many left."

The evening was a both a solemn tribute to a fallen comrade and a joyful celebration of all that those aging musicians had accomplished—and even more that could have been achieved, had fortune and circumstance been different. Looking back fifty years, it is remarkable to think about how those young men made themselves godlike among their peers simply by learning to play guitars, keyboards, bass, and drums. Being stars in their hometown while still teenagers was just a matter of coming up with a catchy song, scraping up a few hundred dollars to record it, and handing the record to a receptive local deejay.

But the window where that was possible did not stay open for very long. Dale Menten blames Arbitron. Begun in the 1950s as a television ratings service, Arbitron started compiling radio ratings for local markets in 1964. As each year passed, the Arbitron ratings became more important to program directors and station managers; consequently, playlists got tighter and tighter. The Top 40 became the Top 30, and there was little room for local records to squeeze into rotation. "The only reason most of the bands in this town were able to break out regionally, or nationally, was because of that loose playlist thing,"

Menten said. "You could walk into any station and a jock would actually play it and give you a chance. Eventually, they could only get you on late at night, and by then Arbitron had arrived. And that's when Amos sold out."

Menten's theory was that the major labels pushed Arbitron as a way to eliminate weaker competition for airplay. "They said, 'We can't get our established artists through these markets, because it's all cluttered with these little Gesture bands,'" Menten said. "'We want to clean that up.' Someone got paid, you know damn well, to make a change like that. Somebody's got a big house somewhere." Menten said local records had a better chance of breaking through when radio playlists were dominated by fun, escapist music. "We were around when it was all this calliope, this fun thing, and then everything crashed, everything got serious," Menten said. "You look at the music—'Liar, Liar,' 'Run, Run, Run,' 'The Crusher,' 'Surfin' Bird'—they're just escape tunes. They're just fun. They're party tunes. All of a sudden, it's 'Uh, you gotta get serious.' It was the 'Eve of Destruction.' It's like someone popped this bubble."

Owen Husney, who achieved regional fame with the High Spirits, thought originality played an important part in the success of Minnesota's first rock bands. "When you see who had the big hits, it was all very original songs," said Husney, who later worked as a promoter, became Prince's first manager in 1976, and established a successful music management business in Los Angeles. "What held a lot of bands back was they were doing other peoples' songs—cover songs. If you had a band that could interpret things in an original fashion, or come up with a totally new song like 'Liar, Liar' or 'Run, Run, Run,' or The Trashmen, even though they got sued by the Rivingtons—those were the bands that broke through. Those were truly original songs."

But even the bands that did make records that broke out of Minnesota found that their home base was not prepared to help them sustain success. "I wish I would have been older and known then what I know now," Husney said. "I could have helped all these groups get to the next stage of their careers. If you moved to L.A. or New York, there were tons of managers who knew how to be honest with groups and how to shape them. One thing that was missing was people to shape groups and be brutally honest. What was lacking was a producer to say, 'No, no, go back into the studio and do it this way.' Staying in Minneapolis is a double-edge sword. In Minneapolis they were all competitive with each other—they didn't know it but they were—but you only tend to rise to be as good as the top musicians in that town. If you go to New York like Dylan, you'll have to rise to a whole different level because there are bands and songwriters there who will knock your shoes off."

In Husney's opinion, Minneapolis was a fertile town with tremendous musicians, and a musical infrastructure just strong enough to make bands think they could succeed on a larger scale even if they stayed in town. In reality, there were built-in limitations that could not be overcome. "Minneapolis had clubs where bands could play," Husney said. "Live music was very well supported. The problem was it was too faraway, and too fuckin' cold. The A&R guys weren't flying into town to hear them and sign them initially. Here in L.A., on any given night there's a band playing Sunset Strip, and the A&R guys on the strip are hunting for the next hit. That wasn't happening in Minneapolis. That's why Dylan left. The infrastructure was good enough to keep the bands from leaving. You didn't get out. The Heilichers [would] record and distribute you. That was all good, but once you recorded your song, there was no active producer who had a few hits under his belt, who could take you to the next step, or could get you out to a much larger swimming pool."

"That happened to everybody," said Denny Johnson of Jokers Wild. "Nobody made it out of here. It's always been that way. Then the ones that did take the next step got screwed anyway. Nobody has anything good to say about the music industry. Even with the hundreds of thousands of records Gypsy sold, Metromedia totally screwed that up."

Despite the disappointments that came later, the musicians remember how exciting it was to play rock 'n' roll music in Minnesota before the business became too serious. "Some of the artists on TV now, they get into all this philosophical stuff about what they're playing, and what it really means," said Andreason. "I watch and I wonder if they are really having fun playing. With The Trashmen, when we get together and play now, people say, 'You guys really look like you're having fun.' Well, we are—just having a ball. Every time it's like, this could be our last time, so we have as much fun as we can. I'm recognized a lot more today than I was back then. People go from this craze to this craze to this craze, and you're just forgotten. Some entertainers get all bothered by that, but that's reality. That's what happens. We had our day in the sun. We looked upon it from the standpoint that there's only a minute portion of 1 percent of people who ever got to experience what we did, and meet the people who we met, do the TV shows that we did, and play the venues that we played. Collectors look at us as one of the greatest four-piece combos of all time. I couldn't believe it—we never took ourselves seriously, even back when we were on tour. It was just one big happy time until acid rock started, and we didn't want to play it, so we stopped."

"The Trashmen led the way for the rest of us," said drummer Jim Faragher of the Chancellors. "They showed us what could be done."

And they're still doing it. The Trashmen—with Bob Reed's son, Rob ("Trashkid #1") filling in on drums for Steve Wahrer, who died of throat cancer in 1989 at the age of forty-seven—drew spillover crowds for two consecutive nights to the Minnesota State Fair in August 2014. Perhaps the younger people in the audience only knew the band from the multiple times "Surfin' Bird" had been featured on the hit animated comedy series *Family Guy*—earning the band more money than any other project they'd ever been involved in. In 1983, The Trashmen had secured all rights to their music from Amos Heilicher through a legal settlement, and starting in 2007—at the suggestion of Bobby Vee—had made a dozen very lucrative tours of Europe, where their music is revered. Yet 2014 was the first time The Trashmen had played the Minnesota State Fair since appearing at the B-Sharp tent in 1963.

This time they appeared at the Schell's Stage with Deke Dickerson, a forty-six-year-old rockabilly guitar whiz who continually gushed about being on the same stage with his seventy-year-old idols. Opening with "King of the Surf," the band worked through most of the songs from their *Surfin' Bird* album, as well as most of the tunes from their 2014 album with Dickerson, *Bringing Back The Trash*. As the set progressed, little kids got up to dance, then their parents began to join them, followed by teenagers who couldn't resist moving to the "Bird Dance Beat." The shows climaxed with Andreason and Dickerson playing fiery duets on the Dick Dale standard "Miserlou," then Andreason growling out "Surfin' Bird." Just like back in the old days, the dance floor was full.

During and after the shows, Winslow's wife, Alta, and Reed's wife, Judy, sold T-shirts that said "The Trashmen: They gave the world The Bird." The band members stayed around signing old and new recordings for a long line of fans who wanted to share memories and take pictures. They stayed until the line was gone and the staff wanted to close the stage. "We have played dozens of fairs in the past from coast to coast, and have played festivals and fairs in Europe, but were never asked to play in our hometown," Andreason said. "It was for sure a blast for us. Living the dream! Like the thrilling days of yesteryear."

Andreason, who also stays busy playing in a bluegrass band, still gets the same feeling he did when he and Mike Jann were playing at church suppers in Minneapolis, and when he was playing for twenty thousand at the St. Paul Auditorium in 1964. "It's a fun business," Andreason said. "There's a lot of bright side to being a guy who can get up onstage and actually play. There's no greater high than being onstage and have everybody stand up when you're done. You back off and look at this audience that really enjoyed what you just did. That's the biggest high there is."

On July 10, 2013, another Minnesota music reunion took place. Bobby Vee, who had scored six Top 10 hits and thirty-eight charted singles before retiring from touring in

2011 due to the onset of Alzheimer's disease, attended Bob Dylan's concert at St. Paul's Midway Stadium. At one point during the show, the normally taciturn Dylan addressed the crowd: "Thank you, friends. I left here a while back, and since that time I've played all over the world with all kinds of people . . . everybody from Mick Jagger to Madonna. . . . I've been on the stage with most of those people, but the most beautiful person I've ever been on the stage with is a man who's here tonight, who used to sing a song called 'Suzie Baby.' Bobby Vee is actually here tonight. Maybe you could show your appreciation with just a round of applause."

The crowd applauded and cheered warmly.

"So we're going to try to do this song," Dylan said. "I've done it with him before once or twice."

Dylan then sang a tender version of "Suzie Baby," accompanying himself and his band on the electric piano—in the key of C-sharp.

ACKNOWLEDGMENTS

MUSICALLY, the 1960s were a time of great experimentation, liberation, personal expression, discovery, and joy. It came as no surprise that the musicians, producers, promoters, and radio personalities who experienced that era were eager to share their memories with me.

The list of people who devoted their time to making this book a thorough and detailed chronicle of those exciting days is very long, but I must start by thanking Bill Diehl—the Deacon of the Discs, and so forth—whom I first met when I started working at the *St. Paul Pioneer Press* in 1980. Bill had already been a newspaperman for more than thirty years, but he was unfailingly friendly and helpful to me and always willing to share stories from his many years in radio as well as print journalism. There isn't a better storyteller anywhere, and it was my great good fortune that Bill was still willing to devote hours to being interviewed for this book. As a Duluth native, I did not have the pleasure of growing up with Bill and the other great Twin Cities deejays, but after knowing Bill Diehl all these years, I feel as though I had.

Tony Andreason, Bob Reed, and Dal Winslow of The Trashmen generously gave me all the time I asked for to discuss the days before, during, and after they were America's premiere rock 'n' roll band. Minnesota could not be better represented by a band or a group of musicians. As Mike Waggoner emphasized to me, The Trashmen were gentlemen—and so is Mike Waggoner. His Bops might have been one wild bunch of rockabilly pioneers, but Mike is one of the kindest men you could meet. Speaking of Mikes, you cannot write about The Trashmen without spending a great deal of time talking to Mike Jann, who has become the unofficial archivist for his friends Tony, Bob, and Dal. Mike answered endless questions and provided a steady stream of images and articles that helped bring the band into sharper focus. I am also grateful to Larry LaPole, who gave me great insight into the peak of The Trashmen frenzy.

I deeply enjoyed my interviews with these members of the following bands: Denny Craswell, Bob Folschow, Jim Donna, Dick Roby, and Dennis Libby of the Castaways (and, in Craswell's case, Crow, as well); Dale Menten and Tom Klugherz of the Gestures; Jim Johnson, Doni Larson, and James Walsh of the Underbeats and Gypsy; Dave Maetzold of Gregory Dee and the Avanties; David Rivkin and Jim Faragher of the Chancellors; Owen Husney of the High Spirits; Zippy Caplan of the Escapades, Litter, and White Lightning; Ron Butwin of the Escapades; Lonnie Knight of the Rave-Ons and Jokers Wild; Phil Berdahl of the Stillroven; Charles Schoen of the Del Counts; Larry Wiegand of the Rave-Ons, South 40, and Crow; Butch Stokes of the Mystics; Arne Fogel and Barry Thomas Goldberg of the Batch; Butch Maness of the Trespassers; Mike Waggoner and the Bops; Bill Lubov of Dave Brady and the Stars; Ken Erwin of the C. A. Quintet; and Chris Nelson of the More-Tishans.

I gained much information from interviews with Sam Sabean (aka Sam Sherwood) and Lou Riegert (aka Lou Waters) of KDWB; David Hersk of Gaity Records; Warren Kendrick, producer and songwriter at Dove Studio; promoter David Anthony Wachter; and Steve Kaplan, editor of *In-Beat Magazine*.

For help in assembling images and information, I thank Bob Irwin and Tim Livingston of Sundazed Records; author and Midwest music historian Tom Tourville; Jeanne Andersen, creator of the fact-rich website Twin Cities Music Highlights (www.jeanne andersen.net); Steve Brown; Mike Gretz; the Velline family; Sharon Johnson and Danny Severance; Sevan Garabedian; Mike Adelson; Shawn Nagy; Steve Moravec; Jim du Bois;

and Rick Hoffbeck. Thanks to Midwest rock music historian Jim Oldsberg, whose interviews and writings over the past several decades were very helpful during my research. My editors at the University of Minnesota Press, Erik Anderson and Kristian Tvedten, were unfailingly excited and enthusiastic about this project from its inception. Every meeting we had seemed more like a record-swap than an editorial discussion.

A special thank you to Denny Johnson, bassist for Jokers Wild and curator of the Minniepaulmusic website, for providing many of the illustrations in this book. The interviews and images he and Tom Campbell have assembled on www.minniepaulmusic.com since 2008 are an invaluable resource for those who want to learn more about the glory days of Minnesota rock 'n' roll—or relive that era.

Arne Fogel told me that Dale Menten was something of a celebrity to him in the 1960s; he was to me, too. I never knew him until I interviewed him for a *Pioneer Press* story about the death of Bruce Waterston in 1996, but I knew Dale's work as far back as 1964, when he and the Gestures had a huge hit with his great composition "Run, Run, Run." Three years later, my older brother Mark met Dale at Dove Studios in Bloomington when the band Mark drummed for, the Soul Seekers, journeyed from Duluth to record a single. The result, "Boom Boom," was a big hit in Duluth, and deservedly so; Dale worked studio magic to bring out the best of the band's voices and instruments. They returned in 1967 to have Dale produce an even better single, "New Directions," which had a harder edge but was also a hit in Duluth. After hearing the two records and listening to my brother talk about his studio experience, I was convinced that Dale Menten was some kind of genius. That might be stretching things, but the musicians I spoke with for this book who know Dale—and that would be most of them—hold him in the highest regard as a producer, songwriter, musician, and booster of Minnesota music. After hours of interviews with him and many exchanged messages, I wholeheartedly agree.

My earliest Minnesota musical influence was my brother. I grew up listening to the radio stations he chose and playing the records he bought, including records by The Trashmen, the Titans, the Gestures, the Castaways, the High Spirits, the Chancellors, and T. C. Atlantic. I would eavesdrop on the Soul Seekers (Frank Bolos, Tom Jones, Tim Koivisto, Dave Slattery, and Bonnie Matheson) when they practiced in our basement, and I tried to figure out how to play Mark's drums when he wasn't around. I quickly gave up; he was just too good. I switched to guitar—and I wouldn't have tried that if Mark hadn't exposed me to so much great music.

Like many teenage boys in the 1960s, I joined a band with five of my high school pals: Steve Aldrich, Robbie Alexander, Steve Gallagher, Bob Hurd, and Bob Husby. We called ourselves the Six Pack, playing upbeat dance songs by the Rascals, the Raiders, the Beatles, the Kinks, the Grass Roots, the Doors, the Rolling Stones, and the Box Tops—and (in my memory at least) we played them very well. Unlike the bands I have written about in this book, we never recorded. We started in the fall of 1967, a few months after *Sgt. Pepper's Lonely Hearts Club Band* had been released, playing school dances and church basements. By the spring of 1968, Cream and Jimi Hendrix had become incredibly influential, and a band playing midsixties Top 40 rock 'n' roll already seemed dated. We broke up and went on to other pursuits.

The Soul Seekers kept going for a year or two, adding psychedelic sounds and playing heavier rock. Eventually, they too split up, as Vietnam, college, and changing musical tastes affected so many bands of the era. Mark went on to drum for a succession of short-lived bands and often filled in with our father's big band, the Hungry Five Society. He served in the National Guard, graduated from college, and raised a wonderful family in Duluth. I can't thank him enough for the musical education and inspiration he has given me, even if he didn't know he was doing it at the time. Without Mark's influence, I would not have thought to undertake this project.

To my brother Mark—Traps, the Boy Wonder—I dedicate this book.

INDEX

RICK SHEFCHIK is a freelance writer and for twenty-six years was a reporter and columnist for the *St. Paul Pioneer Press*. He is the author of four novels and three works of nonfiction, including *From Fields to Fairways: Classic Golf Clubs of Minnesota*, also published by the University of Minnesota Press. Since high school he has been in four bands as a guitarist and singer. His most recent band was Yesterday's News, a '60s oldies band composed of fellow journalists. He lives in Stillwater, Minnesota.